R. L. WYSONG

D0851550

LIVING LIFE
AS IF THINKING MATTERS

Why dissent is crucial
to health, happiness, hope,
and a better world

Published in 2008 by Inquiry Press
7550 Eastman Avenue
Midland, MI 48642

Phone: 989-631-0009
Fax: 989-631-9280
Email: inquirypress@inquirypress.com
http://www.asifthinkingmatters.com

R. L. Wysong, Author
Living Life As If Thinking Matters
Includes bibliographical references and index

(hardcover)
ISBN 0-918112-12-5
978-0-918112-12-5

(softcover)
ISBN 0-918112-14-9
978-0-918112-14-9

Library of Congress Control Number: 2008926076

Distributed by: Inquiry Press

Printed in Canada

DEDICATION

To those unafraid to challenge cherished beliefs, and for whom the open-minded search for truth, no matter where it might lead, is the breath of life.

ACKNOWLEDGMENTS

OVER MY LIFE, and the many years it has taken to complete this book, countless people have influenced me through the experiences I have shared with them and the knowledge they have passed to me. I cannot help but be humbled by the fact that others before me have done so much of the legwork upon which my thinking in large part relies. The reference section in the back of the book catalogs many of those upon whose shoulders I have stood and who have unknowingly contributed.

Additionally, I could never complete such a project without the labor of others. My fellow workers have helped with proofing, graphics, mechanics, and other tasks freeing me to work on research and writing. They help me to multiply myself and make my flow of dreams reality. Although I will leave them nameless, inasmuch as they may not wish to be publicly associated with the controversial nature of the book, they know who they are and I thank them.

My family has had to live with a father and husband preoccupied, even obsessed at times, with a thousand page project (the two books, Solving the Big Questions and Living Life, were written at the same time) that seemed as though it would never end. They more than once observed: "It is a painful thing to watch a perfectionist write and rewrite books…about everything." Since my family is inextricably linked to me by name, they have also had to suffer the same fears as I in releasing books that run countercurrent to many popular beliefs. They deserve thanks, an apology, and always my love.

You the reader also deserve credit. Thank you for reaching out to learn and for responding to a book ostensibly written to help people be better people and the world be a better place. It is upon hearts and minds such as yours that the hope of the future rests.

LIVING LIFE AS IF THINKING MATTERS
Why dissent is crucial to health, happiness, hope, and a better world

SECTION M
Being Good

SECTION N
Finis

INTRODUCTION

EACH OF US IS BORN WITH A BLANK mental slate. Then parents, educators, and society fill it in before we are old enough to do any critical thinking for ourselves. These givens crystallize into beliefs we then hold as true, often carrying them with us for a lifetime. We become very fond and protective of them, cherishing them as if they were a part of our bodies. Throughout life, contrary information is cast aside and facts and experts are selected that agree with us, giving us comfort that we are right. The strength of the beliefs increases in direct proportion to the degree our sense of belonging, comfort, security, ego, or livelihood depends upon them.

This is a book about starting over and skipping the imposed beliefs part. That means, once we are mentally mature, setting aside all the acculturated norms we are invested in. Some of them may be good, some not. How will we know unless we find out?

The kind of thinking we need is not the sort that settles us into an immutable belief and faith. When locked-in beliefs are examined, they are usually found to be quick fixes, easy solutions to a thinking chore that people wish to set aside. Once a belief is adopted, we tend to retire our minds. But living life as if thinking matters cannot tolerate such mental laziness.

Instead of settling on static beliefs, we must engage in a dynamic inquiry using the best and most reliable mental tools we have. I call these tools the SOLVER principles: Self responsibility, Open mindedness. Long view thinking, Virtuous intent, Evidence first, and Reasoning. Using these principles and a desire to find truth, we have the best opportunity to make our lives the best they can be and to transform the world into the peaceful paradise it could become.

But society would rather that we not think for ourselves. "It" wants us to just fit in. "It" would lead us to believe there is something wrong with us if we are not committed to its popular political, social, health, scientific, and religious beliefs. This, and the companion book, *Solving the Big Questions,* will demonstrate that common beliefs are not solutions, they are usually the problem. Since beliefs dictate actions, wrong beliefs, no matter how right they are thought to be, create wrong lives and a wrong world.

In a nutshell, unjustified wrong beliefs are the underlying problem facing us. The solution is to unload belief baggage, back up and start fresh with a clean slate. That is perhaps asking the impossible, but it is the only way we can ever hope to arrive at any semblance of truth—and truth, or as near as we can get to it, is the only real solution.

Why is life so difficult? Why are feelings of frustration, desperation, cynicism, and hopelessness so common? Why are people everywhere engaged in self-destructive behavior? Why, with so much technology and medicine, is our health failing? Why is the world teetering on the brink of disaster from environmental ruination and warring factions? Such threats leave us with feelings of uncertainty, powerlessness, and despair.

Fortunately, there are answers and there is hope. Daring to depart from the givens, and living life as if thinking matters can bring health, longer and more pleasant life, transform the Earth, and solve economic, political, religious, ethical, and social problems. The companion book will even show that by using these tools we can gain a high degree of rational confidence about where we came from, why we are here, and where we are going.

Such optimistic goals may sound naïve and overly enthusiastic. We're used to conceding that complex human problems are to be forever mired in conflicting opinion and disagreement. But before tossing in the towel, consider this. Every person on Earth agrees that 2+2=4, and that heavy things tossed into the air will fall to the ground. So, we must admit, people can agree. We will see that the same thinking process used to conclude the things we can agree on, can apply to all the things we don't agree on.

Unfortunately, education, in itself, does not put us on the path to good thinking. Although school may tell us about reason, it then denies it in practice by teaching us to rely on experts and be herded into the consensus view. But experts can be found on any side of any given subject, and sophistry can masquerade as reason. Tidbits of fact blended with the venom of unreason may create infinite 'truths' that people clutch near to their hearts, but such 'truths' have been the undoing of mankind from our beginnings. Truth cannot be so fickle or treacherous.

Although following the crowd seems a safe haven, we will see, for example, that 'accepted' modern medicine is ineffective in ridding us of the modern plagues of cancer, arthritis, obesity, diabetes, heart disease, etc.; 'accepted' nutritionist-formulated processed foods are killing us; 'accepted' politics can ruin society; 'accepted' unbridled freedom and the 'me generation' are driving people apart; 'accepted' materialism brings no meaning to life and can justify any act; 'accepted' science and the thousands of 'accepted,' competing, and contradictory religions provide no verifiable certainty as to our origin, purpose, and destiny. Almost no matter which way we turn, when the SOLVER principles are applied, we discover that the majority is usually wrong. That's the bad news. The good news is that obvious solutions lie before us.

Making the best of life requires us to take responsibility for ourselves, to never stop learning, and to always be open to change. Thinking, the kind that matters and can bring hope, is an exciting journey, not a boring destination.

This book is structured in sections and chapters dealing with specific subjects to demonstrate the usefulness of open thinking. As you move through the topics—many of which may trigger 'hot buttons'—judge what is said based on the fairness of the reasoning and the evidence, not its consistency with popular beliefs. You will surely find thoughts here that are counter to your present views. I am not asking you to convert to yet another belief, but only to consider where evidence and reason can lead. In so doing, I hope you will be inspired in an extraordinary way.

If you feel it leads elsewhere and wish to express yourself, a special *asifthinkingmatters.com* website has been created for that purpose. The search for truth and improvement in the human condition is always a work in progress, so questions, comments, agreements, and reasoned, evidence-based disagreements are invited and most welcome.

SECTION A

Thinking about. . .

HOW TO THINK

IN THIS SECTION: *Ground rules must be laid before decisions can be made about what is right or wrong, true or untrue. It is not enough to start with a belief and proceed from there. Unjustified belief is in large part the reason the world continues to teeter on the precipice, why so many people suffer as they do, and why we are kept guessing and floundering. If truth matters, thinking must matter. Here are the simple thinking principles anyone can apply to start solving life's problems.*

1

1

WE CAN AGREE

REFLECT FOR A MOMENT on how everyone on Earth can agree that it is reasonable to come in out of the rain, turn the heat on when it's cold, and slip into our pants before putting shoes on. How is it that we can have such consensus but can't seem to come together on other things that have to do with how we get along, or that could potentially ruin health, the Earth, or put us at war?

Television, radio, and Internet blogs teem with animated debate about immigration, taxation, terrorism, nuclear proliferation, racism, social security, healing methods, diet programs, sex offender punishment, socialized medicine, profiling, religion, education, abortion, and free trade. Last evening as I tried to listen through the cacophony of four people on a television panel screaming like a mini version of the chaos on the stock exchange floor, I thought about what a wonder it is that we humans ever agree on anything. Nevertheless, there is no controversy about the rules of arithmetic, the correct formula for determining an unknown angle in a triangle, the value of pi, the atomic makeup of a water molecule, the organ responsible for pumping blood, or the thrust needed to get a satellite of known weight into orbit. Our agreement on such matters cuts across cultures, borders, languages, and political ideologies. We are one world, one people, and one mind on many matters.

Why can we agree that candy is sweet but are ready to kill one another over ideas on politics and what God says? Why the universal schizophrenia? Quite simply, on the one hand, as to whether sugar is sweet, we let evidence and reason lead. On the other hand, with politics, religion, social, economic, and environmental issues we think beliefs come first and tend to use reason and evidence only to the extent that they support these beliefs.

Consider the world's agreement on the science of math. We approach it with an open mind, use reason, apply experience, demand evidence, and change our formulas if the facts demand. There is so much world accord on arithmetic, geometry, and calculus that they have become common property for humanity. From earliest childhood we are taught to respect the rules of mathematics because of their logic, evidence, and proofs. We could neither pass school nor function in society without acceding to their truths.

With social, political, and religious matters, the cry is for freedom to believe whatever we like without regard for proofs, consistency with logic, or evidence. We are free to shoot arrows of belief in walls, paint bull's-eyes around them, and pretend we have hit the mark of truth. Thus the world is filled to the brim with every sort of cockamamie idea. We have even come to believe tolerance and broadmindedness about such flakiness is like an ethical and intellectual badge of honor. But our insistence on the world's right to a vastitude of ignorance and stupidity threatens to hurtle us over the precipice. Thinking, not belief, must come first.

Unproven beliefs are adopted because they may be popular, make us feel secure, or because we're urged by some authority to adopt them. The soft things of the mind and heart, such as desire, will, trust, passion, convenience, herd instinct, ego, and prejudice become sufficient to hammer such beliefs into the intellect, making them well-nigh unassailable. We vote a certain way because that's the way our parents voted, take any pill a doctor tells us to, eat processed foods because the label says they're healthy, and enter the race for money because society leads us to believe that's where happiness lies.

Why on earth are we so intellectually sloppy where it matters most? Why would we buttress a belief that could result in life or death, health or illness, on things as flimsy as "That's what somebody told me," or "It makes me feel good"?

The answer—it should be embarrassing to admit—is our desire for the sense of security and belonging we felt as infants; a euphoric state of comfort we never really forget or recover from. When we are young all the rules are laid out for us, answers are simple, and our every need is someone else's responsibility. But that's not how grownups should behave. There are consequences for nursing on our latent desire to return to the swaddled and carefree security of our parent's bosom. We cannot simply trust the pabulum we are told as adults or lock away the ideas we were spoon fed as children.

We may grow up in the respect that we assume the responsibility for our material needs by getting educated and landing a job. But even then we tend to regress by trying to make our employer and government our mom and dad by lobbying them to secure us with benefits, subsidies, entitlements, and other guarantees. We demand independence, freedom, and the right to take ownership of material things, but we resist exercising the independence and freedom of our own minds by doing the hard work of earning what we put there. We want someone else to tell us what is right or wrong, grace or sin. We want our moms and dads back.

There is a constant tension between taking full responsibility for our thoughts and actions, and our lingering desire to return to the womb. When faced with the hard trials and questions of life, we naturally long for the knowns we had as children. Children panic if there is an instant of insecurity or uncertainty. But retaining the knowns given to us by our parents is to let them live our lives for us. That's fine when we are children, but as adults we must test those knowns as well as any others that society offers up. True knowledge and the security of certainty can only be owned if earned. True peace with ourselves can only come from bravely reaching within to find out who we are, and then acknowledging and living in accord with the honesty we find there.

Clearly, we are capable of finding truths and agreeing on them. It is therefore not Pollyannaish to think the world can be one on all the important matters that affect our lives. The world's consensus on math, science and other mundane matters proves that. The fantastic (peaceful) advances of the modern world owe their existence to the power of putting thinking first. By applying the same thinking process to the issues that divide us, hope, not disaster and hopelessness, can be our lot. This book will explore the very real and wonderful possibilities that lie before us if we will simply behave as grownups, open our minds, put aside the naiveté of unexamined beliefs, and let evidence and reason rule. In other words, live life as if thinking matters.

2

POSSIBILITY THINKING

WE NATURALLY FEAR WHAT AN HONEST, open-minded investigation of our 'sure' beliefs will reveal. It might mean admitting error or ignorance (a most dreaded thing to have to do), or changing how we behave (even more dreaded). It might mean leaving behind a sense of certainty that made us feel safe and then starting over at the beginning. We would be faced with the vulnerability and powerlessness that attends a new journey of unknown destination.

But such hesitations and fears are of no matter since we all must eventually face truth. The universe is truth, and that truth, not our beliefs, is what we are intrinsically a part of and must eventually be reconciled to. Why not sooner than later? Besides, the old uncritically accepted beliefs that pervade our society have not served us well. They lead to only one terminus, a continuing future of error and ignorance.

We have the technological tools to create utopia. The last two centuries of ratiocination in some fields of human thought and industry prove our capabilities. But why does it seem that reason must wear a veil when it ventures out into the arena of public policy? To endure our lot of human misery in favor of a raft of beliefs, makes no sense.

A new approach is obviously needed. To begin, we could stop just reacting to crises. We could also set aside ego, selfish desire, greed, immediate pleasure, fear, nescience, and the flawed and confusing speculative philosophies used to justify them. Leaning on obscurantic institutions (commercial, academic, scientific, religious) as crutches and substitutes for our own minds hasn't worked either. Such convenient and shortsighted approaches to life mire us individually and as a society in the same old human woes—war, poverty, environmental degradation, disease, and meaninglessness.

But it is hard work to gather and ponder facts, deliberate, reason, and be patient for long-term results. So we kick the can along the street of life like this: Hungry? Grab a candy bar. Want more money? Log a virgin forest. Unhappy? Take a drug. Too fat? Look for a pill. Need votes? Lie to voters. Disagree? Blow something up.

We go to school and learn A, B, C, and arithmetic. Parents teach us manners, the church instructs us about sin, college prepares us for a career, and a job creates money. If we mismanage our lives we expect government to step in and save us. Instead of addressing whys, we learn a lot about whats, subscribe to dogma imposed upon us by others, and are swallowed up by the programmed and numbing motion of life. We hear but don't listen; look but don't see; smell but don't sense; speak without saying; and think without realizing. With no fundamental understanding we are adrift, simply following the lazy current of society… and current always runs downhill.

The mindless knee-jerk reaction to life is fine for an animal in the woods where instinct rules and the laws of nature create balance. Although we remain in the woods (from a biological perspective), different rules must apply in our complex society. We are packed together with machines capable of destroying our environmental support, and weaponry that can vaporize all life on the planet. Intelligence got us into this precarious, machine-driven predicament; intelligence can get us out. It's such a simple thought: thought is the answer.

A remedy can't come soon enough. This generation has seen World Wars, the Cold War, environmental and population crises, more wars, terrorism, starvation, and genocide. There is terrible disease, cruelty, untimely death, and social injustice. Even the best-planned life invariably includes great difficulties and tragedies we seem not psychologically equipped to deal with. So much of the misery we visit upon ourselves is because the tendrils of unreason creep into every nook and cranny of the world and our lives.

7

To start anew will require break-ing from a deeply ingrained mold formed over thousands of years. Not only do we continually look for sur-rogate moms and dads to lean on, but institutions have always been on the ready to fill the bill. They give us sub-jugation; we give them obeisance. Like Orwellian glassy-eyed believers, we march to a cadence set by power mongers who have only their self-

"Of course I have the truth. It's what my parents told me and what I learned in school."

interests at heart. It serves neither the institutions' needs, nor our desire to be dependent, for us to break from the line, think independently, and take responsibility for ourselves. So most of us don't.

Think of what would be possible if the world would put thought first and gain certainty and agreement on how to behave, just like we do about the sum of two plus two. We would not need to spend trillions of dollars in response to terrorism, on medical care that is not improving health, and on weaponry to kill and maim one another. If we rationally spent our resources on improving the human condition, there would be no pollution or famine, clean energy would be unlimited, we could manage resources sustainably, rescue the helpless and victimized, and exonerate innocent prisoners. No child would be without a loving caretaker, everyone could have decent opportunities for food, shelter, and self-improvement, we would eliminate unfair discrimination, and could improve the health of all rather than just masking symptoms. It's enough to make one weep when the lost opportunities and waste are contemplated.

As this book examines various topics of life, I hope you will notice that the best of all worlds is not a dream, it is within our grasp. Only our fear of breaking from the ranks and thinking as if it matters stands in the way.

3

THE SOLVER PRINCIPLES

THERE IS LATENT WITHIN EACH OF US, obscured by day-to-day busyness, consumerism, and titillating distraction, a common gift of reason that longs for and is quenched only by truth. The fact that we do not seek or get that truth can only leave us unfulfilled and empty (at least down deep in our heart of hearts), with no real sense of meaning or purpose beyond the next opportunity for gratification. Rather than seek truth, people either defer to others or throw together comfortable opinions about which they stay politely quiet. We make small talk about effects and symptoms and reserve as private our views on the important issues of causes and true solutions.

If we are ever to advance, we must lay bare the taboo subjects, the personal matters of ideas, beliefs, and faith, and make them fair game for open discussion and critical thought. How government should function, what treatment for a disease works best, and whether our distant kin was a monkey or a book was written by God should be just as open to debate as which street corner should have a traffic signal.

What we think regarding the important matters of life is really not personal and private, as if it were sacred skin best kept veiled in public. Nor are we free to hold any opinion that suits our fancy. Thinking dictates how we behave. How we behave has everything to do with whether we live a good or a miserable life, and even whether life on the planet will survive. An effect, or the behavior that caused it, can never be condemned without condemning the belief from which it sprang.

Pilots are not free to believe that there is no law of gravity, bridge engineers are not free to deny the laws of physics, and accountants are not free to hold the opinion that subtraction is the same as addition. Likewise, we are not free to believe that humans cannot impact the environment, that ethics is merely relative, that treating symptoms cures diseases, that criminals are the victims, or that strapping a bomb to our chests and blowing ourselves up in a mall is the shortcut to heaven. Yes, we are free to believe such things in the sense that we can, but not in the sense that we should.

We must get at the heart of the matters that count in life and examine critically the beliefs that underlie them. All thinking should be open and evidence-based because that is clearly the only way to arrive at truth.

To set your mind at ease, I have no agenda here other than to stimulate your own independent thinking. You will not be asked to join anything, subscribe to a doctrine, recant, or send a donation. You will only be encouraged to tap into the common ethical and rational thread that lies within us all and to apply it not only to your own life, but also to the world at large.

To arrive at valid conclusions on anything, we must agree upon a starting point. What better foundation could there be than to agree that human welfare should be given priority in our choices? That is the only logical concession I will ask you to make as we begin our journey. It is the only belief that I will ask you to subscribe to. And I doubt anyone other than deep ecologists, who might argue that a stone is as valid as a human, will have trouble with it.

Given that starting premise, every chapter then presents examples of how any person can proceed toward truth and the goal of healthy human welfare. All that is necessary is that we:

- Take **S**elf-responsibility
- **O**pen our minds
- Think **L**ong-term effects
- Give **V**irtue priority
- Consider all the **E**vidence
- Let **R**eason lead

I call these methods the SOLVER principles. They provide the mechanism by which all human dilemmas can be solved, or at least brought as close to resolution as feasible.

Such an idea of solving the world's problems is, to say the least, lofty and idealistic. But why not? Why not strive for perfection and utopia? If we fall short, then so be it. At least we did not aspire to mediocrity and fail to achieve even that.

Ideally, readers will learn from the information presented in these chapters and the limited personal experience I can share. But I am fully aware that people usually don't listen. We are by and large an unteachable lot. We develop an irrational and obstinate affinity to what already resides in our brains. We protect our minds from the threat of a new idea like we withdraw and protect our hand from a spinning saw blade.

But guarding our thoughts in this way makes little sense since we all, to begin, develop ideas about life quite by accident. Our ideas are formed by the influence of whatever concatenation of circumstances surrounded our childhood. As we come of age and become independent, these accidental ideas should hold no sacredness, regardless of our cathexis, unless we have objectively examined them.

There is no sanctity in prior belief, doing things our way, making our own mistakes, and learning the hard way. Admittedly, life is for living, and the most enduring lessons are taught by experiences forged through the joy of success and the pain of failure. Nevertheless, this is a call to break that pattern. It is the wise who are brave enough to assemble their own examined and evidence-based beliefs, and who can learn from the lives of others without having to go through the fire.

My hope is that there will be something here for you that will strike a chord, cause reflection, embolden you to challenge the givens, and take responsibility for your own mind and heart. The purpose is not to get you to believe a certain thing, but rather to encourage your journey and to demonstrate with numerous and wide-ranging topics that to be right often requires that we be wrong in the popular sense, and how open thinking offers so much promise. Perhaps you will gain a measure of insight and a different perspective that can make life less painful, more hopeful, and healthier, and you can be encouraged to be a part of nudging the world in a better direction.

Techniques of Non-Thinkers	Techniques of Thinkers
1. Uses generalizations – 'Allness' statements (always, completely, only, never) Scanty facts and evidence.	1. Uses qualifiers – Stipulations and limiting statements (usually, sometimes, almost, perhaps), statements supported with specific references and data.
2. One sided – Opposing views are ignored, misrepresented, underrepresented, or denigrated.	2. Circumspect – Issues examined from many points of view. Opposition fairly represented.
3. Card stacking – Data carefully selected to present only the best or worst possible case while contrary facts are concealed.	3. Balanced – Samples from a wide range of available data. Purpose is to reveal.
4. Skews the numbers – Misleading use of statistics.	4. Numbers are qualified – Size, duration, conditions, controls, source, subsidies, and interests are revealed.
5. Lumpism – Ignores distinctions and subtle differences. Lumps superficially similar elements together. Reasoning by analogy.	5. Discrimination – Differences and subtle distinctions are conceded. Analogies are used carefully so as to distinguish where nonapplicable.
6. False dilemma (either/or) – There are only two solutions to the problem, or two ways of viewing an issue: the arguer's way or the wrong way.	6. Alternatives - There may be many ways of solving a problem or viewing an issue.
7. Appeals to authority – Only the selected expert knows.	7. Appeals to reason – Statements by authority are used to stimulate thought and discussion since 'experts' seldom agree.
8. Appeals to consensus (bandwagon) – 'Everybody's doing it' so it must be right.	8. Appeals to facts and logic – Supports arguments with impartially selected data and logic.
9. Appeals to emotions – Uses strong emotional connections and built-in biases.	9. Appeals to reason – Uses emotionally neutral words and illustrations.
10. Ad hominem attacks – Attack the opponents personally.	10. Avoids labels and derogatory language – Addresses the argument, not the people.
11. Ignores and denies assumptions and biases.	11. Explores assumptions and built-in biases.
12. Inhibits inquiry and awareness beyond the approved bias.	12. Language usage promotes greater awareness.

Choosing the Right Thinking - We should be in a constant struggle with ourselves to suppress the tendency toward indoctrination and bias on the one hand, and the open pursuit of truth on the other. The above contrasts the common tactics of those who wish to only support and advance their prejudices, and those who are interested in exploring life and our world as if thinking matters.

SECTION B

Thinking about. . .

HEALTH

IN THIS SECTION: *Health is a decision, not something that happens to us by accident. It is also a moral choice and duty, not just to self but also to those who love us and to society at large. Others should not have to mourn our pain nor pay for our care because we decided to live a life of neglect and abuse. To make healthy choices in life requires that we understand what we biologically are and how we fit into our world. Unlike in times gone by when the rigors of the wild mandated the lives we led, today, with so many choices, we must use intelligence and foresight—the SOLVER principles—if we wish to be healthy. There are as many different opinions on health as there are doctors and books to express them. But opinion is not what we are after; truth is our goal. Truth always lies within, and these chapters will help you think your way to being the healthiest you can be.*

4

OUR OWNER'S MANUAL

To begin our examination of life, there is no better place to start than with health. With it all things are possible, without it almost nothing is. But achieving health seems increasingly elusive and confusing. There are countless opinions and few if any of them work, as evidenced by perhaps the fastest growing industry in our country, modern medicine. (Don't get sidetracked here by the propaganda that we are healthier than ever and living longer today due to medical care. As you will see in the next section, those claims are especially rickety.)

Usually there is no easy answer to terribly important and complex subjects. Although health is most certainly such a subject, the answers to its dilemmas are remarkably simple—if we apply the SOLVER principles and are willing to step apart from the crowd.

Achieving and maintaining our best potential health first requires that we know what we are and where we came from. We need to consult our owner's manual. An automobile has the best chance of long life and optimal performance if the owner's manual is followed carefully. We will have long life and perform best if we follow our owner's manual.

The problem is that people do not follow the manual because they don't even know where it is or how to read it. So, let's put first things first and find the manual.

We don't have to go far in our search. Our manual lies safe and secure within each of us like a yolk in an egg. Our genetics is that manual. Encoded on the genes within each cell in the body is the equivalent of 100 million pages of *Encyclopedia Britannica*. To read this manual requires a short thinking journey.

First of all, let's understand where we are today in the perspective of time. Imagine that we could draw a line 550 miles long that represented the estimated history of life on Earth (3.5 billion years). The final inch of that line would be the time since the Industrial Revolution, about 200 years ago. That's when all this modernity we now find ourselves nestled within really got under full steam. Put another way, if we scaled down to one year the time that life has been on Earth, our modern industrial era would be less than two seconds.

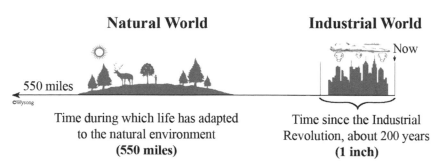

Natural World   **Industrial World**

550 miles

Time during which life has adapted to the natural environment
(550 miles)

Time since the Industrial Revolution, about 200 years
(1 inch)

Time And Adaptation – One inch represents the time during which we have forced our genes to adapt to a modern synthetic world. 550 miles represents the time our genes were incubated and shaped by the natural world. We must return to our genetic roots to achieve optimal health.

Although we have grown up assuming fluorescent lights, polyester, and Froot Loops are normal, ours are totally unique circumstances from a genetic perspective. Clearly our genetic owner's manual instructs about the 550 miles, not the last inch. Sedentary living, diet pop, coffee, morning pep pills, noon tranquilizers, evening sedatives, oleomargarine, s'mores, four food groups (meaning a Big Mac with cheese, lettuce and tomato), and Tums are not in its pages. How could we believe there is no penalty to be paid for not following the manual and altering our environment to such an extent that today virtually no fat in any human body in North America does not contain DDT, polystyrene, or Dioxin?

15

Consider the owner's manual for fish. Fish genes are programmed to accept only specific environmental data, such as a life in water and a cuisine of smaller fish. If a fish is taken out of water and fed lasagna it will become dis-eased—flop, gasp, get sick, and die. Similarly, when we thumb our noses at our owner's manual and take ourselves out of the genetic context for which we were designed, we become dis-eased as well. We succumb to the adult-onset, chronic degenerative diseases such as heart disease, cancer, arthritis, allergies, obesity, autoimmune disorders, dental deterioration, premature aging, infertility, and so on. This is our 'flopping' and 'gasping' from repudiating our owner's manual and living in a world for which we were not designed. Although such diseases may not become manifest until the later years of life, they begin as early as the womb. This makes it difficult to associate them with their true causes: lifestyle, food, and environmental changes—not inadequate penetration of healthcare.

We Are Fish Out of Water – If a fish is taken out of its natural context, water, it will experience "dis-ease" (disease) and die. If humans are taken out of their natural context, nature, they will experience disease and die.

This simple concept—that we are designed for nature—is extraordinarily enlightening and powerful despite its simplicity. Few grasp its full implications. Instead, we eat anything that tastes good and is in a pretty package. We live however we choose, believing modern medicine can repair whatever goes wrong.

This is the simple truth we must understand if we desire health: If things are not used according to the way they are designed, they fail and break. Our parents taught us the proper way to use our toys, and we all know enough to read instruction manuals. These same simple principles of paying attention to our owner's manual and living in the way we were designed provide the master keys to health.

Our genes are an internal code for successfully navigating the external world. When we are born, our genes fully expect to be dropped onto the forest floor and to remain within that context for a lifetime. We should not confuse our origins just because we were born into this new synthetic world.

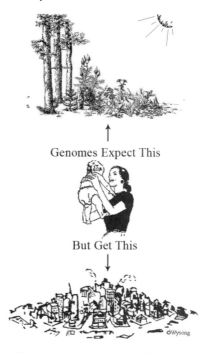

Genomes Expect This

But Get This

So what specifically does this mean we should do? Since 550 miles on the time line (minus about one inch) would represent living out in nature, we need to look to that model. It consists of clean air and water, sunshine hitting our skin, eating food as found in nature, expending considerable energy in obtaining it, finding shelter, and defending against predators. (More specific recommendations will be given in the following chapters.) That is the data our genes understand and thrive on.

Genetic Expectations – All organisms are genetically fine-tuned to the environment and to foods they can eat raw directly from nature. Our new synthetic world creates a genetic stress, manifest in a host of modern degenerative disease.

Our genetic owner's manual does not accommodate so well this new 'better living through chemistry,' synthetic environment we have created in the last one inch of time: air conditioned plastic dwellings, polluted air, receiving almost no sunshine, exercising little, drinking polluted and chemically-treated municipal water, and eating a variety of fractionated, synthetically fortified, processed foods that are barely recognizable as having ever come from nature. We are, in effect, like fish out of water. We pay the price with loss of health. We gain health in direct proportion to the degree we edge our lives closer to the natural world.

Some, arguing in defense of Dr. Pepper, Cheetos, and twelve-position recliners, may say that by now we have adapted to this modern environment. But that cannot be. For one thing, sufficient time has not elapsed for our genetic makeup to change significantly. We are, in effect, in a genetic time warp because one inch is nothing compared to 550 miles.

Additionally, adaptation of the population would require that those with (miraculous) mutations making them suited to modern life produce more offspring than those succumbing to it. But that doesn't happen. The environmental changes to which we are subjecting ourselves are more subtle than a fish put out on land, so we usually survive just fine through the childbearing years. Thus, no natural selection and adaptation to the adult disease-causing modern world occurs.

This is an important caveat to modern living, so let me rephrase it for emphasis. Most believe that the genetic makeup of a population changes through selection of beneficial mutational differences. If diseases caused by modern living killed us before we reproduced, that would be one thing. If that were the case, only the fit—those who had unique genetic strength adapted to this new synthetic world—would survive and pass the trait on to offspring. There would then be a chance of changing the genetic makeup of the population to one more fit for our synthetic modern circumstances. But that's not the case because before we are culled out of the population by adult-degenerative diseases, we have already produced children carrying our disease-prone genetic makeup. (Actually it is not a fault in the genes, but rather a fault in the modern context to which we are subjecting them.) Thus, there can be no genetic adaptation to this new environment because, in effect, the unfit (all of us succumbing to modern degenerative disease) survive long enough to reproduce scions having the same vulnerabilities.

So there is every reason to be 'wrong' about the common 'right' assumption that we are evolving into the synthetic world we have created. As a population, we are genetically doomed to continue to reap the consequences of being out of proper genetic context—with no genetic hope of salvation.* Humans are not going to adapt to living on a couch or to Twinkies and Ritalin. If anything, we are devolving, as evidenced by increasing rates of infertility and the fact that today's children are expected to have a shorter lifespan than their parents.

The solution is not to hope that our genes change, but for us to change. We must understand our genetic heritage—follow our owner's manual—and make life choices appropriately. This simple truth allows us to begin on the road to optimal health and puts control of our health destiny where it belongs—squarely in our own hands.

---

*Although what are known as epigenetic environmental influences, such as diet, can modify the hereditable expression of genes, DNA remains unaltered. Methyl cofactors such as folate, vitamin B_{12}, choline and betaine, as well as plant phytochemicals can attach to a gene and affect its expression. Although this helps prove that how we live and eat can affect our health and that of our progeny (if the changes occur in the sperm or eggs), it does not demonstrate that the underlying genome can be changed. DNA remains DNA, epigenetics just dictates what is or is not expressed.

5

WE LIVE IN A UNIQUE TIME

THE DEGREE TO WHICH WE HAVE VEERED from our genetic design is both remarkable and alarming. We are witness to an unprecedented acceleration of change. It is so exciting and seems so promising that potential consequences are overlooked or ignored. However, as explained in the previous chapter, our genes are not turning a blind eye.

It is essential to keep in mind that our material culture is transmitted and transformed separately from our genes. Our DNA hums along as if we are living in the bush, while we displace our bodies into a new world of environmental disruption, physical ease, relentless emotional stress, artificial light, fabricated food, and pharmaceutical cocktails. These technological and artificial trappings with which we surround ourselves are subjecting us to a gigantic experiment in which we are the willing but unwitting subjects. We may ignore or take the changes for granted, even welcome them with open arms, but our health does not.

The accompanying charts represent some of the dramatic changes occurring in the last 100 years, just in relation to food. They mirror the rate of change in almost every other facet of our world as well. On a broad environmental scale, human activity rivals the natural processes that have built the biosphere. About 40% of the Earth's photosynthetic capacity (plant growth) is now appropriated for human use. The biologically available nitrogen and phosphorus used by humans for fertilizer and chemicals about equals the amount produced by nature. We can also apparently alter our atmosphere on a global scale—think of Chernobyl, the hole in the ozone canopy and greenhouse gases. Huge numbers of species float on the curling tip of a wave of extinction created by human intervention. Every day the planet sees a net increase in population (births minus deaths) of about one quarter of a million people. The speed and scale of human activity even seems to compress time.[1] For example, it took 38 years for the telephone to reach ten million homes, cable TV took 25 years, the fax 22 years, cell phones and VCRs 9 years, computers 7 years, and the Internet only 4 years!

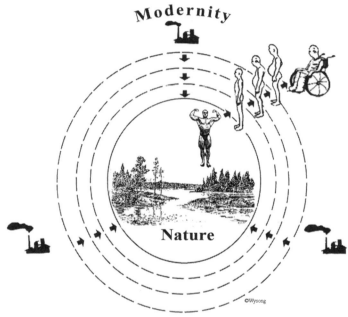

Modernity Robs Us Of Health – We are genetically adapted to living out of doors in nature, eating natural foods as found 'on the vine,' and expending considerable energy with the day to day needs of survival. As modern society with its processed foods and sedentary living encroaches, health is robbed and degenerative diseases take root.

Just an estimated 12 thousand years ago when the total population on Earth was about one million, everyone was hunting and gathering, living in sync with our genetic blueprint. Five hundred years ago, when there were 50 million people, only 1% hunted and gathered. Today, with about 6 billion people, fewer than 0.0001% still primarily hunt and gather for food.[2]

As agriculture developed, society dramatically shifted from the hunter-gatherer mode. Just a few decades ago the family farm was predominant on the rural landscape, telephones were just arriving, lights were new, water was hand pumped at the sink, and outhouses graced backyards everywhere. Many of us have direct experience with and memory of this dramatically different living circumstance.

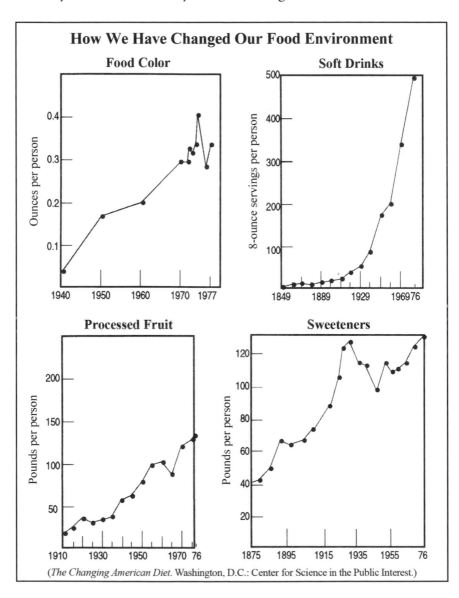

How We Have Changed Our Food Environment

(*The Changing American Diet*. Washington, D.C.: Center for Science in the Public Interest.)

But now, not only our hunter-gatherer, but our agrarian beginnings are receding into dim history. We are being swept along by a whirlwind of change in a direction we know not where. As we leave the verdant vistas behind and replace them with the concrete and haze of our cities, it is easy to accept such 'advancement' as the norm, beneficial, or at worst inconsequential. Our children will especially think so since their entire frame of reference is but a fraction of this last one inch of modern time.

All the changes we make to the natural world alienate us from our genetic design. But our bodies are not changing in tandem—are not becoming artificial as it were. Rather, like rubber bands stretched to their breaking points, we are being stressed to our adaptive limits and beyond. The result is a brave new synthetic world, but old genetics in bodies now wracked with chronic degenerative diseases.[3]

---

100 Years Ago

- Average life expectancy was 47 years
- 14% of homes had a bathtub
- 8% of homes had a telephone
- There were 144 miles of paved roads
- Maximum city speed limit was 10 mph
- A three-minute cross-country call cost eleven dollars
- Average wage was 22 cents per hour
- 95% of all births took place at home
- Women washed their hair once per month with Borax or egg yolks
- The population of Las Vegas was 30
- Crossword puzzles and canned beer had not yet been invented
- 6% were high school graduates
- Marijuana, heroine and morphine were available over the counter at the pharmacist
- Coca Cola contained cocaine

A New World In Ten Decades - Advancing technology permits change on a scale never before seen. In our quest for progress, we must be mindful that biology is essentially remaining static. We are both physiologically and mentally designed for nature. The products of our mind must not create so much imbalance with nature that health is sacrificed. (Adapted from: LibertyPost.org.)

Although it seems presumptuous to suggest that this generation is unique in all of history, the evidence supports that it is. We are a pivotal generation that must now use our technology to return us to our roots.

If we continue to do the stupid thing and keep cracking the safe at our own bank by fueling a degrading environmental and health spiral, we will reach the point of no return. Or we can approach life and our future as if thinking matters.

We are, without a doubt, a very special generation with the weight of the world's future on our shoulders. Intelligence can speed our demise or it can be used with conscience to construct an exciting new world that brings to us the health of the hunter-gatherer along with the security and wonders of advancing technology.

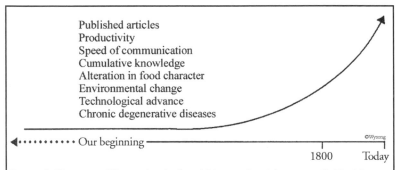

Published articles
Productivity
Speed of communication
Cumulative knowledge
Alteration in food character
Environmental change
Technological advance
Chronic degenerative diseases

••••••••••• Our beginning

©Wysong

1800   Today

Rate of Change – Change in the last 200 years is without parallel in history. Such change reflects our intellectual capabilities to alter the environment but does not reflect any fundamental biological change in our biology. The graph line remains essentially flat back through eons to our beginning.

6

BEING HEALTH SMART

Our great intellect is in large part necessary because of the quest for food. A cow is as smart as it needs to be to figure out how to eat what is always underfoot. The apex predator—clawless, fangless man—needs great cunning, memory, logic, and analytical thought. The spear and arrow have now been replaced with the grocery cart, but even more cunning is necessary in order to survive well and remain healthy in our confusing modern world.

We can no longer rely on instinct, senses, and trust. The healthy choices that were before us in the wild have now been replaced with endless options, most of which can rob our health. More choices mean we must be smarter. Intelligence creates our modern predicament; intelligence must be used to sort it out. Our world is now all about marketing, manufacturing, and science, but much of it is without conscience. The words of Dr. Malcolm in *Jurassic Park* come to mind: "Your scientists were so busy wondering how they could—they didn't stop to ask if they should." It's up to us to discern, cut through the malarkey, and make smart choices.

The heuristic cornerstone for health enlightenment is, to repeat, understanding our proper genetic context. Health is not about a doctor's visit, a cholesterol check, a mammogram, counting calories, or faithfully taking meds. Like any great truth, health truth is right there in front of us, slapping us in the face. It's obvious, simple, and easy. The problem is that it is obscured by the clever deception of modern circumstances such that even a 1.5 trillion dollar medical industry can't see the obvious. The deceptive illusion is that it is right and normal to live without sunlight ever striking our skin, breathe conditioned and polluted air, sit on our duffs the majority of the day, eat a salmagundi of processed trinkets from packages, get vaccinated, swill 'diet' soft drinks, and languish in front of a TV.

We are supposed to be out in the woods, not nestled among oil derricks and snack extruders while scheduling appointments for pap smears and prostate checks. Our genetic fine-tuning to the natural world does not disappear because we invent electricity, plows, hammer mills, and video games. The good life is not achieving a handicapped sticker because we have eaten and lived our life with abandon.

Ignoring our true genetic heritage may not doom us immediately, but the effects over time result in dis-ease: our genes are not at ease with what we are imposing on them.

The wisdom of returning our lives to our genetic roots is an algorithm—a logical framework used to solve problems. Just like a blueprint algorithm can map the construction of marvelous edifices and identify flaws in construction, so too can our genetic algorithm build health and identify the causes and solutions to health problems. There is no need to look for a magic elixir of youth, the right doctor, or an expert to give us a list of dos and don'ts. The only tools we need are our brains and the right algorithm.

If we apply that algorithm, it means we will seek fresh air, clean water, exercise, sunshine, rest, pleasant social contact, physical and mental challenge, and fresh, natural foods in variety to the degree it is possible to achieve this.[1-5]

As obvious as that sounds, it's difficult to apply because our bodies are resilient and permit us, for a time, to get away with cheating. If we were given a convincing jolt of electric shock every time we did something that would bring eventual harm to ourselves, to society, or to the environment, most problems facing humanity would be almost instantly solved. But that's not the way things are. Some lessons are easily learned, like not to pet a snarling dog, and to keep your grip when climbing a tree. But our modern world is more challenging than that. We are faced with many decisions that require intelligent foresight to measure potential consequences that may not come until far into the future—or may only come to our children or theirs.

Therein lies our problem. We are mentally lazy and pleasure-driven, too clever with alibis and excuses, like to play the odds, and are particularly good at self-justification—judging others by their actions and ourselves by our intentions. We continue whatever suits our fancy until eventually we are sufficiently harmed or are humiliated into changing due to the brute force of evidence or public opinion.

The Urban Survivalist

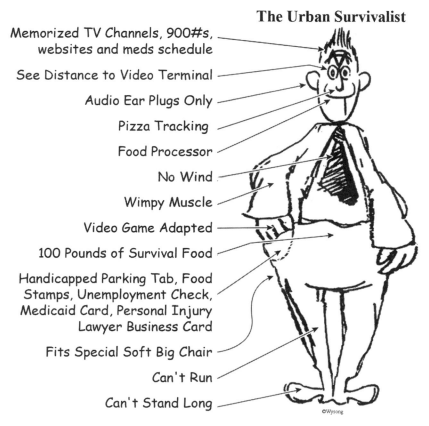

Memorized TV Channels, 900#s, websites and meds schedule

See Distance to Video Terminal

Audio Ear Plugs Only

Pizza Tracking

Food Processor

No Wind

Wimpy Muscle

Video Game Adapted

100 Pounds of Survival Food

Handicapped Parking Tab, Food Stamps, Unemployment Check, Medicaid Card, Personal Injury Lawyer Business Card

Fits Special Soft Big Chair

Can't Run

Can't Stand Long

©Wysong

Although cigarette smoking, industrial smog, water pollution, radiation, toxic gases emitted from modern construction materials, and slothful living are all proven to cause harm, even grievous life-threatening harm, they continue because immediate ill effects do not occur and because change would mean inconvenience and sacrifice. And then there's Uncle Josh. He's robust at ninety-four and yet has smoked cigars, chewed tobacco, and swigged whiskey since he was sixteen. Your brother-in-law works in the nuclear plant and has never developed cancer. A damnable classmate you saw at the recent reunion doesn't exercise, watches virtually

In spite of all this abuse, kids apparently remain healthy. Not just a little, but a lot. They have tons of energy, sleep like logs, can excel in school, and win state sports championships. What's the deal? Adults can't live like that. We'd get sick or kill ourselves trying to keep pace with their antics. If I ate in just one day what I used to eat back when I was immortal and had a stomach of cast iron, I would explode.

Youth *seems* to excuse a lot. But all is not well. Autopsies of young Korean and Vietnam War casualties revealed an extremely high incidence of atherosclerosis, the underlying pathology of heart attacks. Yet there were no detectable symptoms of heart disease in these soldiers as they went through rigorous basic training and fought in demanding wars. Problems lurked hidden within, growing like a slow cancer. If these soldiers had lived out their lives, their wrong choices would have eventually manifested in middle or later years as heart disease or a heart attack.[2]

A 1999 study of autopsies performed on almost 3000 men and women from various races between the ages of 15 and 34 showed the same results. Atherosclerotic lesions (the plaques that plug vessels and cause heart attacks and strokes) in the aortas and most of the right coronary arteries (feeding the heart muscle itself) were observed in the youngest age groups and increased in prevalence with age.[3] As a result of such findings, the American Heart Association released its recommendation that everyone over the age of 20 should be checked routinely for signs of potential heart trouble. (That, however, is not a solution. It is too little, too late.)

Heart disease is by and large a lifestyle and nutritional disease. (No, it's not from butter or cholesterol.[4]) So, too, are most other chronic, degenerative, adult-onset diseases. Their root cause is the dramatic departure we have taken from our genetic roots, and the glut of refined carbohydrates and contaminated nutrient-stripped processed foods that now make up the mainstay diet.

It is a cruel irony that the lifestyle we enjoy while young will create such havoc in adult years. We assume if we felt well and were healthy lollygagging around the house eating junk food as kids, that as adults we should be able to continue to treat food like toys, our body as if it needed no care, and any malfunction as if it were a problem for a doctor to fix. If we engage our minds, however, failed health in the adult years should cause reflection on what *we* have done wrong. The solution, therefore, is not a quick fix from a doctor, but an adjustment in life choices.

So, all is not well just because the young seem to do fine on Mountain Dew, Ding Dongs, and Cocoa Puffs. One of the greatest gifts parents can give kids is intelligent health direction. Children have no idea what's going on; they think food is cotton candy and Kool-Aid, and life is a new video game. Their robust and forgiving bodies should not fool us. Real love is not about being 'nice' by giving kids what they want, or doing what is convenient for us—like getting them out of our hair by sitting them in front of the television with a bag of corn curls.

Our job as parents is to save them from themselves and an adult life crippled with degenerative disease. We can do that by breaking away from the crowd and getting their bodies back in touch with their genetic roots.

8

THE GOOD OLD DAYS

IT MIGHT APPEAR FROM THE ARGUMENTS in the preceding chapters that if we want to be healthy, we should abandon our soft lives and go rough it in the wild. Here's a little perspective on that idea.

The primitive foraging tribe, usually limited to about forty people by the carrying capacity of the land, had an average lifespan of around 22 years.[1] Humans were excellent prey. Not having strength, size, or speed to match the great predators, just trying to stay out of the jaws of the food chain would have been a full time preoccupation. In fact, it is believed that one of the reasons that North America was delayed in being extensively populated was the presence of great carnivores. One was a monster bear that could stand over 10 feet high and had the speed of a horse. Imagine taking a Sunday stroll in the woods with these creatures lurking behind the bushes.*

If you weren't being dined on, even a minor injury like stubbing a toe, embedding a thorn, or getting cut on a rock as you were scrambling to get

---

*To get a sense of what life was like as prey, and to help make the point that we are intimately linked to nature, turn the volume way up on your computer and go to our asifthinkingmatters.com website and click on the "Multimedia" link, and then the "Predator" link. This sound of a predator will create sensations in you including chills running up and down your skin that are almost impossible to control. Such feelings were a part of daily life for our ancestors living in the wild.

away from one of these monsters could be the beginning of the end. No Emergency Room, no disinfectant, not even a Band-Aid. There would be no time to lie around recuperating with someone else feeding you. No entitlement programs, no panhandling. You had to keep going. If death didn't come from the injury, it might from starvation or exposure to the elements. Before that welcome end, you would be in the most dreaded category that predators just love—the weak and disabled, the unfit.

There was every manner of infectious and parasitic disease. To this day in our North American woods there is giardiasis, Rocky Mountain spotted fever, Lyme disease, a cadre of parasitic worms, mycotic and bacterial skin infections, ehrlichiosis, babesiosis, brucellosis, shigellosis, schistosomiasis and Eastern equine encephalomyelitis. Hordes of mosquitoes, black flies, deer flies, spiders, and ticks could make a person want to spend nights plunged neck-deep into leech-infested waters for relief from the relentless attacks.

People today, infected with mosquito–transmitted Eastern equine encephalomyelitis, for example, either get to spend their life propped up in a chair with a bib, or, more mercifully, die. Lyme disease, on the other hand, lets a person experience a smorgasbord of misery: headaches, fever, chills, fatigue, shortness of breath, dizziness, facial paralysis, muscle spasms, mental impairment, loss of control of body functions, depression, and cardiac irregularities. Then there are the hanta viruses, which swarm above the feces of mice and rats. These are killers and can be contracted by just lying on the ground, breathing rodent droppings ubiquitously present on the forest floor (as Bill Bryson put it in *A Walk in the Woods,* after attempting to traverse the Appalachian Trail).[2]

Wild living, the principle we need to apply if we are to have health, is just that—only a principle for modern humans. Primitive times were good in that ignorance and rudimentary technology did limited damage to the environment. Being out in nature, active, and eating what nature provided also gave them robust health because they were living in tune with their genetics. The bad part was that life was hard and dangerous. Their exposed and precarious predicament is not necessarily something to envy. Besides, we have long since grown in population beyond the point where everyone could walk out their door and survive on what the woods and fields provided.

We're kind of stuck in the modern predicament. But on the bright side we can have the best of all worlds if we would just apply thinking. Our technology can bring safety, comfort, security, abundant food, health, and happiness. On the other hand, our advanced tools can strip mine the Earth of all resources, pave it over, and create health-robbing addicting foods and conveniences that turn us into mushy, unfit weaklings festering with chronic degenerative diseases.

We modern hunters must now hunt for the right ideas and be willing to use them. Such intelligence is our ultimate technology and can bring to us the optimal health that only nature obeyed can bring.[1]

9

TIMING LIFE

WE ARE NOT ONLY GENETICALLY TUNED to the natural world, we are inextricably linked to its rhythms in ways that are only now beginning to be discovered. The companion book on *Solving the Big Questions* will explain the science of this truth and its deeper philosophical meaning. But for now, just consider its physical and health implications.

The Earth, moon, and sun embrace one another so intimately that they are best understood as one giant living organism. We are in turn linked to this giant cosmic creature much like a cell is linked to the body. Light, moon, sun, magnetism, gravity, planetary rotation, and orbital periods affect us in subtle, yet profound ways.

The desire to sleep at night and a woman's monthly lunar ovulations are obvious rhythms demonstrating this tie. But don't think it ends there. Well over 100 known bodily functions peak and decline in response to nature. Cell division, hormone release, temperature, blood pressure, mood, energy level, strength, sexuality, creativity, memory, immune function, and alertness cycle daily, monthly, and yearly. Even senescence and natural death are timed.

Since health is actually another word for balance, it is critical to understand and respect these cycling relationships. Unfortunately, the artificial trappings with which we surround ourselves disengage us from the natural environment and our own body's rhythms. Constant sensory overload, snubbing nature, and running our day by a schedule that is set by convenience drowns out the inner voice.

As years pass us in life, we somewhat awaken to the cycling and rhythms in spite of our best efforts to ignore them. If we pay attention we will note:

• Morning and evening (if we have had rest during the day) are usually the best times for active mental and intellectual demands.

• More intense physical activity is best performed in the afternoon. (This may not be entirely true, but since this is a slow mental time it works well to fill it with physical activity.)

• Major meals seem to be tolerated best at mid-morning and evening.

• Energy, immunity, and health are best during the summer or on visits south in the winter when our skin gets a good dose of sun and generates the master hormone/vitamin, vitamin D.[1]

• The shortened days in the fall and winter dramatically increase susceptibility to infection and other ills.

To test these rhythms, notice how poorly the mind works in the one to four o'clock afternoon range as opposed to first thing in the morning. Many find that the morning shower is the most creative time for thinking. Also notice that it is often a struggle to stay out of the land of nod between 2:00 and 3:00 p.m. It is not by accident that some societies close shops and siesta in the early afternoon. Your rhythms may be different than this. If they are, listen to them.

We must pay attention to what the body and mind whisper to us, rather than what convention and society impose. By doing so, our connection with a natural reality is revealed that can help us make the most of life and achieve our best health potential.

10

EXERCISE

THE BENEFITS OF EXERCISE ARE MYRIAD. It makes us feel good, burns excess body fat, grows and maintains muscle, strengthens bones and joints, helps flexibility, deepens sleep, improves appearance, creates a high, provides goals to achieve, lifts depression, relieves stress, increases self esteem, reverses and prevents disease, and helps us feel alive and youthful. There is virtually no measure of well being that cannot be improved by exercise.[1]

In the wild, exercise would be as normal as breathing. If we were not industriously finding food, building shelters, and fighting off predators, we would not survive. In natural circumstances, eating is the reward for exercise. In the modern world we don't have to exercise to get our food. Is a problem not apparent?

We may have cleverly changed our situation and cheated nature with our grocery stores, fast food restaurants, and refrigerators, but we have not changed the rule that eating is the fuel and the reward for exercise. If we are not exercising we should not be eating—or should at least be doing very little of it. (This is not meant to deny that some—very little—food is necessary for moment-to-moment metabolism.) This natural law is rarely cited these days. Ignoring and violating it results in a penalty—obesity and disease.

Unfortunately, with essentially all of today's needs met at arm's length, being sedentary is normal. Getting rewards for physically doing nothing (desk sitting, phone calls, and computer work, for example) is also usual. So thinking must intervene. We must make a decision to exercise because it is what bodies are designed for and health cannot result without it.

There are about as many exercise programs as there are people who exercise and teach it. There are also scientific studies that can be cited in support of almost any choice of exercise program.

"By golly! Every one of the positions, Bev!"

Exploring the options can keep exercise fun and challenging, and make it the lifelong activity it should be.

If weights, aerobics, and athletics seem too tedious or daunting, don't be discouraged. You can still be fit and enjoy the health benefits of exercise with less brawny activity. Regular brisk walks, vigorous housework, lawn and garden activity, taking the stairs instead of the elevator, playing with the kids or grandkids, splitting wood, bicycling or walking to work, and even preparing meals and doing the dishes can be a workout.

Do what you enjoy but look at the results. You don't need a scale or calorie counter. The mirror tells all. If you don't have the results you want (keep in mind that how you look on the outside is a reflection of how you look inside), then adjust intake and output. If you don't want to adjust intake (food), then you may have to readjust your output (exercise) to a more vigorous routine.

The body, like us, is naturally lazy. If the shape it is in is sufficient to do an exercise without effort, then the body will stay as it is. If it is pushed, if there is some physical stress, if we try for steady increases and gains, and even look for the brief pain of strain, the body will respond with a new and better body capable of doing what is demanded of it. When we challenge the body with exercise—not just coast through motions—a signal is sent to the body that it needs to be strong, vigorous, and healthy. It responds to the call. On the other hand, demand nothing and you get nothing.

Like anything else in life that is worthwhile, exercise takes effort. It may mean some sweat, soreness, fatigue and even an occasional injury. In fact, if there is never injury or soreness, there is a good chance intensity is not sufficient. No intensity, no results. I understand this is wrong according to some popular and professional opinions, but just reason on it. Why should the body improve if it is not being asked to do more than it normally could do in the condition it is presently in? Also, the danger for most people is not in doing too much, it is doing too little.

For most of us in modern life, exercise is a special event, not a daily lifestyle like hunting, foraging, or manual labor would be. We go to the gym, put on our running or walking shoes, or do a routine right at home. Regardless, because the event is relatively brief in relation to the rest of our sedentary day, exercise must be done with intensity, like

"Why don't they make fake exercise?"

we mean it, no faking it. To do much good (in terms of sculpting the body, growing muscle, or losing weight), it takes hard work and briefly exhausting muscles two to three times a week. Nothing comes easy. We have to breathe hard and strain and grunt a little if we are trying to be something other than what our body already is. Easy, comfortable, and casual workouts (while sipping on sugared sports drinks and chatting) will produce bodies that look easy, comfortable, and casual.

The idea of a little pain associated with exercise need not be as negative and scary as it sounds. Bodybuilders, in fact, consider their occasional soreness and injuries as clues of success. The soreness I am talking about is not the kind that incapacitates or sends us to the doctor for painkillers. It's more like a gentle awareness of the existence of the muscle, a message from it to us telling us we have done our job. The slight soreness also identifies which muscles were targeted with the exercise and thus tells us the right exercise if we want to condition a particular muscle group. Soreness is not a reason to be discouraged or quit a regimen. It tells us we are not just fooling around, and is a lesson on where our limits are and how to adjust our routine.

There are basic principles that help assure success with an exercise program. For one, lift weights. The extra resistance permits us to gain the benefits of exercise in shorter periods of time. Barbells, dumbbells, machines, or the body itself (pushups, pull-ups, squats,

etc.) create a load beyond normal and call for body improvement. Weight training improves strength, looks, and increases bone density and resting metabolic rate, helping to burn fat calories. The greater the muscle mass, the more calories are being burned at rest.

Women don't need to be afraid of weights. Resistance training can create strength important for day-to-day function, agility, and a more toned and feminine appearance. Another proven benefit of weight lifting for women is decreasing the risk of osteoporosis and bone fracture by increasing bone density and strength. Ladies need not stay away from weights because they "don't want big muscles." Women will not grow big muscles unless they take male hormones. Similarly, an adolescent boy or a man in his eighties cannot make themselves look like Mr. Olympia no matter how much weight lifting they do. For the young boy, that's because the anabolic male hormones have not kicked in; for the elderly man it is because those hormones have ebbed. This fear of big muscles is a common reason (or excuse) why some women do not weight train. It is a myth that should be put aside. Neither should women feel any inadequacy because there are some muscle heads in the gym throwing around big iron. Just do your job and stay within yourself. That will bring the respect of anyone. Besides, the guys really don't want you out-lifting them. They would rather you marvel at how much they lift and swoon at their biceps.

A word of caution is in order for men wanting to use high weights to pack on Herculean slabs of muscle. Hoisting much more than body weight puts excessive stress on joints, cartilage, ligaments, and tendons. Over time, the wear and tear will come back to haunt with arthritis or other limiting joint and back injuries. Staying power in an exercise program is the key, not ego stroking, or just a flash-in-the-pan puffy body.

Two or three times a week, also do 15-30 minutes of aerobic exercise. Alternatively, if you have time, do less intensity over longer time. Regardless, do at least part of it with enough intensity to breathe hard and work up a sweat. Be careful of long distance jogging since the impact on joints can be counterproductive. Impact aerobics is traumatic and tends to tear the body down, not build its strength. Although long sessions of aerobic activity will burn calories, little strength is involved. So, like the wise creature it is, the body slows metabolism and stores the densest form of calories there is, fat. If that isn't enough, it gnaws away at muscles to convert them to calories. Compare the bodies of marathoners to those who run the 100-meter dash in the Olympics. The marathoner's body looks gaunt and malnourished; the face drawn and aged. In contrast, sprinters look strong, vibrant, and athletic. So, if running is the aerobic choice, do series of short sprints. If possible, do it barefoot in sand to give the feet, toes, and calves a great workout and to limit impact. Be careful of intense aerobics on the same days as the resistance work. The body needs recovery.

Standmill

Televisercise

Bicep Curls

Airobics

41

Find an active sport to participate in. Getting up out of a chair, moving about, trying to improve, meeting people, and having fun is a healthy thing to do. The exercise, challenge, and camaraderie can be one of life's greatest joys.

Although pushing toward the limits once in a while may help increase exercise capacity, doing it too often can, over the long term, work the opposite effects. There is potential damage from the shower of physiological free radicals created when demands exceed metabolic capacity. Free radicals are like sparks in the fireplace. If the fire is modest there are few and they are contained. But if the fire is stoked up to roaring, the sparks spitting out into the living room could set the house afire. Extreme exercise is like a roaring fire and the free radicals created can damage body structure and lead to premature aging, structural damage, immune suppression, and disease.

Make accommodations for age, but not before it is absolutely necessary. No 'too old' excuses before your time. Fitness and athleticism can be for a lifetime. Nevertheless, with time, everything does wear and become more fragile. The body at 70 cannot be forced to be what it was at 18, regardless of exercise and diet. New physical levels can, however, be achieved through the 50's. What age takes away in physical vigor and resiliency, it gives in desire and commitment. In the young the body exceeds the mind; in the old, the mind exceeds the body. With advanced age, exercise that is too intense will feel like it is tearing down, not stimulating growth. It is. The fine line between improving or maintaining strength and fitness or doing damage gets thinner and thinner with age. So listen to the body and adjust. Be content with being the best you can be, not trying to be what you cannot possibly be. No ninety year-old has ever won an Olympic event or set a world athletic record.

Most importantly, think about the long term. Staying power is the key. Exercise for life and for health, not for a short spectacular spurt that might cause an injury and then leave you incapacitated.

The human body is a gift and a responsibility. It is a moral duty to take care of it. Exercise like you mean it, but also use the wisdom of moderation. Enjoy the health that results and the wonderful, feel-alive dimension that is added to life by having a fit body.

11

HORMONES AND STEROIDS—
A TWO-EDGED SWORD

WHEN I WAS A YOUNG BOY, seeing muscles bulge here and there was really cool. If a vein popped out a little that was even more awesome. There were no fitness centers or gyms to amount to anything back then. About the only option was to order Charles Atlas paraphernalia from comic book ads, or get muscles the 'legitimate' way by hard work.

I did lots of farm work and construction, but leaving nothing to chance, I built my own weight set with a pipe that I would insert into the holes of cement blocks. I loved the sense of strength that exercise brought and reveled in the pumped muscles that followed a workout. Sorry to sound so narcissistic. But it's the way we young boys thought, particularly those of us involved in sports. We would even compare muscle bumps on the school bus every morning and banter about who could do the most push-ups.

My dad was of the school that exercise could make a person "muscle bound." I guess he must have worried as he saw me in the backyard hoisting my pipe with blocks dangling from each end. He chided and teased me about this and always made me feel like I should have been spending my time hoeing the garden or chopping wood.

I don't mean to bore you with this trip down memory lane, but my own history came to mind as I thought about how far muscle building has come. Now that we are out of the forest and off the farm, exercise is a perfectly legitimate way to replace the physical activity lost with modern living.

The now popular use of anabolic steroids, however, is a perversion of what should be clean and healthy personal development. Use of these hormones totally misses the point. The inflated bodies created through their use do not represent health, yet 'health and fitness' magazines are filled with photo spreads presenting steroid-bloated behemoths as icons we should emulate. The influence on the young is particularly dangerous.

Aside from the dangers of steroids, which I will address momentarily, consider this as well. Although strength and fitness are something to aspire to, musculature of Brobdingnagian (a ridiculous word fitting ridiculous muscles) proportions can be thought of as disease, not health. At the cellular level, enlargement is due to hypertrophy (increased cell  size), and/or hyperplasia (increased cell number). It is a principle in medical pathology that enlarged organs resulting from these cellular changes usually signal stress and disease. An enlarged heart or kidney is an indication that the organ is reaching the end of its adaptive rope. We normally don't think of grossly enlarged muscles as pathology, but we should.

Aside from the fact that natural bodies and developed talents should compete in sports, not drug regimens, the damage these powerful chemicals can do is enormous. And there is a lesson here for anyone taking hormones for any purpose. Of all the drugs dispensed in medical practice, hormones are among the scariest. They can create dramatic and immediate results (and that is their allure), but hormone treatment continued for any length of time comes back to haunt.

An example in humans is the use of testosterone patches to increase libido in women. If they are taken for any length of time, passion may be triggered but so too will the voice start to deepen and a beard blossom—not so good for the libido of the husband. Corticosteroids taken for allergies or injuries can result in extremely serious adrenal gland diseases, immune suppression, and vulnerability to infection. Birth control hormones are fraught with dangers, yet their use has even become fashionable to limit the inconvenience of menstruation. Hormone replacement therapy in menopausal women is directly linked to breast cancer.

The same dangers apply in veterinary medicine. One situation I am reminded of is related to hormones that were given to dogs for birth control. Years after discontinuing the drugs, treated dogs would present to veterinarians with life threatening illness, extreme thirst, and white blood cell counts off the charts. Their abdomens would enlarge due to the uterus swelling gigantically with pus (pyometra). Pints of it could accumulate, all just because a little ol' hormone was given years ago, with nary a hint of any ill effect at the time.

To better understand the dangers of taking hormones, we must remember that the body is extremely wise. It is not fooled, enamored of fad, or forever forgiving. For example, if an arm is broken and put in a sling, the muscles don't grow bigger, they atrophy. This is because the body is also efficient and will not do what is not needed. Why grow muscles, or even maintain them, if they are not needed? When the sling is removed the arm will have withered and lost most of its strength. The body shuttled its resources into building bigger muscles in the arm that had to perform double duty. It's a very pragmatic thing. The body doesn't pay attention to your agenda, it just does what it must to stay alive, make do, and meet everyday stress.

The same thing would happen to both arms—to the whole body— if servants did everything and we just reclined in our easy chairs. If we then suddenly had to get out of the chair and run a mile, or lift 200 pounds to survive, we wouldn't make it. An atrophied and weak body could not rise to the challenge.

Hormones are metabolic slings. They replace the hormones that the body normally produces. When this happens there is a negative feedback mechanism: the more that hormones from the outside are introduced into the body, the less the body does what it no longer needs to, which is synthesize its own hormones. So the metabolic 'muscles' that create hormones atrophy. If all of a sudden the outside source of hormones is withdrawn, the organs that are now withered from the easy-chair life do not have the strength to produce their own hormones. Since almost every function in the body is hormone influenced, and every hormone interacts with every other hormone in some way, catastrophe results.

So what would be expected with massive doses of hormones at a level the body would never produce on its own? In the case of anabolics, what happens to the digestive system that cannot grow digestive muscle paralleling the pecs, but is being forced to digest and assimilate massive amounts of food daily? For example, some body builders try to consume 600 grams of protein per day. That's about 20 chicken breasts—and represents only the protein fraction of their diet.

Gregg Valentino – was featured in "The Man Whose Arms Exploded," a TLC documentary highlighting the use and abuse of steroids. He is reported to have the largest biceps in the world. He not only consumed every imaginable steroid, but injected them directly into muscle. (With permission: http://greggvalentino.net/index.cfm?pageID=12&picSectionID=4)

Is it also any wonder that over time modern anabolic bodybuilders are racked with heart disease, cancer, immune weakness, atrophy of the testicles (in effect, they are put in a sling when hormones are taken), digestive failure, and metabolic disorders?

A huge number of high school kids are now trying to 'get big' with steroids. What an incredibly dangerous proposition for them. Parents need to be aware that this fad is prevalent and not innocuous. If the argument is that taking hormones is the only way to excel in a sport, then have them change sports. Insist.

Adults who are toying with the idea of taking hormones for one reason or another should think long and hard. Read the contraindications and cautions on the drug insert sheets. Take heed. Find other ways to stimulate the body's own natural ability to enhance or improve itself through exercise, lifestyle, and nutrition. We can't put our organs in slings by taking hormones and then expect long-term benefit. The disease piper will always be paid if we ignore, attempt to supercede, or defy nature.

12

THE FEMALE
HORMONE PROBLEM

WITH INCREASING POPULATION PRESSURE, modern independent lifestyles, and economic limitations, interest in child
bearing is waning. However, nature does not change just because
we exert our right to make a choice. What seems perfectly 'right,'
turns out to be 'wrong' from a biological perspective. Women are
designed to have children. Additionally, if children are conceived,
opting for synthetic milk formulas also disengages women from
the natural biological function of nursing. Not having children,
as well as having them and not nursing, have profound hormonal
effects and potential health consequences.

Contraceptive hormones, hormone replacement therapy, an increasing load of estrogenic pollutants in the environment and food,
and a diet that has veered significantly from its natural design all
set the stage for hormonal pandemonium, metabolic dysfunction,
and disease. The results are manifest today in early menses in children (beginning as early as eight and nine years of age), infertility,
abnormal and erratic menstrual cycles, cervical dysplasia, fibroids,
endometrial cancer, breast cancer, premenstrual syndrome, dramatic
mood swings, depression, osteoporosis, exaggeration of the hot
flashes, psychological problems, decreased libido, and thinning of
the vaginal wall common in menopause.[1]

These health problems would by and large disappear if women would bear children naturally, nurse them for years as they are designed to, eat natural foods (what those are, exactly, will be covered in a following section), and live in a more pristine environment. But the likelihood of that is like hoping money will flow out of the tap to solve financial problems.

Thus there is a dilemma. Women need to fulfill their reproductive role to achieve metabolic balance and health. At the same time, they don't want to be restricted by the burdens of large families, may not feel financially capable, or may be impeded by social or environmental responsibilities. In an attempt at a solution, women have turned to the quick fix of hormones. There are hormones to control conception, modulate abnormal menstrual cycles, improve sex drive, and fix menopause. But there is no free lunch. For example, since the 1940's when estrogen therapy became popular, hundreds of thousands of women have succumbed to estrogen-sensitive cancers. Women on estrogen are 13 times more likely to get endometrial cancer and there is a 30% greater risk of breast cancer. The two top preventable breast cancer risks are now known to be oral birth control pills and estrogen replacement therapy.[2]

Some women justify the use of estrogen for the putative benefits of decreased risk of osteoporosis and cardiovascular disease. But they have succumbed to marketing, not good science. Proper exercise, diet, and lifestyle choices can have the same beneficial effect without the potential consequence of cancer.

Here's what nature intended and why living in accord with it is protective against the modern plague of female cancers. The average mom today gives birth to about two infants. On the other hand, women in the primitive natural setting who may not even know what causes pregnancy or how to prevent it, on average would have started menstruating and ovulating at age 12 and would have delivered 9 babies during their lives and breast-fed each one for about five years. Pregnancy stops the reproductive hormone cycles that generate estrogen. Nursing also impedes the cycle because the body 'knows' that lactation and caring for an infant is about all one body can endure.

The modern woman who has only two children and bottle feeds them would reproductively cycle and ovulate approximately 438 times during her lifetime. On the other hand, the combination of more numerous pregnancies along with extended breast-feeding would have decreased the number of ovulations in a primitive mother to about 9.

This means that women today cycle through their menstrual periods about 429 times (438-9) more than they were designed to. This causes repeated surges of estrogen that increase the risk of estrogen-sensitive cancers. The cancer-estrogen link is also proven by the fact that such cancers in humans and animals are decreased if the estrogen-generating ovaries are surgically removed. (I am merely making a point, not advocating the procedure since the absence of estrogen creates problems as well.)

Primitive Woman
9 eggs/lifetime
9 estrogen surges

Modern Woman
438 eggs/lifetime
438 estrogen surges

The resting periods of lower estrogen levels that women experienced in the pre-modern setting during pregnancy and lactation served as protection against cancer. But how can this knowledge be applied in our modern setting? For one, women can dramatically decrease their risk of breast cancer by nursing their young for as long as possible. Even as little as two years can make a big difference. A healthy lifestyle and remaining relatively lean is also very important. (Body fat accumulates environmental estrogenic toxins.) Eating natural foods is also protective since the natural diet contains compounds known as phytoestrogens—particularly high in cruciferous vegetables and legumes—that are able to attach to estrogen receptor sites and prevent the stronger ovarian estrogens from attaching to tissues. These plant estrogens do not promote cancer since they only exert a mild estrogenic effect and they inhibit oncogene (tumor gene) expression. This is the logic behind plant-based nutritional supplements (nutraceuticals) to help women with estrogenic problems and cancer prevention.

Clearly, child bearing is an extremely important decision and an enormous responsibility for women. Merely following popular trends and being a ready customer of the latest pharmaceutical hormone or baby formula is not the proper basis for decision making. On the other hand, having nine children may not be socially or environmentally responsible. Nor does the modern woman warm to the picture of nine children underfoot, clinging to hems and scaling her like small mountaineers. Some balance of all the opposing factors must be made. But in that process, and as compromises are decided, women must always keep in mind that health is nature obeyed. Edging life as close to that ideal as possible is living life as if thinking matters.

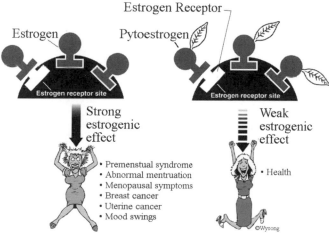

Good - Bad Estrogen – Modern living forces women out of their natural ovulation, pregnancy, and nursing periods. This unnaturally impacts levels of hormones which in turn increases susceptibility to disease.

13

GROWING OLDER

WHEN WE ARE YOUNG we assume that being old won't happen to us. Old age is so far away we think it doesn't matter, or maybe the event will forget us when we get there. Getting old happens to us in spite of ignoring it. It's not an easy process, either, and is not usually done gracefully. To compound the biological problems, there is the pervasive and ignored 'ism' of our day, ageism, where the elderly are essentially ostracized. (More on this later.) It's a tough row all of us must hoe one day. The actress Bette Davis summed it up like this: "Growing old is not for sissies."

Not only do physical capabilities ebb with the years, but mental skills do as well. The elderly can cycle back to the physical and mental incapacities of being an infant. The time in the center of life when we are fully capable is but a brief window. Our problem is that in this window of the middle years we think old age is way off in time. So we don't store up health treasures to be redeemed later on in life. Living for the moment, adopting an if-it-feels-good-do-it attitude, and traipsing through life under the mistaken assumption that the wonders of medicine will fix anything that breaks, is the formula for health disaster in the golden years.

To harvest health in the latter years requires cultivating it in the early ones. As previously explained, most of the chronic degenerative diseases that rob life begin in childhood. The good news is that most of them are preventable with proper lifestyle and diet.

We hear reports of how science will extend life to 150 years and even beyond. Aside from the fact that science has not extended life at all, and is nowhere near that capability (proof of this follows), in the state many people find themselves at even 50 or 60, who would want more time of that? Life in a nursing home crippled, demented, incontinent, breathing tanked oxygen, or on life support is not particularly attractive.

Although I discuss at length whether death is really *The End* in the companion book, Solving The Big Questions, let me here say that there is a time for the end of life on Earth and that is not necessarily bad or something to fear. When life brings more pain than pleasure, death is surely a welcome relief. In fact, when you think about it, all of life is filled with a series of deaths. The innocence of childhood, the thrills of the high school years, the security of life at home with parents, young love, children of our own, the excitement of a new career, a first car and home, the 'stuff' of boats, clothes, tools, furniture, etc., is temporary. They all, in effect, die because they pass or lose their glamour. My daughter recently remarked to me as she was moving through young adulthood, "Everything is becoming more real, less fantastic."

If these deaths in life are not offset with new adventures they can mound up as only memories to make life a very depressing ordeal in the later years. The trick is to not let life degrade to nothing except an accumulation of memories. Life is a participation sport requiring that we fill it with new challenges, never stop growing, and that we make a point of becoming a better person. That is the only way to make growing older worthwhile—yet another beginning chapter to look forward to, not a final one we wish would end.

Aging is, in part, self-imposed because as we get older we convince ourselves we're supposed to slow down. We don't grow old; rather we become old by not growing. We are not an exception to the rule that all things like to take the route of least resistance. It's easier to not learn more, not be creative, not develop a new skill, not become fitter, increase strength, or develop athleticism. Being 'too old' is a convenient excuse to not apply the force to life to improve it and prevent its slide downhill.

Our body and mind rise to the challenges we place upon them. If we do something, we will be something. Do nothing and we become nothing. Be increasingly inactive and we will achieve the ultimate inactivity—death. The best life of all is to not permit the decrepitudes of old age and die old as young as possible.

Forget the numbers attached to life. Don't assume that forty means easing off, fifty means retiring, sixty means incapable, and seventy means being just an observer. Life is about pushing ourselves mentally and physically, always seeking new horizons. That's what can make life fulfilling to the end. If we plan to live forever every day, we can always say, "So good, so far."

This is not to say that age does not slow us down and decrease capacity. At age 80 we can't run the same time in the 100-meter dash that we did at 25. Nor should we try since the inherent strength and resiliency of an older body is less and thus more prone to getting broken. We're like rubber bands in that regard. Stretch a new one over and over and it doesn't matter. Get one out of the back of the drawer that's been there for a few years and try the same thing and it will break apart. But that's okay. We can still stretch our lives; we just have to be more careful.

Also consider that what we lose due to physical attrition we gain in experience and savvy. It's pretty satisfying to get to the point in life where there's nothing much left to learn the hard way, and most everyone around you is younger and therefore less experienced. With age we don't have to guess so much about things or embark on time- and energy-consuming adventures that are fruitless. Having been there and done that gives us confidence, even smugness, with respect to the frenzied and dead-ended activities of all the young gaffers.

Living a full life means deferring less and less to teachers and mentors. We become the teacher and mentor. It is no longer necessary to be in awe. We can discern, be critical, and perhaps even make better sense of things than most of the supposed experts out there—if we have lived as if thinking matters. Although humility and learning are always in order, shifting roles from life's student to teacher and leader—from taking to giving—is something to welcome as one of life's wonderful rewards. It is a reward only possible if we *grow* older.

54

Here's proof and encouragement that it is never too late to be what we might have been:

- At 100, Grandma Moses was painting.
- At 94, Bertrand Russell was active in international peace drives.
- At 93, George Bernard Shaw wrote the play Far Fetched Fables.
- At 91, Eamon de Valera served as President of Ireland.
- At 91, Adolph Zukor was chairman of Paramount Pictures.
- At 90, Pablo Picasso was producing drawings and engravings.
- At 89, Mary Baker Eddy was directing the Christian Science Church.
- At 89, Arthur Rubenstein gave one of his greatest recitals in New York's Carnegie Hall.
- At 89, Albert Schweitzer headed a hospital in Africa.
- At 88, Pablo Casals was giving cello concerts.
- At 88, Michelangelo did architectural plans for the Church of Santa Maria degli Angeli.
- At 88, Konrad Adenauer was Chancellor of Germany.
- At 85, Coco Chanel was the head of a fashion design firm.
- At 84, W. Somerset Maugham wrote Points of View.
- At 83, Aleksander Kerensky wrote Russia and History's Turning Point.
- At 82, Winston Churchill wrote A History of the English Speaking Peoples.
- At 82, Leo Tolstoy wrote I Cannot Be Silent.
- At 81, Benjamin Franklin effected the compromise that led to the adoption of the U.S. Constitution.
- At 81, Johann Wolfgang von Goethe finished Faust.
- At 80, George Burns won an Academy Award for his performance in The Sunshine Boys.

14

SQUARING THE CURVE

IT IS A MISCONCEPTION that medical technology is increasing the potential life span of humans. In fact, it has done nothing to alter our genetic limits. No, medicine will not save us from ourselves by giving us immortality with an injection or pill.

This misplaced hope derives from the insidious and erroneous philosophy of materialism. The body is seen as a mere machine, and as such, perpetually salvageable. Although it may be true that parts may be repaired and replaced, life is not reducible to matter (see the companion volume), nor can the decline of any organism be circumvented. The Second Law of Thermodynamics demands that all physical things move toward ever increasing entropy, that is, toward ever increasing decay and disorganization. Like a home will become disorganized if unattended to, so too will the universe one day be cold, dark, still, and random. Every living organism's low entropy and highly ordered state is only temporary and must comply with this law and thus experience an inevitable decline. To achieve physical immortality would mean to defeat this absolute universal law. That is not going to happen.

Science has also discovered that our organs and systems have a finite reserve capacity. For example, the heart can increase its output by a factor of 6, the kidney can function with about 80 percent of its filtering nephrons lost, and a person can survive with one lung and one quarter of the liver. We live because we are in homeostasis with our environment and can endure its threats—to a degree. As we lose organ reserve, including immune capacity—over 50 percent is lost by age 85—every stressor becomes more life threatening. When organ function declines below the level necessary to withstand even minor stress, death will result.

In 1961, research demonstrated that the life span of fibroblast cells in tissue culture reached a limit of 60 divisions and no more. This is known as the Hayflick Limit. The cells did not stop dividing as a result of toxins, infectious agents, or problems within the growth media. Instead, there was found to be an inherent limit to cell division. If the cultures are frozen and then thawed several years later, the cells continue where they left off and complete their normal number of doublings up to the limit of 60. The maximum cell doubling number is proportional to the maximum life span of the species. For example, the Galapagos turtle has a maximum life span of 175 years and a maximum cell doubling of 125. Human maximum life span is about 120 years with a maximum cell doubling of approximately 60. The mouse has a life span of about 4 years and a maximum doubling of about 28.

The mechanism of aging has long been studied but was dramatically invigorated with hope when DNA was discovered and then sequenced. After all, if life is nothing more than an arrangement of chemicals along a nucleic acid strand then chemists should be able to figure that all out and shut down the aging process. That's the theory, but that is not the way things have worked out. Life is far more than DNA and, in fact, is not reducible to matter at all. That is why life has never been created in a laboratory starting with lifeless inorganic chemicals.

Health is not solved by blind faith in science's promises of immortality. While we are alive and healthy we must address the loss of life by such things as chronic degenerative diseases, infirmity, and senescence. Getting dead is the problem, not being dead.

We need to square the curve on a graph that plots vitality on a vertical axis and aging on the horizontal. For those experiencing degenerative or debilitating disease beginning as early as their twenties, the curve begins a downward slope in proportion to the frequency of trips to the doctor, hospital stays, and growth of the pharmacy in the bathroom cabinet. In effect, the death process begins with the first trip to the doctor.

Our goal should be to be active, alive, and vital until the very end of our genetic life limit and then to die rapidly, much as a leaf falls from a tree. Health is not the slowest possible rate at which one can die. It is thoughtless to cash out vitality and health during youth and then surrender to a disease-ridden decline. A life that is only made tolerable by pharmaceuticals that temporarily relieve symptoms is not how life should be.

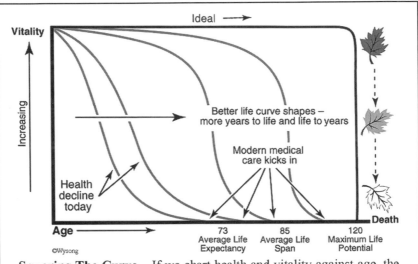

Squaring The Curve – If we chart health and vitality against age, the curves to the left on the chart represent typical loss of health and languishing for decades under medical care. The goal should be to maintain optimal health and vitality right out to our genetic limit (squaring the curve) with life ending like a leaf falls from a tree.

Hope does not lie in technologies such as gene splicing to create perpetual cells. The idea is to add life to years and not just years to life. To do that, we must overcome the debilitating killers that slope the vitality curve prematurely. These include such conditions as atherosclerosis, cancer, diabetes, arthritis, emphysema, and cirrhosis that cause almost 90% of all disability and premature death. Such conditions are not inevitable and there is much we can individually do. And, you guessed it: it all has to do with matching our life choices to our genetic design.

In societies that do seem to have many long-lived individuals—such as certain groups in Russia, the Hunzas, and the Vilcabamba—fancy hospitals are nowhere to be found. Rather, there is a high level of physical activity into old age, such as farming by hand. There is also an absence of obesity, no retirement, strong families, moderation, and usefulness and purpose to the very end.

But even under the best of circumstances there are aging changes we have to concede. The decrease in skin elasticity, graying and thinning of hair, loss of muscle, decrease in bone density, energy, and stamina, and increased rigidity in arteries and the lens of the eye are inevitable. But affecting the rate and degree of such loss—changing the shape of the curve—is within our grasp.

Heeding all the dos and don'ts of the next chapter is a good start in squaring the shape of the graph. Proactively making health happen, instead of waiting for science to save us from our laziness and bad habits, gives us the best chance for a full and productive life culminating in a death that is natural and healthy.

15

HEALTHY DOS AND DON'TS

THE PREVIOUS CHAPTERS provide the philosophic basis for making healthy decisions. The purpose of this chapter is to show several specific ways that philosophy can be implemented.

Here goes, one idea for each week in the year:

1. Responsibility—Take responsibility for yourself. You alone are the master of your own health destiny.

2. Philosophy—Without the correct roadmap to health, how can that destination ever be reached? Evaluate all life choices with the knowledge that you are a natural creature, designed to live in nature. Veer from this roadmap the least to have the most health.

3. Prevention—Prevention is not a vaccine, pill, or check-up. Obey your genetic design as closely as possible so when illness does occur you can know you have done the best you could.

4. Illness—The first thing to do when you feel ill is to stop eating for the first twenty-four to thirty-six hours. The digestion of food requires immune system attention and diverts the strength and energy the body needs to fight the disease and heal. Drink lots of alkaline water at room temperature or heated (see #6). When the fast is broken, eat no carbohydrates at all. Infections thrive on carbohydrates and in the acidic environment they create. Take probiotic (see #11) supplements immediately and antioxidant supplements after the worst part of the illness has passed.

5. Injury—Heat is a super healer. Heat is life, cold is death. Heat the whole body or the body part to speed recovery. Only use cold for the first few hours after trauma to a body part. Exercise the part as soon as it can be done without undue pain. Heat and exercise improve circulation and bring healing elements to the injury, speed their activity, and ferry debris, toxins, and pathogen carcasses away. For overuse injuries, there is no substitute for resting the part for a time.

6. Water—Try to drink 3-4 quarts of purified (preferably alkaline) water each day. Do it regardless of thirst. Drink more if sweating. Get it all done before supper so you don't have to race to the bathroom all night. Squeeze fresh lemon juice in the water to help reverse acidemia, which virtually everyone in modern society has

"It's a great new diet...
I can eat all I want of anything that tastes awful."

and which is a fundamental, underlying cause of disease.[1-2] Don't wash food down with water. This can lead to overeating and inhibit digestion.

7. Processed oils—Avoid hydrogenated and all other heat processed oils as much as possible. Hydrogenated oils are toxic and heat processed oils are oxidized, making them toxic as well. Best choices for cooking are natural, more heat-stable saturated fats such as butter, and oils such as from coconut, palm, sesame, and olive.

8. Sun—The sun is not the enemy, it is the energy that underlies all life. It has a critical impact on mood, immunity, general health, and vitality. Try to expose as much of the skin as possible to the sun every day for at least 30 minutes or so. In sunlight the skin synthesizes the most important vitamin/ hormone in the body, vitamin D. Do not get burned since that can cause genetic damage to the skin. Use natural sunscreens, shade, and clothing to prevent overexposure. Use sun-mimicking, full-spectrum lighting in the home.

9. Cosmetics and personal care products—Read the labels. If the ingredients are not, in principle, edible, don't use them. The skin absorbs similarly to the intestinal tract.

10. Living food—Make raw food the predominant part of the diet. It is what every other creature on the planet eats, so why not learn from their wisdom? Supplement with food enzymes if eating cooked or processed, and therefore enzyme-devoid, foods.

11. Probiotics—Supplement the diet with probiotic cultures and eat foods such as yogurt (non-sugared) and other cultured and fermented products. These friendly bacteria fight pathogens, boost immunity, and synthesize vitamins, enzymes, and other nutritional factors. They are destroyed or thrown out of balance with the use of antibiotics and pharmaceuticals. There are more microorganisms in the intestinal tract than the total number of cells in the body. Grow the right kind and nurture them properly with these 52 principles.

12. Vitamins and minerals—Take full spectrum supplements every day. Modern factory farming and food processing diminish these nutrients in the food supply. The stresses of modern life also increase our needs. Larger doses than contained in the average diet have been proven to prevent and reverse a number of diseases.

"Just take half of one of these in the morning, and it will decrease your appetite all day."

13. Antioxidants—Take antioxidant supplements (at least vitamins A, C, and E) and eat fresh fruits and vegetables. The huge oxidant (acid) burden on the body caused by modern living needs to be counteracted.

14. Organic and free range—Foods raised in this way are higher in nutrients and lower in toxins. Such farming methods are environmentally friendly and more sustainable. Send a message to the industrial, petrochemical farm by diverting dollars to those who have foresight and conscience. Free-range foods are more nutritious (they follow the principle of #2) and are raised more humanely. A clear choice.

15. Nontoxic home—Choose the least toxic home construction materials and cleaning supplies.

16. Lab tests—Avoid medical tests unless there is a manifest problem and a test will make a difference in terms of effective treatment. False positives can kill with the stress of worry; false negatives send a person on their merry way while disease continues to grow. Also, if you feel healthy, be very skeptical of any test that attempts to tell you differently, and most certainly be hesitant to begin dangerous medical interventions based upon it.

17. Clinical tests—Do not assume tests such as prostate, colon, and breast screenings are necessary. They are unproven and are not 'prevention.' They put a person in the medical mill and divert attention from where it belongs: taking control of one's own health destiny. (This 'anti-medical' advice will make more sense after the next section.)

18. Variety—Eat a variety of foods but not at each meal. Variety decreases the odds of toxicity and broadens the spectrum of nutrients. It is not necessary to get every nutrient in the universe at each meal. Relax, your body has reserve capacity. Try to eat no more than two categories at a meal. For example, for supper, eat meat and a salad.

19. Cooking—Do as little of it as possible. Heat is the enemy of nutrients. When cooking, use high temperature for short time to preserve the most nutritional value. Quick grilling, double contact table top type grills, and the new steam ovens are good choices.

20. Dairy—If you choose to eat dairy products, get raw, non-homogenized, and non-pasteurized milk, cheeses, and yogurt if they can be found. If not, eat whole milk yogurts. Some people find a dairy farm where they can buy part of a cow and then legally obtain raw whole milk from it.

21. Omega-3 fatty acids—The modern diet is deficient in this critical class of fatty acids. To increase them, eat more cold water fish (if they are not laden with mercury or other toxins), wild meat, grass-fed meats, raw vegetables, and tree nuts. Fatty acid supplements are also a good idea to make up for the deficit, but be sure they are of the highest quality, properly protected with natural antioxidants, kept in the refrigerator, and protected from light and air.

22. Dental health—Diseased gums and teeth can seed the body with infection and depress the immune system. Keep teeth clean and do not permit dental procedures that destroy or remove tooth structure unless there is no alternative. If repair is needed, do not use toxic mercury/silver amalgam; use porcelain or gold instead and find a dentist who understands this. Find a holistic dentist who uses new technologies such as tooth-preserving laser.

23. Vaccines—Avoid them. Health is the best immunity. If taken, the killed varieties in oral or nasal form are most natural and safe. Don't believe the promotion of flu vaccines which studies have shown to be ineffective.[3-4] Use natural supplements with scientifically proven immune

stimulating and antipathogen properties, such as selenium, quercetin, tumeric, echinacia, astragalus, burdock root, goldenseal, vitamin D, and probiotics. Hydrating with a gallon of alkaline water per day does wonders in preventing and reversing infections.[5-6]

24. Pharmaceuticals—Avoid symptom-based medications if at all possible. Removing symptoms does not cure disease, and there are just too many potential adverse side effects. No disease was ever caused by a deficiency of

> "I feel sorry for people who don't drink or do drugs. Because someday they're going to be in a hospital bed, dying, and they won't know why." -Redd Foxx

a pharmaceutical and therefore a pharmaceutical cannot be the answer.[7]

25. Radiation—Avoid it if at all possible. All radiation is harmful and cumulative.[8]

26. Don't diet—Just change foods, eating habits, and lifestyle. That will automatically solve weight problems. Skip a meal unless it is deserved due to physical exertion. Eating is not recreation, and to eat more than deserved is unethical (as explained in a coming chapter).

27. Eat less—Eating less does more to extend life than almost anything else that can be done. Don't eat unless hungry, and stop when the feeling of fullness *begins*.

28. Avoid sugar—Refined sugar is an unnatural food and is addictive and toxic.

29. Avoid grains—Grains are an unnatural food (in their raw form they are toxic) and in their refined white flour form are just another form of sugar. If they are eaten, whole grains are more nutritious. Sprouted grains are the healthiest form since sprouting converts grains to vegetables which can even be eaten raw.[9]

30. Avoid hospitals and doctors' offices—More disease and death is created in this environment than cured. (Proof follows in the next section.) Except for emergencies, stay away and learn how to take care of yourself.

31. Nurse infants—The breast is the fountain of health, not just an item of adornment for adults. Formula is the granddaddy of all junk foods. Children raised on it suffer in innumerable ways throughout life. Even the incidence of something as obscure as myopia (nearsightedness) is decreased by breastfeeding.[10]

32. Circumcision—Just say no. Circumcision is mutilation and removes functional aspects of the penis. If circumcised, learn how to uncircumcise (restore the foreskin). Those who do this come to understand what was lost.

33. Four white poisons—White flour, sugar, processed oil, and refined salt are unnatural, nutrient-stripped toxins. Avoid them or replace them with their whole natural counterparts.

34. Sunscreens—Don't use the synthetic versions unless there is no alternative. They permit overexposure and potential skin damage. If in danger of burning, cover with clothes, seek shade, and limit sun exposure until acclimated.

35. Sleep—Getting at least seven to eight hours of sleep or closed eye rest each day is essential. If sleeplessness is a problem, get more physically active during the day. If unable to sustain sleep at night, be sure to take a nap during the day.

36. Nap—Take a mid-day nap for rejuvenation. Even a few minutes can make a huge difference in the rest of the day.

37. Timing—Mornings are usually best for mental activity, afternoons for physical. Listen to your own rhythms and obey.

38. Nature—Try to get outside for a time every day. Take vacations in nature. The mind and body need rejuvenation by regularly getting reacquainted with where we came from.

39. Serious disease—Act now to prevent it. If stricken with cancer, heart disease, diabetes, arthritis, or the like, reflect on what YOU have done to cause it. Do not just surrender to the medical machine. Get many opinions, study hard, and research all alternative therapies. Give acupuncture, herbs, natural diet, homeopathy, naturopathy, and other natural therapies a chance. Alternative medicine at least tries to address causes, which is a leg up on conventional medicine that focuses on naming and categorizing diseases, and treating their symptoms.[11]

40. Beverages—Avoid them like the plague. Soft drinks and the like (including fruit drinks) are addictive, acidifying, and a sugar and chemical assault. Drink water. Juice whole fruits and veggies if chewing is too much of a chore.

> "I always keep a supply of stimulant handy in case I see a snake, which I also keep handy." -W.C. Fields

41. Glasses—Avoid them until there is no alternative. Glasses are like crutches in that they weaken the very organ needing strength. Explore exercise methods to improve vision. (There are several methods available. Search the Internet under "natural vision improvement.")

"Could you drink that caffeinated coffee someplace else, please?"

Consider pinhole glasses to relax the eyes and permit close vision more naturally. Use them for reading and computer work.

42. Don't be silly—Smoking, drinking, drugs, not wearing a seat belt, and standing on the top of a stepladder are invitations for disaster. Do the common sense things to give life and health the best odds.

43. Local foods—Whatever the climate, the foods that are grown there are the healthiest for residents there. Tropical foods are best in the tropics and northern foods best for the cold.

44. 100% complete—Don't be fooled. Talk is cheap. Nobody knows how to make a 100% complete food since nobody has 100% complete knowledge of nutrition or our biology.

45. Swimming pools—The skin is an absorbing organ. Unless you're of the opinion that a whopping dose of chlorine (a potent oxidant), algaecides, and colorants are a good idea to have circulating in your bloodstream, find natural water or pools that have been ozonated, treated with ultraviolet light, or otherwise maintained. If using a chlorinated pool, limit the time in it and shower thoroughly after.

46. House plants—Grow lots of them. They filter the air, produce oxygen, and add life to the home.

47. Fat and cholesterol—Eat it so long as it has not been unduly heat processed. Natural fats, oils, and cholesterol (the body makes this every day to create hormones and other healthy biochemicals) are the premier energy source. If dietary carbohydrates are displaced by fats and proteins on a calorie for calorie basis (not that you should count calories), the body will store less fat and be more inclined to burn the fat that is trying to hide in those pudgy little rolls.

48. Ventilate—Bring fresh air into the home and exhaust the old. Use a heat exchange unit to capture the heat. To freshen indoor air use negative ion generators and filters. Use a central vacuum system that exhausts to the outside.

49. Fever—The heat of fever is the body's mechanism for destroying pathogens and speeding immune response. So why run for an aspirin to bring the temperature down so the pathogens can proliferate? Believe nature, not a pharmaceutical company.

50. Food for age—The young and the old have the highest demands for quality food. Supplements and nutrient dense foods high in protein and micronutrients are critical for the young because of their growth demands, and for the elderly because of their decreased ability to assimilate nutrients.

51. Garbage—Judge health by garbage. The more compost created (veggie, fruit, meat, nut, egg, and dairy scrap), the healthier. The more processed food packaging garbage at the curb, the less health can be expected.

Know Your Food Groups

The Donut Group

The Jolly Ranchers Group

The Coffee and Pop Group

The Sugared Yogurt & Pudding Cup Group

52. Birthday suit—We were not born with, nor designed to wear, clothes. Live where the least amount of them are required. Get them off at every opportunity such as in bed and for full body sun and air baths wherever you will not get arrested.

You will note that healthy choices are usually not in accord with conventional wisdom, commercial interests, and popular practices. You must be wrong in order to be right by paying attention to your natural genetic roots, and the SOLVER principles—self-responsibility, open thinking, long-term view, virtuous intent, evidence, and reason.

Taking control of your own health destiny becomes particularly important when faced with the tremendous pressures, propaganda, and dangers of the modern medical machine.

SECTION C

Thinking about . . .

MODERN MEDICINE

IN THIS SECTION: *The modern commercial world would lead us to believe that experts, technology, and industry can fill our every need. All that is required of us is money. This mindset dangerously pervades healthcare, partly because medicine is a profitable business, but also because consumers are lazy and want others to take care of them. Yet health is not something somebody else does to us. It comes from within and cannot be purchased. It is a garden we individually sow and nurture. Letting our health go to weed and wither and then expecting medicine to fix it is unrealistic. Even if free insurance, drugs, and medical services were in limitless supply, the idea that humans are a mere assemblage of material parts and pieces, and that broken health can be serviced like a washing machine, remains dead wrong—and deadly.*

16

THE MEDICAL PROFESSION

PEOPLE GO INTO THE HEALING PROFESSIONS with high ideals. Most certainly, nothing could be much nobler than relieving pain and suffering.

But there is a slip between the cup and the lips. Medical schools (human and veterinary) inadvertently teach compassion and creativity right out of students by indoctrination in reductive materialistic science and the allopathic (symptom-based) version of medicine. Students are subjected to an antiquated lecture–note-take–regurgitate pedantry that overwhelms them with minutia, much of which they will never retain nor need. Upon graduation they are institutionalized, licensed, and regulated like cogs in a machine. Then the long hours and demands of internship, residency, and practice never leave room for reflection or altering thought patterns. Even the obvious is ignored: standard care often fails, and does harm far too often.

Once the new physician is in practice, the bloom comes off the rose. Surveys show that more than 40 percent of physicians would not go into medicine if they had it to do over again. An even larger percentage say they would not recommend the career to their children. Boredom, infrequent therapeutic success, and the high costs of assuming liability are credited with the dissatisfaction.[1] Doctors also face the frustrating and depressing daily reality of patients who expect miracles but will do little to help themselves.

Doctors who retain the high ideals that brought them to the profession are a wonder. This is true not only because the effect of the system schools, regulates, and sues the idealism out of them, but because feeling genuine empathy and compassion for every single patient day after day would require superhuman emotional capacity. In the end, money, job security, protecting an educational investment, and prestige begin to displace ideals as motivation. But the money is being siphoned off by liability insurance premiums and the doctor pedestal is cracking as alert people are becoming resentful of escalating costs without improved health.

If we examine day-to-day results for people with multiple problems and degenerative diseases—not the heroics of sewing a finger back on, giving an antidote to a poison, or stopping hemorrhaging—it becomes apparent to any thinking medical professional that there is little they do to truly help patients. Nevertheless, doctors continue in the belief that what they were taught is the only 'scientific' way, and may even vigorously condemn or ridicule colleagues who veer from the accepted standard.

Things are not well in modern medicine. Not only is it largely ineffective (and highly dangerous, as will become apparent in the following pages), it is draining the economy. This dismal and failing state of affairs is primarily due to the flawed paradigm of naming and categorizing diseases, diagnosing them with elaborate technology, and then focusing on treating their symptoms. Modern medicine is not a health profession, it is a disease profession.[2]

Treating symptoms is like turning off the smoke alarm while the fire smolders in the closet, or yanking out the wires to the low oil gauge in the car when it flashes red. The immediate issue may be temporarily and dramatically removed, but the underlying problem remains and usually compounds.

The degree to which this medical philosophy is skewed, even perverted, is typified by an article in the *New England Journal of Medicine* entitled, "Efficacy of Bilateral Prophylactic Mastectomy in Women with a Family History of Breast Cancer."[3] The study concluded: "...prophylactic mastectomy can significantly reduce the risk of breast cancer." "Prophylactic mastectomy" means to

Medical Advice Through the Ages
3000 BC ... Eat a root.
500 AD ... Roots are evil. Say a prayer.
1850 AD ... Prayer is superstition. Take this pill.
1980 AD ... That pill doesn't work. Swallow this antibiotic.
2000 AD ... Antibiotics cause super-infections. Here, eat this root.

surgically remove healthy breasts so they will not become cancerous. The article states that only 36% reported decreased satisfaction with their appearance, and 25% reported decreased feelings of femininity. In other words, one of modern medicine's ideas of prevention is to cut off any part of the body that might one day get diseased. Doctors can then claim they have conquered the disease and rest confident that the majority won't mind their missing parts. What a heyday this could create for surgeons if they were to remove all the parts and organs that *might* become diseased. Of course this would kill virtually any patient who participated since there is no part of us that might not get disease. Nevertheless, the medical profession could produce a statistical analysis proving how they have vanquished all disease. Such is the tragic saga of modern 'miracle' medicine, over a 2-trillion dollar industry that has as its profit center our continued pain, suffering, and disease.

71

The solution for the medical profession is to start thinking outside the box. That means seeking and welcoming change and innovation. Doctors must begin their true education after school. That requires becoming an autodidact through wide reading, exploring alternative therapies, philosophic pondering, putting principle first, bringing base scientific knowledge up to speed with cutting edge holistic physics—which is about 100 years ahead of the medical school materialistic paradigm—and keeping an open mind. It means applying the SOLVER principles.

But that's largely a pipe dream. It takes an unusual person to break from the medical fraternity, admit that how they were trained is incorrect, face the reality that they may be doing more harm than good, and spend time and energy to search for the truth. The inherent busyness of medicine, paperwork, regulations that force conformity, the threat of suit if non-conventional treatments are used, and the momentum of a gargantuan industry ensure that change will likely not come from within.

Additionally, unless a doctor makes a diligent effort to explore all realms of knowledge, he, like the public will be swept along in the current of conformity. For example, Medline is the online medical search engine for the National Library of Medicine. It is funded by tax dollars through the Department of Health and Human Services and the National Institutes of Health. It permits free access to millions of scientific papers and about two million people use it every day. But not everything is indexed. How and who decides what gets into the database is a secret. While it includes *Time, Newsweek, and Readers Digest,* not exactly cutting edge scientific literature, it excludes *The Journal of Nutritional and Environmental Medicine,* the *Journal of American Physicians and Surgeons, Medical Veritas, Fluoride,* and the *Journal of Orthomolecular Medicine* in its thirtieth year of publication. A person can find over 1,200 on flatulence and articles demonstrating that espresso kiosks can be a profitable addition to hospital foodservice (*Health Foodservice Magazine),* but has to struggle to get full information on megavitamin therapy, raw food benefits, and alternative cancer therapy. Medline's screeners don't burn books, they just make it difficult to access literature that threatens medical status quo.[4]

So health consumers must take matters into their own hands. By taking control of their own health destiny—learning, questioning, and thinking in terms of prevention rather than cure—doctor visits become largely unnecessary. When people stop or redirect medical spending and demand health rather than symptomatic relief, the profession will perhaps begin teaching and practicing true health and prevention.

There are inklings of such progress. Several medical schools now teach some material on alternative medical approaches. But don't think this is because they saw the error of their ways. It is in direct response to patients shunting dollars to alternative practitioners. Presently, thirteen of the top fifteen paying jobs are in the medical industry. That is not by accident. Modern medicine is a cash cow and jobs and salaries follow the money. Regardless of 'rightness' or 'wrongness,' cash keeps things in place. But money should not reign when it is our pain, suffering, and lives that are on the line.

In the meantime, there is no need to wait for an institution that feeds on money to be dragged by the heels toward change. Start getting healthy today. Health begins with how we think. The first step is to understand that we are responsible for our own health, and then think about changes that bring living in accord with nature. A more true, simple, and wise course cannot be found in any medical school.

17

THE GREATEST
THREAT TO HEALTH

THERE IS A PREVAILING BELIEF that modernity translates into better health. A corollary of this logic is that we can live our lives pretty much as we want because we can always buy a repair. You know, the car won't start, the TV is broken, and the telephone is dead, no problem. Just call in an expert, spend some money and all is well. So then, if our ticker falters, joints creak, or an unwanted growth pops up, no problem. Buy some modern medical care. If that doesn't work, then the problem will surely be fixed with more money, better insurance, increased hospital funding, more research, more doctors, and better equipment and technology. Wrong.

The following is taken right from the pages of the *Journal of the American Medical Association* (July 26, 2000): "Of 13 countries in a recent (health) comparison, the United States (the most modern and advanced in the world) ranks an average of 12th (second from the bottom)..."

Additionally, the U.S. ranks:

• Last for low birth weight

• Last for neonatal and infant mortality overall

• Eleventh for post neonatal mortality

• Last for years of potential life lost

• Eleventh for female life expectancy at one year of age, and next to last for males

• Tenth for age adjusted mortality (life expectancy after age 40)

The World Health Organization, using different indicators, ranked the U.S. 15th among 25 industrialized nations.

Some might say these dismal results are because of smoking, alcohol, cholesterol, saturated fats, and poor penetration of medical care across economic strata. Not so. Epidemiological studies prove that overall health is greater in countries where economies are poorer and these health risks are worse.

Nor is failed American health due to lack of technology. The U.S. is, for example, second only to Japan in the number of magnetic resonance imaging units (MRIs) and computed tomography scanners per capita. Neither can lack of medical personnel be blamed since the U.S. has the highest number of employees per hospital bed in the world.[1-2]

So what is the problem? Here are some clues as revealed in the same journal:

• 12,000 deaths per year from unnecessary surgery

• 7,000 deaths per year from medication errors in hospitals

• 20,000 deaths per year from other hospital errors

• 80,000 deaths per year from nosocomial (originating in a hospital) infections

• 106,000 deaths per year from adverse effects of medications (total adverse drug reactions yearly: 2.2 million)[3-6]

That totals 225,000 medically caused deaths in hospitals per year. Another study estimates 284,000 deaths per year. An analysis of deaths due to outpatient care jumps these figures by 199,000 for a new total of 483,000 medically related deaths per year. Other studies based upon the expected mortality from over 16 million unnecessary medical and surgical events combined with unnecessary hospitalizations estimates 783,936 deaths, another totals 999,936, and yet another 1,189,576. These numbers are conservative since, of course, doctors and hospitals are not going to eagerly report all their mistakes. Nobody is particularly proud of error, no one is anxious to get sued, and many are afraid of reprisals if they whistle blow on others. So, only about 1.5% are reported, at most only 20%.[7-11]

Keep in mind that these figures are not a reflection of the precarious health of those visiting a doctor or admitted to a hospital. The deaths are the direct result of the medical intervention, not the presenting illness or malady of the patient.[12]

Think about those numbers for a moment. It's like every day of the year five of the largest airliners filled to the brim with passengers crashing and killing everyone on board. How many would take to flying if that were the case? The public outcry would be deafening and the airlines would go bankrupt.

It goes virtually unnoticed, however, that when people get on board the medical juggernaut they are at such great risk. Instead of being up in arms, people clamor for more high-risk medical planes and free tickets to board them. Like lambs led to the slaughter, medical consumers just keep piling into doctors' offices and hospitals, bloating the medical industry with profits and importuning politicians for more insurance and social programs enabling them to do it even more.

The poor health ranking of the U.S. is not because of lack of modern medical care, it is because of it. Aside from the fact that ANY medical intervention is dangerous, it is estimated that some twenty percent of diagnoses are wrong and result in serious injury or death. Over a quarter of all radiological tests, including CAT scans and MRIs, are misread. People are dying to get healthy.[13-14]

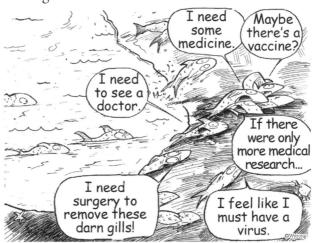

We behave like fish out of water - The obvious fact that we are flopping around out of sync with our genetic context is ignored. Instead we just look to medicine to patch us and cover up symptoms. We need to jump back in the 'water' of our natural biological roots and breath clean air, exercise, drink pure water, and eat natural food.

This does not deny that each person's life choices impact health as well. People cannot live with abandon and then expect someone else to fix things. Imagine the frustration that physicians must feel as they are faced day to day with patients wanting a quick fix to cure a lifetime of unhealthy life choices. By attempting to satisfy the unquenchable appetite of a public that refuses to live as if thinking matters, modern medical tinkering has become a huge threat to life and limb.[15]

Why do we not hear more about this disaster? Months are spent ana-
lyzing the death of Princess Diana, yet we do not hear a word about the
hundreds of thousands dying at the hands of modern medical care. Perhaps
it's just too difficult to come to grips with the inevitable—and unbelievable—
conclusion that when all the deaths reported and not reported are tallied,
medical intervention is likely the leading cause of death in America! And
this does not even take into consideration the hundreds of thousands of
people who are maimed or otherwise harmed but don't die.[16]

Time to splash some cold water on our society's inebriated faith in
and reliance on modern medicine. And remember, the above are just cold
statistics. Take any one of these medical 'accidents' and humanize it to the
real pain, suffering, financial devastation, grief, and family disruption, and
a heart rending and tragic story could be told. It is a disaster of a magnitude
unequalled by anything in human history. And it's repeated every day. By
sheer numbers, it makes 9/11, all the deaths in all U.S. wars, deaths by
automobile accidents, homicides and everything else pale in comparison.

The media should be shouting about medical risks from atop their
broadcast towers. Instead there is mostly silence because news organizations
are made of people who have been buffaloed like the rest of us. Besides, such
information is best left on the editor's cutting room floor where it will not
insult drug and medical advertisers. But the facts remain, albeit in obscure
(to the public) medical and scientific publications. To a crystalline degree,
the evidence there proves the disproportionate dangers of modern medical
care. In the meantime, instead of standing before the world in a posture
of shame, the medical industry promotes itself as the only beacon of hope.
Rather than shackling it and sending it to the Hague for crimes against
humanity, the public just bows and pays the escalating tithe.

From just 1995 to 2002, pharmaceutical sales jumped from
$65 billion to over $200 billion. From 2002 to 2006 sales jumped
to over $600 billion. That's about one prescription for each man,
woman and child in the country every 10 days. There are at least
36 million adverse drug events per year.[17] We can only expect that
to escalate since the AIDS-interest groups have now forced the
FDA to speed the approval process. Little wonder that in just the
six years following the turn of the millennium, 65,000 product
liability lawsuits have been filed against drug makers.

The risks from drugs that the FDA has approved are so great that Harvard University professors are advising that physicians not prescribe any new medications. In the professors' evaluation of 548 new drugs introduced over a 25-year period, it was found that at least 20% could cause life-threatening reactions and several had to be withdrawn from the market because they were lethal. The problem is the effects were not discovered until years after the drugs had been widely prescribed and used by naïve and trusting doctors and patients.[18]

Prevention – The Key To Health – True health can only be achieved by addressing all things that can impact health from a holistic preventative standpoint. Symptom-based interventions will never solve underlying health problems.

One must wonder how this could be when the FDA is a government agency charged with protecting consumers. Like all organizations, the FDA is comprised of humans, many of whom have a vested interest in protecting the medical paradigm and speeding products to market. Some even have direct links to the pharmaceutical industries they are supposed to be policing.[19]

Pharmaceutical industries that spend hundreds of millions in research exert tremendous pressure on regulators. The pretense is that it is unconscionable for a bureaucracy to hold back drugs that are life saving. So, in just eight years during the 90's, drug approval rates jumped from 60% to 80%. In the meantime, new diet pills, heartburn medications, cholesterol drugs, and antibiotics prescribed for non-life threatening conditions are killing people by the thousands.[20]

The philosophy of symptom-based, reductionistic, episodic, after-the-fact, crisis care medicine is seriously flawed—and very deadly. Wrong philosophical premises are hamstringing good and well-meaning doctors. Doctors are crippled every bit as much as explorers who once believed in a flat Earth. Trying to achieve health with modern allopathic medicine is like trying to fix computers with a hammer because that's the only tool one is taught to use or believe in.

Don't wait for the system to change. Old ideas die too hard. The mega-medical industry is not going to be quick in either admitting error or revamping itself. Your health is at stake. Think prevention and natural holistic cure. Study, learn, grow, be skeptical, change lifestyle, be self-reliant…be a thinking person. That's the best and only road to health.

SHOULD GUNS OR DOCTORS BE BANNED?

- Not everyone has a gun, but everyone has at least one doctor.
- Number of physicians in the US: 700,000.
- Accidental deaths caused by medical care per year: 500,000.
- Accidental deaths per physician: 0.71
- Number of gun owners in the US: 80,000,000.
- Number of accidental gun deaths per year: 1,500.
- Accidental deaths per gun owner: 0.0000187
- Statistically, doctors are over 60,000 times more dangerous than gun owners.

(Adapted from Internet circulated e-mail.)

18

DON'T SURRENDER
TO MEDICAL CARE

CONSIDER THE CASE OF THE INFANT who was to have a routine circumcision ("so he will look like all the other boys"). The surgeon used an electrocautery that was set too high and burned the infant's penis completely away. The medical staff then recommended to the young parents that the boy be surgically converted to a girl. The parents were assured that all would be fine so long as they reared him as a girl. What the heck, the only difference between a girl and a boy is the presence or absence of a penis and a few hormones, right?

In the end, the young boy never thought of himself as a girl and never behaved like a girl in spite of intense and devoted nurturing to the contrary.[1] (Another nail in the coffin of nurture over nature.) It is hard to even imagine the physical and psychological stress this poor youngster and his parents went through. Eventually he was surgically rebuilt as a male, but normalcy never came to his life and he committed suicide as a young adult.

I recently visited an 83-year-old friend in the hospital. She was having a bout of fluid buildup in the lungs from congestive heart failure. The dieticians were feeding her pudding, instant potatoes, and a slab of some nondescript canned 'meat.' None of it was edible to her and her frail and wasting frame was starving. The nurses, however, made sure she took her 17 different pills—yes, 17—with a cup of water. Down the hatch they went on an empty stomach.

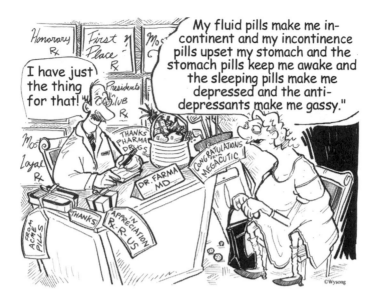

She had placed her care and life in modern medicine's hands and it was killing her. She pleaded for us to go out and bring back some "real food." So we did and she promptly inhaled it. I encouraged her to get home as soon as possible. When she got home she began to promptly improve.

I investigated the 17 medications and discovered that the total number of contraindications and side-effects reported on the drug inserts was over 350. No doctor could have any idea what all these medications taken in combination were really doing to this poor lady. But every time she had a complaint, off to the doctors she'd go. They would oblige with yet another medication insisting that the meds were what was keeping her alive. My friend, like some torture victim that had finally caved in with total surrender, would do whatever the imperious masters of her life (the doctors) said.

Thinking people should not cave in to medical authority. Buyers (this is a buy/sell arrangement, don't forget) must beware, skeptical, and informed.[2] Today, with the Internet and the plethora of alternative medical opinions, ignorance is no excuse. But people in the main put less effort into choosing medical care than they do buying a car. They just submit.

As a society, we surrender to medicine because of the presumed validity of the system. Couched in esoteric technology and vocabulary as it is, both doctors and patients assume there is precision and safety. Yet hundreds of double-blind tested drugs supposedly proven safe and effective have had to be withdrawn from the market after they maimed and killed enough people. Are the profit driven sponsors of such science, the pharmaceutical companies, unbiased? Are they going to want to release results that present them in a negative light, or will they redesign a study that is not going their way so that the result they want is achieved?[3-4]

Another wild card in all medical testing is the placebo effect. How does one control for the fact that the results hoped for may occur even in the sugar pill cohort? If, for example, a person can lose their hair or experience cancer remission when they think they are receiving chemotherapy, but are in fact receiving sugar pill placebos (which has happened), then all blind studies are shadowed by doubt.[5-7]

"And now, without further ado, the one you've been waiting 3 hours for, straight from the Mega-Pharma-sponsored golf outing and luncheon, prescription pad in hand, deigning to give you, oh lowly lay person, 3 minutes, offering the promise of a fancy diagnosis you can brag about and a pill to mask the symptoms... the one... the only... your doctor."

Disregarding commercial bias and the power of mind over body is a serious modern medical error. It results in blindness to anything other than conventional thinking wherein the results desired are the only ones accepted as true.

Here are further examples demonstrating that modern medicine is by no means an exact science, but most certainly is a business—and a risky one at that:

• More money is spent on marketing drugs to doctors than is spent on education in all medical schools combined.[8-10]

• A new growth market for pharmaceutical companies is the creation of 'diseases' that conveniently need drugs. Examples would include "restless leg syndrome" (RLS), erectile dysfunction (ED), and high cholesterol. Cholesterol medications now approach twenty billion per year in revenues and ED drugs are the most successful (profitable) pharmaceuticals ever invented. This is not to say that there may not be some who are affected by RLS, ED, or high cholesterol, but it is difficult to argue that they are serious medical conditions requiring potentially dangerous drugs. Also, each of these conditions can be remedied either completely or to a significant degree by safe exercise, lifestyle, and dietary changes. RLS can often be resolved by supplements of iron, folic acid, magnesium, and antioxidants like vitamin E, or simply abstaining from caffeine, cigarettes, or alcohol. On the other hand, if people take the drug designed for this condition (Requip), they are putting themselves at risk of over 20 side effects, including compulsive gambling and eating, as well as hypersexuality. The same applies to drugs for ED. High cholesterol, as presently defined, is neither a disease nor a symptom, nor has it been proven to cause heart disease and strokes. Little wonder that cholesterol drugs have not been proven to prevent heart disease or heart attacks.[11-16]

• After pathological review of removed tonsil tissue began, the number of removals decreased by two-thirds. Surgeons decided to stop the surgery if they were going to be called on the carpet by review boards for doing it unnecessarily.[17]

• Biopsy tests to determine cancer of the prostate showed a 25% incidence, but no more than 3% of those who have a positive test manifest the actual disease by age 70. (Tests themselves can create 'epidemics.') Digital screening of the prostate is of no proven value. Canada, Australia, Sweden, and Denmark are against the more sophisticated PSA (prostate specific antigen) test. The inventor of it says, "It's over," meaning it's no longer worth using. Hundreds of thousands continue to be performed.[18-21]

• The stethoscope has never been proven to benefit patients. (Meaning it is no more effective than placing an ear to the chest or simply observing patients.)

• At least 65% of operations are unnecessary.[22-24]

• Adenoidectomy has been proven to be of little or no benefit.[25-28]

• Antibiotics for sinusitis are ineffective.[29]

• The neonatal ICU is no better than mom and breast. Use of a bilirubin light in preemies can result in a heart defect (PDA). Oxygen therapy in preemies can result in retrolental fibroplasia, a potentially blinding condition affecting the retina.[30-35]

• In spite of hundreds of thousands of cervical smear tests performed over the years, there is no change in the death rate from cervical cancer.[36-38]

• Mammography can spread breast cancer to the rest of the body. A study of 50,000 women demonstrated that the procedure did not improve mortality for women aged 40-50.[39-49]

• Computed tomography scanners (CT scans) were introduced in 1973 with no FDA safety or efficacy studies. By 1992 there were over 6000 scanners in the U.S. Their overuse is proven by the fact that in some institutions over 90% of scans are negative.[50]

• Carotid endarterectomy is a procedure that supposedly decreases strokes and helps some 35 other conditions. But it has never been proven to be of value. In 1971, there were 15,000 performed; in 1985, 107,000. The number continues to grow.[51-58]

• Getting a check up before engaging in an exercise program has never been proven to be of value.[59]

• Wearing an eye pad for corneal damage is of no proven value.[60]

• Screening for colorectal cancer is of no proven value.[61-67]

• The number of surgeries decreases if surgeons are on a salary.[68-71]

• At least one-half of all pacemakers are unnecessary.[72]

• Most C-sections are unnecessary, yet the number continues to climb. The U.S. delivers 24% of babies by this method while the Netherlands only does 8%. There is no evidence that moms and babies are different in the two countries. There is evidence that the U.S. maternal and infant mortality is higher either in spite of or due to the cesarean section pandemic.[73-74]

• Amniocentesis performed on a healthy pregnancy can result in miscarriage.[75-78]

• Fetal monitoring is not supported by studies and not recommended by the Centers for Disease Control. It results in a higher incidence of cesarean section.[79]

• Circumcision is unnecessary and harmful.[1,80-89]

• It is estimated that 85% of all disease that is treated is self-limiting. That means that 85% of treatments are no better than giving a placebo, and potentially far worse than doing nothing.[90]

• Mortality is not decreased with coronary by-pass operations, but it is a 100 billion-dollar per year business. The procedure is increasingly performed even though clinical trials have not proven its safety or effectiveness. By-pass surgery and angioplasty (not clinically proven either) rates vary with skin color, type of medical insurance, and geography—factors having nothing to do with the disease condition. The cost per patient over five years for either procedure is about $40,000. Angioplasty patients also receive massive doses of carcinogenic x-rays during the procedure, up to 1580 mrem (a routine chest x-ray is 2 mrem).[50,91]

• Laparoscopic cholecystectomy was introduced in 1989 and in five years 85% of all gall bladder surgeries were performed by this method. There was an associated increase in cholecystectomies of 30%, indicating that the mere introduction of a new procedure can increase the rate of a disease. Mortality for people with gall bladder disease has not declined with the new procedure.[50,92]

• The earlier a person is released from the hospital, the faster the recovery.[93-94]

• The average senior receives 25 prescriptions annually, yet there is no physician or pharmacologist anywhere that can predict how they all interact.

• X-rays, CT scans, mammography, and fluoroscopy are a contributing factor in 75% of new cancers. 100 million premature deaths over the next decade are estimated to be due to ionizing radiation. X-rays used to measure the pelvis of expectant mothers and diagnose twins resulted in a 40% increase in cancer in the children.[95-96]

• Vaccines are now the cause of all cases of polio.[97-104]

• In 1900, one in thirty got cancer. In 1971, President Nixon declared war on cancer and hundreds of billions have been spent on research and therapy. Now almost one in three get cancer. All so-called improvements in cancer mortality statistics (with the exception of a few leukemias) are attributable to changes in lifestyle (decreased smoking, dietary supplements, etc.), not medical intervention.[7,105,109]

• Scalp irradiation can result in breast cancer.[110-112]

• Induction of ovulation can result in neural tube defect in the newborn.[113-115]

• According to the *New England Journal of Medicine*, one in 50 physicians is an imposter. Whether they do more or less good than the legitimate ones has never been determined.[116-117]

• Yearly checkups do not improve health.[118]

• Doctors going on strike have resulted in decreased mortality in the community.[119-121]

The list could go on, way on. *Caveat Emptor* – let the health buyer (you) beware.

This critique of modern medical practice is not to lay blame. It is a wake-up call that salvation at others' hands does not await after a thoughtless life of self-abuse. You, not someone else, are the master of your health destiny. Take control, starting today. Use the principles outlined in these chapters, the library, Internet, bookstore, and get outside of mainstream popular press. You must be wrong (in the eyes of standard medical care) in order to be right. Go about achieving health as if thinking matters. You can prevent and heal and are your own safest and best doctor.

"You need to trust me, those vitamin pills could make you sick and if you go to that alternative quack, you may not get the life-saving therapy you need."

19

"BUT WE LIVE LONGER TODAY"

THE MEDIA, medical community, academia, drug companies, schools, parents, and friends all chime in with the same mantra about how blessed we are that medicine extends our lives. People are as confident that medicine increases life span as they would be if they had a fistful of aces. But when everyone smiles and agrees, they are usually wrong and progress weeps.

The force field of "truth" surrounding this popularly held "but we live longer today" meme exempts the foundations of modern medicine from criticism regardless of their shortcomings. After all, if everyone gets to live into their seventies, on average, as opposed to dying in their twenties as a result of medical progress, what's a few shortcomings? (That would, according to the previous chapter, require the word *shortcoming* to mean the equivalent of five jetliners of people dying each day from medical intervention, and at least ten times that number being damaged or maimed.)

Average lifespan (take note of the word *average*) was indeed shorter in the distant past. But *why* is the question. For one, life used to be staggeringly difficult. People weren't pointing and clicking sitting at a computer back then; they were hunting, gathering, laboring, and were prey themselves. With the advent of agriculture, toiling in fields from sun up to sun down with little to eat but moldy, mycotoxin-laden bread during many seasons, was a sure trip to an early death. Life was impoverished and brutal, perhaps even making death welcome. In the early cities people lived in windowless huts, on dirt floors, and were under constant threat from starvation or from the elements. Even the aristocracy in the middle centuries, died at about age 20. The cause of shortened life had nothing to do with the absence of vaccines, cholesterol medication, or MRI machines. It had everything to do with the reality of nature and the brutality of trying to eek an existence out of the land without the advantage of modern inventions.

If today we toiled manually every day from the time we could walk, and were sustained with only meager insect-infested crumbs and rotten potatoes, we would not last long either, in spite of any modern medical measure. Infants, with their immature immune systems, would be particularly vulnerable and easily succumb to deadly disease. The 'old' (beyond about 35) would not have the resiliency and energy of youth and would succumb to the sheer stress of trying to stay alive. There would be no retirement or old folks' homes. If today we lived in crowded, vermin-infested cities where people threw the contents of their bedpans out the window into the streets (a common practice then), if we believed disease was caused by demons, and if it was also a matter of piety to keep the vile body filthy (it was 'sinful' to bathe), we would be dying like flies at an early age too, no matter how much medicine and surgery was offered.

Pregnant moms weren't exempt from the hard life, either. They toiled in the fields and would barely take a break to give birth. Mothers were nutritionally and immunologically debilitated and passed those weaknesses to their children. The meager and often toxin-laden diet they consumed did not make for the highest quality milk for the child either. As society advanced into the Victorian era, women found nursing inconvenient or just plain did not have time due to the daily drudgery. The advice they got from the health experts of the time was to feed children the following recipe: baked flour, bread crumbs, a little sugar, and water boiled for up to five hours. They would feed this through a calf's teat stretched over a bottle and used for a "fortnight" (ten days).[1]

Couple these circumstances with the total lack of public utilities and hygiene in an increasingly congested society and it's no wonder infant death was astronomically high. Infant death was also a natural mechanism to decrease the drain on resources. In a similar fashion, wild animals will not reproduce or will produce stillbirths if the mothers are starving. High infant mortality was a part of life back then. It was not because the peasants could not whisk children off to the ER and ICU.

The average life span number that is increasing and being credited to medical advances is the average age at death of the entire population. If there is a population of two, and one dies at one year of age and the other at 80, then the average life span for that population is about 40. In pre-modern populations, early deaths for adults and infants, for the reasons cited above, would make the average lifespan very low.

Even in 1900 with all the advances that had accrued by then, the average lifespan was only 47. Today it is about 73. Why? Primarily because infant mortality has decreased by some fifteen-fold since 1900. Infants have fared better in modern times, as have adults, because of the ease of life, the ready availability of adequate and safe food, decreased physical stress and danger, and public hygiene created by utility infrastructure.

So yes, the average lifespan has increased, but note that modern medicine cannot lay claim to that success any more than a rooster can boast responsibility for a sunrise. It is a simple play on statistics, bringing to mind George Burns' humor, "If you live to the age of a hundred, you have it made, because very few people die past the age of a hundred."

The delicious irony here is that the heroes of the *average* increased life span we now enjoy are food truckers and plumbers. Not quite as sexy as high-tech medicine, but true nonetheless. In the meantime, modern medicine attempts to take credit. Like a cheerleader taking responsibility for a team win, modern medicine just happens to be at the right place at the right time in history.

Besides, when we think about living longer are we really concerned about a statistical average of deaths or do we want to know if individually we have more potential for living longer? Potential for long life is called longevity. If we have moved into adult years and beyond the risk of infant death and starvation, are the odds better today for living into advanced old age?

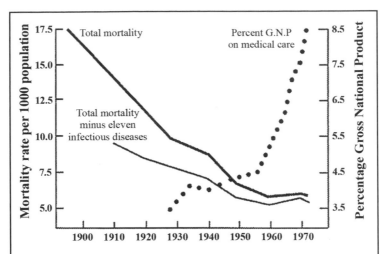

Is Decreasing Mortality Due To Modern Technology? – The graph represents the age and sex-adjusted mortality rates for the United States, 1900-1973, including and excluding eleven major infectious diseases. Mortality is contrasted with the proportion of the Gross National Product expended on medical care. Notice how the majority of the drop in mortality occurred prior to the burgeoning cost of modern medical care. Today, the costs are almost vertical but health is not improving. (McKinlay, J. R. and McKinlay, S. (1977) The Questionable Contribution of Medical Measures to the Decline of Mortality in the United States in the Twentieth Century. The Milbank Memorial Fund Quarterly, 55 (3): 405-428.)

To examine this, let's get some terms out of the way. Maximum life potential is the age at death of the longest-lived member of a species. For humans this is believed to be about 115-120 years. It has not changed. Life span is the age at which an average individual would die if there were no disease or accidents. That is about 85 years. It has not changed. Life expectancy is the expected age at death of an average individual at a given age in a population allowing all factors for mortality such as disease and accident. That is approximately 73 to 74 years at birth. After a person reaches 40, there has been very little change in life expectancy. After 75 there is none.

So, removing decreased infant deaths from averages, and omitting the role of plumbers and food truckers in giving us health, there is really no reason at all to be heartened by the capabilities of medicine in helping us to live longer today.

If one considers quality of life, that is, life lived free from debilitating disease (disease that medicine should be preventing and curing but is not), we are in fact headed in the wrong direction. For example, more than one in three die from cancer today and about one in two die from heart disease.[2] And no, it is not because we are living longer.

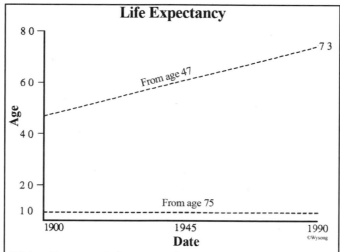

Living Longer – It is commonly assumed that we are living longer today as a result of medical intervention. The facts do not bear that out. For as far back in time as data can be collected, each individual's potential for living has not significantly changed. And since medical intervention is the number one killer, that can hardly be credited with whatever improvement there may be. Infant death has been decreased due to hygiene from public utilities and food distribution. This increases a population's average life expectancy but that is not the same thing as people expecting to live longer.

Prior to 1900, atherosclerosis (heart attack) was practically unheard of. Obesity, diabetes, arthritis, cancer, autoimmunities, and the whole range of modern day degenerative diseases sucking the life out of people and the economy were rare. It is true that understanding of disease back then was poor, lumping many things under "evil spirits" or "consumption," but there is no paleopathological evidence suggesting that they experienced anywhere near the incidence of these diseases we now do. Moreover, extant primitive societies today with no medical care whatsoever, given adequate natural food supplies, predictably do not get these diseases to any extent.[3]

91

Although we have more years to live in our modern day, we have less good life in those years. We are a society of walking wounded. Like a heavy November cloud descending upon us in midlife, we must greet our remaining years with the sense that we are living the adverse reactions listed on a drug bottle insert. Meanwhile, the focus of medicine has become keeping people alive in a hospital bed as long as possible.

The medical lobby would rather that we not know this sad state of affairs and that we continue under their spell. It's in their vested interests for us to continue to believe they hold the key to long life. To them health is, you know, mammograms, pap smears, prostate checks, angioplasty, yearly checkups, gobbling pills like a famished chicken pecking up corn kernels, and, of course, always a new vaccine or drug just on the horizon to save us all.

Better to put aside the fairy tale that modern medicine is going to save us from degenerative disease and extend our lives. It won't, but we individually can.

20

DOLLARS DON'T
MAKE HEALTH

AMERICANS NOW SPEND over 2 trillion dollars annually on medical care. There is no end in sight to rising costs.[1] From the medical community's vantage point, they would hope not. If you have a cash cow you milk it for all it's worth. Since expansion is the goal of free enterprise—and medicine is free enterprise—what else could be expected?

The only protestations there seem to occur when there isn't enough money to feed the monster. The question is not about the rationality of drugs, vaccines, diagnostic machines, lab tests, surgeries, and hospital facilities, but rather, how will they be paid for? The medical behemoth is considered as essential to life as food and water and thus it is petted, pampered, and protected. While it stuffs itself and swells to obscene size, everyone clamors for unlimited access to it by way of insurance and government entitlement programs. Consumers may wonder why modern medicine is getting so rotund, but then, awestruck with its techno-wizardry, continue to feed it by marching right into its mouth.

Now then, if the medical system we had in place were truly decreasing disease, optimizing people's health, increasing healthy life span, and decreasing mortality, that would be one thing. But that is not the case. As previously shown, it is arguably the number one killer.[2] The medical gorging and human sacrifice are ignored because esoteric medical science is seen as our only hope. To the public, sensational successes—separating Siamese twins, transplanting organs, removing tumors from brains, reattaching limbs—seem like sure proof that medicine is on track. We therefore easily overlook its glaring failings in preventing and reversing diseases and assume that all that will be necessary for everyone to be recipients of miracle cures is more dollars. It's a very modern thing to do. If there is a problem, throw money at it.

I had to chuckle when a radio announcer recently expressed concern about declining participation by employers in providing health care benefits. He said to his guest, "Do you realize what a devastating effect it will have on hospitals when people don't so readily seek medical care because they don't have coverage? Hospitals, like hotels, need beds to be filled or they go bankrupt." Obviously they are echoing the very American sensibility that business is the greatest good, so what is good for business is good. Heaven forbid that people might increase their odds of being healthy by being more discretionary in seeking medical services, or even staying away altogether.

It is pure propaganda that health solutions are in a pill, on a surgery table, or just around the corner—if we would just fund more research. Doesn't the outrageous growth of medical expenditure in the absence of proportionate salubrious results speak to the failure of the system, not its success? Health care, by definition, should be moving people in the opposite direction and be self-eradicating. The fact that this is not happening proves that modern medicine is first and foremost a business.[3]

Nothing is in place to curtail costs. The Food and Drug Administration (FDA) is the primary watchdog but its only charge is to ensure the safety and efficacy of drugs and devices. It gives no consideration in its approval process to the costs of therapy, nor are comparisons made to existing drugs or to non-drug alternatives.

When something is so clearly amok, it's time to take a close look at the philosophical underpinnings. Modern medicine is based upon the materialistic assumption that we are a mere amalgam of data generated by parts and pieces that can be manipulated at will. But we are not a chemical soup held in by a membrane, a sort of test tube made of skin. I will discuss this in greater detail in the companion book, but the evidence clearly demonstrates that health is a holistic affair and can

no more be reduced to a number on a lab test than happiness can be explained by the electromagnetic forces in brain cell chemicals.

This flawed materialistic explanation of life in turn leads to the quick-fix, life-as-a-machine approach: If a chemical in the body is out of whack, take another chemical to neutralize it; if your gizzard is acting up, get a gizzardectomy; if the medicine you are taking is making you sick, take another medicine to counteract it; if eating fries and pop cause a burning in the gullet, take a pill. We are an instant-gratification society, and a favorite son of materialism and consumerism—modern medicine—offers up easy solutions.

Materialism is an intellectually simplistic philosophy and eliminates probing into people's lives to see where causes really lie. What could be simpler than to run a test, check a number, give a pill, and send a bill? But this is counter to the way the body operates. We are a self-healing organism, infinitely complex and finely tuned, not just an assemblage of pulleys, pipes, levers, valves, and proton pumps. Modern medicine's attempt to ignore the body's complexity and to force it into submission with drugs and mechanical alterations is about as smart as oysters.

The failure of the approach is most glaring in the face of the epidemic of chronic degenerative illnesses—cancer, heart disease, arthritis, and so on. Yes, modern medicine is fantastic at crises such as anaphylactic shock or an operable tumor pressing on the heart. That is not disputed. Successes with such mechanical conditions, as opposed to metabolic and systemic failures, are to be expected. In contrast, the great degenerative disease killers today result from longstanding problems of lifestyle imbalance. They are not simple mechanical problems and are not solved by syringes, pills, or scalpels.

The system is closed to change not only because of the torrent of dollars flowing into it, but because people who spend years in costly medical training don't figure anyone else has a right to speak with authority on the subject. So closed medical minds arrogantly puff themselves up like sails on a ship and march millions down the gangplank to their medical end. This is not to impugn the efforts of the many hard working health care workers. But intent does not erase result.

Most doctors come to intuitively understand that disease is self-inflicted through improper lifestyle choices. Few, however, have the financial courage to tell people that they need to change their lives, not get another pill or have surgery.[4] Such advice would just drive patients elsewhere where they will be told what they want to hear. Or the doctor might even be threatened with suit for offending a patient. A recent case in point is a New Hampshire doctor who was turned in to the Board of Medicine and the Attorney General for telling a patient she needed to lose weight.[5]

As hard as doctors may try to do what is right, financial pressures and incentives are woven into the way they treat patients. There are bills to pay and the potential for a lavish lifestyle. Doctors also feel entitled. A long and costly education, long hours, lawsuits, malpractice insurance, and putting up with an endless procession of patients who will do nothing to help themselves surely merits more than average pay. More pay comes from doing more to patients. Conveniently, the medical standard of care (what doctors are taught to do to avoid liability) encourages more of almost everything: more lab tests, longer hospitalization, more diagnostics, more drugs, and more surgery. So, although in many cases the best advice to a patient is to go home and make life changes, doctors too often do that which is safe for their career and income. Defensive medicine (an escalation of services to avoid out of control malpractice litigation) just so happens to be what the patient wants anyway.[6]

Although medical insurance is heralded as a solution, it is in large part the blame for the explosion in healthcare costs. The public sees insurance as a bottomless vat of money that promises cure. If patients were made to pay as they go, out of their own pockets, there

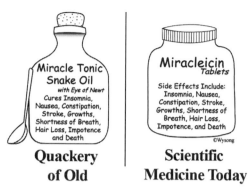

Quackery of Old   **Scientific Medicine Today**

would be more shopping and discernment. Facing crippling medical costs, they would decide to stay home with their chicken soup (a statistically good idea anyway). Moreover, if doctors faced the real-life financial circumstances of patients they would be forced to use judgment as well. The net result would be a lot less unnecessary medical care. Putting the responsibility for health on the individual where it belongs would mean more health and a lot less medical injury. One sure way to affect that result is decreasing the scope of insurance so that it covers primarily catastrophes, not increasing it so that people can run to the doctor every time they burp.

Since everything seems to move by the force of dollars, let's shift the rewards. The ancient Taoist doctors were paid only if the patient was well. If they became ill, payment was stopped and the doctor was considered ignorant.[6] But that's too rational. There are not only too many money interests fighting tooth and claw to keep things exactly as they are, but it also does not fit the fable that disease is 'just one of those things' to which we may innocently fall victim. Why hold the doctor (or ourselves, more appropriately) accountable for an act of God?

As philosophically flawed as modern medicine is, it is by and large an effect, not a cause. Medical commerce is driven by consumer demand. If the market were not there, the business of increased profit for increased health failure could not exist. If people would learn how to take care of themselves and take ownership of their own health, the medical sinkhole would shrivel and the tidal wave of chronic degenerative diseases would dry up to a trickle.[7]

Don't wait for things to change. You change. Decide not to participate. Learn to take control and optimize health by giving your mind
and body the lifestyle and food it was designed for. Money really has
nothing to do with the solution to the problem. In fact, money can
spell your demise by not only the unhealthy lifestyle of indulgence it
permits, but by making it too easy to obtain the most and best that
modern medicine has to offer.

21

DISEASE DOES NOT STRIKE US

NOTICE HOW THE CHANGE OF SEASONS seems to trigger illness. Traveling across time zones can do the same. We are like finely tuned machines and even small stresses can increase our vulnerability. Disease results from an imbalance with our physical and social environment.

We become vulnerable to organ failure, mental dysfunction, loss of vitality, cancer, infection, and even death when stressed. Cattle that are gathered into feed lots or shipped often succumb to shipping fever, a deadly viral and bacterial infection. Baby elephants offered the best of food and conditions will die without social contact. Infants not lovingly handled are immunologically weak and suffer emotionally. Plants grown on nutrient-depleted soils are attacked by pests and weed competition. Creatures, organs, tissues, and cells are tuned for specific conditions. When this tuning is disrupted, balance is lost and disease takes root.

People today commonly see disease as something that strikes us from the outside. But disease is not an attack. It is the body's reaction to the stress that is usually caused by some life choice we have made. If we are weak nutritionally, physically, mentally, metabolically—out of tune with our physical and social environment—we will not endure stress, and disease is the result. We are to blame for making ourselves the fructuous soil for disease to take root and flourish. Cancer, heart disease, arthritis, and even infectious diseases do not suddenly appear out of nowhere to inflict hapless souls. The potential for disease is always there. We change it from potentiality to actuality by the choices we make.

That is the reality, but it is not what modern medicine promotes and its consumers want to hear. An easily identifiable enemy is more commercially viable. It opens the door for surveillance (lab tests) and weapons (drugs, antibiotics, and surgery). If the public can be led to believe we are at war with disease, there is no limit to the medico-military budget that can be justified. Additionally, people would rather think in terms of disinfecting doorknobs and getting vaccinated than changing their habits.

We also cannot assume that apparent health is real health. The World Health Organization has even admitted that health is not the absence of disease. This is because any rational investigation of the facts proves that disease can, for a time, coexist with seemingly normal function. Serious organ disease begins small and undetected, only to manifest itself after the majority of the reserve of the organ has been lost. For example, a large percentage of the kidney and liver can be destroyed with little outward evidence of disease. The body is marvelously capable of adaptation and resistance, but only to a degree. When the stress continues, the body exhausts its ability to compensate and adapt. Breakdown—disease—results.

Recall from a previous chapter the young vigorous soldiers who were killed in battle. Upon autopsy, their hearts were found to have the beginnings of heart disease normally only associated with older men. They had passed the military physicals, endured boot camp, and faced the rigors of war. The atheromatous swellings (plaques) on the interior of their coronary (heart) vessels were the result of an improper diet that began in their infancy. The resiliency of youth masked the problem and permitted the young men to function normally even though the heart muscle was not receiving optimal blood flow.

But such adaptation—margin for error—has definite limits. If a correction is not made in the lifestyle choice that is causing the stress to the body and its organs, disease becomes manifest. When the outward symptoms of the disease finally do appear, we do not suddenly 'get' a disease. If the soldiers had survived war and had a heart attack in their later years, the cause would not have been high cholesterol detected when they were 50. It would not have been from not having a yearly physical, not being diligent in taking an aspirin a day, or faithfully consuming cholesterol medication. The cause was a nutritional stressor that began way back in early youth resulting in the slow growth of the lesions in the coronary vessels. In other words, disease is self-induced. We are not victims other than of ourselves.

If we wait until symptoms of illness appear and then attempt repair or make the appropriate life alterations, we may be too late. This is not to say that there is no hope—even in advanced illness. But if we understand that illness is the end product of the incubation of a pattern of improper living, the earlier we make changes the better. Obesity in the young will increase the risk of heart disease by almost fourfold, but there may be no overt signs of heart disease through

"Good news. All the tests were negative. You'll be just fine."

decades of early life. It takes as much as four years after changing the diet to natural foods to convert tissues assaulted from unhealthy oxidized and hydrogenated fats to their healthy fatty acid form. Cancer usually incubates in the body for twenty to thirty years before becoming manifest.

Obviously the time to do something about disease is before symptoms ever appear, during the window of opportunity the body affords us. We must do the hardest thing of all: put a lot of effort into staying healthy when we are healthy. If we don't, we are putting ourselves in the position of having to solve a problem at the end of the problem. That is not living life as if thinking matters.

This then brings us to a basic truth: health is best served by prevention, not attempted cure. The problem is, when we are apparently well it is difficult to work at fixing what doesn't seem to be broken. After all, what is prevented if there is no disease? So prevention seems boring because when it's done well nothing happens. It isn't nearly as spectacular as getting a ride in an ambulance, staying in a $2000-per-night hospital room while a fleet of medical technocrats poke, prod, and dote over us, and then being whisked off to have a heart transplant or a section of the colon removed. Unless that's the kind of excitement we are looking for, then we better begin doing the boring thing now. It's a matter of pay now or pay dearly later. The best way to think of prevention is this way: If we are not right now doing something to create health, we are causing disease.

Prevention is such an incredibly worthy, even ethical, pursuit. It's a crime to our very being not to engage in it. The dysfunction, pain, inconvenience, and economic damage from disease so dwarfs the relatively small requirements to build and maintain health that it is insanity not to pursue health now. Even Pasteur (credited with the germ theory of disease) reflected, "Whenever I meditate on disease, I never think of finding a remedy for it, but rather a means of preventing it."

Good food, joining a health club, and learning how to properly care for ourselves can cost some money and time. Unfortunately, when we are well it seems like we are paying for nothing. We have no problem spending money on cures or wasting time in a hospital bed. We spend without limit on dying but little for living. This mindset is reinforced— even forced—by medical insurance that does not pay for prevention, and a government that prefers to entitle disease care rather than health care. So we continue to chase but never catch.

The word *prevention* is perverted when it is attached to such things as lab tests, mammograms, prostate screening, check-ups, lumpectomies, and medications. Finding a disease and attempting to then treat it is not prevention. That's like saying a police report describing how you ran a red light, and a body shop that repairs your smashed vehicle, prevents a car accident.

The medical community cannot help with true prevention because they are brainwashed into the mechanistic view of the body. They can do only what they are trained to do: name diseases, treat symptoms, and attempt repair. Furthermore, people think they have a manufacturer's warranty. If things go wrong it's someone else's problem and all it will take is money and an expert to make things all better.

For doctors to help patients with true prevention would require teaching and counseling. But that requires a deeper philosophical understanding of the body at its most fundamental level—who humans are, where we came from, and our place in the world. But doctors are no longer philosophers (as they were long ago), but rather materialistic technicians, mechanics, and machine operators. Most know no more about the deeper philosophical issues of life than the average welder or gardener does.

People are thus deceived into thinking that health is about being a dutiful consumer and paying for early detection and symptom removal. Health, an honorable thing that people can only do to themselves, is profaned to a mere purchasing decision. It's crazy stuff.

Don't go along with the craziness. Health is not consumerism. It is the wisdom of self-management and the foresight to do the hard things now that will bring dividends later.

For starters:

1. Eat foods you were designed to eat

2. Exercise and work hard so you deserve to eat

3. Get outside in nature

4. Drink clean water and breathe fresh air

5. Sleep plenty

6. Question all dogmas

7. Hug somebody

22

GERMS DON'T CAUSE
DISEASE, WE DO

At one time at our office we had a day care. It was complete with a classroom, an area sectioned off for indoor play, kitchen, and outside playground. There was a full-time monitor/teacher and lots of little munch-kins around the office interrupting us during the course of the day.

It was great for moms and dads to be able to interact with their children during the day. If you own a business, think about doing this. If you are an employee, get together with coworkers to see what you can do to help the business you work for get one established. We operated ours for almost a decade, until most of the youngsters grew up. Several of them have even come back to work with us as young adults. We became like a home away from home.

I was the official sliver surgeon for all the kids. Our office is in a wooded area and we had wooden playground equipment, so almost every week there was a sliver drama. That's when I got to perform my magic with terrifying instruments like a scalpel, forceps, needle, and magnifying glasses. My little patients tried to be real brave and fight back tears but their dilated pupils and clammy trembling hands revealed the true life threatening state they found themselves in. All the other kids were a wide-eyed and awed audience for these major surgical events. Once my patient's survival was assured, there were lots of hugs and thanks. Then off they would all skip, relieved that their friend had survived one of life's dire calamities. They could be heard around the building all abuzz with, "Did it hurt?" "I saw the blood!" "You were brave!" "How big was it?" "Glad that wasn't me!"

Actually, everyone would be pretty brave about this except my own kids. To listen to them when I was removing a sliver not even visible except with magnification, you would swear I was working on a two by four with vice grips, or sawing their limb off with a chain saw. No need to be brave when it's Dad who's working on you.

As I would work on sweaty, grubby little hands, it brought to mind the wonder of how kids ever survive childhood with all the filth. If germs were really the true cause of disease, how could any of us survive?

Contrary to popular belief and commercial propaganda, germs are not kept at bay by washing with antiseptic soap, disinfecting toilet seats and telephones, wearing surgeon-type face masks on the streets, or getting vaccinated. One *E. coli* bacterium (a resident of our digestive tract) in the evening can produce four billion offspring by the next morning. Viruses, bacteria, fungi, protozoa, and parasites are ubiquitous throughout nature in air and water, and on surfaces, skin, food, and ground. Just one gram of soil contains over a billion microorganisms. In a small pile of one cubic meter of dirt, 35 pounds of it would be these microscopic critters.

Some microorganisms are pathogens, others are necessary for our survival. Without bacteria to consume garbage, for example, we would have long ago been smothered under the refuse created by nature and us. Good bacteria (probiotics) on the skin, in the mouth and intestinal tract actually help thwart the bad bacteria. Over fifty percent of the dry weight of feces is comprised of microorganisms. The number of such organisms in the digestive tract outnumbers the total cells in the body by 100 fold. The thing that it seems medicine is trying to achieve—no bacteria at all—with obsessive disinfection and sterilization, is neither possible nor beneficial. Germs are not the problem.

Disease-causing pathogens can even exert a beneficial effect by stimulating immunity. In one study of the relationship between stillbirths and urinary infections in the mother, it was found that pregnant women who had such bacterial infections while pregnant were 70% less likely to have a stillbirth. Evidently, the antibodies the mother produced in her blood in response to the infection were passed to the fetus to exert a protective effect.[1]

In another example, scientists attempting to rid chickens of salmonella (food-borne pathogens) tried a sterile environment. The result was that mortality increased because the chick's immune system could not develop properly without exposure to the pathogens it needed to be protected against. Germ-free (gnotobiotic) chickens were fine so long as there were absolutely no germs around. But since that would never be possible, once exposed to the pathogens, the chicks easily succumbed to disease. They didn't just get sick—they'd die. The solution was to feed baby chicks the salmonella-infested droppings of the mother hens. After all the sterility failed, the cure was in the filthy poop![2]

It is commonly thought that we would be dropping like flies from the plague and other epidemics if it weren't for medicine. There is no doubt that infectious disease can be devastating. For example the 1918 Spanish bird flu pandemic which began among military recruits in Haskel, Kansas, spread throughout the U.S. killing 675,000. It then moved across the Atlantic killing millions of soldiers and on to colonial India taking 20 million lives. Contrary to popular belief, however, diseases like the flu, polio, measles, and typhus were not conquered by humans. Note in the accompanying graphs that the vaccines or chemotherapeutic agents that are credited with vanquishing the scourges were introduced *after* the majority of the decline in the diseases had already occurred![3] For modern medicine to claim responsibility is like a person taking credit for dropping the level of the ocean by bucketing water out as the tide was receding. Infectious diseases have a natural ebb and flow and so does the general immunity of the population. That is the reason epidemics decline, not because of human intervention.

We can't even eradicate the mosquito, a creature which we can see and for which we can examine every life stage in detail. How are we going to eradicate microorganisms, which, if crowded side-by-side, would require numbers in the trillions to occupy the space of one mosquito? Creatures in the wild thrive in filth. Rabbits eat their stool, vultures eat rotten carcasses, and dogs will roll in the most putrid, decaying material they can find and then lick themselves clean.

Children constantly have their fingers in their mouths after wallowing on the floor, playing in the toilet, or exploring the garbage pail. We adults aren't exactly sterile in our habits, either. Up until relatively recently, a bath once a year was considered plenty in western society. That frequency of bathing, or less, is common elsewhere in the world to this day. Billions wipe themselves with their fingers (usually with the left hand, a reason it is customary to shake with the right) and yet live in societies that rank higher on health scores than nations with bidets, perfumed toilet paper, disinfectant aerosols, and soaps.

Modern Medicine Did Not Vanquish the Great Plagues

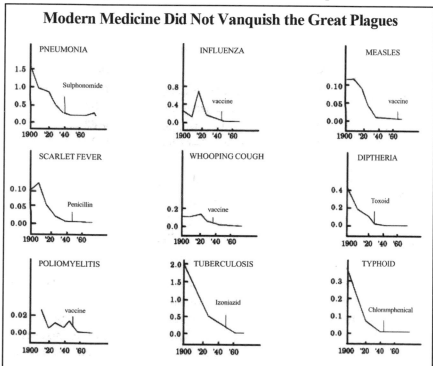

Too Little, Too Late - These graphs represent the fall in the standardized death rate (per 1,000 population) for nine common infectious diseases in relation to specific medical introductions. Note that the medical measure commonly credited with the decline of the disease occurred after the majority of the decline has already occurred. (McKinlay, J. R. and McKinlay, S. (1977) The Questionable Contribution of Medical Measures to the Decline of Mortality in the United States in the Twentieth Century. The Milbank Memorial Fund Quarterly, 55 (3): 405-428.)

Don't buy the simplistic germ-based view of how we get disease. True, certain pathogenic organisms can be associated with disease, but likewise so are crows and buzzards associated with road-kill. Buzzards are not responsible for road-kill, neither are pathogenic organisms responsible for disease. They are both opportunists. They wait until prey is weakened and then they dive in.

The resistance of healthy tissue is demonstrated by the effective medical use of maggots to clean infected and necrotic tissue from wounds. These revolting little creatures will digest all the rotting tissue but leave the healthy tissue intact. In microcosm, infectious disease is like the carnivore-prey drama occurring throughout nature. Predators always choose the easiest meal: the unfit, the weak, and disabled.

We are not victims. Germs do not 'get us.' Well, yes, they potentially can, but they will find a far less willing host if we take care of and boost our defenses. No matter how much money we give experts (who have a vested interest in our illness), they will not protect us from the dark germ forces in spite of their Star Wars antiseptics, vaccinations, antibiotics, and chemotherapeutic agents.

We are in control of our own defenses. We either create the setting for health or the meal for pathogens. It is our choice.

23

FROM WHERE DOES
HEALING COME?

THE PREMISE OF THIS BOOK is that the difficult issues facing humans can be solved. Surely you must have wondered at my optimism. But reflect on these two health and medicine sections and notice that problems arise simply because the correct method of thinking has not been employed. First off, human welfare is not given priority, and secondly, every one of the SOLVER principles is violated: Self-responsibility is not fostered; Open-mindedness is not encouraged; Long term consequences are not measured; Virtue is not the objective; Evidence of failure and of better systems of healing are ignored, and Reason is put aside for the sake of profits and protecting old ideas.

As will be repeatedly shown in this and my book on *Solving the Big Questions,* we get into trouble again and again when we marry ourselves to unproven beliefs and retire our minds. It is also a curiosity of the human psyche that often the more dubious the belief, the more that people are certain of it. Such certainty is murderous because there are consequences to the antics that arise out of wrong thinking. As the number one killer today, medically certain beliefs prove this point. Our pain, suffering, and death at our own and medicine's misguided hands are ghastly consequences for the sake of belief.

If we want to solve health problems (effects) we must attack the beliefs (causes) that are getting us into trouble. The faulty philosophy of materialism looms over medicine as it does essentially every other facet of modern human thought. Medicine begins with the assumption that the body is a mere material thing, a machine that is simply the sum of its material parts. Starting with this faulty premise, it is reasonable to assume pretty much everything else that follows in medical reasoning. If we are a machine, why would we not assume that if something goes wrong all that is needed to fix it is the right tool? If there are cancer cells, then we need mini-medical missiles to fire at them. If a plugged coronary vessel can cause a heart attack, then roto-root the plug out. If germs can feed on tissue, then kill them with poisons. If life is nothing more than a sequence of nucleotides on a DNA coil, then we should be able to gene splice, graft, and clone ourselves to immortality.

Injecting venom antitoxin, reversing anaphylactic shock, destroying infection with antibiotics, and sewing, screwing, and pinning people back together if they fall off ladders are life saving and remarkable medical successes. Credit is due where it is deserved. However, exuberance over medical heroics and good ol' American can-doism should not replace reason and evidence. It is one thing to replace a joint, fix a valve, reroute plumbing, and fumigate pestilences in the body. It is quite another to claim such acts deserve full credit for creating health and that all disease and even death lie within the reach of drugs and scalpels.

The small successes of medicine have worked a narcotic effect on the profession and the masses giving open license for medical intervention. The result is immeasurable misery that is excused because the alternative, us taking care of ourselves, is too unthinkable.

Modern medicine is like a malodorous rose that appears beautiful at a distance but then presents its contradiction up close. To clear our heads we need to go beyond the medical bluster and hubris and examine the beginning materialistic assumptions, as well as look at the real record, not the imagined one. For one thing, notice that medical successes are episodic and singular events for which a specific cause is identified and a specific remedy is clear. You cut yourself with a kitchen knife (cause) and a doctor sews you up (remedy). Medicine can be pretty good at fixing accidents that happen to an otherwise well-functioning mechanism. Fixing them is like patching a hole in a tire. After the tire is re-inflated, off you can go again like nothing ever happened.

Such events, however, are different in nature from heart disease, stroke, Alzheimer's, arthritis, obesity, dental disease, diabetes, cancer, autoimmunities, and other chronic degenerative diseases. These are not simple accidents but rather complex systemic maladies for which no specific ultimate cause can be identified other than something as abstract and complex as wrong living. They encompass the entire being and can incubate undetected for decades. Attempting the mechanistic fix to such problems is like having the hole in the tire patched (removing the symptom) but then going back out on the road of broken glass and nails. Modern medicine ignores the condition of the road and just keeps attempting fixes until eventually the tire is so weakened that no patch will work.

Repair does nothing about cause, and diagnostic tools only give knowledge of effects, they do nothing to prevent or cure anything. The skill to diagnose arthritis and replace a knee joint should not be construed as skill to affect the 'climatologic' conditions within the body that led to the arthritis that destroyed the joint in the first place. Working within the philosophical constraints of their materialistic view, it is little wonder that the best that modern medicine can do is deal with effects and symptoms.

Successful stopgap medical repairs only serve to create an illusion of knowledge and mastery. The resulting exhilaration then becomes manic when it is used to justify limitless expenditure: If human health is the jurisdiction of modern medicine, and no limit can be put on the value of a human life, then no expense should be spared. In spite of the fact that this reasoning clearly does not work, it continues unabated, threatening to bankrupt not only our economy but our health as well.

The common tools of medicine are by and large useless in changing the course of degenerative diseases or preventing them. Viewing the inside of the body with diagnostic machines, starting a stopped heart, measuring chemicals and cells in the blood, and replacing organs neither prevent nor reverse disease. That's because degenerative diseases are insidious, pleomorphic, idiosyncratic, and progressive with almost a life of their own. They are whole body affairs not amenable to measuring, replacing, or fixing a part or piece, because a part or a piece is not the cause. Similarly we cannot affect climate or dissipate hurricanes by repairing wind damaged homes, welding together a weather vane, or reprogramming a digital thermometer to measure degrees out to the sixth decimal point.

The materialistic symptom-based approach to health is wrong in practice and contradicted by history and the success of other healing methods. The modern materialistic approach assumes that without diagnosing and naming a disease, there is no hope of cure. But effective treatment can often exist long before there is knowledge of the cause and course of a disease. Ancient civilizations had methods of healing long before germs were even conceived, and when anatomy, physiology, and biochemistry were only dimly understood. With ritual, prayer, and access only to things found in the forest, primitive cultures today also perform healings.

The emerging alternative medical fields also offer proof that approaches other than diagnostics, drugs, and surgery are not only effective, but are also safe.[1] Such success is in spite of the cries of foul by the medical faithful who insist that before any claim can be made about the benefits of carrots, multimillion dollar controlled trials must be performed. But who is going to embark on such an expensive project when the results could never recover the costs? Carrots cannot be patented and sold in a capsule. And besides, is it not this supposed charmed circle of third person experimental science that has given us drugs that, according to the Centers for Disease Control, kill at least 100,000 and injure two million people each year? (A Harvard professor insists those figures are way too conservative, and says thirty-six million drug related injuries per year are more like it.)[2]

Forgetting that for the moment, even the most fantastic drug or surgical procedure is for naught without the body's own healing resources. No drug could ever hope to exert anything other than a toxic effect without synchronizing in some way with the staggering complexity of body biochemistry. If defensive immunological forces did not rush to a scratch in our skin, we would all become nothing more than a tasty culture media for microbes. And where would surgeons (mechanics) be without the body doing the heavy lifting of reorganizing tissue, removing clots and debris, destroying infective agents, joining membranes, tissue, bones, and skin, and even weaving tissue into synthetic fabrics? (Let's not forget the ability to wall off in fibrous capsules the sponges, needles, instruments and other surgery room debris left behind.) Sutures would never hold without the miracle of first intention healing (inflammation, then scar tissue, then reorganization to original anatomical state). Even casual activity would result in sutures tearing through tissue, undoing all the surgical work and permitting tissues to fall apart. The body must be functioning properly to bring to a finale the most spectacular of surgical feats. On the other hand, the healing ability of the body can make even the most inept and sloppy surgeon look good.

This is the reality every physician faces every day: without the healing powers of the body, no salubrious outcome ever occurs. But rather than this truth hitting them squarely between the eyes, their ingrained materialistic beliefs leave no room for the obvious: If healing comes from the natural body, then every means available should be used to aid and support its natural functions. Instead, nature is ignored, manipulated, and pushed around with machines, chemicals, and scalpels.

Modern medicine takes far too much credit. Notwithstanding palliation, limited repair, and relief of pain, there are few medical measures that positively impact the course of a disease or improve patient outcome over the long haul. So-called 'preventive' measures, like early diagnosis and even such cherished paraphernalia as stethoscopes, thermometers, and reflex hammers are little more than props. There is no proof that they have ever resulted in changing the course of disease in a beneficial way even though routinely used by every medical practitioner. Although the public has come to assume that medicine is cold and sober hard science, the vast majority of its practices are plucked from the ethers of unproven beliefs and faith.

The saga of medical errors and tragedies is virtually endless. Not because medical personnel don't try. Many are wonderful at what they do and are compassionate and self-sacrificing. But they are human and rooted in a social/cultural/educational/institutional/economic context. They are not automatons driven to external truths and altruism. Like everyone else, they are ultimately self-serving and never lose sight of the cash value of their beliefs. If the present medical system serves their individual financial and ego needs, that system will be held sacred regardless of its cruel and lethal effects. It is not that white-coated, stethoscope-draped medical technicians are barbarians; they simply must shrug off contradictions and be stoic in the face of failures that they can only see as an unintended consequence of 'progress.'

Failure is the function of the ignorance that springs from the grandiosity of a belief system not derived nor restrained by reason and evidence. From the gilded prison of faith in a belief, even the embarrassing fact that medical expenditure is disjointed from success is lost on virtually everyone. Instead, there is a pomposity and arrogance that either assumes immunity from error and accountability, or endless forgiveness because of how much effort is being put forth. Modern medicine is a failed system (in terms of creating health). That is not changed by some of its headstrong, self-congratulatory, and elitist practitioners. The system must be seen for what it is: a threat and danger that must be employed with careful discretion and extreme caution.

I have cited much evidence in the previous chapters to make this point. To illustrate let me here just single out one of the many disasters. Let's consider what modern medicine does to birth. The U.S. ranks last (meaning worst) among developed nations for infant mortality, and first in terms of technological intervention. Should this not make one think that present medical solutions may be the problem? Although medical intervention in high-risk pregnancies can save lives, that should not mean that intervention in normal pregnancies is indicated. But in true form, when an inch is given a mile is taken. A natural process (birthing) is illogically turned into a disease needing treatment.

Epidural blocks are given for delivery pain which in turn increase the likelihood of a dangerous Caesarean section. The blocks can also cause fever and headaches resulting in more medication and increased risks to mother and child. Epidurals and the practice of whisking the child away immediately after birth interfere with child-mother bonding which can delay breastfeeding and open the door to vastly inferior formula feeding.

Episiotomies are routinely performed but statistically do more harm than good.[3-4] Electronic fetal monitoring is of no proven benefit and often brings harm.[5-6] Clamping the umbilical cord immediately after birth so that medical personnel can do their sampling and chart recordings, deprives the child of blood intended to flow from the placenta to the newborn. For about three minutes while the cord is still pumping, oxygenated iron rich blood and stem cells are delivered to the newborn. This bounty of nutrients helps jumpstart the child's respiratory metabolism, prevents anemia, and contributes to brain development.[7-8]

In short, every medical intervention is fraught with danger to mother and child. This story is detailed in the doctors' own medical journals but by and large ignored. Since medical intervention is the only tool they have, if there are problems, doctors can only assume that they just need to figure out how to use their tools better. And on and on the endless cycle goes because nobody will step back and ask the hard and embarrassing questions about whether the tools themselves, and the thinking that creates them, are wrong.[3-7]

Disastrous examples could be enumerated regarding every facet of modern medical care. Turning things around will require thinking deep enough to recognize that the body is neither a machine nor an extension of human technology. Better technology, making more donations to research, national free healthcare, and increasing the percentage of our gross national product expended on allopathic (treating symptoms) approaches is not where healing will come from.

The U.S. spends more on health care than any other country but has the highest infant mortality among 24 industrialized countries and the lowest life expectancy after age 60.[9] No matter how much sincere effort is expended to repair and tweak the present system, it will continue to fail until the underlying materialistic bias and philosophy of healing are changed. In the meantime, modern medicine is only punching at its own shadow.

If we put thinking first, wonderful new vistas of health and healing open to us. Survival of the sickest rescue medicine, the mentality in diseasecare today, must become just a withering branch of a new focus on true healthcare that explores and supports the reasons why people can be well. That change will not come from within a system that has inverted priorities in order to sustain its own unquenchable economic thirst. It must come from the bottom up, from the medical consumer once they decide to pay for results rather than complexity.

IN ALL ASPECTS OF LIFE we come to learn that we are what we choose, not what others do to or for us. Health is no exception. After over two trillion dollars are spent on medical care each year, it turns out that simple things like stopping smoking, exercise, natural and safe remedies, and eating properly (as discussed in detail in the next section) are the only causes of any decline in dreaded diseases like cancer and heart disease.[10]

WYSONG

The solution to the present health crises is clear: Living in tune with nature and humbly recognizing that all healing ultimately comes from within. Thinking things through clearly reveals that wellness is not a product of a medical industry and its technology, but rather lies where all good things in life reside, in our own grasp.

SECTION D

Thinking about. . .

FOOD

IN THIS SECTION: *Although there exists every imaginable diet, and everyone has advice about what to eat, there is only one healthy option. It is neither a mystery nor is it a problem for technology and commerce to solve. We are finely tuned, genetically programmed creatures that have specific requirements. All we need to do is open our eyes to let nature teach us. It is a matter of becoming reacquainted with what we already intuitively know but have been distracted from by the modern world. Armed with correct thinking we become our own best nutritionists without ever having to count calories, think about cholesterol, fiber, protein, or carbs, and without being misled by any other fad that comes along.*

24

THE BEST FOOD

MOST PEOPLE BELIEVE THE AVERAGE diet based upon the official food pyramid is just fine. Some eat predominantly fast food. Others advocate veganism (eating only plant foods), or lacto-ovo vegetarianism (plants plus dairy and eggs). Others set their eating practices by the standards of holy writ that proscribe or sanctify foods. Others just eat what tastes good and that's logic enough.

People in general feel guarded and pretty jealous about their food choices and don't like others meddling. But eating is not recreation. Food choices are health choices. By and large, however, diet is a topic essentially ignored by the medical profession other than just to parrot what the public already hears on the television set. This includes marketing sound bites about cholesterol, calories, fat, fiber, or whatever else is making money for an industry at the moment. In conventional medical school curricula, doctors receive no special nutritional training and generally eat just as poorly as everyone else.

The bewildering wonder of the body is to blame for the murkiness about what is or is not correct food. The human organism is so amazingly adaptable and forgiving that it will do its best to survive on whatever it is given. If the food is incorrect, there is usually no immediate harm because the body will call on its reserves. This buffer the body provides means wrong decisions may not manifest their full impact until late in life. Nutritional damage can even be delayed so long as to pass genetically to later generations.

Yet the body's forgiveness is not bottomless. If the stress from improper food continues beyond the ability to adapt, disease, degeneration, and loss of vitality will result. Unfortunately, such consequences are so far removed in time from the eating regimen that caused them that few understand the relationship or can trace the connection. Nevertheless, like old bills turning up that you thought you would never have to pay, bad eating habits will come back to haunt us.

The true test of any health idea lies so far out into the future that almost any claim can seem valid since there are apparently healthy people doing and eating just about anything—for the moment. So we must be cautious before subscribing to bold claims about what is or is not good to eat.

A well-grounded philosophy needs to be in place if health is the objective. To sort through the competing ideas, all we have to do is put thinking first. A simple and reasonable principle emerges that is so logical that everyone can agree.

Consider the following three premises:

1. Just like a tree is genetically adapted to absorb certain nutrients from soil, and a lion is genetically adapted to thrive on prey, and a deer is genetically adapted to browse on vegetation, so too are humans genetically adapted to certain kinds of food.

2. Most of the foods we are presently exposed to are a product of the Agricultural/Industrial Revolution and occupy a small part of the genetic history of humans. (Refer back to the 550-mile time line in which less than an inch represents modern eating practices.)

3. The natural diet to which humans are genetically adapted must predate them. In other words, how could humans exist before the food they needed to survive? We were completely developed biologically prior to agriculture and any method of food processing. That means whatever diet archetypal humans ate was the perfect diet. It was the diet responsible for the existence and development of the incredibly complex human organism. That diet was the milieu, the environmental nutritional womb from which we sprang.

The logical conclusion we must draw from these three premises is: *The best food for humans is that food which they would be able to eat and survive on as it is found in nature.*

119

That means no dyes, preservatives, synthetics, nutritionally barren cooked starches, or refined sugars and oils. Our tissues were obviously designed to be bathed in food nutrients derived from natural living foods found in nature. Make no mistake, if we are not eating according to this principle our bodies are being constantly stressed by deficiency, imbalance, and toxin exposure. The result of generations ignoring this principle is the current epidemic of obesity, chronic degenerative diseases, the exhaustion of digestive processes, and premature aging.

Food First? or Chicken First?

This is the price we pay for becoming consumers—unthinking, passive, and dependent. Wendell Berry wrote, "Our kitchens and other eating places more and more resemble filling stations, as our homes more and more resemble motels…Food industrialists will grow, deliver, and cook your food for you and (just like your mother) beg you to eat it. That they do not yet offer to insert it prechewed into your mouth is only because they have found no profitable way to do so… The ideal industrial food consumer would be strapped to a table with a tube running from the food factory directly into his or her stomach."[1]

Which Came First, The Chicken Or Its Food – Food is that which nourishes and sustains life. Food, by definition, must preexist the life forms which depend upon it. Which came first, the chicken or its food (a new version of an old conundrum)? The food had to have been there first or life would not have been possible. Natural food fits this definition. New forms of 'synthetic' foods are new arrivals from a geobiologic perspective and thus do not fit the definition of food.

We race through life on the money trail hell-bent on increasing life's quality by affording more and bigger toys and replacing foods nature intends us to eat with industrial artifacts that bear no resemblance whatsoever to anything coming from nature. This race after things, convenience, and time off (to recreate with as much speed, ease, noise, and violence as possible) ignores the true cause and effect relationships of our body in nature. We thus have become exiled from biological truth and come to think that life is only about economic transactions and that food is only about recreation and sating appetite.

Certainly modern industry is to blame for their beguiling advertising (brain washing) and adorned food creations that, as Berry quipped, smell as prettified as the actors promoting them. Our industrial benefactors have replaced nature, quality, and health with throughput, economy of scale, and profit. We, in turn, buy the pig in the poke.

If we awaken our consciousness we will find that food and health really have nothing to do with the dyed, breaded, sauced, and sterilized creations of profiteers. For one thing, a feature of all natural foods is that they are raw—alive if you will. Let me make the connection here, in principle, to a law in biology. The Law of Biogenesis says life can only come from pre-existing life. Life begets life. If we eat living foods we enhance our own life. If we eat dead devitalized foods (virtually all cooked and processed foods), we become devitalized and dead. Granted, this will not happen at once, but as the adaptive reserves within the body are exhausted we become just like the lifeless food we eat.

Processed Goop – Food processors continue to shrink the natural diversity of food starting materials. It is economically advantageous for them to merely fractionate a few easily tilled crops and then modify them into a variety of 'value added' products cleverly packaged and marketed.

Studies of the diets of past cultures and today's primitive societies reveal that they ate exactly as their genes and the environment dictated: natural and raw.[2] Yes, even the meats, organs, eggs, and insects . Remember, we're looking far back in time to the prototype, even before the use of fire (much less the microwave, stove, oven, grill, deep fryer, or extruder).

Raw foods make so much sense. After all, we were not suddenly dropped from outer space onto Earth with fry pans, matches, and rotisseries. We began on the forest floor, not in a line at a fast food counter. We had only our natural bodies in a natural world. Every other organism on Earth eats raw foods exactly like they are found in nature. How can we think nature doesn't notice our decision to flout her instructions and change all that?

All of the mystery about what is or is not proper to eat vanishes if we just imagine ourselves placed in nature in the total absence of modern technology. Ask yourself the question: What would I eat and what could I eat? Humans can eat and digest fruits, nuts, insects, a few plants, honey, worms, grubs, eggs, milk, and animal flesh. These are about the only food substances in nature that humans are capable of digesting without technological (including fire) intervention. These are, in fact, the very foods that are the mainstay of nomadic primitive societies. Only when these foods become scarce do unpalatable foods such as grains and some otherwise inedible vegetables get cooked and processed to change their taste, neutralize toxins, and increase digestibility.

What would have been the single most predominant human food in the wild? Likely prey. With a family to feed we would look for the most calorie- and nutrient-dense food we could find. That would not be a few wheat seeds, some grass, or a root. We would let the herbivores do all the grazing and digestion with their specialized stomachs that are capable of converting essentially any plant material into edible protein and fat. Then we would eat them. Some people are repulsed by this idea. I must say that I cannot easily find comfort in it either. But that's the way things are on planet Earth in this biological web we are entangled in. It is reality and solutions can only come from facing reality.

The simple truth of nutrition is that we should eat what nature provides that we can digest. Yet this is never explained in nutrition textbooks, and PhD nutritionists graduate without even grasping it. The understanding that we are designed to eat raw, natural food we can digest cuts through all the theory, belief, lore, and guesswork. It matches our natural bodies with our natural food.

Modern cookery and food processing has misled us. Foods such as granola, soymilk, and rice that are marketed as the ultimate health foods are in fact not natural human foods at all. These products either do not exist in nature, are so scarce in the wild as to never possibly be a sustaining food, or in their raw precooked form are unpalatable and even toxic.

For example, raw soybeans contain a variety of chemicals that can stunt growth and interfere with the body's digestive enzymes. Eat enough of them and death is the result. Grains in their raw form are unpalatable, indigestible, and also potentially toxic. In nature one would never find enough kernels of rice, wheat, or barley to make up a meal, even if they were edible in their raw form. (Sprouted seeds and grains are an exception since they are digestible, raw, and nutritious.)

Now then, these understandings create somewhat of a dilemma. Knowing what our natural food is and consuming it are two different things. We are so acclimated to the modern diet that the notion of eating raw meat, for example, is nauseating to most. Never mind grubs. Nevertheless, as evidenced by primitive (but nutritionally advanced) peoples, raw meat and organs can be eaten with great nutritional benefit and they are totally digestible. Some cultures even bury raw meats and let them rot (ferment), and then consume them with gusto. These societies are robust and healthy until modern foods encroach. Then, like a dirty and toxic bathtub ring, modern degenerative diseases decimate those people at the periphery where there is contact with modern foods.[3-4]

If you are panicking at the thought of eating raw foods, yes, there is danger of food-borne pathogens. But if careful and clean about preparation, the danger is far less than the danger of a lifetime eating devitalized processed foods. Raw natural foods must be safe or our ancestors would not have survived and we would not exist.

Granted, it is very difficult today to achieve the ideal raw natural diet. But we can at least steer our choices in that direction. This doesn't mean no processed or cooked foods should be eaten. Look around the grocery store (usually the outside aisles) and consider what it is that could be eaten in its natural state. Increase the proportion of those foods. Choose processed foods that compromise natural principles the least and are as close to nature as possible. They should be whole foods, packaged carefully to protect nutrient value, and be free of synthetics, hydrogenated oils, refined salt (natural is okay) and sugar. Meats and eggs should be cooked as lightly as possible.

Choose foods requiring the least alteration and adulteration. For example, whole raw milk yogurt is ideal. The same thing pasteurized would be next best. The same thing pasteurized and homogenized next.

Worst would be non-fat, pasteurized, homogenized, artificially flavored and sugared yogurt (which is, of course, what the majority eat because it tastes most like what we are used to—candy).

Eat in variety and moderation the best foods that can be found. (More specific guidelines are in a following chapter.) Don't sweat the small stuff or panic when a meal is not perfect. Freshness, rawness, and variety are the principles to reach toward. That is not something that can be easily or perfectly achieved in our modern day. Thankfully, the amazing human body is forgiving if small compromises are made here and there. Just keep the ideal goal in sight and don't worry about veering off the path now and then.

25

FOOD ETHICS

THE THOUGHT OF A CREATURE, any creature, dying in order for people to eat is very unsettling for many. It is also puzzling that humans seem to be the only ones who make a fuss about it. Other creatures just eat what they are designed to eat and apparently never give it a second thought.

Vegetarianism is a choice many make because they feel that taking animal life is wrong. But how is it logically valid to assume that the life of a plant is of less merit than that of an animal? *Plant* and *animal* are mere words humans have devised. There is no such labeling in nature. The arbitrariness of the two categories particularly becomes apparent at the microscopic and biochemical levels where meaningful differences can be almost impossible to discern.[1]

Evidence is also now in hand that plants have feelings, can communicate, and are perhaps sentient in their own unique way.[2] Just because plants don't have legs or a brain like ours does not justify an anthropomorphic moral distinction between them and animals.[3] For example, starfish don't have a brain and yet are very social creatures—making them eerily like many people we know.

The crisp categories and labels we impose on nature may make it appear like a tidy taxonomic department store, but that is not the reality. As science progresses it becomes more and more difficult to differentiate plant and animal. Nature, although apparently heterogeneous and divided by cell walls, plasma membranes, and skin, is inherently homogeneous and interlinked. We and every other creature are just eddies in the great river of life. Life is joined and blends within itself with symbiotic, commensal, parasitic, and predatory food chain relationships keeping nature in balance and intact.[4]

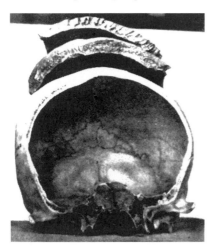

Losing Our Thick Skulls - Notice the thickness of ancient Florida Indian skulls (the two on top) compared with a modern skull. Bone density is very much dependent upon a healthy outdoor lifestyle and mineral-rich, raw natural foods. Little wonder modern people suffer from osteoporosis and bone fractures to the degree they do. Heat processed, starch-based, and sugar laden diets literally strip bone out of the body due to the chronic acidemia (high tissue acidity) they create. (Price, W. (1982). *Nutrition and Physical Degeneration*, California: The Price-Pottenger Nutrition Foundation. Used with permission. Contact at (619) 462-7600, www.ppnf.org, info@ppnf.org)

If one is of the opinion that the taking of life is immoral, accordingly, the taking of any life should be deemed immoral. How is it we humans get to decide which life is more valid than another? But taking life for food clearly cannot be immoral for that would make life itself immoral, since in order for any creature to live other creatures must die.

In nature there is a predatory hierarchy. Cows kill grass, lions kill zebras, and big fish kill little fish. If all creatures decided to contravene their nature and draw arbitrary lines about what to eat, or all decided to only eat vegetation, populations would grow unchecked, resulting in massive die-offs and ecological disaster. The web of life requires death at all levels. So attempting to moralize about food based upon which categories of life we decide to kill has little to do with logic or science, and everything to do with emotion, feelings, sentimentality, and anthropomorphism.

Although humaneness and consideration for all life is important, so too is the ethic of human health. If we start with the premise that human life and health are to be respected and protected, certain ethical decisions follow. As discussed in the previous chapter, healthy food is that food we are designed to eat. It would therefore be unethical to refuse to eat a food we are designed to eat, thus causing our own disease, pain, suffering, and death. If we voluntarily choose the wrong foods (even if motivated by an ethic we devise) and cause the protracted suffering from a disease like cancer, for example, how is that not unethical as well? In other words, we can choose the ethic of sparing the life of a food animal, or we can choose the ethic of preventing disease, suffering, and death of humans.

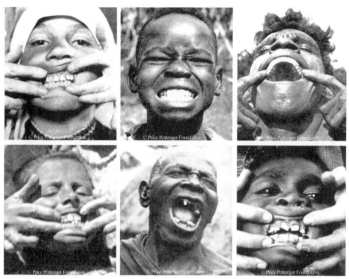

Dental Degeneration - Converting the diet to its more natural form is not just a theoretical thing to do. These pictures compare the dentition of isolated (pre-advanced), as opposed to modern, Swiss, Africans, and Aborigines. Notice the broad and healthy mouths holding a full complement (including wisdom teeth in most cases) of well spaced and beautiful teeth (top photos). The diets are predominantly raw foods and constructed similarly to what is being outlined here, as opposed to the modern, heat processed, carbohydrate saturated fare (bottom photos). (Price, W. (1982). *Nutrition and Physical Degeneration*, California: The Price-Pottenger Nutrition Foundation.)

If human health and life is the primary objective, the most critical ethical issue is determining what we are genetically designed to eat. In our early history, humans were opportunists. We would hunt, as well as scavenge animal remains killed by carnivores. No ancient civilization was absent animal foods. Even primates, formerly believed to be strict vegetarians, occasionally engage in carnivorism and cannibalism. Humans lost in the wild, surrounded by vegetation, will even cannibalize.

Only when animal foods were exhausted did our ancient forebears resort to plant foods as a staple. Strictly vegan diets (no meats, eggs, or dairy) have only been possible since the Agricultural Age. With the invention of the plow (probably the pivotal invention converting nomads to farming communities), stone mill, and bake oven, inedible and toxic raw grains became a mainstay. If the population of prey animals had grown to keep pace with human population, farming and grain production might never have occurred. If it had, it would have been in condiment measure, not as a staple. Veganism is not the archetypal and healthy model. Hunting and scavenging is.[5]

Our present Agricultural/Industrial Age represents a miniscule portion of the 550-mile long time-line of life. It is only because of the burgeoning human population and its decimation of natural prey food sources that agriculture and processing became necessary. Agriculture is not the natural order. It is an artificial manipulation of nature in order to accommodate swelling societies with grain-based foods.[6]

A vegetarian diet of rice, bread, granola, and the like would never be possible in the wild absent fire and technology. No other creature on the planet bakes or microwaves their food. Humans not only do this, but then assume that it is the natural and healthy way to eat—as if Mother Nature had it all wrong and we have fixed her with our fancy processing machines and agribusiness.

It is an experiment that has had disastrous effects for those who do not understand how a vegan/vegetarian diet must be carefully orchestrated. For example, a young couple fed their infant a diet of soy milk and apple juice. At six weeks of age it weighed only three and a half pounds and died of malnutrition. The parents were sentenced to life in prison. This makes it painfully clear that we do not get to do with our diets whatever we please—regardless of our good intentions—without consequences.[7]

This is not to say that vegetables (by vegetables I mean any non-animal or non-fruit product) are not nutritious to some degree. They are just not what we are best adapted to as a mainstay. To make our diet predominantly foods we could never find in the wild, or digest if not processed, is at best a risky experiment.[8]

Nevertheless, even doctors, nutritionists and governmental agencies—who should know better—promote unnatural foods as natural and even place them as the predominant food in nutrition pyramids. Notice how grain-based products are featured in these models. The results of this illogic are manifest everywhere today, from rampant obesity to every imaginable degenerative disease condition.

The reason our modern processed food experiment fails is three-fold:

1. Raw animal products contain a variety of essential nutrients not found in vegetation.

2. Heat processing any food diminishes its nutritional value and produces a host of toxins.

3. In order to replace the concentrated calories of animal food, addicting grains and sugars have become the mainstay, resulting in a carbohydrate load human bodies were never designed for.

Dr. Dulltool ponders an experiment to determine what foods creatures require.

Hunger solves the question of what we should eat. As mentioned previously, with a family to feed and with the energy demands of an in-the-wild existence, humans would not focus on lettuce, a few seeds, or seasonal berries while ignoring concentrated food sources such as rabbits, fish, and deer. With survival at stake, we would forget the luxury of devised principle, and eat whatever we could find or catch, particularly that which was energy-dense and digestible.

Arguments about stomach size, length of the intestinal tract, construction of dental arcade, food transit time, and the ability or inability to synthesize various vitamins are all interesting in the debate about whether humans are carnivores, omnivores, or vegetarians. But these polemics do not cut to the chase: what would we eat, what could we eat if turned loose in the wild and faced with survival? The answer to that simple question tells us precisely what we are designed to eat.

Incidentally, no modern human has ever survived for any length of time if lost in the wild without eating other creatures, including some unthinkables such as bugs, grubs, worms, and maggots.

Research shows that hunter-gatherers ate (as a percentage of total energy consumed) as much as 35% protein, 58% fat, and as little as 22% carbohydrates. They ate the entire edible portion of a carcass (no carbohydrates there at all, except some glycogen in the liver and possibly the tongue and kidney). Plants consumed, in order from most to least, were: fruits, seeds, nuts, tubers-roots-bulbs, and then the leaves-flowers-gums of miscellaneous plant parts.

Of 226 hunter-gatherer societies studied and reported in the Ethnographic Atlas, 133 derived at least 2/3 of their subsistence from animal foods. None were largely or entirely dependent upon gathered plant foods. Hunter-gatherers were found to only eat cereal grains as a last resort if in a state of starvation.

Yet grains in their many processed manifestations are the most common food today. Compare the percentages above with current U.S. eating patterns and 'recommended' healthy diet touted by the experts: protein 15%, fat 30%, and carbohydrates 55%.[9]

It is of no small importance that societies and animals on raw natural meat-based diets are virtually free of chronic degenerative diseases (heart disease, cancer, obesity, arthritis, diabetes, etc.). In contrast, we experience them as an epidemic in direct proportion to our grain-based agriculture. In other words, the proof is in the pudding (complete with sugar, colors, preservatives and artificial flavors).

Put simply, if long-term health is the objective, raw natural foods must be a significant part of the human diet. If health is not the objective, then any food choice that fits one's arbitrary ethical fancy would be fine.

"Yep—us modern people just keep gettin' smarter and smarter..."

Arguing for vegetarianism because of one's compassion is one thing. Insisting that it is healthier than meat eating requires that logic and a lot of evidence be ignored. All the shortfalls of meat eating commonly cited are related to processing, agricultural practices, and over consumption, not of the diet itself. For example, it is not the cholesterol found in animal products that is detrimental to health, but rather the processed oxidized form of cholesterol that plays havoc on health. The processed form of cholesterol is toxic in that it causes free-radical pathology to various tissues. The result is cancer, atherosclerosis, and the host of other degenerative conditions. Cholesterol in raw natural food is not oxidized and is a beneficial nutrient. If we do not consume it, the body produces it since it is the starting point for the synthesis of hormones essential to life. Also, farmed and grain-fed meat tainted with antibiotics, pesticides, and herbicides is unnatural and unhealthy. But the perversion of meat foods by human intervention does not deny their healthfulness in the raw wild state.

In spite of the compelling arguments that we are omnivores, killing animals for food is troublesome for many people, including me. It's as though our bodies, our biology, are of this world, but our psyche and our ethical sensibilities are from somewhere else. What possible survival value is there in having an aversion to foods we are designed to eat? (This paradox is addressed further in *Solving the Big Questions*.)

Even if it does not make sense from a nutritional, health, and biological perspective, vegetarianism and veganism are to be respected for the sensitivity to life they represent. Such sensitivity is much better than a dominionist predatory attitude where killing is recreation, and marauding the Earth's resources to exhaustion is considered a right.

Regardless of how we choose to eat, conscience can always be exercised. For example, one can use animal products that do not result in the death of the animal, such as dairy and eggs. More vegetables, fruits, and nuts can be used thus sparing more animals. By using organic and free-range products, not only are we supporting more humane farming practices, the animals so raised are healthier, less stressed, and produce healthier food.

We could also eat less and by so doing improve health, increase longevity, and decrease the demand on animal food production. Killing creatures in order to survive is one thing, killing them to support gluttonous eating is quite another. Each of us must keep in mind the carbon footprint we place on Earth. Any food we eat and do not need is not a matter of our 'right,' nor is it innocent recreation. Fields have to be planted, animals raised in pens and slaughtered, herbicides and pesticides sprayed, trucks put on the road, fuel consumed, exhaust produced, and stores built just to support such excess eating. A single person can consume tons of unnecessary food over a lifetime, enough to support a tribe in an underdeveloped nation. Neither is the ethical high ground achieved just because the fat we are layering on our bodies is from organic eggs or free-range beef. Is it not also unethical to cause obesity-related diseases, and then place demands on society for the medical care and maintenance that then become necessary?

Eating is great fun. But fun does not mean license without responsibility. Just because we can, doesn't mean we should. What we choose to eat and how much are daily ethical choices that permit us to exert sensitivity to all life, discharge our fiduciary duty to the Earth, and create the best health it is possible for us to achieve.

26

HEALTHY WEIGHT

FOOD IS FUEL AND MATERIALS. It provides the building blocks for organic structure and the energy input for the dynamics of life itself. Interestingly, the sun is the ultimate source of the energy we derive from food. Through photosynthesis the sun's energy makes the bonds between atoms in food plant molecules. In turn, food animals consume plant molecules. When we digest and metabolize plant or animal tissue we break the carbon-to-carbon bonds in the molecules, releasing the sun's energy for our own use in building tissue, fighting disease, keeping warm, and moving about.

That's all kind of peripheral to the point of this chapter but it is quite fascinating that the source of the energy keeping us at 98.6 degrees and for every move we make is the sun. We, and all life, are solar powered. It is yet another fact demonstrating our inextricable link to the natural world.

Eating is a very practical thing, transforming the energy of the sun into the energy we need for life. It is not just recreation. We enjoy food because our bodies know it is necessary for life. Otherwise we would take it or leave it. Since great effort is required to obtain food in the wild, without the satisfaction of eating, our ancestors would have long ago starved and we would not now exist. So the urge to search out food and enjoy its pleasures is a good and necessary design.

The problem is that this design for survival can get perverted when all the food we want is available by simply opening a cupboard or refrigerator door. In the wild, food was usually scarce and only found with great difficulty and effort. When we made a find we would gorge ourselves, enjoy doing it, and our body would release hormones such as growth hormones and insulin to build tissue and store any excess into the densest form of reserve (sun) energy, fat. The body reasons: "Who knows when another meal might come, so better pack as much fat away as possible."

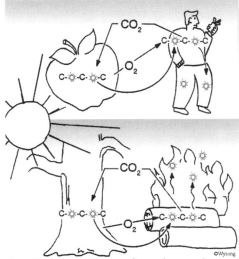

What happens when food is not scarce? What if we don't have to be hard bodied and swift footed like our food gathering Paleolithic ancestors? Since we are still physiologically, genetically, and instinctually back in the wild, our body tells us to eat aplenty, enjoy it, and store as much fat as possible for those future bouts of starvation. And boy, do we listen.

Another mechanism designed for the wild—not discarded just because we have become civilized—is the 'on' eating switch. Notice sometime when you are not even hungry that if you start to eat, all of a sudden you do feel hungry and wade in with gusto. In the wild the eating 'on' switch assures that if food is found we don't just take a few

Sun Energy – Energy from the sun is converted and stored as bonds in carbon chains (C- -C-☀-C) in plants. These chains are found in carbohydrates and lipids. Once consumed, the chains are broken by use of oxygen, produced by plants, releasing the sun's energy for the body's needs. CO_2 is expired in the process. Similarly, wood is comprised of sun energy contained in carbon chains released as heat when wood is burned. Oxygen is consumed and CO_2 released in the process in the same way as in energy production in the body.

nibbles and walk away. Remember, food was difficult and scarce in the wild. When it was found it needed to be taken full advantage of. But today, when food is available 24 hours a day, the switch is flipped on entirely too often. The result is storage of emergency fat with no emergencies to spend it on.

Aside from abundance, the most aggravating factor in modern obesity is the shift to a carbohydrate-based diet. In the wild, cheese puffs, Jolly Ranchers, and Big Gulps would not exist. We would be primarily metabolizing protein and fat because that is the makeup of natural foods in the wild.

When we fill the intestinal tract with carbohydrates (all of which convert to quick energy sugars) and keep it full, there is no need for the body to ever call upon reserve fat in tissue to supply energy. Additionally, the fat that is eaten is shuttled off to fat stores since it is the prized storage fuel. There is no need to waste this prized fuel for energy since all the moment-to-moment energy needs are being taken care of by an intestinal tract that is constantly laden with carbohydrates. Carbohydrates in excess of moment-to-moment energy needs are then also converted to fat for storage.

As the body gets used to this skewed form of metabolism, it becomes dependent on it and will feel discomfort if it is not continued. The craving for sugar and starches (another form of sugar) is a universal symptom of the obese. Their inability to imagine a day without soda, some candy, bread, cereal, pastries, potatoes, and rolls is not a matter of mere food preference, but of addiction and should raise the red flag that those are the foods they should abandon. This craving for processed carbohydrates, when the body obviously does not need more food, is an addiction every bit as powerful as nicotine, caffeine and street drugs. The carbohydrate junkie is enslaved and self-destructive like any other addict.

The "on" eating switch is meant for this...

...not this.

The Eating-On Switch — In nature, when food is found, the pleasure of eating causes creatures to eat to fullness. Once we start to eat there is a biochemical switch that stimulates us to continue. The ready availability of food in the modern setting permits repeated triggering of the eating-on switch and resultant overconsumption and obesity.

135

That brief explanation is the long and short of the cause of the modern epidemic of obesity, as well as the many other modern chronic degenerative diseases.

Since it is intelligence, not our biology, that has created the convenient modern abundance, it is intelligence, not biology, that must dictate how we eat. Reason tells us that we should be selecting foods as close to nature as possible and expending sufficient energy by work or exercise to balance what we take in. That is a matter of thinking and judgment, not feeling— feeling like we want to eat and feeling like we don't want to exercise.

Actually, little thought is required if whole natural raw foods are the focus. Such foods will automatically regulate weight. High levels of body fat do not exist in the wild other than to serve a functional role in insulation or as a reserve for hibernation. Natural food—any food that can be found in the wild and digested raw exactly

Food addiction is like drug addiction.

like it is without any form of processing—also contains all the vitamins, minerals, enzymes, accessory nutrients and undiscovered essentials to process the food and permit the full expression of health. Unnatural food—that which can only be eaten if processed or synthesized—is cosmetically enhanced to fool us into thinking it is good. It is usually laden with toxins and easy calories stripped of vital nutrients. Modern processed foods are too much of too little. The obese are in fact starving, famished for the critical nutrients found only in raw natural foods.

Excess weight is such a pervasive problem and an inciting or aggravating factor in so many diseases that its prevention should be on everyone's mind, and it pretty much is these days since the majority of people are overweight and at least a third are obese. Excess weight is neither innocent nor harmless for the individual or society. Since excess weight boils down to eating more than one's activity justifies, it is a form of theft in that we are taking what we do not deserve. In a world of limited resources, including those necessary to farm, process, transport, and store food, why should we consume more than we need? Moreover, while children here and abroad starve, we are killing ourselves by overeating. Instead of the counsel echoed in households across the land: "Clean up your plate, don't you know there are starving children?" it should be: "Don't put so much on your plate; don't you know there are starving children?"

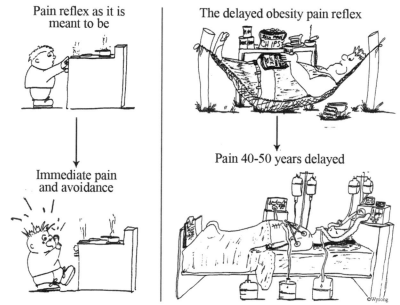

Pain reflex as it is meant to be

Immediate pain and avoidance

The delayed obesity pain reflex

Pain 40-50 years delayed

Obesity Pain Reflex – It is unfortunate that the pain that is felt from obesity is delayed so long. In the meantime, a lot of pleasurable eating can take place. If every time we ate more than we should we experienced pain, obesity would be nonexistent. It is thinking (technology) that puts us in a position where food in abundance is but a few steps away. It is therefore thinking that must be engaged to measure long term consequences. Eating for modern humans is a mind thing, not just a "what tastes good" thing.

We owe it to our body to properly care for it. It is a moral and ethical responsibility as much as caring for children, parents, pets, and the environment. Some justify being overweight as a life choice. But no choice is made in a vacuum. Society ends up paying for handicap facilities, healthcare, and social aid for those who, under the burden of their own weight and the attendant health decline, cannot stand on their feet for any length of time or sustain a job. It is also not fair to family and friends to impose upon them the emotional anguish of watching a loved one self-destruct.

Excess weight predisposes those who carry it to myriad diseases and mobility problems. Decreased agility increases the risk of physical injury from falling and decreases a person's ability to escape quickly from threatening situations. The load stress on the joints erodes them and inflicts arthritic changes requiring pain medications (a sure downward drug dependent and side effect spiral) and joint replacement surgery.

If a person simply calculates how much they are overweight, say it is 50 or 100 pounds, and goes to a gym and picks up dumbbells of that weight and carries them around for a short time, it will be clear why the joints are failing. Such a person is not a 'victim' of arthritis, and it is not 'in the genes,' even though many physicians and surgeons will tell their patients such an outrageous story.

If an obese person requires surgery, risk is increased because of the difficulty of reaching target tissues, the danger of ligatures slipping, and the sheer frustration of attempting precise work in a corporeal vat of grease. Furthermore, if the goal is to reach the maximum lifespan of about 120, or at least live healthily for the years lived, few things can be done that will increase the chances more than eating less and being reasonably lean.[1-2]

EXCESS WEIGHT IS A PROBLEM that lies within any person's power to solve.[3] Even when people feel up against the wall and resort to highly dangerous bariatric surgery (stomach stapling and the like), success does not come from the surgery; it results because less food is eaten. Eating less food can be a choice; choice does not require surgery.

Life is best lived as a challenge to be won. By following the simple principles outlined above we can meet and win the challenge of excess weight with a wind at our back. All that stands in the way is thinking and the will to become a better person.

So don't see excess weight as an impossible burden or a reason to concede defeat, nor to resign oneself to a lifestyle of masochistic self-loathing. Don't be discouraged by the feeling of emptiness and frustration from failed diet programs that center on some expert or product. They provide no true foothold because they center on an outside agency, not personal enlightenment. See the problem and your new understanding of it as a fount of action. It is a wonderful opportunity to take control, watch your body transform, and experience the health it is designed to have.

27

HEALTHY EATING IDEAS

MODERN LIVING, individual circumstances, and tastes that have been formed over a lifetime may not permit us to eat perfectly. That's okay. If we keep our sight on the goal of matching food to our genetic design, we can slip here and there. The body is forgiving and health does not require that we follow a precise eating formula.

Nevertheless, since the type of diet explained in the previous chapters (undereating with overnutrition) is a dramatic departure from common fare and style (being overfed and undernourished), you may wonder what to do next. This chapter will provide some specific daily eating ideas on returning to nature.

EARLY MORNING

Drink a quart or two of purified water before eating anything. Squeeze in ½ lemon to help with combating acidemia. (Since lemons are acidic this may seem like a contradiction, but once digested and metabolized the citrate in lemons buffers tissue acid. The malate in apples can do similarly.) Warm the drink if you would like. Everyone today is prone to acidemia (high body acid) due to modern circumstances and diet. It and the free radical pathology it promotes underlie most modern degenerative diseases.[1] Drinking a significant amount of water first thing also helps flush out accumulated toxins and staves off appetite. Increasing water intake will help with virtually any health condition and is a great preventive as well. It even helps burn calories since the body must expend them to warm the water up to 98.6 degrees.

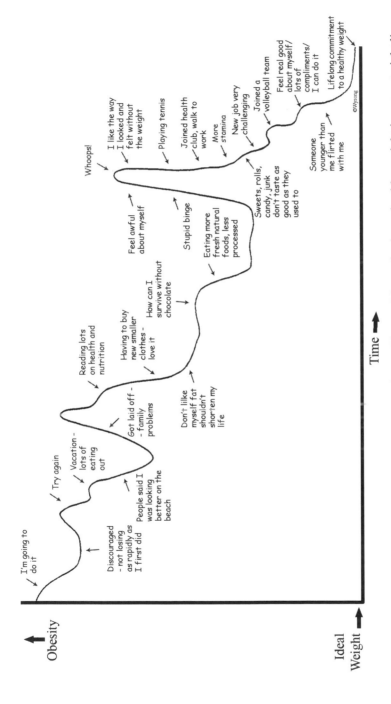

Obesity

I'm going to do it

Try again

Discouraged - not losing as rapidly as I first did

Vacation - lots of eating out

People said I was looking better on the beach

Got laid off - family problems

Reading lots on health and nutrition

Having to buy new smaller clothes - love it

How can I survive without chocolate

Don't like myself fat - shouldn't shorten my life

Eating more fresh natural foods, less processed

Feel awful about myself

Stupid binge

Whoops!

Sweets, rolls, candy, junk don't taste as good as they used to

I like the way I looked and felt without the weight

Playing tennis

Joined health club, walk to work

More stamina

New job very challenging

Joined a volleyball team

Feel real good about myself/ lots of compliments/ I can do it

Someone younger than me flirted with me

Lifelong commitment to a healthy weight

©Wysong

Time ➤

Ideal Weight ➤

The Ups And Downs On The Road To Healthy Weight – The road from obesity to healthy weight is not a straight line. A person must understand this before embarking on a new diet program so that setbacks are not taken as a reason to abandon the effort. The objective should be health, not a specific amount of weight lost in a certain time. If health is pursued, weight will fall in line automatically over time.

140

BREAKFAST

Unless engaged in demanding exercise, there should be no true hunger until late morning. Don't eat breakfast out of routine. Again, remember your origins and the fact that we are not designed for limitless food within easy reach. (Children are a different matter in that their needs are greater and must be constantly met to accommodate growth.)

Make it a personal challenge, no matter what you eat, to not get full. This is difficult because the eating switch remains on long after we have had more than we need. We have to consciously make the decision to turn it off. Walk away, brush your teeth, or do some enjoyable activity. After the desire to eat subsides (it will), you will have a great sense of satisfaction once you realize you didn't need more food after all.

Options:

1. Poach eggs or lightly cook an omelet with whatever natural foods you would like inside. And/or have some plain yogurt mixed with fresh fruit and raw nuts. Any of the ingredients mentioned in option #2 can be mixed in as well.

"I know it's my glands because I run three miles daily and only eat a couple of apples and a bran muffin."

2. Make a shake in a blender or just stir the ingredients together by hand:

• Whole protein powder, and/or one or two raw, organic, free-range eggs—a perfect protein.

• Two or three prunes that have been soaked until soft (just put some in a capped jar, cover with water, and keep in the fridge). Prunes are nutrient- and antioxidant-dense, have activity against possible food-borne pathogens, and help keep bowels regular.

• Part of a banana and/or other fruits like dried dates, figs, blueberries, cherries, raw honey, etc. These are great raw nutrition and the various flavors permit you to make the drink to taste.

• A slice of avocado will help thicken the drink and add important nutrients.

• Flax, pumpkin and virgin coconut and palm fruit oils—sources of important fatty acids, phytonutrients, and fiber. They are important for the immune system and help the body relearn how to metabolize fats rather than carbohydrates.

• Whole food dried concentrates, such as from wheat and barley grasses, spirulina, algae, and the like are sources of dozens of raw plant-based antioxidants and phytonutrients. Vitamins and minerals in food form like this are the most beneficial to health.

• A cup or so of plain organic yogurt (not the cloyed, fruit on the bottom, or otherwise flavored varieties)—a source of probiotics, protein, minerals, and immune factors.

• One-half cup or so of raw nuts and seeds—excellent protein, minerals, and essential fatty acids. These could include macadamia, cashews, Brazils, almonds (with the brown skin peeled off after soaking them in water long enough for it to easily peel away), walnuts and pecans (soaked overnight and  drained of the dark colored, bitter, and anti-digestive tannins, and rinsed), sunflower and pumpkin seeds, and coconut meat. Keep the nuts in the freezer (coconut in refrigerator) to help protect their fragile fatty acids.

   ◦ Alternatively to the above dry ingredients for the shake, use prepared, raw, grainless, sugarless, 'un-cereals' and snack bars. Just mix with fresh fruit and the yogurt and blend into the drink. If you cannot wean from cereal, use a non-sugared (read the ingredient list), whole-grain cereal topped with the nuts as prepared above.

• Blend a little. If a few chunks of nuts are left, that's good. It will force chewing the shake rather than guzzling it. Chewing slows down eating and increases salivary flow and digestive action.

Rotate the ingredients so the shake/meal is not exactly the same every day. This helps decrease the likelihood of developing food sensitivities. Vary the fruits to create different flavors. Make the shake small enough that it creates comfort but not fullness. Take half of your daily supplements with this meal. Encapsulated supplements that don't taste awful can be opened and sprinkled into the shake before blending.

This nutritionally dense meal is extremely satisfying and will hold through the entire day until supper.

It's also a wonderful meal substitute anytime. When I travel I make this shake at home and put it in a capped jar packed with a gel cooler bag. No hunting for a restaurant, no getting desperate and eating junk, and no hunger for the rest of the day.

Alternatives to the above would be anything you can think of that mimics natural foods and could be eaten raw. Just don't cave in to starches and sugars by filling up on bagels, pancakes, cereals, breads, and the like.

THROUGH THE DAY

If truly hungry, snack on fresh fruit and/or fresh coconut, or other tree nuts and seeds. Always ask the question as to whether you have done sufficient activity to justify what you are eating. If not, do some exercise and there is a good chance the desire to eat will subside. There is no crime in being hungry once in a while. It is not a disease needing an ER raid on the refrigerator. As the body adjusts to the new diet, you will also find that food has much more staying power.

If possible, take a little nap around noon. Even fifteen minutes of shut-eye can make a tremendous difference in the rest of the day. Otherwise, you may see your tiredness as a result of not eating, 'hypoglycemia,' or some other food-related cause remedied only by, of course, eating.

SUPPER

Skip it if not hungry. Remember, there is no law that says you must eat at every mealtime. Who decided there should be meal times anyway?

Here are some options, with a hunt and gather flair: (These are all just suggestions to give a feel for what you are naturally designed for. Do what you can.)

1. 'Pick and gather' a fresh raw salad of your liking. Dress it with extra virgin olive oil. Add some seasoning and shredded raw organic cheese for variety. Try different veggies and rotate ingredients. Four to eight ounces of meat with this meal will be sufficient. Lightly broil or grill. If you can do steak tartare, fine; if you can't, high temperature/short time is the best way to cook to preserve nutrition and decrease toxins. Remember, in the wild there is no cooking at all.

2. Next day's dinner could be just a salad with some nuts, vegan style (because you found no prey that day).

3. The next dinner could be just eggs, perhaps as a veggie-filled omelet (because you found a nest to rob). An alternate dinner could be yogurt and cheese (from the tamed goat, buffalo, or camel), plus a salad perhaps.

4. Another dinner is nothing except water. (It was a day off from food hunting and there wasn't that much hunger anyway.)

Supplements are important because we never eat perfectly, many modern foods are nutritionally weak, and modern living creates extraordinary stresses. Supplements are not a very wild thing, but then neither are we being totally wild. Take supplements during meals with chewed bites of food. Do not take the same supplements without letup. Vary them as you do your meals.[2]

For an example of how to do this see the Optimal Health Program I have designed.[2]

Do not drink with meals since that shortens chewing time, allows gulping, and dilutes digestive juices. Coffee, booze, and pop do not come along with wild meals.

Have some chocolate or other small dessert.Make ice cream with eggs, cream, vanilla, fruit, honey, nuts, etc. Experiment making non-cooked pies with a nut crust, fruit, whipped cream, honey, etc.[3]

EVENING SNACK

Only if really hungry. Some choices:

• Air popped popcorn topped with extra virgin olive oil and seasonings

• Natural peanut butter as a dip for carrots and celery sticks

• Raw nuts and dried fruits as in a trail mix

- Fresh coconut

- Fresh fruit

- Raw organic cheese

• Dips made with blended organic cream cheese, fresh peppers, garlic, whole sea salt, lemon and lime juice, cashews, tomatoes, avocados, or whatever—have fun. Yes, you can cheat with some whole grain, organic corn, or potato chips to deliver this wondrous concoction. No hydrogenated oils, though.

Again, don't get full and don't eat out of bottomless bags. Set out a reasonable amount before beginning and let that be it regardless of how good it all tastes and how on the eating switch is.

SKIP A DAY

Don't eat for a day every now and then. Just drink the water. Not eating is one of the healthiest things to do! Decreasing food intake is the only consistent variable scientists have found that can extend life.

If you do less physical activity on any particular day, eat less. Think in terms of 'deserve.' Do more, eat more. Do less, eat less. It means getting the mind engaged and using discipline.

If there is a problem with parts of this regimen, or a problem digesting certain components, or you can't bring yourself to do the raw egg thing, that's okay. Just use this as a model along with the principles explained in previous chapters to tailor things to your liking.

There is no hard and fast rule other than to break from convention and eat as if thinking matters.

SECTION E

Thinking about . . .

MENTAL HEALTH

IN THIS SECTION: *The health of the mind is directly linked to physical health, which in turn is determined by lifestyle, exercise, and nutrition. On the other hand, the mind can influence the health of the physical body. Mood, hope, happiness, and fulfillment affect our lives and at the same time are products of how we live them. Modern life has made us increasingly dependent for even our basic needs. When things go wrong, such dependency makes it easy to blame others and feel victimized. But we are never really pawns, nor is life a guarantee. Seeing life as an opportunity over which we have control is the key to mental health.*

28

FIRST THINGS FIRST

THE MEDICAL VIEW OF THE MIND is that it is just a product of the electrical currents flowing across neurons. This hamstrings approaches to mental health. Effects are focused upon, diseases named, symptoms treated, but cures are elusive.

Contrary to popular belief, although the mind is related to the brain, it is not a mere product of neurons (much more on this in *Solving the Big Questions*), nor is the mind disjointed from bodily function. Depression and psychological stress can sap the will for a productive life, suppress the immune system, and open the door for infectious and degenerative diseases. On the other hand, happiness and optimism can imbue life with health, creativity, and purpose.

Because mind and thought are nonmaterial sorts of things, the demanding physical needs of the brain are often ignored by psychologists and therapists. On the other hand, the psychiatric profession sees the mind as closely allied with matter, but only insofar as it relates to pharmaceutical manipulation. All such professions, as a matter of course in their conventional approach to mental illness, miss the point.

If the mind is not working properly, the obvious matters of health must be taken care of first. Remembering our origins is key. Daily exercise, sunlight, proper natural nutrition, and pleasant social interaction directly affect the function of the mind. It is remiss to attempt emotional repair using drugs or talk therapy if the patient never sees the light of day, sits in front of a television for hours on end, and consumes only processed junk food. Not living properly affects the body, which in turn affects the brain, which then affects the body, and on and on.

While in a dark mood, we may be convinced that the entire problem is our job, mate, or upbringing, and that our inactivity, diet, and lack of sun have nothing to do with how we feel. But vitamin D deficiency from insufficient sun striking our skin, B vitamin deficiency from food processing, insufficient minerals from factory farmed foods and from being leached out of the body with sodas and metabolic acidosis, imbalanced amino acids from a protein-poor diet, toxicity from environmental pollutants, drugs, starches, and sugars can dramatically affect the brain. Toxicities, deficiencies, excesses, and imbalances can make us vulnerable to, and even create the gamut of mental illnesses ranging from mild depression to psychopathic acting out, even murder and suicide.

Although the relationship between overall health and brain function is obvious, millions of people are on drugs or live life in silent psychological misery, while the body endures constant abuse from poor life choices. Why feel like a helpless victim of depression or take a drug that could create dependency and produce side effects when something as simple as a multiple vitamin and mineral supplement, eating fresh natural protein-rich foods, drinking lots of pure water, achieving healthy weight, and taking vigorous walks in the sun might be the cure? Unfortunately, a mind that is in an unhealthy setting and not properly fueled cannot be trusted to make such rational decisions about lifestyle.

So while well, like right now while reading this book, make the decision to take the healthy steps outlined in the previous chapters at the first sign of mental illness. Giving nature a chance is not only the first thing we should do when physical or mental illness strikes, it is often the only thing we need to do.

29

HOPELESSNESS

PEOPLE OFTEN PERCEIVE HOPELESSNESS as an effect rather than a cause of mental and physical disease. Hopelessness creates a despair that descends upon us when we sense that there is no apparent way out of a situation and we fear an outcome over which there seems to be no control. Not only can depression set in, but physical illness almost always follows the stress of hopelessness.

Seemingly hopeless situations could be things like the death of a loved one, being sued, receiving news of a serious illness, losing a job, a marriage that seems unworkable, a child going astray, discrimination, or conflict with friends, relatives, or coworkers. Looking backward can also affect us negatively because it is hopeless to try to change the past or bring it back.

Hopelessness can work a deadly toll. It is an insidious, potentially lethal disease. There is an antidote: determining not to cave in or accept victim status. Hopeless situations are a signal to exert diligent effort to take control. One must immediately become proactive and get at solving the problem even though the inclination is to roll over and expose the belly.

The very act of engaging in the battle gives a sense of control and the healing power of hope. For example, a wrongly convicted prisoner could sink into hopeless despair or rise up, learn the legal system, study the case law, and spearhead appeals. The death of a loved one from disease or violence could spur activism to alert the public and encourage preventive measures. One person's singular misfortune could save the many.

Mothers who lost children in car accidents involving drunk drivers founded Mothers Against Drunk Driving (MADD). Their activism helps save lives. Doing something worthwhile, making something good come out of tragedy, gives meaning and purpose, an essential ingredient for a healthy mind. The *America's Most Wanted* television program was started by a father who lost a child to a psychopathic predator. His activism results in the capture of violent criminals and saves lives—including his, by giving him purpose and hope.

Recently (2006), Ken Lay, the founder of Enron, died of a heart attack while awaiting sentencing for corporate fraud. One can only dimly imagine the hopelessness that he felt in facing the prospect of jail after a life awash in power, money, and luxury. It would be hard not to associate his death with the stress and seeming hopelessness of his situation.

But it does not have to end like that. A young farmer (called "Farmer John") faced economic disaster on a farm that had been in his family for generations. He was forced to sell land and equipment dear to his heart just to survive. The situation seemed so hopeless that he locked himself away and sank into a deep depression for over a year. He came out of it only when he started writing his story, produced a movie on it, and began to convert what was left of his farm to an organic venture that people from a nearby big city could come and participate in. It is now a successful and growing enterprise that teaches people about sustainable agriculture. His life now has far more meaning to him than the former commercial farm ever could have.[1]

The key to reversing hopelessness is to learn, study, reach out, change, grow, be creative—to do whatever it takes regardless of the situation, and to get at it right now with great industry. Remember, too, that no matter how terrible it may seem, we learn and grow from experience. If we see life as an opportunity to grow—not just a comfy secure ride with others at the helm—we will learn to expect adversity, failure, and difficulty. Such experience is the forge that can make us better people. Being better people is the only worthwhile reason to be here.

We can do a great deal to prevent hopelessness. Perhaps the circum-stance we find ourselves in is of our own doing and the penalty we are enduring is what we deserve. If that is the case, then fess up and "take it like a man." Place the blame where it belongs, resolve not to do it again, and teach others so they do not make the same mistake. Be thankful. Life lessons, even painful ones, save us from even greater disasters in the future. There is always a bright side.

We get ourselves into hopeless situations particularly when we don't follow conscience and listen to the inner ethic. To prevent most hopeless situations—don't cheat, lie, steal, harm others, get lazy, or stop thinking. To avoid the hopelessness of prison—obey the law; of bankruptcy—don't overspend; of enemies—be nice; of disease—get healthy; of being paralyzed—don't drive drunk; of addiction—don't get started; of a failed relationship—choose well and put some effort into it.

The greatest danger of hopelessness is that those who have it do not recognize or respect it as of their own doing. Instead we live lives on the edge in the belief bad things just happen to other people and that we are special and will escape penalties. Then, when con-sequences befall us, we play victim, pout, withdraw, blame others, and lose control of our lives.

Blaming others is futile and counterproductive. All seemingly hopeless circumstances we find ourselves in are often of our own doing in one way or another. When we come to recognize this it should give us the wisdom and foresight to live life in a preventive mode and take responsibility for whatever life presents.

Hopelessness is not hopeless. Its cause, cure, and prevention lie in understanding that life is not surrender or reliance on others. We are the masters of our own lives.

30

DEPRESSION

DEPRESSION SENDS APPROXIMATELY 25 million people to the doctor each year. Some 90% of these visits result in medications with usually little or no attendant advice on lifestyle or nutrition. Prescriptions for depression have doubled in less than a decade even though studies have shown that most such medications are no more effective than placebo (sugar pills).[1] Even children have become a growth market for such medications.[2]

It is estimated that fifty million Americans are on SSRI antidepressant drugs (selective serotonin reuptake inhibitors), such as Zoloft, Paxil, and Prozac. Research has shown that 40% derive no benefit, 30% have diminishing effects after initial benefits, and almost 90% will experience withdrawal symptoms. Amazingly, not one of these fifty million people developed mental illness due to a deficiency of the drug they are taking. But many reap dire consequences once they are hooked, such as violence, aggression, suicidity, heart damage, liver failure, and breast cancer. Nevertheless, these dangerous drugs (some of which are banned in other countries) are prescribed like candy. Psychotherapeutics may help in certain instances, but should never be used without addressing causes.

At the onset of mental illness, most people will make an attribution to some circumstance in life, such as a problem at work, a marriage going bad, a death, parents who were not loving enough, financial woes, and so on. But these are the things of life. Difficulties cannot be escaped because they are part and parcel of life for everyone. Try as we might, we cannot perfect life and live happily ever after with no bumps in the road. How we handle difficulty, our inability to rebound, or being incapacitated by problems has to do with our mental and emotional strength and health. That, like the strength of a muscle, the heart, liver, and lungs comes from how we care for the body's—and brain's—physical needs. Don't expect to be able to sprint a mile without proper conditioning, rest, freedom from toxicity, and good nutrition; don't expect the brain to handle the marathon of life without such care as well.

Aside from rare instances where there is a genetic predisposition to mental disease, the cause of the brain's inability to generate healthy mood and balance is, as you might have guessed by now, our modern lifestyle. Rather than recognizing and fixing the problem, a huge percentage of the population lets themselves be convinced that mental problems are due to drug deficiency problems. We will spend a few moments on this with specifics to demonstrate, yet again, that with regard to popular and medical opinion, we must be wrong in order to be right.

Mental illness can result in violence, self-mutilation, suicidal thoughts, depression, eating disorders, panic attacks, insomnia, addictions, intolerance of heat or cold, self hatred, the blahs, worrying, irritability, cravings for caffeine, sugar, and chocolate, SAD (seasonal affective disorder), and virtually any other negative, aberrant, or obsessive mental state. Since the brain is an organ dependent upon specific nutrients, any imbalance in those nutrients, or toxicities, can cause the brain to malfunction and manifest these kinds of symptoms.

Biochemical neurotransmitters in the brain include serotonin, catecholamines, GABA, and endorphins. Each of these can be influenced by toxicities and diet. For example, it is estimated that over ninety percent of those seeking psychiatric help are serotonin deficient. This chemical helps us feel cheerful, emotionally flexible, not obsessive or worried, and able to relax and sleep well. It is manufactured in brain tissue from the amino acid tryptophan, which converts to 5-hydroxy-tryptophan (5-HTP) and then to serotonin. Serotonin in turn forms melatonin, the sleep chemical. (This is why depression is usually associated with insomnia.) Tryptophan is found in proteins, but the modern sugar and starch based diet is low in

154

tryptophan–containing proteins. SSRIs fool the body into thinking it has lots of serotonin by preventing its reabsorption (reuptake). But the body cannot be fooled for long, and will not tolerate us fooling around with its chemistry with drugs either. Changing lifestyle, getting sun exposure (stimulates serotonin production), converting the diet to natural foods we are genetically tuned to, and taking amino acid supplements (5-HTP usually best) address actual causes and promise cure. Even a genetic poly-morphism that causes depression by interfering with the conversion of tryptophan to 5-HTP, can be addressed by supplementing with 5-HTP.

The catecholamines (epinephrine, norepinephrine, dopamine), responsible for the feeling of energy for life, are derived from L-tyrosine, a conditionally essential amino acid which is particularly high in meats. The catecholamines also stimulate the adrenal glands to produce cortisol, another feel good chemical. Coffee and other caffeine containing drinks create the temporary highs we seek when catecholamines are low. But they inhibit serotonin and melatonin, and exhaust stress hormones.

The neurotransmitter GABA (gamma butyric acid) is produced to help us cope with stress and to relax. It, too, requires dietary amino acids. Chronic stress depletes GABA. Proper diet, supplements of magnesium, potassium, green tea, St. John's wort, vitamins B1, B6, B12, methyl donors (SAME—S-adenosyl methionine), theonine, GABA, and adrenal support with glandu-lars and licorice can counteract the depletion of catecholamines and GABA.

Endorphins are neurotransmitters that give pleasure, enjoyment, and joy. Without them we are oversensitive to pain, melancholy, and easily cry. They are released in response to stress and create the high from exercise. They are also responsible for why we may not feel pain at the time of trauma. Chronic pain—experienced by many with degenerative diseases—uses them up, and is why so many people are on addictive pain killer medica-tions. Some nineteen amino acids are necessary for endorphin synthesis. The amino acid phenylalanine (a precursor to tyrosine), in particular, helps sustain endorphins by decreasing the brain's destruction of it.

These natural dietary and supplement remedies are safe and can result in relief within ten to fifteen minutes. Although SSRIs can be discontinued immediately, the anti-anxiety benzodiazepines (Halcion, Centrax, Valium, etc.), capable of causing permanent, Alzheimer's-like brain injury, need to be more carefully withdrawn.

Although the majority of the medical profession prescribes drugs hit and miss to cover symptoms, there are some health practitioners who rationally evaluate lifestyle and brain chemistry and can actually cure psychiatric disorders such as depression, ADHD, schizophrenia, addictions, anxiety, and panic attacks with no risk of side effects. Aside from dietary deficiencies of amino acids, omega-3 fatty acids, vitamins, and minerals, modern living disrupts stress hormones, sex hormones, thyroid hormones, digestive function, and places a toxic, stimulatory (sugars, caffeine, Aspartame, alcohol) and oxidative burden on the body.

A drug designed to bully the brain into submission is not the answer. Returning to nature, and, if necessary, seeking help from professionals who understand brain chemistry and respect nature, is.[3]

Aside from seriously crippling episodes of depression, being down once in a while is something that happens to everyone. It is estimated that the typical American is in a bad mood approximately 110 days each year. Depression is part of the cycle of day-to-day life and not a unique circumstance. It just has to be dealt with intelligently if we are not to become our depression.

Clinical depression can ruin life. It can also end it. About two thirds of all suicides are depression related. The pain a person must feel to get to the point of suicide is surely immense—more overwhelming than most of us can even imagine. But when we think of pain, be it from a heart attack, arthritis, cancer, or depression, we should think about causes and prevention, not temporary fixes. That's the intelligent and humane approach that is virtually ignored by the medical establishment.

What follows is not to minimize the seriousness of clinical depression or the need for some people to have short-term medical intervention. But here are some cheap and safe things to try that will give the body and mind a chance to heal itself:

• First off, to repeat, eat properly and take nutritional supplements. The brain requires fuel, and lots of it. Pump water into a car's gas tank and the engine fails. Put the wrong fuel into the body and the brain fails.

• Before resorting to drugs, explore the various nutraceuticals, vitamins, minerals, and amino acids such as mentioned above that have proven effects on the brain and virtually no side effects. There is a world

156

of information and help a few clicks away by searching on the Internet under terms like, "natural mental health," "supplements for depression," "amino acids for the brain."

• Get outside every day if possible. Take a vigorous walk. If there is snow, cross-country ski or trek on snowshoes. Take in the fresh air and let the sun's rays, even if dulled by the clouds, hit the eyes and skin. We belong in the sun just like plants do. If we cloister ourselves in plastic caves under artificial light we will suffer just as plants do when so deprived.

• If possible, consider spending more time in the sunny South during the winter. Vitamin D—the anti-depression vitamin—is synthesized in the skin in response to sunlight. It is deficient in just about everyone who lives above 35 degrees latitude (level of Los Angeles). Further aggravating the national vitamin D deficiency is the skin cancer paranoia fostered by the medical profession. People are treating the sun as an enemy, staying indoors, and slathered with sunscreen when they go outside. Eating foods that are fortified with vitamin D is not the solution. Current recommendations for vitamin D (40 IU) are underestimated by a factor of about 100.[4] Not only is mood affected, but the host of degenerative diseases, including breast and prostate cancer, osteoporosis, autoimmunities, and musculoskeletal pain (themselves an aggravator or initiator of depression) are directly linked to vitamin D deficiency. We must get in the sun where we belong. Don't use sunscreens and don't stay in the sun so long that you burn. Take high-dose vitamin D supplements during the fall, winter, and early spring. Letting the sun into life makes for sunny people.[5]

• If doomed to the inside for the winter, convert to full spectrum light bulbs and consider obtaining a phototherapy lighting unit.[6]

• Engage in regular exercise. Be serious about it. Work up a sweat and get a muscle pump. The endorphins released from this activity will give an immediate boost. The social interaction from joining a gym will also lift the spirits and motivate you. Join a team for any sport and try to get good at it. Study, train, and teach others.

• When there are feelings of loss of control or being victimized, focus on figuring a way out (see previous chapter). Until that is done, depression will linger and deepen. Don't acquiesce, don't resign, don't play victim, and don't give up. Change things. Fix it. Gaining control of life is absolutely essential to health of mind and body.[7]

• Spend more time with a pet, or get an additional one if it can be cared for properly (see coming chapters). They are excellent mood therapy and can literally save lives. The ancient Greeks believed in the healing powers of dogs and used them as co-thera-pists. Asklepios, the principal healing god of the Greeks, exerted his healing power through dogs. The use of pets in nursing homes, hospices, hospitals, and for withdrawn

or chronically ill children has proven to be effective when nothing else will work. Pets give the unconditional love we all desire and serve as wonderful social lubricants. For these reasons, there are over 2000 programs in the U.S. alone using pets as therapy ("P.A.T.," as it is called).[8]

• Make work challenging and interesting. Yes, you. Don't wait for a better job description or the boss to take the lead. If there is no such opportunity, find another job or start a business. But there are few jobs that could not take creative input. So do it. Don't wait for a raise, don't wait for prodding, just get after it. Creative work is essential to a good life and a feeling of worth. It is not something to carefully measure in terms of dollars returned. Its reward is in the pride, fulfillment, optimism, and sense of accomplishment and worth it brings. Don't take on the employee mentality of measuring output to be sure it does not exceed pay scale. Don't be a nine-to-fiver. Dig in to work and think about increased efficiency or improvements of any sort. Make work like a hobby. That is what it should be. Take work home. Bring things to completion speedily. Think about ways to improve. Learn how to get better at job tasks. Treat a job as if it were your own business. Increasingly, as our economy becomes global, high wage/low skill (or performance) jobs will be a thing of the past. American glut will be leveled as vast third-world populations compete by gratefully working 12-16 hours per day for a few dollars. American employers will be more and more selective. So avoid yet another reason for depression—joblessness—by being useful, productive, and invaluable.

• Be creative at home. Refurbishing, decorating, cleaning, organizing, or starting a home business can all be wonderful uplifting challenges. Get engaged with organizations that are trying to make a better world. Spend more time with the kids in play, teaching them, or helping with their homework. Mentor or adopt a child.

• Learn to play a musical instrument and practice every day.

• Read and learn about self improvement and taking responsibility. Do not seek counseling that reinforces our desire to feel like a victim, prods us to selfishly assert ourselves without regard for the feelings or welfare of others, or makes us dependent on such therapy because, although we are simple ordinary people, we have become convinced we are complex.

• Turn the focus out, rather than in. Reach out to help others. Do a kind deed every day. Write thank you notes. Call someone to see how they are doing and do not permit the conversation to drift to you. Don't be right all the time and don't judge. Smile even if you don't feel like it. Hug someone. If something nice comes to mind about another, say it.

THE EFFECTS OF SUCH LIFESTYLE choices are not always immediate and they may not be the total solution to depression. At the least, however, they will help, may reduce the need for medications and counseling, and are without any dangers. Note that every one of the suggestions means action. Real and lasting solutions do not usually come by others doing things to or for us. Take control. Make your solution happen. Start today. Take the attitude that depression will only be allowed to be an occasional fleeting problem because living a good, healthy, and productive life leaves no time for such annoyance.

31

MEMORIES

RECENTLY I BOUGHT A BLUEGRASS CD because I find some of this music very enjoyable and uplifting. I usually don't pay much attention to lyrics, but one of the songs was so enjoyable I found myself trying to sing it. To do that, I had to pay attention to the words. This is what I ended up with:

"The wind is blowing around the cabin. I hate to hear that lonesome sound. I'm all alone and so downhearted since my true love has up and gone. I hate to see the sun a sinkin'. Another night to toss and turn. Another night to be without her, another night for her and him. She had no cause to go and leave me, for I had never done her wrong. She left our home and little children and with another man she is gone. The children they are sound asleeping, for they don't know their mother's gone. What will I do when they awaken? Can I tell them their mother's gone?"

The tune was catchy and the beat was fast, but what a downer story to be tapping the toe to. Why would anyone want to memorialize such a miserable situation by putting it to music? When you think about it, many popular songs and movie stories are similarly depressing.

It's not just lyrics, but music itself can send many people into depressive and melancholy moods. As life accumulates behind us, genres of music remain associated with each stage of that history. There are the songs of our parents' time, of high school and college, music we watched our children enjoy, and so on through every stage in life. Music can elicit powerful memories and sentimentality.

We naturally want to revisit our history, but by and large it is not a very healthy thing to do. A school reunion can make some people depressed for months. The music, sights, smells, tastes, and social events experienced year after year during holidays are powerful memory stimulants as well. These seasons often bring depression and even increased violence and suicide rates.

Holidays, birthdays, movies, television, and music all take advantage of our sentimentality. If there is a dollar to be made, no matter how miserable it may make people feel, it's going to happen—again and again, year after year.

There is no way to avoid all sad memories, but neither is it smart to seek out reminders of them. Think about it. Why voluntarily pay to see a tear-jerking melodramatic movie that leaves us feeling awful? Will we not face enough problems in our own lives without being entertained by those of others?

If we've ever lost a true love, already know we're going to die, face aging every day in the mirror, watched our children grow up and move away, and face trauma and tragedy in our own lives, why would we want to voluntarily seek situations, music, and entertainment that would remind us of this? So true is the aphorism, "The key to happiness is a bad memory."

Sometimes we think we must revisit the past in honor of it. But if the memory isn't refreshing and does not create optimism, it's not a wise place to go. The past cannot be relived, nor can it be changed. Pay respects and try to move on.

The trick, as we get older and have more life behind than in front of us, is to keep facing forward. We need to fully engage the present and put things into our lives that have a future.

By being active, socially engaged, always creative, inquisitive, reading, listening to audiotapes, watching instructional videos or television, going to lectures, sitting in on classes, and engaging in challenging hobbies or sports, we make life present and forward, not backward. The present and the future, unlike the past, hold events over which we have control. Control has everything to do with mental well-being.

If we stop growing, being challenged, and reaching out to the future, our mind will necessarily settle in on the only thing it has remaining, the past. The result is hopelessness, helplessness, despair, depression, and lost health.

Get engaged in the here and now. Do things that create prospects for fun in the future. Plan a project, work toward it, and determine to be the best. Whether the goal is grandiose and worldwide in scope or humble and in the kitchen, yard, shelter, or local gymnasium, start today. Take control of life. Don't linger in the past and permit hopelessness to take root. Such a positive, forward-looking life can do more for health than almost anything else we could do.

The present is the time we can do something about. The past is history but today is a gift; that's why, as the saying goes, it's called present. Use it to make the future bright, fun, challenging, hopeful, and healthy.

32

ADDICTION

THERE IS WIDE CONSENSUS that addicting drugs are a bad idea. They can obviously suck the life right out of a person. But what is not generally recognized is that there are many other ruinous addictions, many of which are not even recognized as such because of their social acceptance.

Actually, life is filled with addictions. We are addicted to eating and sleep, for example. Also, to lesser degrees, we can be addicted to exercise, sex, work, and interpersonal relations. The body and mind are designed to feel comfortable if we do these things. Pleasure chemicals are released to the brain by doing them, and discomfort results when we don't. Addiction to the things that keep us alive and healthy is a survival mechanism.

But the leisure and technology of modern life permits the perversion of this pleasure chemical mechanism. In the wild we would never be able to brew coffee every morning, smoke packs of cigarettes a day, drink pop, take drugs, overeat, play video games, snack on sugars, jog obsessively, and the like. Almost anything can become addictive and ruinous to health if we permit it to monopolize life and let society and commercial interests convince us it is hip and normal.

How do we know if we are addicted? The thing enslaving us is one of the first things that comes to mind in the morning and the last at night. Life seems incomplete without it. Any threat to its continuance brings on a sense of panic or a defensive rage. Criticism of it results in twisted self-justifying logic. Creative ambition and self-exploration are compromised. Everything is subordinated to the addiction. When health problems arise, they are almost always attributed to something other than the addicting thing.

Nobody sets out to be addicted, but we are given to ease; ease creates routine, and routine fosters repetitive acts that lay the seeds of addiction. The modern world also gives us every means and opportunity. Even seemingly innocent behaviors and foods can ruin health over time. The dose makes the poison. Without breaks—which addiction does not permit—the body cannot detoxify and recuperate.

Over time, irreversible damage and crippling disease can result. Runners can destroy knees and feet, soda drinkers erode their teeth, caffeine addicts exhaust metabolism, television and computer slaves cripple their minds and subject their eyes and bodies to radiation of unknown danger, and smokers age their skin, loosen their teeth, and ignite the germination of cancer.

Since virtually all addicts are in denial, it takes honest self-examination and an open ear to clues from those around us who have our welfare at heart to recognize our addictions. Admit them and break the pattern. Everyone knows enough to rotate the tires. Life needs rotation too or it will wear unevenly.

Be alert to addictions creeping into routines and the danger they present not only to health, but also to the freedom we must maintain to be the best we can be.

33

BLAMING THE PARENTS

HAVING CHILDREN BRINGS RESPONSIBILITY. That responsibility is to provide for their needs until they are capable of taking care of themselves. If your parents did this for you, they did their job. If they did not and you are now an adult, then what does it matter?

But no, therapists' offices are filled not only with young adults, but people in their 50's and beyond moaning about how they were potty trained too early, once got a spanking, lived through a divorce, or weren't loved as much as siblings. Rodney Dangerfield lamented, "When I was a kid my parents moved a lot, but I always found them."

We need to get over it, get a life, take control and responsibility. A salesman stuck in an elevator for a day can complain, get angry, blame everyone and everything, and call his psychotherapist on the cell phone—or determine to sell the elevator operator a new Cadillac before the door opens.

Parents are not the cause of our failures, we are. We are free moral entities who must make the choice to have a good life and then get at it. There are people who rise up out of far more miserable and oppressed circumstances than ours, no matter what they were. Many successful adults never had active parents in their lives at all. Some people were forced into factories when they were tiny children to help the family survive. Starving, diseased, abused, and crippled children have found a way to earn a PhD, head successful companies, contribute to society, rear their own children, and have a fulfilling marriage. Parents don't make or destroy us.

165

We can also look at it this way. Without adversity, pain, and suffering it is very difficult to grow. If sympathy is to be extended, it should go to those who have been excessively sheltered and pampered by parents. Having a mommy wiping our nose into adulthood sets us up for failure in the real world, not success. Life is tough. Getting eased into it as children girds us for the heavy licks we all experience as adults.

If we don't like the way our parents treated us, then we should be thankful for the lessons learned about what not to do. Their failure can be our success if we set about forgiving them and taking responsibility for building our own happy life and family.

The Modern Adult

34

SURVIVING TRAGEDY

THE LOSS OF LOVED ONES IS INEVITABLE. The tragedy is not so much for the one who has passed as it is for those who remain and suffer guilt, regrets, and loneliness.

There is no way to escape tragedy other than to die before anyone else does, be a recluse, or not permit close relationships. However, close loving relationships are a wonderful and even necessary part of a full life. Perhaps the pain we feel from the loss of a loved one is to teach us the very meaning of life, love, and the importance of respecting relationships when we have them.

But everything should be in measure. To throw ourselves totally into another person and lose self and independence is a formula for disaster. When the loved one is gone, meaning can be lost, which in turn can jeopardize health and life. We must love well, but always keep a part of ourselves that can survive in the absence of the loved one.

Rejection by a loved one can bring almost the identical pain and suffering as losing someone to death. It can be even worse since the lost person's presence continues as a constant reminder. The wound is irritated, scraped, and reopened again and again.

The best way to survive tragedy is to plan for it. For one thing, a creative and challenging life gives us something to fall back on. It's also critical to be aware beforehand that there will be no quick or easy healing. Pain and sorrow are part of the healing process. Do not assume life is ending or that the acute pain will remain forever.

Think of a tragic loss as if it were a deep knife wound to the brain. First there is the sharp and excruciating pain (for this metaphor forget that brain tissue has no pain receptors). Then there will be less, but more chronic pain. Healing of such a wound has inevitable ups and downs like any physical injury. The wound can be reopened (like stubbing a toe on the mend) by a memory, a song, a visit, or acquaintance, and then re-closed. The further the distance in time from the event, the more quickly the wound re-heals when re-injured.

With more time—at least two years—the wound closes more completely. Once the 'scar' is in place the pain is duller and continues to fade. Life becomes livable again even though the scar is never totally gone.

This natural healing process, in which time is the most essential element, is a reality all of us must understand to survive well through such an ordeal. The pain we feel is not unique and is not the most anyone has endured. Time must be allowed for the healing. In the meantime we must do smart things that will speed the process and ease the suffering.

That is, of course, easy to say but almost impossible to understand or implement when tragedy strikes. So we must resolve beforehand that when tragedy strikes we will do certain things even though we will not feel like it at the time. Exercise, social contact, rest, sunshine, and good nutrition are essential. These are the therapeutic factors the mind needs as building blocks for the healing process. Stopping a healthy routine will only prolong the healing. We need to buy time, and the best currency for that is to continue with smart living.

People who stop eating and shut themselves in their room to mourn only prolong the pain and may even create life-threatening disease. The mind-body connection must be respected. If we give up and wish death, our body listens. That is why so many people fall victim to serious illness and even die close in time to the loss of a loved one. Although we may feel like giving up, others love and need us. We have a responsibility to them and to our own person to treat our own gift of life with the respect it deserves.

Becoming active in a cause that helps others, or a cause relevant to the loss can speed the healing process. As mentioned in a previous chapter, Mothers Against Drunk Driving (begun by a mother whose child was killed by a drunk driver) and the America's Most Wanted television program (begun by a father who lost his child to a murderer) are two excellent examples. Helping to right a wrong and assisting others is the best form of distraction. It helps us think outside of our own circumstance to the feelings and needs of others. This gives that all-important sense of control and purpose. Using our misfortune to ease the suffering of others can also help us to see one of life's most important lessons: everything in life, no matter how awful or tragic, can work toward good.

35

TOUCH

ONE OF THE MOST GENEROUS, meaningful, and memorable gifts we can give to another person is to kindly touch them. There is an unidentified energy conveyed to another when they are touched in a caring and loving way. It symbolizes the unity, oneness, and belonging we all seek deep down.

Booths set up at fairs that offer hugs can have the longest lines. Teachers who move about the classroom, touching, adjusting collars, patting, and holding the hands of students, create a learning experience unexcelled by any other method. Doctors and nurses can speed the healing process by caring touch.[1] Business people can create life-long loyal clients by making touching contact with them. Not just a perfunctory handshake, no glad-handing, but a handhold that communicates genuine care, or a pat or a hug that tells others they are special and that you can be trusted.

Our litigious society has everyone now afraid of touching for fear of being slammed with a sexual harassment suit. Discretion is in order and nonsexual intent must be apparent and sincere or there can indeed be trouble. Nonetheless, touching is so important that it is a risk that must be taken.[2]

I remember when my children played sports and would line up after a game to shake hands with the 'enemy.' It was the best part of the game. Adult players do the same. In two-on-two sand volleyball, so neither side is advantaged by sun or wind, players switch sides of the court when the points total certain multiples. As opponents pass one another under the net it is a common practice (practically a law) to slap or shake the other's hand. No matter where the game is played, regardless of nationality, language, age, race, or sex, it is the same. Even in professional sports where big money is on the line, there is always the friendly hug or handshake. It's wonderful to do and heart-warming to see.

Sport is a model in miniature of life in general. We may be at odds with others for one reason or another, but that does not mean we cannot put things into perspective and let people know that friendship is still there and fundamentally important. Touching is an excellent way to do that.

Infants in sterile nurseries propped up to bottle-feed will languish. Those in filthy, backward, third world countries, who have a mother/nurse to hold, caress and coo at feeding time, will thrive. There is evidence that withholding touching from children can even increase the likelihood of early sexual experiences. Unfortunately, as teenage children pass through puberty parents think it is time to withdraw the touch. In fact, during these tumultuous years, teens need the contact more than ever. There is also evidence that violent criminals often have a childhood devoid of loving touch. This is not to excuse any behavior as an adult because we weren't hugged enough as a child, but does emphasize the important role parents can play in nurturing.

Loving and caring touch can help build a society of gentleness, kindness, compassion, unity, and trust rather than one of coldness, alienation, enmity, division and suspicion. Touching does something to

This Is Your Brain on Hugs

the mind and heart that is healing and helps make life worth living. We all have known the warmth of a caring touch. So why be stingy with something that costs nothing and can bring warmth and love to the world?

36

MUSIC AS HEALER

APPRECIATION FOR AND CREATION OF MUSIC (beyond the few programmed notes of songbirds) appears to be a unique human quality. Nobody knows why or how it has come into being. My theory is that it has to do with the fact that we are not really substance—as quantum physics has proven—but rather, at the fundamental level, waves and vibrations. The unseen reality is one all-encompassing harmonic symphony. (I develop this more fully in *Solving the Big Questions*.) Our bodies naturally seek balance, a form of harmony. Music can help us achieve that.

Music has a powerful and very real effect beyond just giving pleasure or causing a toe to tap. Universities now offer classes on music as therapy. Researchers also report breakthroughs on difficult mental conditions through the use of music.[1-3] Music can delight, impassion, lift the spirit, calm, depress, anger, or irritate. National anthems can inspire people to love and war. Different flavors impact each individual differently.

Although culture and family can influence our music preferences, by and large our likes and dislikes appear to be individualistic. Appreciation for a variety of music styles can be developed but first choices seem to remain. Within my own family, raised under the same roof, there is wide diversity. When I take my five-string banjo out, some come and listen, others run and hide. When the hiders play their rap or hip-hop, to me they might as well run their fingernails across a chalkboard. I must have bluegrass genes while they have hip-hop genes.

But that's okay. Enjoy but be aware, as mentioned previously, that music can also send one into a depressing melancholy. If a song does this, change the tune. Find something that lifts the spirit, is happifying, energizes, and puts one into the moment rather than reeling into a history about which nothing can be done.

Actively playing an instrument is very effective at relieving stress. Find an enjoyable instrument and begin to learn. Spend some time at it as often as you can, particularly when feeling down or overwhelmed with life. Take lessons or use self-teaching aids. Don't worry about being perfect or accomplished right away. The process of learning and achieving even little gains is an end itself.

The mental, creative, and emotional engagement of playing an instrument, or just enjoying music others make, can give a lifetime of fulfilling pleasure. It can also provide a place to go when we need a haven where we can rest, heal, feel better, and lift the spirit.

37

HUMOR

WHY WE LAUGH AT THE THINGS we do is not well understood. It must have something to do with advanced intelligence. The more intelligent we are, the more we understand relationships and anomalies and this is what humor is about. This wonderful gift can both expand the mind and relax the brain. It should be used as much as possible.

Don't let life hammer you into a corner. Don't take yourself too seriously. Always be willing to laugh at yourself. Humor helps us keep things in perspective. It elevates mood, relieves stress, improves optimism and just plain makes life more enjoyable. The good friends and mates we choose are usually those who help us laugh and enjoy life. Remember how popular the funny classmates were back in school. Keep this in mind if you wish to make yourself more attractive to good companions.

Laughter is also therapy. In fact, researchers suggest 'humor rooms' in hospitals to help people who suffer from painful and depressing degenerative conditions. One study put a group of people through group humor therapy. The subjects were exposed to funny books, records, and films, and learned to give humor high priority in their everyday lives. As a result of this unique 13-week program, their overall state of psychological well-being definitely improved.[1] Humor therapy increased the general quality of life for patients and was therapeutic in relieving symptoms. Laughing also makes people more self-confident,

174

better able to cope with symptoms, and helps them enjoy life regardless of their particular medical circumstances.[2]

Look for opportunities—movies, books, cartoons, tapes, friends—to have a chuckle and lighten the day. Laughter is even good physical exercise and tones facial and abdominal muscles too. It also releases good-mood hormones, making it very difficult to remain angry or grumpy.[3] See if this doesn't lighten your day:

Church Bulletin Bloopers:

1. The Scouts are saving aluminum cans, bottles, and other items to be recycled. Proceeds will be used to cripple children.

2. Ladies Bible Study will be held Thursday morning at 10. All ladies are invited to lunch in the Fellowship Hall after the B.S. is done.

3. The pastor would appreciate it if the ladies of the congregation would lend him their electric girdles for the pancake breakfast next Sunday.

4. Low Self Esteem Support Group will meet Thursday at 7 PM. Please use the back door.

5. The pastor will preach his farewell message, after which the choir will sing, "Break Forth Into Joy."

6. A songfest was hell at the Methodist church Wednesday.

7. Pray for those sick of our church and community.

8. The eighth graders will be presenting Shakespeare's Hamlet. The Congregation is invited to attend this tragedy.

9. Thursday night Potluck Supper. Prayer and medication to follow.

10. The rosebud on the altar this morning is to announce the birth of David, the sin of Reverend and Mrs. Adams.

11. Tuesday at 4 PM there will be an ice cream social. All ladies giving milk will please come early.

12. A ham and bean supper will be held on Tuesday evening in the church hall. Music will follow.

13. At the evening service tonight, the sermon topic will be "What Is Hell?" Come early and listen to our choir practice.

14. Weight Watchers will meet at 7 PM at the First Presbyterian Church. Please use large double door at the side entrance.

15. Mrs. Johnson will be entering the hospital this week for testes.

16. Please join us as we show our support for Amy and Alan who are preparing for the girth of their first child.

17. The Lutheran Men's group will meet at 6 PM. Steak, mashed potatoes, green beans, bread and dessert will be served for a nominal feel.

18. The Associate Minister unveiled the church's new tithing campaign slogan last Sunday: "I Upped My Pledge—Up Yours."

19. Our next song is "Angels We Have Heard Get High."

20. Don't let worry kill you, let the church help.

21. James and Rachael Sims were married last Saturday. So ends a friendship that began in Junior High.

22. For those of you who have children and don't know it, we have a bus to take them away at the south end of the parking lot.

23. This being Easter Sunday, we will ask Mrs. Lewis to come forward and lay an egg on the altar.

24. The service will close with the Little Drops of Water. One of the ladies will start quietly and the rest of the congregation will join in.

25. Eight new choir robes are currently needed, due to the addition of several new members and to the deterioration of some older ones.

26. The senior choir invites any member of the congregation who enjoys sinning to join the choir.

27. Attend and hear an excellent speaker and heave a healthy lunch.

28. The kids made nutritious snacks and everyone got full of them.

29. The dropouts from the Bible study have been cut in half.

30. The men's bizarre exchanges anything—mowers, bicycles, washing machines, etc.—so why not bring the wife along and get a bargain?

31. The toilet in the hall is out of order so please use floor below.

32. This evening at 7 P.M. there will be hymns in the park across from the church. Bring a blanket and come prepared to sin.

They who laugh, last.

SECTION F

Thinking about. . .

PETS

IN THIS SECTION: *Pets are wonderful reminders of our origins. They tell us that although we may have conquered nature in many respects, we are still a part of it. Without speaking a word, they can also teach us about love, devotion, kindness, compassion, and responsibility. Pets are also mentally and physically therapeutic. But with the decision to, in effect, take pets from nature and remove their options, comes the serious responsibility of providing for their mental and physical well being. To do that requires more than packages of food and shelter. We must do for them what we must do for ourselves in order to achieve health: return to nature.*

38

PETS AS LIFE SAVERS

As our modern world becomes more urbanized, populated, and technologically dependent, we can feel lost in the crowd and isolated. Our electronic era makes personal contact less and less essential in day-to-day life. Telephones, faxes, and computers have replaced handshakes, hugs, and face-to-face friendships. The Internet Age is exponentially speeding this fundamental change in interpersonal relations.

When we separate from one another by wires and antennas we leave something behind. There is an inherent need in each of us to experience social and physical contact. Warm, personal friendships and loving and caring touch create feelings of worth and security not replaced by e-mail or soap operas.

Impersonal distance in modern life can also create pathologies ranging from road rage to overt violence. Enemies are easily created when they are nameless and faceless. That's why the best way to defuse an attacker is to talk with them, make eye contact, and get personal.

Modern life also estranges us from our natural environmental roots. Asphalt, drywall, and fluorescent lights are a far cry from meadows, trees, and stars. There is a yearning within each of us, a biophilia as it has been called, to connect with nature. A walk in the woods, planting a garden, feeding birds, visiting a wilderness, and catching a glimpse of wild creatures does something quite indescribable for the soul. The peace, inspiration, and pleasure brought by contact with nature are downright therapeutic. Nature draws us to it like a magnet. The further we get from it, the less whole and healthy we feel.

Our need for love, closeness, touching, and connection with nature is what draws us to pets and makes that contact so beneficial. Pets are still quite wild with retained senses and abilities that make them yet suited for survival in nature. Our close relationship with them keeps nature ever near—and in a very convenient, safe, cuddly, and loving form.

The simplicity of the human-animal bond is what makes it so endearing, particularly today in our complex world. Feed them, treat them kindly, clearly define expectations, and they become a friend for life who will never criticize and who will love unquestioningly.

I knew a sand volleyball player who had a terrible personality problem. He would barely acknowledge the existence of anyone around him other than players he liked playing with. You could say something to him and he would just avert his eyes. When new players would approach him and ask him to play, he would just walk away. He was insulted that rookies would have the audacity to think they could play with someone of his caliber and stature. He was awful on the court as well, criticizing opponents for any tiny rule infraction and expressing disgust for any error his partner would make. If there was an argument somewhere, he was always in the middle of it.

In spite of such obnoxious behavior, he was wonderfully kind to a little terrier companion he always brought with him. If it was cold he put a little coat on him. If thirsty, he would pour water into his cupped hand for the dog to lap. When he would lie down on his back to rest between games, his little friend would run over and jump up on his belly, curl up and rest with him.

As difficult as it was to think well of this person, you couldn't help but be warmed and marvel at the love he and his dog shared. The little signs of humanity he showed to his pet made it seem as though there was hope for him. One could certainly wonder though, how socially misfit he might have become if it were not for the love of his dog.

The psychological and physical benefits to humans from pet companionship are enormous. A pet in a nursing home environment can breathe new life into those who have given up. Almost every measure of improvement in the disabled is benefited by pets, including motor skills, balance, self-esteem, mood, attention span, memory, vocabulary, and overall health.

Children who are physically ill or socially maladapted similarly benefit. Pets can make life happier and easier for youngsters having trouble with studies, classmates, or family. A pet can help a child keep a positive outlook on life since it serves as a positive, non-judgmental companion. Caring for a pet also teaches responsibility and gives a mentally healthy sense of importance.

Remarkably, anyone can experience health benefits from companion animals. Recovery from any illness is hastened, blood pressure reduced, will to live increased, immunity enhanced, and mental balance strengthened. Even watching fish in an aquarium can decrease heart rate, blood pressure, and anxiety. Heart attack fatalities are 30% greater in a given population for those who do not have a pet as opposed to those who do. For just this one disease, pet companionship could mean about 30,000 lives saved each year.

Pets can bring out the best in us. They help us empathize, focus outward, nurture, develop rapport, have fun, get up off the couch, socialize, stimulate us to think and reflect, provide unquestioned nonjudgmental acceptance, and teach loving touch. Pets put us near that good and kind inner being we so sparingly let out.[1] As Anatole France stated, "Until one has loved an animal, a part of one's soul remains unawakened."

39

PET KEEPING—
A SERIOUS RESPONSIBILITY

PETS ARE REMARKABLE CREATURES. They are:

• Masters of life in the moment and in the art of simplicity

• Reflections of a world forgotten, presynthetic, more complete

• Reminders of the quiet strength and dignity of creation not tinkered with

• Keepers of gifts we have lost or never had

• Ambassadors of loyalty, love, forgiveness, acceptance, fun, and truth that are neither measured nor withheld

• Recipients of our wonder, respect, love—and needful of the care that will bring them the fullness of health that comes only from nature obeyed.

Animals are not best served by imposing all the elements of modern life upon them. All the principles discussed earlier about genetic context, medical dangers, and preventive care apply equally well to pets. Our choice to live unhealthily is a crime against our own person. To impose such unwise decisions upon others—children and pets—who have no real options, is an even greater crime.

Although pets are often treated like surrogate human infants, that is not what they are. If we pamper them with modernity we will condemn them to the cruelty of modern-living diseases. Obesity, cancer, allergies, arthritis, dental diseases, and the like, ravage modern pets just like they do their owners. Such preventable conditions are essentially absent in wild populations.

Pets deserve our understanding and respect. They are not what we are. We may be superior in our factories and at our computers, but they are superior in their tool-less senses and intuitive skills to survive in nature. Life for them is meant to be challenging and interesting. That cannot happen at the end of

Having Pets Because You Love Animals

a chain or on a couch. If they are to be healthy, they must be allowed as much freedom as possible, and we must engage with them every day.

The healthiest place for animals is in their natural setting. But given that we are not all going to release our pets into what's left of the wild any time soon, the onus is upon us to create for them as much 'wild' as possible. That would include exercise, fresh air, sunshine, real natural food, fun, excitement, and companionship. If we choose to have a pet, maintaining its life and health is a moral duty.

Dogs and cats are carnivores, retaining all the wild skills we have forgotten. They are intelligent because that's what they have to be to catch prey. If that is not evident, leave your clothes and provisions behind and set out into the woods for a couple weeks' stay. See if it's easy to catch the food your pet could easily catch if released into the same setting. Their intelligence is one of the things attracting us to them, but it is also something that places demands upon us. Imprisoning people is a severe punishment because of the intellectual and social needs of humans. Imprisoning animals as pets is also a punishment unless we modify their prison with the appurtenances they naturally need.

The right to have pets doesn't mean we should, anymore than our right to have children means we should. We should not bite off more than we can responsibly chew. A pet is not a toy, appliance, or piece of wood to whittle. We don't have the 'right' to carve them to our liking with spaying, castrating, declawing, defanging, vegetarianizing, ear cropping, dewclaw removing, and tail docking. (This is not to say that the pet population problem we create may not require a remedy such as neutering surgeries.)

Cat Pens For Fun – I built these cages out of dead cedar trees gathered from our wooded property. Climbing posts were put together sort of randomly and logs hollowed out for hiding. The 'guys' have great fun playing tag and watching all the other critters that venture out of the woods. One of the pens abuts the house so we can just crank a window open for them to go in and out.

183

They are not disposable things to obtain on a whim and then cast aside when the novelty wears off or when they become inconvenient or burdensome. This doesn't just apply to dogs and cats, but to all creatures including horses confined to pens where every bit of sod is trodden to dust, and goldfish purchased in a baggy as a surprise 'for the kids.' Just because an animal is different from us is not an excuse for abuse or negligence. How we treat fellow creatures is a direct reflection of what we are inside. Gandhi wisely said, "The greatness of a nation and its moral progress, can be judged by the way its animals are treated."

Dogs and cats are a 15-20 year commitment. In that span we are responsible for the needs of a baby, adolescent, pubescent, adult, and senior. Although they grow older, the daily demands upon caretakers are not unlike those demanded by an infant that never grows up. They must be fed every meal, their dishes must be washed, and their potty needs tended to. We must bathe and groom them and perhaps contend with fleas, ticks, and worms. Their nails may need to be trimmed, their messes cleaned up, and any damage they may cause repaired. We must respond to their crying, take them to the doctor, and give them almost constant attention.

Compressed into their years are most of the things we experience in our own lives. They can be 'good,' they can be 'bad' (in our terms). They can bring joy, sorrow, fear, and love. They will require doctoring (little, however, if things are done properly), have accidents, and can succumb to disease. We will have to experience their death and perhaps be faced with a choice of whether to cut their pain short with euthanasia. We will suffer greatly at the loss of a wonderful friend.

Having and properly caring for a pet for its entire life is a personal decision because of the commitment involved. Giving pets as gifts to kids or friends is therefore presumptuous and irresponsible. Sending pets off for long stays at caged boarding facilities (the equivalent of human prisons) is not commitment or responsibility either. Yes, this may occasionally be necessary, but it can be a great trauma to pets. They have no idea if you will ever return, and their stay in a pen or cage is not home no matter how well they are tended to by caretakers.

If a pet is obtained to teach the kids responsibility, forget it. No matter how much they plead that they will do all the tending, they won't. Figure on about one or two weeks of enthusiasm for the work of pet keeping at best. Afterwards, guess who gets to take care of the pet.

The point is, the thrill of getting something new, like a car, television, or coat should not be transferred to obtaining a pet. They are not low maintenance and cannot just be set aside when the excitement wanes.

Now then, if you personally decide to shoulder the responsibility, save a life at the same time by getting a pet from the local humane or animal shelter. These facilities are usually filled to overflowing from discarded pets dropped off by people who did not put thought before emotion. (How people can abandon the family pet to such a facility is incomprehensible. It's like putting an innocent person in prison to be executed.) Demand should not be placed on breeders until there are no shelter pets left. There is already a pet overpopulation problem, so why not help solve it rather than contribute to it?

It is also better and kinder for everyone involved to have two pets. This will decrease the demands to occupy their time since they will enjoy one another's company. It is arguably inhumane (should be illegal) to imprison in solitary confinement a creature designed for the freedom of the wild. A pet left alone in a cage, in the house, or on a chain for extended periods while we go about our interesting work and social life is hardly fair.

Pets are a responsibility, a burden, a worry and a lot of trouble at times. But what they return in guileless love and devotion, and health benefits for their owners, makes the costs one of the best bargains in life.

What we get out of it aside, pet keeping is a serious responsibility that extends far beyond the euphoria of watching the antics of a kitten or puppy. It requires serious commitment as well as the circumstances and knowledge to care for them properly for their lifetime. If that is not possible, then vent the affection for animals by helping at the local shelter or humane society, pet sitting, or volunteering at the zoo.

Another option is to think of animals in terms other than as 'pet.' Possessing animals is not the only way to show affection and concern for them. Become active in environmental actions that restore and protect natural animal habitats. Just observing animals in the wild and respecting them for what they are is love too.

40

THE MYTH OF 100% COMPLETE PET FOODS

THE PET FOOD INDUSTRY has been running in place and causing immeasurable harm to pets for at least 75 years. It presents an egregious example of scientific hubris and commercial irresponsibility. Whether you have pets or not, what follows will underscore and substantiate everything the book has said thus far regarding how wrong society can be. Only in this case, our wrongness falls upon innocent pet victims.

Companion animals were once fed table scraps and also ate whatever they could find or catch in the barn or fields. This was fine until leash laws were enacted and pets became more urbanized and house bound. As we became swept along with consumerism and convenience, it was only natural that we would seek convenient pet foods from the grocery store. Alert entrepreneurs in the food processing industry noted this and saw an opportunity to convert waste (much of it still highly nutritious) in the growing human food industry into pet food. These converted scraps proved to be an efficient use of resources otherwise wasted and a profitable solution to keeping the pet's bowl full.

There are now extruded, pelleted, baked, canned, freeze-dried, semi-moist, frozen, lifestage, breed specific, high protein, low protein, natural, holistic, USDA approved, human grade, organic, fortified, anti-allergenic, and disease treatment processed pet food formulas. In a race to create new market niches, profiteers roll out an endless array of purported 'special' ingredients, and demonize a growing list of 'bad' ingredients. Each manufacturer argues that their food is the best and can offer either un-supported claims playing to myths and public ignorance, or proofs such as analyses (% protein, fat, water, etc.), successful AAFCO (American Association of Feed Control Officials) feeding trials, digestibility studies (how much comes out compared to how much is fed), and testimonials and endorsements. All such claims and proofs constitute a fallacious life support system keeping, as you will see, a very dangerous idea alive.

The commercial pet food imbroglio is confusing and frustrating for consumers trying to make conscientious choices. After all, how can food A be better than food B, while B is better than A, with each side providing proofs? Rather than get into the confusing debate, most people just go with the flow and swallow current marketing razzle-dazzle. Myth, lore, faith, convention, clever advertising, convenience, trust, and tales of pet food ingredient dos and don'ts have become the basis for pet feeding. But virtually every processed pet food claim intended to lure consumers is found to be deceptive upon close examination.

For example, "human grade" ingredients sound good, but virtually all pet food ingredients come from human grade processing facilities. (There are no "pet food ingredient" factories.) "No by-products" sounds good, but the trimmings, organs, and scraps you and I can't find at a meat counter turn out to be some of the most nutritious elements for pets. "No corn, soy, or wheat" is a common scare tactic, but the brands that omit them usually use some other ingredient that is just as starchy (sugary), and often nutritionally inferior.

Some brands, in an attempt to scare people into their coffers with a "no-grain" claim, use tapioca for their starch. But that can contain the poison hydrogen cyanide. Some make boasts about being holistic, natu-ral, and the like but are essentially the same as all other brands. The "no preservatives" claim would mean that the nutrients are unprotected from oxidation and would generate toxins worse than the preservatives that have been left out. One brand, implying by its name that it is "raw," lists the raw ingredients it contains after fifty or so ingredients that are heat processed (ingredients must be listed in order of quantity), and below an ingredient that is in the food at one ten-millionth of an ounce in a normal meal. The raw part of the food could be at billionths of an ounce, trillionths, or just a few molecules per twenty-ton truckload.

People are easily led and deceived because they tend to believe anything on a label and assume pet feeding is mysterious and needs high tech solutions. Let's think about this for a moment using the same common sense we would use in choosing our own best foods.

Because of the nondescript nature of the mush and nuggets in cans and bags, pet owners must extend a lot of trust to manufacturers. But the balm of blind trust and faith never turns out to be a solution for anything. For example, consider the following approved ingredients from the official AAFCO regulatory publications:

- dehydrated garbage (you read that right)
- polyethylene roughage (plastic)
- hydrolyzed poultry feathers
- hydrolyzed hair
- hydrolyzed leather meal
- some 36 chemical preservatives
- peanut skins and hulls
- corn cob fractions
- ground corn cob
- ground clam shells
- poultry, cow, and pig feces and litter
- hundreds of chemicals
- a host of antibiotic and chemotherapeutic pharmaceuticals
- a variety of synthetic flavorings
- adjuvants
- sequestrates
- stabilizers
- anticaking agents

This is not to say these ingredients are commonly used, just to point out that they can be. Obviously these 'approved' ingredients prove it may not be such a good idea to blindly trust regulators, manufacturers, and nutritionists, and assume they know better about how to feed your pet than you do.

The absurdity of official nutrition deepens because at the same time regulators approve dehydrated garbage, they ban natural ingredients like pollen, chondroitin, Coenzyme $Q_{10,}$ and other nutraceuticals (natural substances with health effects). Any health food store and grocery has foods and nutraceuticals approved for humans that are banned from inclusion in commercial pet foods.

This sad state of irrationality—approving feces and garbage but banning chondroitin—can only be explained by the fact that regulators are trained in old school nutrition using textbooks parroting 100-year-old nutritional ideas. They are taught and come to believe that the nature of the food makes no difference, just the percentages of protein, fat, vitamin A, and the like. If dehydrated garbage and feces is made sterile (safe?) and has 12% protein, then to them that equals nutritious food. Similar thinking can be found in human hospitals where old school nutritionally trained dieticians feed diseased and starving patients instant potatoes, Jell-O, canned meat, and Diet Coke. Any claim about special merits of natural ingredients is voodoo to them.

Both human and animal nutritionists can be so caught up in their science of percentages that no room is left in their brains for common sense. If that's the way they want to eat, that is one thing. It's quite another for consumers to follow along just because nutritionists and regulators promote themselves as expert, authoritative, and immune from error.

In a classic case of government run amok, pet food regulators carefully purge the industry of natural ingredients that may have health benefits, and then call manufacturers to task over picayune matters on package labels that have nothing to do with nutrition, health, or safety.

Here is just one example of how regulators fill their time policing pet foods. A commercial food that had chicken and organs in it claimed on the label that it had "meat." The regulatory Gestapo swooped down and declared it illegal. They considered neither chicken nor organs to be "meat" because of a terminology technicality they had created. It took thousands of dollars and months of work for the manufacturer to make the changes to the packages. For what? So the public would not be 'misled' to believe that the "meat" mentioned on the label was chicken and organs (even though the ingredient label clearly identified what was in the product). This was an action taken by the FDA, the same regulatory body that permits drugs into the market that maim and kill hundreds of thousands of humans and animals every year. In contrast, never has the word *meat* on a label harmed a pet. And most certainly, no pet has ever been harmed if their owner understood meat to be chicken and organs.

Pet food regulators busy themselves refereeing precise label verbiage, size of print, where on packages certain things must be said, and promoting the disease-producing "100% complete" label claim I will get into in a moment. They are stuck in their own deep bureaucracy, oblivious to the real world, and convinced of their self-importance by monitoring silly nonsense.

In the meantime, against such a massive background of agreement among industry, regulators, medical professionals, and nutritionists, how could the public help but be bamboozled into thinking that pet food manufacturing is some sort of high tech wizardry their pets need. Yes, processors can soup-up their twin-screw extruders and make things like white flour, textured soy vegetable protein (TVP), dye, and flavoring look and taste like a real pork chop. But the best of technology is being used to fool owners and pets and to make profits, not to create truly healthy foods.

The results speak for themselves. After countless generations on the new fangled diets, pets are plagued with every manner of modern degenerative disease, including obesity, cancer, dental disease, and the whole list described in previous chapters that plague humans on their fare of processed foods.

The tragedy is greater for pets because people can at least choose foods for themselves; pets can't. Even though people may think they are being really smart by relying on the pet expert industry, stop and think about this for a moment. Nobody in their right mind would ever eat the same processed food, meal after meal, day after day for a lifetime. Nobody would make his or her child eat the same processed food at every meal. So why on earth would we ever think of doing it to our pets? Yet virtually every pet owner feeds the same processed food, meal after meal, day after day, and does so thinking they are doing their pet a favor because the label says "100% complete and balanced."

Recognizing this contradiction and then using the same intuitive sense to feed our pets as we do ourselves is the key to healthy pet feeding. It also provides another striking example of the fact that what the majority thinks and does—including all the experts—is usually wrong.

Aside from the fact that the singular feeding of processed foods spawns illness and disease, it is a cruelty to force a captive animal to eat the same food at every meal. Try eating a bowl of dry Cap'n Crunch as the only food at every meal for the next 15-20 years, the lifetime of pets. Or eat a can of Spam at every meal for the same time.

The exclusive feeding of processed pet foods takes advantage of people's desire for convenience and their unwillingness to trust themselves or take personal responsibility. As for the pet industry perpetrators, it all began innocently and well-intentioned enough. Entrepreneurship is the American way. All pet food producers needed to do was convince the public to throw their "non-nutritious and imbalanced" table scraps in the garbage, and to feed their pet the new modern way. But heat-processed, starch-based foods had all sorts of nutritional imbalances and deficiencies. Pets were dying, developing rickets, and going blind, just like starving children do in a third world country.

To save the day, regulators stepped in to force manufacturers to balance the foods better. So manufacturers consulted nutritionists who hold the belief that almost any mix of base ingredients can be made whole by adding protein and fat from virtually any source, along with synthetic vitamins and minerals. (The recent massive pet food recall of products containing an ingredient that was evidently spiked with toxic melamine to boost its nitrogen percentage—interpreted as protein—is an example of the danger of a focus on percentages.) They 'fortified' and 'balanced' the foods so they would meet the 'known' standards. To prove that the resulting foods are wholesome and healthy they decided to devise an experiment, known as the AAFCO feeding trial. This is an example of something called science that is not that at all.

It goes like this: If after a few weeks of eating the specific diet to be proven, the caged experimental animals don't die or show signs of deficiency, toxicity, or sickness, the food passes. The manufacturer can then claim "100% Complete and Balanced" on the label. Monitoring this claim and making sure manufacturers meet the standards surrounding its presentation on labels is pretty much the central focus of pet food regulation: the FDA, USDA, AAFCO and every state feed control agency.

With a passed AAFCO test certificate in hand, the manufacturer can tell everyone that their new 'scientifically proven' food is all that a pet owner should feed and if they feed anything else nutritional imbalance and disease may result. If the manufacturer flashes scientific looking graphs and charts in front of veterinarians, some of them might endorse the products as well. (Veterinarians, like physicians, get little if any nutritional education. What they do get comes primarily from the biased "100% complete" pet food industry.)

By performing such testing, all was supposed to be well and science served. But as it turns out, the claim of "100% complete" is a pretense of science because it assumes that which cannot be true—100% complete knowledge.

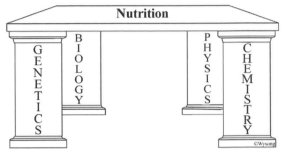

Nutritionists, caught up in their cognitive chauvinism about percentages, totally miss the fact that nutrition has long-range impact that cannot be measured in a several-week AAFCO feeding test. Measuring such things as body weight, general condition, and a few blood values only gives the

The Pillars of Nutrition – Nutrition is an aggregate discipline resting upon many basic sciences. Since nobody could argue that these basic sciences are completely understood, how could nutrition be? If nutrition is not completely understood, then the claim cannot be made that any fabricated food is '100% complete.'

process the flavor of science, not its substance. They forget that prisoners have been known to survive for years on little more than water and a little rice or bread that is deficient and imbalanced by every nutritional measure. They overlook the body's ability to adapt to and tolerate all kinds of nutritional abuses—for a time. Their so-called proof of a food's perfect completeness is a mockery of logic, evidence, and science. Since AAFCO science and experiments are really not worth doing, they are not worth doing well.

The commercial gambit of claiming 100% completeness is nothing new. It was also attempted in the baby formula industry. After all kinds of assurances that scientifically designed baby formulas were the "100% complete" smart choice for modern moms, the breast was retired to its 'proper' place as a cosmetic appendage. Physicians were indoctrinated by industry propaganda to push baby formula as the new, advanced, modern way. Then disaster struck. Hundreds of thousands of babies suffered serious nutritional diseases. When the breast was brought out of retirement, health was restored. Surely with such a terrible lesson, food processors would not again try to supplant nature.

But they have, and on a grand, worldwide scale. With clever subterfuge the pet food industry—under the tutelage of official nutritionists and regulators—is doing exactly the same thing the baby formula industry did. The difference is that it is now illegal for mothers to be told that baby formula is better than natural food (in this case, breast milk), or that formulas should be fed exclusively. Why? Formula can cause disease and death.

But the lesson learned has not been transferred to pet feeding. The "100% complete" claim is now the bread and butter of a multibillion-dollar pet food industry and pays the salaries of countless nutritionists and pet food regulators. The scam has caused disease and death from its beginning, but it continues unabated while regulators harass manufacturers about how to place words on package labels.

What's Wrong With This Picture?

Mrs. Jones Goes to the Veterinarian

Later... Mrs. Jones Goes to the Pediatrician

Think about it. Our world is complex beyond comprehension. It is not only largely unknown, it is unknowable in the "complete" sense. In order for nutritionists and manufacturers to produce a "100% complete and balanced" pet food, they must first know 100% about nutrition. But nutrition is not a completed science.

In fact, although nutrition is rapidly being developed as a science, it has always lagged behind the other sciences. This is in part because it is a field of study that has not stood side by side with the other sciences

193

in universities. Rather, nutrition has more or less been considered an incidental branch of homemaking or some other applied field such as animal husbandry. Additionally, because of its almost infinite complexity, the science of nutrition is not easily developed.

The fact of the matter is that the "100% complete" claim is actually 100% complete guesswork. At best, one could say that such a claim is the firm possibility of a definite maybe.

As proof, consider that each time regulatory agencies convene to decide how much of which nutrients comprise "100% complete," debate ensues and standards usually change. This not only proves that what they claimed to be "100% complete" before was in fact not, but should also make us highly suspicious about what they now claim to be 100% complete.

So don't believe the claim on any commercially prepared pet (or human) food that it is "100% complete and balanced." It is a specious, unsupported boast intended to build consumer trust and dependence on commercial products—not create optimal health. It is a marketing slogan and nothing more.

Modern, heat processed, food-fraction-based, additive-laden pet foods sold as supposedly "100% complete" foods to be fed exclusively have caused serious illness and the death of untold thousands.[1] Take the case of cats fed thoroughly approved, AAFCO proven, "100% complete and balanced" premium branded foods. These poor cats ended up with eye maladies and dilated failing hearts (dilated cardiomyopathy), among other things. *Science,* perhaps the most prestigious of all scientific publications, prefaced a study of this disaster with this: "Thousands of pet cats die each year with dilated cardiomyopathy..."[2]

When such nutrient problems strike, the exigencies of public relations and profits prompt the industry to quickly search out a solution. In this case, to make up for the damage heat processing was doing, they added the synthetic amino acid, taurine. This action had the virtue of being relevant to the matter at hand (animals dying from taurine deficiency) but was generally unimportant in that it did not fix the underlying cause: the pompous mindset that all is known and that good nutrition is just about percentages. This intellectual cul-de-sac creates mental cobwebs preventing the understanding of the single most essential element of health: nature cannot be replaced nor improved upon.[3-4]

In spite of the continuing disasters, the pet food industry—including nutritionists, veterinarians, and regulators—continues mired in its wrong thinking and parading out before the public an endless array of new brands that are heralded as the fix to all the pet disease and dying going on. The market is flooded with "100% complete" diets by prescription, for life stages, for specific breeds and sizes, and those featuring high protein, low protein, no-carb, low-carb, organic, no corn, no soy, no wheat, high fat, low fat, lamb, potato, rice, avocado, persimmon, tapioca, quail eggs, buffalo and on and on. But they all miss the point: a heat-processed food cannot be "100% complete" and should never be fed exclusively.

Occasionally there are disastrous failures in commercial foods such as with taurine, and more recently with "100% complete" and "natural" foods containing the toxic plastic, melamine.[5] In this latter case, although the poison was purposely added to an ingredient imported from China, only those animals being fed the same food meal after meal received a lethal dose. This tragic situation, affecting thousands of animals and a variety of brands, resulted in an almost hysterical reaction by the public. Their trust had been violated. Unfortunately, most pet owners just searched for a food without the poisoned ingredient and went about feeding the new brand meal after meal.

The lesson to be learned from such disasters is that no food can be totally trusted. The only safeguard is to ignore the "100% complete" claim and do the common sense thing: vary the diet.

More often, deleterious results from feeding singular foods meal after meal are not immediately apparent. Subtle nutritional problems can cast long and insidious shadows. Many of the degenerative diseases striking animals—particularly in their middle and later years after perhaps years have passed with no apparent problems—are directly related to following the "100% complete" pet food myth. Since these degenerative diseases are the primary reason people flood veterinary offices with their pets, this is no small matter. The pain and suffering for both pets and their owners, and the financial loss, is a tragedy of incalculable size. It will not end until the "100% complete" claim is banned from labels or people recognize it for the fraud it is.

When people are no longer under the assumption that a packaged food is perfect, they will hopefully begin to think and find a better way. It will have little to do with nutritionists and regulators pretending they have complete knowledge, and everything to do with applying the SOLVER principles (Self-responsibility, Open mindedness, Long view thinking, Virtue, Evidence, Reason). It also will have to mean respecting and listening to nature, and gaining the courage to be 'wrong' when everyone else is '100% complete' right.

41

FEEDING PETS AS NATURE INTENDED

THIS CHAPTER WILL REVEAL what nutritionists, veterinarians, and regulators are not taught, and what pet food manufacturers would prefer you didn't know. Unlike the standard information about animal nutrition, I will not talk about percentages of nutrients. You know, the tired old stories about how calcium is good for teeth and bones, vitamin A is good for vision, essential fatty acids make a smooth and glossy coat, and so on. After all, why pretend as if the road to health is a matter of playing the nutrition percentages game? It hasn't worked to prevent all the degenerative diseases plaguing animals (or humans), so why give it credence as though it did? Instead, let's look at pet feeding as if thinking matters.

Most premium pet foods appear polished, official, safe, and regulated in their enticing packages. It would appear there must be good science and know-how behind them. Although the previous chapter should have put that belief to rest, consider this little tightly held pet industry secret: Anybody off the street (even you) with some money and ambition can go to any of dozens of manufacturers across the country and have them make a "new improved" pet food in short order. No special license or credentials are needed. There is not certification, no governmental oversight of what goes in the package, and even a second grade education will do just fine as long as you have the start-up money. You could set up your office in the corner of the bedroom, think of how to spin your 'new and improved' story, send it to a graphic artist to create brochures and labels, and you'd be on your way.

Private label manufacturers (manufacturers for hire) have all kinds of standard formulas on the shelf ready for use. These stock formulations have already been tweaked for palatability and 'balanced' with vitamins and minerals to make them '100% complete.'

Let's say you decide to do this. To make your product stand out from the pack, you want the label to say "all natural filet mignon, rack of lamb, and caviar." No problem. Just sprinkle a tiny bit of these ingredients in, carefully metering so as to not cut into profits too much. Heck, you're not lying. Gullible and trusting consumers will not even do the math and discover that there is a slight problem with your product selling at 50 cents per pound and caviar selling in the grocery store at $200 per ounce.

The Premium Food Myth – The truth: Premium pet food has caused disease and death due to imbalances of taurine, carnitine, potassium and other problems related to the rigors of food processing and singular feeding.

If they are taken aback for a moment, it will pass when they just reflect on the marvels of modern technology that must be going on in pet food manufacturing plants. Your secret (scam) is safe because people like to believe what labels say and shopping is not always the most muscular moments of inquiry for excited consumers looking for easy solutions and convenience.

You can even advertise about how bad all of the pet foods are that don't contain caviar and rack of lamb. There is no better motivator than fear, so you can also put something like, "no corn, soy, grains, or chicken fat" on the label. Then tell people that these nasty ingredients cause allergy and cancer. You can verily raise yourself to sainthood by declaring that your product contains "no by-products, road kill, or euthanized pets." That will work really well. People love myths. The more sensational, the better.

To lend credibility to your pet food company you can cut small checks to some local veterinarians. Ask them a couple of questions and give them samples to feed. Now you can say, "designed, approved, and fed by veterinarians." No fibbing there.

You are on your way to becoming yet another pet food mogul, rising to power on sheer confabulation. Even though you know no more than the average Joe who learns nutrition from reading the back of cereal boxes, you now become a pet food nutrition expert. The unthinking consumer doesn't mind so long as you capture and keep their attention with some clever marketing and advertising pizzazz. Particularly beguiling are claims about being "healthy," "natural," "raw," "organic," "holistic," and how your products leave out all the supposed nasty things all the other producers put in.

The pet food industry abounds with such companies. At the helm are homemakers, breeders, movie stars, used car salesmen, bankers, investors, lawyers and profit seekers from every imaginable background. Conspicuously absent in the leadership positions are people with expertise, like food scientists, engineers, holistic nutritionists, and health professionals. Not that such credentials guarantee product merit or healthy motives, but at least such people would be starting with basic tools of knowledge.

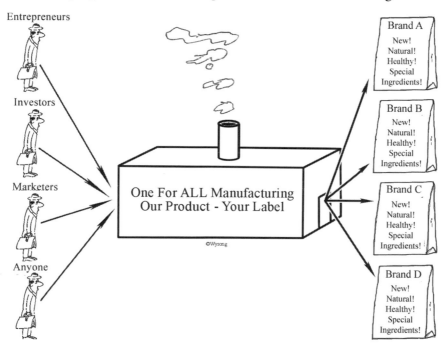

This is not to suggest you, movie stars, or plumbers don't have every right to enter a business where there may be profit. But isn't nutrition a serious health matter? Shouldn't consumers concerned about health scrutinize the credentials of those at the helm of companies claiming to be able to make "100% complete" and healthy pet foods that are to be fed exclusively? No claim should be taken at face value. You wouldn't trust brain surgery to car salesmen, actors, and plumbers. Don't trust pet food feeding to car salesmen, actors, and plumbers.

At best, pet food companies are displaying willful ignorance; at worst, they are engaged in moral fraud. Those strong words can be said because producers attempt to convince consumers to feed processed foods at every meal. They attempt to divert attention (knowingly, and even worse, unknowingly) with their special ingredients and absence of boogeyman ingredients, from the disaster of feeding one food at every meal.

What common perilous feature is held in common by all processed foods? Fire. Although it is an enigmatic quirk of human nature to overlook the obvious, think about it. Why do we fear fire and pay taxes for fire departments, but unleash it on our foods? Fire may create flavor, may sterilize, may make tolerable that which is not, but it is the consummate enemy of nutrition.

Food is made up of infinitely complex and fragile biological elements, not stone and ore needing a blast furnace to yield their contained bounty. It will at once be clear then that if we light a fire to anything biological (food, by definition is biological) it is destroyed, not improved. You or your pet cannot survive for any length of time if body temperatures exceed 118° F. Neither can food. All conventionally processed pet foods are subjected to temperatures far above this threshold.

Pet foods are baked, extruded, retorted, fried, and dried, often repeatedly so. Consider, for example, the processing of the most popular dried kibble form: Some ingredients are precooked, then precondition cooked, extrusion cooked, and then again cooked and air blasted to get dried. It is pressed at over 600 pounds per square inch, and reaches temperatures from 200 to over 300° F four different times before reaching your pet's dinner bowl. It is all done with impunity because the sacred nutritional percentages needed to make the claim of 100% completeness can practically stay the same practically no matter how much the food is brutalized.

If producers want to make money selling pet foods all over the world—which they understandably do—the cheap and easy way to do it is with fire. Fire turns perishable food into nonperishable cardboard-like food artifacts. It destroys germs present in contaminated and rotten ingredients, permits fabrication and molding into every manner of cute shape, and enables production at the rate of many tons per hour. Nutrition and health are not the true objectives in these manufacturing food torture chambers.

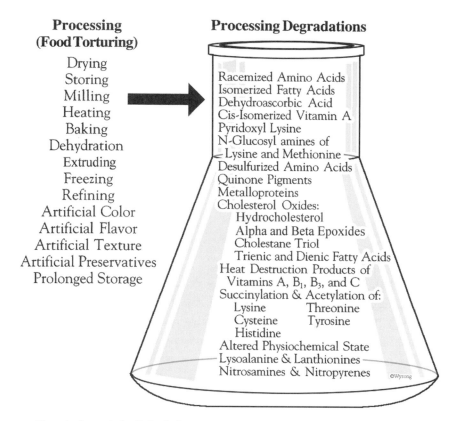

**Processing
(Food Torturing)**

Drying
Storing
Milling
Heating
Baking
Dehydration
Extruding
Freezing
Refining
Artificial Color
Artificial Flavor
Artificial Texture
Artificial Preservatives
Prolonged Storage

Processing Degradations

Racemized Amino Acids
Isomerized Fatty Acids
Dehydroascorbic Acid
Cis-Isomerized Vitamin A
Pyridoxyl Lysine
N-Glucosyl amines of
Lysine and Methionine
Desulfurized Amino Acids
Quinone Pigments
Metalloproteins
Cholesterol Oxides:
    Hydrocholesterol
    Alpha and Beta Epoxides
    Cholestane Triol
    Trienic and Dienic Fatty Acids
Heat Destruction Products of
    Vitamins A, B_1, B_3, and C
Succinylation & Acetylation of:
    Lysine   Threonine
    Cysteine   Tyrosine
    Histidine
Altered Physiochemical State
Lysoalanine & Lanthionines
Nitrosamines & Nitropyrenes

©Wysong

Food, by rightful definition, is naturally fresh, not torched. Animals in the wild eat everything raw and would never think of cooking it, even if they could.

Do we really think we can reinvent nature without her noticing and calling us to account? Commercial deception, the desire of consumers for ease, and the shifting of responsibility to 'experts' have a Faustian price: loss of vitality and resultant disease. Pets and humans pay the price of heat processed food with the panoply of modern degenerative diseases. Such diseases are not just in the cards or one of those things over which we have no control.

Surely a pet's body will notice if we thumb our noses at nature and pour vitamin-fortified, compressed and scorched food artifacts in the feeding bowl meal after meal. Animals were designed for natural foods, so health will be best achieved by feeding natural foods. When scientists succeed in making animals in their laboratory—they can't even make a single cell—then they can feed them foods made there.

But alas, pet owners throw their hands up in dismay thinking that pet feeding principles are different than what common sense would dictate for them and their children. Is it reasonable, as nutritionists would have everyone believe, that the only way we could know what lions, or bears, ants, elephants, or robins should eat, is to cage them and perform placebo-controlled, double-blind, crossover scientific feeding studies? Should we not reasonably say, "What? I already know what they should eat. It's what they're already eating out in nature!"

We don't need a nutritionist to tell us how many milligrams of vitamin B$_6$, international units of vitamin E, or grams of protein creatures need. They obviously get what they require by eating their raw, whole, natural foods. The simplicity of this truth is overwhelming, yet it is essentially passed over by the entire food industry, medical community, and the public.

So then, to the question of what do pets need to eat? The answer: What they would eat if released into the wild. Granted, today's companion animals cannot be turned loose, but that does not mean we should not model their diets to retain as much of the character of the archetypal pattern as it is possible to achieve. The best pet food is clearly that food which animals are genetically adapted to, the food of the pre-modern "550 miles" as previously explained. For cats and dogs that would primarily be prey—whole prey, uncooked, including their viscera filled with vegetation and probiotic matter.

Modern, cooked, carbohydrate-based pet foods are a far cry from that, even when they call themselves super-premium, organic, human-grade, and natural. Armed with this understanding we can begin to take charge and sort through the abundant pet feeding fables and lore. Don't assume that a high priced food solves this problem just because it was recommended by a veterinarian, breeder, or pet store clerk, or because it claims to be natural. Claims are cheap. Uninformed recommendations abound where money can be made. In fact, it is usually the high priced 'premium' foods that have the most lore and nonsense attached to them. But perception is everything and profiteering pet food marketers know this.

Use the same intuitive sense you should use when feeding yourself and the family. You know that fresh, whole, natural foods eaten in variety are healthy. That's not nuclear physics. But people will subject their pets to something they would not ever tolerate for themselves—eating the same fired and lifeless processed food at every meal for a lifetime.

Since we cannot open the door in downtown Chicago or New York to let the pet out to seek its own natural food, we must bring the proper food from nature to them. That means fresh raw grocery foods, at least in part or in rotation. The most healthy foods are those an animal can eat and digest without requiring cooking. This would include, meats, organs, bones (raw bones are not dangerous, obviously, or carnivores would never survive in the wild), and some fruits, veggies, dairy, eggs, and nuts.[1]

Pretender Raw Pet Foods – To attempt to capture the raw food market, some producers attempt to deceive consumers into believing that no grains means the same thing as raw, or they sprinkle a few raw molecules of something on the product after it is cooked and imply the whole product is then just like raw.

Conventionally processed pet foods and supplements can be used but are a compromise and therefore require discrimination. Manufacturers should be carefully scrutinized to determine whether they are truly committed to health first, and whether they have the competency at the helm to achieve it. Feeding a variety of well-made processed foods in rotation with raw grocery foods is not a problem. But note the words *rotation* and *variety.* Feeding anything day in and day out, regardless of its health merits, creates a dose that can be a poison.

Fresh and dried raw packaged foods are also now commercially available and combine convenience with raw. Caution is advised with regard to fresh frozen pet foods since about anyone can produce these in their kitchen and introduce them into commerce. The potential dangers of food-borne pathogens are greater with such products. Additionally, many freeze-dried foods are not really raw since they have been heated above the 118° F threshold that destroys many important food elements.

Discernment is critical since there are now marketers who say their products are just like raw because they contain "no grains." Examine closely and you will discover that they have merely substituted another starch for the grain and are in fact cooking their dried and canned foods just like everyone else in the industry. Some, as mentioned in the previous chapter, try to cash in on the 'raw' idea by simply sprinkling a few molecules of raw something or other on the product after it is cooked. Important words—like raw—are not regulated at all. You must be smart enough to flush out the pretenders and charlatans.

No matter how good meals are, variety is critical. That means variety from meal to meal, day to day, not a smorgasbord at one sitting. Every essential nutrient does not have to be fed at every meal. In fact, fasting a day here and there to mimic the natural fasts forced in the wild is beneficial as well.

Think about what pets would (could) eat in the wild and try to mimic that as much as possible. What to feed will then become self-evident. But don't make the project so tedious that you give up and go back to the cruel and non-thinking practice of pouring "100% complete" pseudofoods in the bowl every meal. Understand the principles outlined here and do the best you can.

THAT CLOSES THE PET SECTION. But let's not end it on such a serious note. Pets can bring so much joy to life, so here is a more fitting conclusion that brings pets, Adam, and God all together in one big happy family:

In the beginning God said unto Adam, "Behold, out of love for you I have created Dog. Regardless of how awful and self-centered you will be at times, this companion will accept and love you in spite of yourself. And because I have created this animal to reflect my love, his name will be a mirror image of my name." And it was so and Dog was pleased and so was God. And Dog showed his love for Adam by wagging his tail. And it came to pass that God saw Adam's heart harden with sinful pride, as he thought himself worthy of adoration and worship because of the obedience and love of Dog. And God said, "Behold! Adam now thinks he is like me and worthy of worship. I must go down and make his pride fall and confound and humble the man to save his soul." So God created Cat. And Cat taught Adam his true place in the universe, and that man's voice is puny, his wishes a joke, and that there are those superior to him. And God was pleased with Cat. And Adam was brought down from his high place and humbled before Cat. And it was good that man had a companion that taught him that he was inferior. And Cat became worshipped by Adam's begetted Egyptians and to this day Cat has not forgotten this. And Dog is still happy and wagging his tail. And Cat really does not care one way or the other.*

*After L. T. Pilgrim and M. Lee Young

SECTION G

Thinking about. . .

ENVIRONMENT

IN THIS SECTION: *We once thought that we were separate from our environment, from the trees, sun, animals, and air. We once threw garbage out our car windows without a care. The world was so vast it could absorb anything we did and not be phased. As population swells, Earth's resources bottom out, refuse piles up, and we choke on our own exhaust we begin to see that the environment and we are one and the same. Harm to one brings harm to the other. Expansive thinking, foresight, compassion, selflessness, and love are the tools we need to sharpen if we are to survive on planet Earth.*

42

INDUSTRY VS EARTH

THE INDUSTRIAL REVOLUTION began at a time when the Earth was not yet fully explored. It still seemed limitless with an absorbing capacity far beyond human reach. Waste was simply dumped on the ground, in water, or billowed into the air. The enthusiasm for the wonders that the industrial/technical era could bring caused everyone to think as far as the goodies and no further.

We now know civilization's capacity to disrupt environmental balances cannot be ignored. On the other hand, neither can we stop industrial/technical advance. It's a heck of a pickle. Industry wants to proceed as if there are no environmental consequences, and others, not wanting to gag on exhaust, want to put the brakes on. The debate between profits and jobs on the one hand and environmental concerns on the other will continue to heat up as population swells, consumerism flourishes, and emerging economies struggle for their share of the industrialized good life.

Environmental crises are a testament to the fact that people are always inclined to live as if the moment is their only concern. Extrapolating the consequences of actions out into the future might get in the way of cherished habits. So we live with insouciance and wait for disaster to stare us in the face. Then, when it is hopefully not too late, we attempt to take intelligent action.

The smart thing from the very beginning would have been to never engage in industry that fouled our environment or consumed resources in a non-sustainable way. Safety and sustainability should have been first priority, not seeing how fast we could crank up assembly plants to create products (most of which are unnecessary) and line pockets.

Maintaining wild areas, renewable energy sources, sustainable agriculture, and being sure recycling technology keeps pace with production and packaging are not insuperable difficulties. As evidenced by emerging green technologies, our ingenuity could easily overcome the problems. By pausing as a society to look at the long-term, we could have all the modern conveniences but without the attendant environmental threats.

But "would've-could've-should've" is not where we are today. Although we face environmental concerns on every front, many politicians, consumers, and industrialists deny that there is a problem. They argue that environmentalism is just a silly reason to interfere with

"Maybe we better slow down before this gets out of hand."

progress and prosperity. The attitude seems to be that unless people are choking on smog, growing tumors from drinking the water, or have to pay ten dollars for a gallon of gasoline, all is well.

The economy and the environment are intimately linked. A robust economy as well as poverty can be ruinous to the environment. When starving or freezing, people eat and burn whatever is available. Perfect examples of this can be seen right now where refugee camps are set up. Every piece of wood and every edible plant or creature is obliterated, creating a dust bowl perimeter that expands out from the camps in proportion to time. A thriving economy solves such desperation. Also, by improving the standard of living, people start to think in terms of maintaining their quality of life. That means looking to the future, the view that is necessary for sustainability and long-term health. In turn, environmental sensitivity engenders health, without which a prospering economy makes no difference.

It is now politically correct to demonize industry and money rather than see their potential synergy with a healthy environment. Although this extreme view is not totally reasonable, it is a safer approach than industry without limit. On the other hand, the pro-industry, anti-environmental view has a beguiling appeal because it tells people what they want to hear: Everything is okay—so eat, drink, and be merry. Ozone holes won't get you, nor will bad food, species extinctions, deforestation, water pollution, tobacco smoke, factory farms, herbicides, pesticides, genetic engineering, or automobile and industrial exhaust. Forget the radical environmental stuff and enjoy yourself. Humans are puny and the Earth is big, so don't worry about it.

Proponents reinforce and justify this environmentally blind, pro-industrial view with arguments such as these: humans create more greenhouse gasses than cars; water is cleaner than it has ever been; trees are on the increase; volcanoes cause more pollution than industry; oil slicks are not a concern because oil is a natural product constantly released on the ocean floors anyway; the Earth can heal almost anything; life would reemerge eventually even if all nuclear plants and weapons exploded.

Do Your Part

Population Control

No War

Clean and
Renewable Fuels

Recycle

Even God enters the fray. Some argue that stewardship is really not that important since God is coming to save believers and create an Earthly paradise, or take them to a pristine heaven. They are confident that God would never permit things to get so bad that the saved would not be saved. Besides, there is a Biblical command to subdue the Earth so why not have fun doing so?

We all share guilt for environmental degradation, regardless of our philosophical or religious views. If we live in and support the modern world we are culpable by our very existence. Each one of us tends to use up and

209

waste more than we restore. At the same time, we want to feel comfortable that our conveniences and industrial actions will not harm us. Therefore, there is strong emotional pressure in all of us to believe that everything is okay and that we need not worry because the Earth is so big and forgiving and all we are doing, after all, is just trying to enjoy life. In the back of everyone's mind is the hope that science and technology will always be able to come save us. It's the "really bad things won't happen to me" syndrome spread across whole societies and the whole Earth.

But environmental problems are real and can destroy us. History abounds with evidence that we ignore the environment at our peril. We should be living on our income, not the Earth's savings. For example, primitive cultures became nomadic because they exhausted the resources in their surroundings. (Where will the U.S. move when it exhausts its resources?) Archaeology shows how settlers to islands first killed all the animals for food, and then felled all the trees for homes, boats, and fires. With no life support left, their society either perished or moved to another land. (Where will Africa move if it does the same?) Ancient civilizations around the globe suffered under environmental ruination and either met their demise or moved on to despoil yet another area. (Where will Europe move when it ruins its land, air, and water?)

Environmental ruination and human suffering are not just events of the past, or abstractions to ponder for the future. For huge third world regions these stark realities are present right now in an endless cruel cycle of environmental degradation, over-population, and poverty. Millions send their toddlers out across barren areas searching for the last twigs of firewood. Some walk for hours every day just to find potable water. They have no place to move and only misery to look forward to. (Where will Earth's inhabitants move when we reach the bottom of the planet's barrel?)

Every Home Needs A Rain Blower

Here is the essential point that seems to be missed: If we care about humankind, all planetary issues are important. Therefore, all sociopolitical, economic, biological, and environmental issues must be evaluated on the basis of how they impact human welfare, both in the short-term and long-term. This evaluation should then be the filter through which the merits of competing ideas are judged.[1]

For example, the issue is not whether chlorofluorocarbons emitted from spray cans are destroying the ozone layer, but rather *could* they if their use were unbridled? What if emissions increased a thousand, a million, or a billion-fold? Would that not, in fact, jeopardize the atmospheric canopy that protects human health? It's not a matter of concern for the canopy; it is a matter of human health.

Similarly, the issue is not just whether a spotted owl is exterminated by deforestation. If deforestation continues without restraint, won't humans be adversely affected? Don't trees, in fact, beneficially affect the air and temperature of the planet helping to create homeostatic balance that permits human life? If a forest is going to be logged and turned to wasteland or a paper pulp tree farm, doesn't that have meaning for human welfare? Should extending the paycheck for a logging industry for a few months be given priority over maintaining pristine natural areas, which generations into the future could enjoy and benefit from?

Since plankton creates far more oxygen than all the Earth's forests, then shouldn't we be concerned about pollutants in the oceans that can destroy these air-regenerating creatures?

Throwing trash from car windows is not a question of how long it would take to make mountains of debris along roads that would impair the vision of drivers. The point is that private despoiling should not take priority over the common right to the aesthetics of a litter-free highway.

Oil is a natural product of the Earth and may be spontaneously released at the ocean floor, but does that justify decreasing controls that could result in more oil tanker breakups? Although past oil tanker spills have resulted in some environmental recovery, what if the spills increased ten-fold or a hundred-fold? What if no part of the ocean could be found without an oil slick and no beach could be safely enjoyed? Wouldn't this adversely affect human welfare? Should not the potential for such disaster be nipped in the bud? Is not more concern better than less?

211

Because environmentally ruinous practices may be seen as necessary for business, profiteers tend not to voluntarily reform. This is a case where governmental controls can serve a needed function. Only 0.1% of all large-scale layoffs nationwide have resulted from environmental regulations such as the Clean Air Act. By contrast, changes in company ownership accounted for more than 35 times that number of jobs being terminated. This is not to say regulatory bureaucracy should not be trimmed and made more rational. For example, while only 18 hazardous waste sites were cleaned up by the EPA's superfund in the approximate ten years following 1980, some $600 million of the fund went to lawyers.

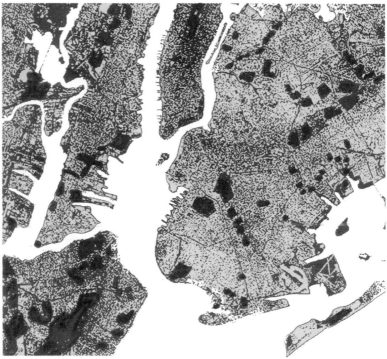

A satellite view of New York City – White is water, grey is building and asphalt, black is remaining vegetation areas. The entire region was originally forested and green – all black. This demonstrates the incredible capacity of humans to remodel Earth. (earthobservatory.nasa.gov)

Ultimately, jobs will not be diminished if there is a reorientation of industry away from environment-wrecking technologies. Although that is not comforting to those who profit from things remaining as they are, the big picture must be viewed. When industry shifts focus, jobs are not lost, the skills necessary to fill them simply change. For example, if virgin forest logging is curtailed, jobs are not eliminated; they are redirected toward sustainable timber practices and industries which create alternative construction and paper products. A clean renewable energy source that replaces oil and gas would also just shift jobs to the new technology.

What about the argument that because humans are natural, whatever they do is natural and therefore can't be considered as anti-environmental? Indeed, natural human activity is fine until human intellect and creativity are attached to it. If we dig at the branch we are sitting on with our fingers, no big deal. Put a chainsaw to it and we have an entirely different matter.

Problems arise when ancient habitat meets modern capability. Put humans in the woods without access to any machinery, just like all other creatures, and no irreparable harm is done. In the rain forest, aborigines make baskets out of leaves without destroying the plant. They eat fruit and cultivate more fruit by spitting out or defecating the seeds. What they consume ultimately re-fertilizes or plants in an endless cycle of death and regeneration as nature designed. But give them bulldozers, a food processing plant, and garbage cans, and we have another matter entirely.

So the wild card usually not taken into account by those who deny human impact on the environment is the unique (unnatural) compounding element of technology. It potentiates and accelerates our ability to destroy resources and upset balances by a factor of thousands.

Let's also not be distracted by arguments about the insignificant worth of trees, spotted owls, or obscure endangered fish. Yes, on the surface it can seem foolish to shut down an industry because of a minnow. But to ignore the importance of biodiversity is to violate the principle of interdependence: we will ultimately suffer harm if we harm the intricate natural web of which we are a part. It's really not about the minnow; it's about the mindset that knows no limit in terms of what can be destroyed in the name of 'progress.' To eradicate species, as we are doing, is to burn a gigantic genetic library before we have read the books.

The course of human history is ultimately shaped by paradigms, the prevailing philosophic thought, the zeitgeist. The Inquisition, Dark Ages, Renaissance, and the Industrial Revolution all were created by ways of thinking. While some paradigms advanced the human condition, others have brought immeasurable human suffering. The paradigm of unbridled

213

industry and resource consumption has proven to be naive. Not because progress is bad, but because the scale of industry is now so enormous. Human encroachment and destruction continually grow, but the Earth's capacity remains the same. The problem is one of limits. Human destruction of resources and life support systems will eventually meet Earth's capacity. Blind faith that technology will somehow at the last critical moment solve any problems is no solution. A paradigm shift of Earth first, consumerism second, is needed. We either change our philosophic approach from industrial hedonism to fiduciary responsibility, or we will make Earth uninhabitable.

Humans did this.

Humans can do this.

Is the ozone hole growing or shrinking? Is the Earth warming or cooling? Should the spotted owl take precedence over logging jobs? Should a natural area be explored for oil? Environmental answers always lie in measuring long-term consequences. It's simple. Human activity that would eventually threaten humans must stop.

Unfortunately, the distance in time between cause and effect too easily lulls us into complacency and self-justification. In this regard, how we treat our relationship to the environment is not unlike how we tend to reason on health. Cigarettes and processed food cause no immediate harm. Pollution doesn't either. The lag in impact on the environmental organism is just like the lag of degenerative disease impact on individual organisms. Just because we cannot measure immediate harm from an act does not validate it. That's the difference between intelligence and wisdom, on the one hand, and simple neurological reflex on the other—which coincidentally is the difference between us and other life forms.

It is the unreasoning forms of life that populate and exploit without any concern for the future. The result is starvation and calamity as populations come and go, exhausting resources or poisoning themselves with their own waste. Shouldn't we humans, with our apparently unique ability to reason toward the future, figure out something better than a ruined environment for our children?

Do we just continue until the Earth is blacktop and rivers course in tamed concrete channels? Isn't there obviously more potential harm in destruction of natural areas and industrial pollution gone unabated than prohibiting any further degradation? Isn't despoiling nature like whipping our own mother? Should we not err on the side of overprotecting rather than attempting to balance on the narrow edge of disaster?

We are living through an Earth-scale revolution because technology has permitted us to reach some of Earth's limits. Our choices will ultimately determine if we become victims of myopic and selfish acts or founders of a future of hope and promise that can only happen if we live our lives and govern our world as if thinking matters.

GASOLINE

Simply applying some thinking can dramatically save resources, emissions, and dramatically blunt rising gas prices

1. Stop driving. Let's say you would normally make two car trips today. If one was not really necessary and you didn't do it, you just effectively doubled gas mileage.

2. Think in terms of total fuel used, not just gas mileage. Arrange life to use less fuel and you will beat the price increases, and reduce waste and emissions.

3. Car pooling does the same. Also, rather than you making a special trip, have a family member or friend pick up the item you need on the way.

4. Group your needs and preplan trips so you get all your running done in one trip with an efficiently planned route.

5. Get a smaller car, and use a bike, scooter, roller blades, or just walk. Stop and think about how ridiculous it is to use a three to four thousand pound vehicle to haul your little self to the store to pick up a twelve ounce box of cereal. Consider the resources and energy used to make and move your two ton vehicle, and then to scrap it one day. Sometime, put the car in neutral, get out and try to push it. That will give you an idea of the tremendous amount of energy used each time you run the roads. If resources and fuel were infinite, and if population were stagnant, that would be one thing. But that is not the case. The United States' gluttony is a shame on us. If the whole world consumed like we did it would take four Earths to support it.

6. Drive smart. If there is a red light or a stop sign up ahead, why accelerate toward it and then slam on the brakes? Braking effectively cancels all the fuel energy that was used to push the car up to speed. If you could coast to all your stops, you would be getting maximum efficiency out of your vehicle. Capturing this lost energy is what hybrids do, but you can do it without a hybrid by using this simple technique. Yes, you will tick other drivers off who are hurrying up so they can stop, and you will have to use judgment based on traffic, but do it when you can.

(Modified from an Internet circulated e-mail.)

215

43

POPULATION

WE LIVE ON ONE FINITE WORLD with finite resources. Population growth, potentially, is infinite. Is that not a problem? This Malthusian dilemma has been debated in the closets for over a century, but almost nobody seems to want to talk about it openly other than to insist everyone has the right to reproduce endlessly. Imagine the fate of a politician who told us we needed to curtail reproduction, even if it might be the bold-faced truth?

Aside from the ability of humans to accelerate technological development and the exploitation of Earth's resources, consider the sheer magnitude of the human population explosion. It supposedly took 2 million years for the Earth to reach its first billion in population. It will now take only about 11 years to add another billion.[1-2] This, too, is made possible by technology. But technology can only squeeze so much out of a finite Earth. Reproduction, on the other hand, seems to know no limits and is the engine that ultimately drives environmental destruction.

We talk about conserving, recycling, reusing, and curbing pollution. But mum seems to be the word about population growth because the issue is intertwined with religious beliefs (God says to "fill the earth"), evolutionary philosophy (each of us should breed as much as possible to give our individual genetics the most chance to be "selected"), and fear of Orwellian governmental controls (we have our "right" to breed as much as we like).

Food resources and predators tightly control animals in the wild. But humans have controlled their predators and, through agricultural technology, expanded food resources to enable population growth where resources do not even exist. Consider the desert communities of Las Vegas and Phoenix, or any modern urban area for that matter.

Creatures in the wild multiply until resources are ruined or exhausted. Then they die back. Some therefore argue that there is no real population problem since we will die back too, if not by starvation, then by disease and war. How is that more humanistic than to encourage decreased procreation? It's also doubtful that those who argue that disasters will take care of our population problems would be quite so flip if the die back included them or their loved ones.

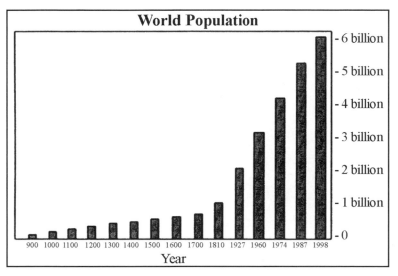

The dilemma is that any solution sounds awful. But, for starters, at least all parents should have to shoulder the full burden of responsibility for the children they bear. That, rather than ever-expanding social aid to relieve parents of their duty, would be a real deterrent. If parents prove unfit, then the state must take over but the parents must foot the bill.

If the citizenry does not solve the problem on their own—which they never do—Big Brother will when the situation reaches crisis proportions. Government will either force us to stop having children, mandate abortions and infanticide, or society will face the death of vast segments of population as it collapses on itself.

China (about 34 births per minute) has made a rational effort to intercede and control its population in spite of vigorous international protest. Chinese citizens are told how many children they can have and this is determined on the basis of the resources available within the particular community. Individual human rights are secondary to the good of the whole. One-child families receive subsidy and priority housing incentives, while two-child families lose these. In some Chinese communities, parents who have more than two children are fined 10% of their income. Yes, that sounds draconian, but is the Western world more moral by permitting unbridled reproduction, giving financial incentives and tax benefits for larger families through social programs, and not holding parents responsible?

Admittedly, there is enough room on Earth to comfortably fit far more people. In fact, the entire world's population could live in the state of Texas with each family having a 2000 square foot home on a good-sized city lot. Japan has 125 million people crammed on a landmass the size of California. But the problem is not one of square feet (yet). People need resources and their waste must be carried away. Japan does not prove that the world is under populated. It must import almost everything and export its garbage. Left to support themselves with their own resources, tens of millions of Japanese would

PARADISE or BUST!

Salvation – Some believe we can treat Earth with impunity and then expect technology to provide space travel to a new pristine paradise when our environment becomes unlivable.

have to die. If the whole world were to populate like Japan, where would the resources come from and where would the garbage go?

A nation should, it can be argued, be left to solve its own problems. If it has created population beyond the capability of its resources, then it must solve the problem or take responsibility for the consequences. Look at it this way. Let's say a people choose to live in an oasis in the desert. There are enough coconuts, bananas, and water to sustain 25 people. They insist on their right to procreate without limit. Now there are 50 people and 25 are starving and diseased. Being kind people, we send food to save the extra 25. They get full and healthy and begin rolling in the hay again. Now there are 100 people with 75 starving. We send more food, and on and on until there are a 1000 people on the tiny oasis. We continually send them aid and they are all happy and fat. We feel wonderful that we have done so much good. Meanwhile, our own population has increased and there is a drought. We now have high unemployment and are hungry and impoverished. When the 1000 from the oasis need another shipment we can do nothing. Now, instead of 25 starving and dying, 975 do. All because they did not take responsibility for themselves, and we let emotion and stopgap solutions get in front of thinking.

It should be noted that the United States is experiencing the largest population growth (never mind unbridled immigration) of any industrial nation in the world. We will not escape the consequences of our 'right' to indefinitely procreate. Yes, the U.S. is the breadbasket of the world, but that is only a climatic shift or environmental disaster away from drying up.

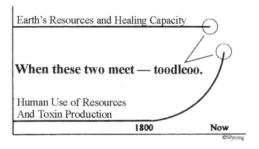

It is easy to slay messengers of the stark reality that people must match reproduction to resources. Proposals that don't work are acceptable because they sound warm and cuddly—such as sending food where countries have out-swelled their resources, and not interfering with anyone's right to have as many children as they wish. Solutions that will work—such as teaching societies to be self-sufficient and to control their numbers, or leaving them to starve so that their numbers retract to match their resources—are considered inhumane and unacceptable.

219

Watching starvation as populations retract to meet existing food resources seems incredibly cruel, even unthinkable. On the other hand, feeding such populations so that they grow further and then perhaps face even greater catastrophe in the future is even crueler. Such terrible dilemmas are the price to be paid when foresight is not used.

Of course we must do all we can to feed starving people and address crises. Extending a hand to our neighbor is part of what being human is about. But such aid must be obligatorily linked with long-term solutions: "Here is food to feed your children, and here is the know-how to irrigate your fields, rotate crops, and do some planned parenting."

> *"China has a population of a billion people. That means even if you're a one in a million kind of special person, there are still a thousand others just like you."*

Unfortunately, any approach to overpopulation is a search for the lesser of evils. Nobody wants to be told what to do, much less have their 'right' to have children curtailed. At the same time, everyone wants peace, security, space, nature, food, and health. The reality is that the two desires are not endlessly compatible. The Earth is finite.

Human intelligence has given us the capability to create societies separate and apart from nature, permitting population growth that would have never been possible in the wild. That same intelligence must be used on a local, national, and international scale to create humane solutions, not apply Band-Aids that only deepen the problem and ultimately put more at risk.

Where Does the Responsibility Lie?

44

MODERNITY'S DECEPTION

ALTHOUGH IT IS CHARACTERISTIC of every generation to think of itself as unique, ours truly appears to be so. As explained in the section on health, the speed of change since the Industrial Revolution is unprecedented. Time itself seems to be compressing.

We must keep in mind, however, that material culture is transmitted and transformed separate from our genes. The technological and artificial trappings with which we surround ourselves are all a gigantic experiment in which we are the subjects.

Our genes remain back at the hunter-gatherer stage, but our body has been displaced into a new world of environmental disruption, pollutants, physical ease, relentless emotional stress, and fabricated food. We may mentally ignore the changes we are subjecting ourselves to, even welcome them with open arms (and tummy), but our body, mind, and health do not let them go unnoticed.

The key to humanity's future and to health is to not forget our beginnings. They are firmly anchored in nature, in prehistory, and should not be severed with impunity. That is what environmentalism is really all about.

The new artificial world is, in effect, toxic. What makes a toxin is the body's unfamiliarity with it. For example, synthetic chemicals are not, in themselves, noxious. It's just that we are not designed for exposure to them. Our biology has not had time to adapt to them by developing metabolic pathways that either utilize or detoxify them.

It may be reasoned that evolution may save us. But the evidence proves that we can adapt and change only to a degree in the face of a changing environment. Additionally, organisms modify primarily as populations over many generations. But the rate of cultural change we are now seeing is not being spread over many generations, it is occurring within one. That is why our modern world is dangerous and we must be concerned with the speed of change and the distance from nature those changes take us.

The principle that we are inextricably linked to the natural world by a lifeline is so simple, yet so profound. We ignore it for the sake of technological progress and limitless consumerism at our peril.

Future Urban Landscaping

THE GRAND EXPERIMENT

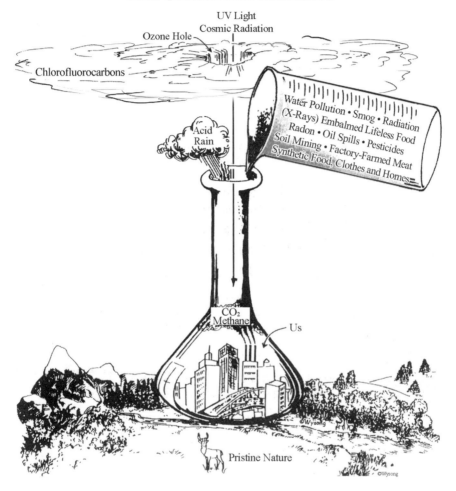

The Grand Experiment – Although we may think that modernity is business as usual, it is not. We are genetically designed to be out of doors, in the fresh air and sun, eating foods exactly as they are found in nature. Instead, we are being subjected to a gigantic experiment in which we are the unwitting subjects. Our air, water, land, and food have been dramatically altered. We live in synthetic buildings shielded from the sun, and breathe, drink, and eat a variety of toxins our immune system has not had sufficient time to develop mechanisms to detoxify. The result is the panoply of degenerative diseases that are now of epidemic proportions.

45

ANIMAL RIGHTS

FROM A PURELY BIOLOGICAL PERSPECTIVE, no creature inherently has rights beyond that which it has the power to impose. What is able to survive does, what cannot does not. But our world is not just biology. It is ethics as well. "Might makes right" cannot be the operating paradigm in a world where freedom, compassion, humanity, and love are desired. Nor are we removed from consideration of the rights of other creatures just because we are paying somebody else to create drugs, scent a deodorant, or raise our food.

Humans with the ability to use their technology to affect and control the world so widely and deeply are constantly faced with ethical choices. Modern life is not a matter of mere survival as it was when we were in the wild. It is an opportunity to develop and grow as introspective, sensitive, and ethical people. For example, walking in the woods requires no rules, but driving in traffic does. Drinking from a stream is not a problem, but damming the stream and flooding thousands of acres is. Breaking down brush with our hands to make a lean-to for shelter is one thing, but denuding the planet with machines is quite another. Hunting animals in the wild for food using only ingenuity, strength, and speed is a matter totally unlike wiping out whole populations with rifles (for 'sport') or with our urban encroachment. Farming animals to feed a swelling population is necessary, but denying them any form of natural or decent life, or subjecting them to abuse or cruelty is not a right we can claim.

Living in the wild would present few ethical choices. Causes and philosophy have a way of taking a back seat when life is consumed with day-to-day survival. But an advanced society with almost limitless technological capabilities is another matter. Our ability now to practically cage and control every creature on the planet and virtually destroy the Earth's life-supporting environment on an Earth-wide scale requires choices and ethical responsibility.

The first choice to be made, it would seem, is whether we wish to survive here long term or not. Assuming the answer is yes, we must take fiduciary responsibility for the planet and its web of life. But it does not end there, as some humane and green movements would seem to argue. In order to survive we must also take the lives of the plant and animal food we consume. That is a reality we face, and, assuming we wish to survive, it is not a matter of ethics. On the other hand, our management and behavior toward other living things—including our food—do present moral choices. It also creates a mood, if you will, setting the tone for how we treat one another. If we find it easy to treat life with insensitivity, it is a small step to treat one another the same way. If we extend care, compassion, and decency out toward the rest of the world, we are far more likely to treat fellow humans similarly.

Killing animals or plants for fun or just because we have the power to do so is neither rational nor ethical. It is a form of psychopathic behavior that threatens the web of life upon which we depend and desensitizes us to the value of all life.

People who take joy in the pain, suffering, and death of other creatures, or justify it because of dollars to be made, threaten civilization itself. It is not that great a leap for those who behave in this way to extend similar insensitivity to humans. Would we rather live next door to someone who creates habitat for wild creatures in their yard and live-captures house mice to set them free outdoors, or someone who stomps on any bug they see, chains their dog to a stake in the yard, yahoos about shooting songbirds from their window with a pellet gun, and hunts for trophies leaving carcasses to rot? It is not a coincidence that serial killers often have a history of torturing and killing animals.[1]

Creatures raised for food should not be treated as nothing more than production units, confined so as to never see the light of day, and then be handled and slaughtered inhumanely. They should be raised kindly in a free and open environment where they might enjoy the life they have. Arguably hunting should be reserved for the singular purpose of obtaining food, not for the pleasure of killing. If there is opportunity to show compassion, why not take it rather than abuse and exploit just because we have the power to do so?

Scientists and much of the public justify animal experimentation as necessary in order to find disease cures, test toxins, check mascara safety, and so on. I am reminded of an experience in a toxicology class. The lesson for the day was to show how topical products could be screened for safety. For a demonstration, the professor held a rabbit by the nap and put some drops of a chemical in the rabbit's eye. The rabbit squealed and struggled in pain. It was a miserable thing to see. As days went by we were shown the progression of the caustic chemical on the rabbit's cornea. The extreme ulceration that resulted was grotesque and the pain the rabbit was enduring was gut wrenching. To this day I remember vividly and regret that I paid tuition for this needless cruelty—although to show any reaction at the time risked being viewed as unscientific and emotional, a definite no-no in medical schools.

The lesson to be learned from this pathetic display of human insensitivity was that noxious chemicals will ulcerate and dissolve eyes. How profound. There wasn't a student in the class that could not have guessed the outcome before the macabre demonstration was done. The real takeaway was that life could be treated with disregard. If we wanted to be good doctors we needed to suck it up, put aside silly compassion and bravely mutilate life for the sake of the greater good of medicine.

Torture aside, such experimentation is unnecessary and really quite embarrassingly sloppy science. Those who participate in it become desensitized to suffering, lose compassion, and learn to hone the skill of obtuse justification. Medical experimentation upon animals is unnecessary because every species reacts to toxins, drugs, and even surgery differently. For that matter, every individual is different biochemically. What might be true for one goose is not for a gander. So a scientific result from a lab in which thousands of mice, dogs, or monkeys are tortured does not give certainty about an effect in humans or in other species. Biological differences skew all results.[2]

Aspirin causes birth defects in rats but not in humans. Humans and guinea pigs require vitamin C in the diet but most other creatures manufacture it themselves. An opium dose that will kill a human is harmless in dogs and chicks. Allylisothiocyanate will cause cancer in the male rat, but may not in the female, or in mice. Penicillin will kill a guinea pig but potentially save the life of a person. Most drugs, nutrients, and toxins have a reverse effect: a benefit at one level is a danger at another. Measuring such things is near impossible.[3] Even kindness in the lab can alter results as demonstrated by atherosclerosis (the heart attack factor) being reduced by as much as 60% in rabbits that are handled, compared to those ignored.[4]

The point is that nobody knows all the variables when conducting such research. They can only control for some, guess at all the others, and then make an extrapolation, a huge leap in faith timed precisely to occur before the budget runs out. This is the reason drugs go through years of FDA trials at a cost of 360 million dollars, and then can kill and maim when introduced to the population.

Nevertheless, such heartless experimentation proceeds in the name of science and the promise of cures. It's a shame. Using a little logic, or other laboratory tools such as tissue culture techniques, could as well have led to the same conclusions gained from animal experimentation. For example, researchers used 24,000 mice to prove that 2-acetylaminofluorene was carcinogenic. Based on genetic context logic, you or I could have told them the result without caging or torturing one mouse. Why would a synthetic chemical such as this *not* be harmful?

What is most frustrating is that the result of all the animal experimentation is not cures. Rather, there are hundreds of thousands of maimed and killed humans who bought into the faulty science of such 'proven' drugs. Animal research brings us drugs with side effects, dependencies, prescription errors, cross-reactions, and removal of symptoms while the cause of the disease continues. Animal experimentation is a bad idea at its start and a tragic disaster in practice.

The popular idea is that our environment, including all of its creatures, is a mere resource for our exploitation. That is irrational if long-term human welfare is to matter and denies that humans have a higher purpose than might makes right.

Predator Catch And Release

46

BIOPHILIA

WHAT IS IT THAT CAUSES that warm glow inside, the sense of peace and exhilaration when walking through the woods or sitting by the ocean and watching the sunset? Why are we spellbound by the beauty of a fresh snowfall clinging to trees, the smell and feel of the first warm day in spring, and the vistas of unspoiled prairies or mountain ranges?

Watching animals in the wild or even the behavior and antics of our pets can affect us similarly. Virtually everyone is touched by such experiences, even though we seem to be increasingly alienating and isolating ourselves from nature. Biologists call this phenomenon biophilia—defined as the human need for and love of natural places and creatures.

If we canoe a beautiful crystal clear stream, note how the mood changes when we come upon an old tire lurking in the depths, a broken beer bottle gracing the forest floor on the wilderness backpack adventure, or the plastic bags entangling our bare feet as we stroll the ocean shore. Note how the view of the open prairie or desert is ruined when billowing factory smoke is seen in the distance, how offshore derricks interrupting the ocean's horizon diminish the wonder of the sunrise, and how spoiled the dead silence of the forest is when pierced with the irritating sound of a chain saw?

The interjection of human activity into these natural settings ruins them. It can change the mood from peace, wonder, and personal reflection to disgust, anger, and a sense of despair. Tripping over a pop can in nature is like spoiling a beautiful symphony by starting  up a Harley Davidson. The chaos of centuries of forest refuse strewn about is a thing of beauty, but human refuse and junkyards are ugly and repulsive.

The reason for this double standard is that at our core we are part of nature, not synthetics. Just as birds of a feather flock together, we are attracted to our own kind as well. Nature is our kind. Synthetic and industrial artificiality are not.

"Over the polluted river and through where there used to be woods, to grandmother's house we go."

Everything in nature is connected. Neurons and blood vessels course through the body interconnecting every single tissue with what is sensed from the external environment. As we breathe, lung tissue connects us to the atmosphere. Seeing and hearing is connection of light and sound to the body via chemical reactions in the tissues of our eyes and ears. Smelling, tasting, and touching similarly put us in contact with our environment. When we feel the wind in our face, the crunch of snow underfoot, listen to a bubbling stream, breathe the aroma of a forest, marvel at the flight of geese in formation, or gaze in awe into the infinite nighttime heavens, we are connecting. Joining with nature is like coming home, harmonizing with the world, connecting to that which is familiar, and touching our very origins.

Biophilia speaks to protecting nature, but it is also key to understanding illness. Health is a balance that requires connection to our source of life. There is a direct proportionality. Break the interconnections with nature, and illness will result in lock step. Restore these balances, and physical, mental, and spiritual health is the reward. That does not mean we must return to caves and hunt for food, nor is it sufficient to only turn our face toward the sun during a lunch break in Central Park. It is something in between that we must make a special effort to work into our lives.

Nature is a fragile treasure essential to our well-being. We should treat it as such.

47

RESPECT FOR ALL LIFE

LABELS EXIST NOWHERE IN NATURE, and nowhere in nature can we find rules about how things should behave toward one another. But that reality is just too unsettling and untidy for us. So we create words that artificially frame reality and provide markers for behavior. Even *living, dead, plant,* and *animal* are concepts that exist as clean categories only in the heads of word makers. Nevertheless, once labeled as *living, dead, plant,* or *animal,* we then behave toward the thing defined in a certain way. We treat *dead* things differently than *living* things, and *animals* differently than *plants.* The problem with this categorization is that nature is homogeneous and continuous. Naming things does not change that.

For example, we tend to think of *plants* as dumb, insensitive, photosynthetic food producers. Yet, researchers have electrically monitored plants and discovered a sort of nervous system that is sensitive to and responds to its environment. Studies also show that tenderness in the care of plants—singing and talking to them, touching them fondly—results in the plant's enhanced growth and better health.

Plants and animals even communicate. For example, certain parasitic wasps must find appropriate caterpillars to incubate their eggs. A wasp paralyzes a caterpillar and inserts an egg that then develops into a larva that slowly consumes the living host caterpillar. Although caterpillars have developed a variety of hiding mechanisms within plants, wasps are still able to find them by tuning to signals that plants emit when caterpillars feed on them. That means insects listen to plant communication.[1]

So, plants are neither inert nor insensitive, even though the word *plant* implies otherwise.[2] Who is to say plants do not have a form of feeling and intelligence, and that they deserve to be treated with ethical disregard? This is not to suggest that we should all start petting lettuce heads—at

Disregard for some species leads to disregard for them all.

least not that we spend a lot of time on it—but it does mean ethics and considerations do not end when we call a thing *lettuce* or *plant*.[3]

Similarly, things we label as inert, such as dirt, rocks, air, and water are tied into the intricate web of life. If all things are interconnected to life, then treating anything with disrespect is never justified. A wise person comes to see that reality is a continuum, not disconnected parts and pieces. *Self* and *other* are different manifestations of the same thing. Disregard for *other* is disregard for *self.*

This is not to suggest that a dust ball in the corner of the closet, a carrot, and a neighbor should all be treated the same. Ethics is not a matter of one action toward all things, but judgment and discernment in determining the role that all things play in reality. Using trees to build a home is one thing; cutting down all trees on Earth just because profit can be made is another. Growing food is one thing; using toxic chemicals in the process that then leach into the water supply is quite another.

Word labels oversimplify reality and provide excuses for behaviors. Labels are easier than exercising conscience or thinking. Justification for abuse and destruction is always linked to mere words like: *plant, animal,*

233

pagan, witch, Buddhist, Indian, enemy, evil, bloods, whites, blacks, and so forth. Once the label is in place, thought stops and mindless behavior begins. How else, through the millennia, could people have visited such inhumanity on one another and on nature? Labels cannot and do not define the bounds of ethics.

A label-based mindset lies at the root of disrespect for and dismantling of the environment at large. *Water, air, dirt, animals,* and *plants,* become just labeled commodities for our use and disregard. Things not extended the courtesy of the *human* label are thought of as inconsequential and not deserving of ethical treatment.

If we excuse abuse because something is just *sod* or *animal,* it's not that far of a reach to excuse abuse of *Eskimos, whites, Taoists,* or *capitalists.* All that is necessary is to construct word definitions and word rules. That line of thought and manipulation of reality with words can then transition to the psychopathology of disregard for anything other than *me.* On the other hand, those who worry about consideration for bugs, trees, dirt, air, and water, are less likely to have trouble seeing the immorality of harm to fellow humans.

Seeing beyond the artificial words humans impose on reality is necessary for a truly compassionate, sustainable, and better world. It fosters respect for the oneness of all things and provides hope for a better future.

Only when the last tree has been cut down

Only when the last river has been poisoned

Only after the last fish has been caught

Only then will you find money cannot be eaten.

— Cree Prophecy

SECTION H

Thinking about. . .

ECONOMICS

IN THIS SECTION: *Business, money, and jobs are the life-blood of modern society. Although economics occupies so much of life, little thought is given to its methods and impact. By going with the flow and racing for dollars we too easily lose sight of the ethics that must be employed in their accumulation and use. Economics is not a neutral human activity. It has limitless potential for both good and bad.*

48

DOING GOOD
WITH BUSINESS

THE PREVAILING OPINION IS that business cannot succeed without a cold, dollars-first, impersonal approach. But a profitable end cannot justify any and all means. The power to affect the world that comes along with business transactions can result in a tyranny that can ruin health and the planet.

Modern business attitudes can mimic addictive behavior. Addicts first lie to themselves, then they lie to their families or their organizations, then they lie to the world. The lie to self is that amassing fortune will bring meaning or purpose to life. The lie to family and organization is that money should be life's only duty. The lie to the world, through advertising and marketing, is that business endeavors that create worthless and harmful products should be supported.

Profit-driven business addicts, like street addicts, cannot feel the world around them and thus they are numb to the impact of their irresponsible behavior. The high from their money fixes keeps them coming back for more and more. The euphoria of prestige and materialistic gewgaws feeds a never-ending destructive cycle.

There are finite resources on Earth. So why should anybody be able to have at them with the only qualification being money? The anything goes, free market heyday has consequences. Not only does it consume planetary life support, it will ultimately result in economic destruction since it creates an artificial economy based upon dead-end businesses and dead-end jobs.[1]

Money Means Choices Of Conscience

On the other hand, it is possible to interject conscience into virtually any business endeavor. It begins with the motive of leaving a better world behind after one's footprint. Consumers who encourage businesses that are environmentally ruinous by purchasing their products, buying their stock, or working for them are culpable as well. It is encouraging that an increasing segment of thinking consumers thirst for better options and will even pay a premium for them. Note the rise in popularity of organic foods, recycled products, energy efficient cars and appliances, and natural alternative medical therapies.

Consumers have a right to look to business for leadership and direction. In turn, business has the responsibility to become expert in their field and lead consumers to healthy and environmentally responsible choices, not merely to follow market whims.[2]

Business is actually like a gift, a wonderful opportunity to make a better world. Business leaders should view the profits they create not as an end, but as a by-product of the good that is being achieved and as fuel to do more of the same. When seen in this light, business is a serious, even solemn responsibility and opportunity. It is not so much a chance to be profitable, but to be human.

49

THE GLOBAL ECONOMY

EVERY SO OFTEN there is a global economic shift. When it happens, it unfolds quickly and lives are changed dramatically. For example, in Thomas Jefferson's time 83% of the people in America lived on farms, whereas by the mid twentieth century only 3% did. Today we are in the midst of a similar transition that will put us in a new, almost unrecognizable world. Just a few decades ago America was the manufacturing capital of the world. Even workers of low skill could get good jobs and support their families with only one parent working. But manufacturing is not only being increasingly automated, it is being moved elsewhere in the world. As a result, notice how few one-working-parent families there now are. More dollars are floating around, but the value of those dollars is less and less. To maintain a standard of living they think they deserve, both parents must work or try the financially ruinous acrobatics of credit.

Large companies are also now struggling to survive and tens of thousands of workers are being laid off. Inflated wages as well as corporate waste and extravagance cannot compete in a world market. In contrast, manufacturing and economic power is blossoming in parts of the world that had been considered backward and impoverished twenty years ago.

These remarkable changes are a manifestation of the inevitable pressures toward one world. The globe has finite resources so if in one area the standard of living rises, in another it must fall. This historic global shift is the macro-cause for the job disruptions and lowered standard of living in communities across America.

The nations now growing the fastest in the new Industrial Revolution (perhaps better termed job dislocation) are those in Southeast Asia, China and India. People there are working hard and saving—something Americans used to do. Instead of reinvigorating a work ethic and innovation, many Americans are attempting to sustain the lifestyle they think they are entitled to by second mortgages, consolidating debts, maxing out credit cards, lotto ticket purchases, get-rich quick schemes, lawsuits, and playing the market. Industry is moving elsewhere, while banks, credit institutions, and investment venture groups make hay with the artificial manipulation of domestic wealth.

In 1991, Singapore's national savings rate was 43%, compared to 3.2% in the U.S. From 1980-1990 there was an annual budget surplus in Singapore of 10.5%. In the U.S. deficits averaged 4%. If we had Singapore's surplus instead of our deficit, Washington would now have trillions of extra dollars in their coffers instead of owing that much.[1]

The American middle class is taxed to death to support the progression toward socialism. The starting income tax rate in Singapore is 3%, and half of their taxpayers pay less than $150 per year. In America, a person's combined taxes can reach 60% or more. Per capita annual income has increased five-fold in Singapore since 1975, while our income has actually fallen in real terms since 1973.[2]

Similar revolutionary things are happening in Thailand, Malaysia, and China. China, in fact, if it attains even the per capita wealth of Taiwan, will be a larger economy than the rest of today's industrial world combined. Presently almost one-half billion dollars per day are being invested in China by foreign interests.[3]

"How 'bout more jumbo and less mumbo."

There are many reasons for the rising success of these economies. These reasons provide empirical proof that short-sighted socialistic trends do not work. Only to the degree that China subverts its socialism with free enterprise does it become economically prosperous. Also, the cultural beliefs of these developing nations do not accommodate free rides. People there are much closer to the reality of what is required to survive: tend the chickens, gather the eggs, hoe the fields, or starve. They think paying people welfare for not working is a drug that has sapped the vitality out of the West. Asian governments also spend very little on health and social security. This creates a mindset in workers that they are responsible for themselves and must work hard, save, and manage money wisely. American entitlements and union guarantees create the exact opposite mentality.

For those who might believe that life is unduly harsh in these countries, consider that a baby born in Hong Kong can expect to live two years longer than an American or British baby. Families in the Far East save and provide for their own and let government spend its budget on education, industry, and infrastructure. Asia's secret is this: Get skilled, work hard, save, tax little, make quality products the world wants at affordable prices, and invest in good schools and a strong infrastructure.

This global economic shift is an attack on status quo in America. Our immediate reaction is to keep things as they are and deny the inevitable. This is manifest in the "buy American" movement and the outcry about outsourcing jobs to other countries. But these are like the final convulsions of a sinking ship. We are sitting atop a historical correction that is bigger than any cries of protest.

Prosperity will not return or be secured by a union vote, a law mandating economic isolation, or refusing to buy anything manufactured in whole or in part outside the country. This would be like a company trying to save its market share and fat salaries by sending a letter to customers demanding that they continue to purchase the company's products.

America became prosperous because of entrepreneurship, creativity, and hard work. Once prosperity came, its inertia permitted a generation to ride the tide and receive much for very little. But a something-for-nothing economy is a bubble that must burst. The fat prosperity America once enjoyed will never return to its inflated size. But we can at least be competitive if we return to the ethic of value given for value received and if government unleashes free enterprise by curtailing socialistic parasitism and disincentives.

How Companies Think

American businesses and their employees cannot have the high failure rates they do in the face of a world economy. Businesses fail in principle, if not literally, when money, rather than a worthwhile idea, is the objective. Employees fail in large part because they do not see that they are in the business of selling worthwhile services and are not merely entitled to wages.

Business owners are often frustrated by not being able to give employees a sense of what it is like to start a business from scratch, that jobs do not just appear out of thin air, and that success is not automatic or just the result of being 'busy.' A business is like a living creature that needs understanding, nurturing, kindness, creative feeding, and protection. It is not a horse to ride into the ground.

How Companies Should Think

Unfortunately, many people have come to believe that mere presence at a job, past experience, or academic credentials are sufficient to justify wages. The notion that they should actually produce something that could at least translate into their wage does not even register. This is in large part because there is this chasm of understanding between those who have the responsibility of business on their shoulders and have no guarantees, and those who receive a guaranteed wage. Couple this lack of employee understanding with politically fueled class warfare—corporations vs. public; rich vs. poor; white collar vs. blue collar; salary vs. hourly—and the seeds for malcontent and business ineffectiveness are sown.

Everyone must see the reality: Something must be accomplished or produced quickly enough so that return exceeds the costs and wages of the project. Otherwise, expenses are not covered, there can be no wages, no growth, and ultimately no jobs or business. It's a simple equation but few people take it to heart in our guaranteed wage and entitlement-leaning age.

Businesses must be especially careful to not become part of the 85% that fail within the first few years. Such a dismal statistic is not by accident, bad luck, or fate. If the beginning idea is good and there is a market, there can be success. But there is much more to it than a good idea, printing a logo on pens to give away, and calculating that if only 0.001% of the population buys a product and the margin is X%, that profits and success are a cinch…so why not borrow money and enjoy the fruits of success now?

Succeeding in business is neither easy nor glamorous. Too often, aspiring entrepreneurs look glassy-eyed at effects: the envious lifestyle and income of those who have succeeded. They don't see the hard work, failures, sacrifice, disasters, risks, and time that even modest success requires. Nor do they see the litter of dashed dreams and devastated personal assets scattered over the failed business landscape.

Business and employees must face the reality that there are no guarantees other than that good results come from hard, smart, and relentless work. That employees and employers find themselves at odds makes no sense, particularly in the face of the limitless competition of the new global economy.

> Jack Benny is walking down the street, when a stick-up man pulls out a gun and says *"Your money or your life!"* An extremely long silence follows. *"Your money or your life!"* the thug repeats. Finally Benny says *"I'm thinking!"*

50

THE POWER OF MONEY

EVERYONE THINKS ABOUT MONEY. Few, however, stop to think about how money originated and then evolved into a mechanism of power that institutions and any common person can wield to exert great good or bad.

Money's original purpose was to serve as a convenient medium to replace barter. It represented hard work on a one-to-one basis. The blacksmith toiled for a day shoeing horses and got five dollars. The farmer harvested for a day and got five dollars. Each of them could then take their five dollars and go buy whatever they needed, understanding that what they bought would represent fairly the fruit of their day's labor. Back when money was only hard currency that could be held in hand, it was an accurate reflection of the useful work that had been performed. But money could only accrue in a very limited way since a person could only work so much.

Over time, money has transformed from coins and bills providing functions of exchange, into abstract units of account. Money can now take on a life of its own through clever buying, selling, and financial schemes of multiplication. This was particularly enabled when the dollar was taken off the gold standard in 1972 and the financial world became interlinked with computers. The dollar trading pit at the Chicago Mercantile Exchange was opened and from that point the value of money was determined by a few

243

thousand speculators sitting at their computers around the world betting moment to moment on how the value of the dollar would change relative to other currencies. There are 1.3 trillion speculative dollars exchanged every day, thirty two times that which is spent on work and production. That is a bubble that one day must burst.

The simple solution to globalization and falling income

Arguably, it is unfair to accumulate money disproportionate to the work used to create it. However, instead of marching in lockstep with work, money has careened off on its own to create a monetary world that behaves like a gigantic casino. Luck, inheritance, lawsuits, working financial markets, fraud, and graft can create huge amounts of wealth. It is now possible to amass enough money totally apart from work, that one never has to do useful work at all. Those who are successful at this sleight-of-hand are envied and considered clever heroes of capitalism.

Cash in hand has become obsolete. Money has transformed into cyber digits in a banking computer program. This tends to separate money from the value of work it is supposed to represent. One could potentially become fabulously wealthy in an instant by an error that simply moves the decimal point to the right in a bank's computer. When hard money was the only unit of exchange, such a thing would not be possible without a lot of work figuring out how to rob the bank and enough manpower to wheelbarrow the loot away.

The point being, once money changed to mere numbers on a ledger and then to electronics, it became more easily manipulated and construed as something other than a representation of work. People can now rob banks sitting alone in the living room with a computer accessing credit cards that are not theirs. If they are clever and lucky enough they can legitimately become wealthy trading stocks, bonds, and futures, playing on-line poker, or by any number of other means using nothing but a keyboard.

Such undeserved largesse may seem innocent enough at first glance, but money has become the prime mover, the power that shapes the world. Money is the medium of essentially all interactions. It affects roads, schools, utilities, environmental protection, social aid, medical care, defense, industry, religion, and even close personal and family relationships. The leading cause of divorce, for example, is money. The flow of dollars directs and shapes society and every individual's life.

Since any individual can fall into wealth and the power it wields, any hare-brained idea can take center stage in society. Barbaric ideologies can threaten the world just because those holding them happened to have pitched their tents on sand that boiled up black gold, or conquered a land

Which Is The Meaning Of Life?

rich in agricultural fertility, minerals, or gems. Money is like the sword in the stone of King Arthur legend. Once it is pulled out, special powers come to its holder. It's also a Golden Rule—whoever has the gold rules.

Institutions that have gained ascendancy because of money can be particularly dangerous because of their reach into society. If an idea is profitable for enough people, regardless of how it may eventually harm, it remains. The gasoline-powered automobile is a good example. Although born out of the need for better transportation and the ideal of improving society, it remains in spite of much better ideas. Efforts to use more recyclable materials, stop obsolescence from cosmetic model changes, and create nonpolluting and more efficient engines are stymied because those who reap money from the system hold the reins of power.

Modern medicine is another example. The medical system began with the ideal of healing. But now, with over one and a half trillion dollars annually circulating through it in the U.S. alone, its way of conducting patient care remains. This is not because of merit but because of the sheer weight of the many dollars holding it in place. For example, drugs that are known to kill persist in the market until the cost of litigating deaths exceeds profits from sales. In the meantime, the FDA, not wanting to disturb billion dollar industries, may do little more than require re-labeling—like requiring stronger warnings that the drug may cause serious harm or death.[1] There are far better approaches to healthcare than naming diseases and treating symptoms. But such ideas remain on the fringes and are not afforded the opportunity to establish legitimacy because they threaten status (money) quo. In the meantime, millions die and suffer from preventable and reversible diseases. Even epidemic death and suffering caused by the medical monster itself has not forced rational clarity.

It is tragic that the only way things usually change is when crises force us to rethink our position. Our motto seems to be: Money first and solve no crisis before its time. For example, if oil ran out or enough people were suffocating from pollution we would have a new form of automobile engine. But until then (even though pollution is a problem and oil reserves are clearly finite), economic forces will keep things as they are even if things as they are clearly take us down a slippery slope.

The course of history follows the money trail. The corruption and demise of every developed civilization stems from powers with the financial reins to keep bad ideas in place. The situation is far more critical today because human problems are global, not local.

Once we come to understand that many of the ideas and institutions in our world are in place because of money, we can begin to see things as they are. It becomes clear why nonsense can seem to be ruling our world. Money can make bad ideas look good, and good ideas appear evil. The burden is therefore on each of us to measure the merit of any idea with thinking, not by a popularity that can come from nothing other than the power of money.

We, the people, can also use money rationally by supporting those individuals and institutions that set ethics and principles before profit. Money must not be used in a moral vacuum. It is within our reach to use reason and principle to create utopia or spend our way into environmental, social, political, or military oblivion. Industrial, political, medical, and other institutions are not destroying our health and world—we are by giving them our money. Purchasing power is the most influential power ordinary citizens hold. All we need to do is exert it as if thinking matters.

"Oh no... last week's stuff!"

246

51

FINANCIAL AFFAIRS

IT IS EVERYONE'S PERSONAL RESPONSIBILITY to save sufficient money for future security. Nobody should place the burden of their care on government, family, or children. But, contrary to popular belief, getting to that point is not a matter of loaning and borrowing. Shakespeare wrote: "Neither a borrower nor a lender be; for loan oft loses both itself and friend, and borrowing dulls the edge of husbandry."

Nevertheless, borrowing has become standard practice. Note how many advertisements there are from banks, loan agencies, debt consolidation companies, credit score services, and attorneys who will help you declare personal bankruptcy (legally renege on all your debts) or help you get out of an IRS obligation for pennies on the dollar. All of this economic mismanagement subculture is spawned by people who insist on living beyond their means. Now about 50% of all earnings goes to service debt. As a result, the majority of people will end up outliving their assets.

Saving should be hammered into children and practiced throughout one's work life. Saving is one thing, investing is quite another since it puts money in others' hands. Yes, there is that tantalizing prospect of having money create more money without having to do anything other than give someone money. The something for nothing carrot is usually a trap. Perhaps that's why those who invest our money are called brokers.

Investing is gambling; it is just not stigmatized that way. Also, once the control of money is relinquished to another person, there is the very real concern about whether the money will be returned when it's asked for. Money is like glue in that it sticks to whoever has it. Its adhesion gets particularly aggressive when possessed by those who do not own it. Like a vast sea, money can drown truth, honor, and conscience.

Certainly not everyone is dishonest. But that is never known until money is surrendered to another person. Then all bets are off. And don't think that our legal system and governmental controls will prevent an investing disaster or being outright defrauded.

Even mainstream, publicly traded, governmentally scrutinized, blue chip company stock is risky. Bonds, futures markets, precious metals, bank debentures, oil and gas leases, and high yield investments are all gambles, other than for their sellers. If investing were a science, as it is often marketed—complete with impressive charts, graphs and mathematical formulas—then it is a science that would have long ago been used to drain the entire market.

Fair warning: if it seems too good to be true, it is. That is sage advice we have all heard countless times. But it is wise counsel nobody wants to heed until they are burned enough times to see its truth. You think that you could be the lucky one, that your situation is different, and that the people offering you the opportunity are honest and trustworthy. Then like a balloon loses air and a watermelon seed squirts from the fingers, you will lose your money.

The greatest responsibility faced with a nest egg is to keep it from being stolen or devalued. Just keeping money, not having it grow through clever investing, is the primary challenge. So before turning savings over to another, be skeptical, ask for proofs, take time, talk to references, see pressure and deadlines as a sign of scam, get it in writing, know the recourse if things go wrong, search the Internet forums, take more time to ponder, consult bankers (a very conservative voice), and listen to friends, family, and intuition, not greedy desires.

Forget the stories about people getting rich quick. It won't happen to you. Banks are happy getting only a few percentage points on loans. Do you know more about investing than they do? Banks do everything they can to not gamble. Result? Banks flourish while get rich quick investors file for personal bankruptcy in unprecedented numbers.

Companies and people succeed not because they gamble, but because of industry, frugality, and sound, conservative business and financial practices. Yes, people have struck gold in 'them there hills' but you will not be one of them. Persist in thinking in this way and all you will do is strike it rich for the vultures ever present to prey on you.

Hi again Ralph! I'm Bill, that telemarketer you just hung up on... About that special stock you just have to get in on...

©Wysong

Be careful and very conservative with hard-earned money. Getting money is like digging with a needle, spending or losing it is like water soaking in sand. Be content with security rather than dreaming of investment windfalls. Don't gamble with money needed for survival now or in the future. Also, try to be a productive person as long as you are physically able. You are your best investment. When all else can fail, your honest hard work is something that can always be banked on.[1]

It is one thing to fulfill the responsibility for future security, but the ladder-climbing pursuit of money can be so distracting and consuming that we can come to believe that it in itself is life's purpose.

Making our financial way in life by becoming self-sufficient and caring properly for our families is certainly one of life's most important responsibilities. Poverty and hand-to-mouth existence leave little room for moral development, healthy decisions, ethical concerns, or environmental stewardship. Saving trees, stopping pollution, doing cancer research, and protecting endangered species are not high on the priority list of a population that is starving and freezing.

Moreover, not properly caring for personal responsibilities shifts the load to society at large. This in turn plays into the hands of governments always eager to steal from others in order to dole out to you to save you from yourself and secure your vote. The end result is socialism, which ultimately destroys economies and lives. Without a free economic infrastructure, nations cannot have healthy commerce with other nations. Healthy international trade is the most effective impediment to war. Nations don't find it very beneficial to kill their customers.

We all have a financial responsibility to rise above poverty. But being fiscally sound is one thing, chasing an alluring pot of gold is another. Everyone can agree that being poor is not the place to be, but few understand that being fabulously wealthy may not be all it's cracked up to be, either.

It would appear that the rich and famous, movie stars, and sports heroes have it all. But would we really want the responsibility of always being under public scrutiny, being perfect, managing mountains of money and possessions, and having no privacy? Not one of these icons, after having arrived, if they have anything other than a nub on top of their spinal cord, feels they have achieved life's purpose.

The wisdom of all the great sages is that money is not life's answer. But people insist that they would like to prove to themselves that money does not bring happiness. So on to the money chasing treadmill they go, convinced that when magnate status is achieved all woes will end and happiness never known will surely appear—blossoming out of a mound of riches.

It is a grand cultural illusion that the prestige, power, position, and goodies money can create bring happiness or meaning. Such things can be occupying, challenging, and fun for a time. However, money is unlike most other physical things. Like a child, it never just sits in a chair and behaves itself. Something is always happening. Even when we try to put it in a bank to go to sleep it is either losing or gaining value.

The love of money may be the root of all evil, but the mere possession of it in excess can be the root of a whole lot of misery. Riches look like a beautiful present, but when the pretty packaging is unwrapped there is a list of burdensome chores. Because of the options it creates, money is a tremendous responsibility. It forces us to make choices. The more money, the more choices. Fine, you think. Making choices between models of Ferraris would be no problem whatsoever. But if one's whole life becomes a matter of constant choices, what fun is that? A Ferrari will not just sit there. It needs care, an ongoing stream of choices.

Our imagination and the media present phantasmagoric images of idyllic lives in mansions, yachts, and limousines. But this is but a veneer of what life is really like for those who have to manage such onerous material monstrosities.

Copious non-necessities can also nag the conscience. How is using up Earth's resources for superficial pleasures justified? We know there are philanthropic purposes the money could be better used for. Excess money (money beyond basic needs and that needed to secure future independence) is an opportunity to do good, not just lavish oneself. It is even arguable that personal use of money that squanders Earth's resources and is used for anything other than basic survival is immoral.

Bob got smart and worked the system. A little scheduling using vacation, sick leave, disability, unemployment, flex time, e-mail, teleconferencing and job sharing, and he could stay home all day, play video games and still rake in the big bucks.

However, if we listen to the inner voice and decide to give money away, we are faced with a big chore. How do we know the money is going to the target need or lining the pockets of con artists or 'administrators'? The graft that occurs in supposedly non-profit organizations is now well-known. But even the legitimate siphoning of funds in such organizations is astonishing.

I formed a non-profit organization in part to try to ferret out organizations where donated money is efficiently used. We wrote queries to organizations that advertised that they helped victimized children, asking for an accounting of how donated money was used. Here are a couple of the results. One Christian organization was paying their president $360,000 per year. Another group had six "vice presidents" each making over $150,000 per year, and their president got $250,000. (Proving that although some people make counterfeit money, more frequently, money makes counterfeit people.)

An interesting and satisfying life has to do with what we do, not what we have. Exploring, growing, and doing good are the things that are fun. The life of the 'rich and famous' is only wonderful from the outside looking in.

Once a person has 'arrived,' it is an empty state of affairs unless he or she is busy being useful, active, creative, challenged, and helping others. If leading an interesting and engaging life is what fulfills us, then what is the point of all the obligating toys and ambience for leisure and sedentary living? As we look back on life, will a memory of a purchase or the memory of hard work and sacrifice be more fulfilling? Buying something is empty; it's something anyone can do. Accomplishing something is what life is really about. Few live life well in that regard.

Perhaps the best advice is to try to die poor by using up the fruits of life in helping the true victims in society. Victims are those unable to change their bad circumstances, or who are not responsible for the hopeless situation they find themselves in. True victims are homeless and abused children and animals, the environment, and the legally or politically oppressed. Giving money to those who are not true victims only robs them of life's duty and greatest pleasure: taking responsibility for ourselves.

Money is not all it's cracked up to be and certainly not a cause for envy. More appropriate would be a deep thankfulness, that oh, but for the grace of God, there we be. True wealth is taking responsibility for one's own life and knowing that we have enough.

"Miss Jones, phone someone and have them hold for me."

52

WORK AS FRIEND

BUSINESS, WORK, AND THE FLOW of money they create are the lifeblood of society. A person in the wild must work hard constantly in order to survive. There is no choice. Although modern economics permits some to do no work and yet bathe in the lap of luxury, we cannot forget our roots and the fact that it is not natural to get something for nothing. Society can remain viable only if honest work and pay are exchanged. Unfortunately, it is a common inclination to be lazy, to want to return to the nest where moms and dads provide our every need and our most important responsibility is to have fun.

Socialism feeds these desires, leading people to believe they have every right to expect to have a mommy and daddy forever. That leads to feeling entitled to government, wage, and benefit handouts. A handout is something for nothing. That may be fine in philanthropy, but business and work are hard reality, not philanthropy. Reality is cause and effect. It is a false reality when an effect, money, comes without its proper antecedent cause, productive work.

Our country is clearly sliding into the false economics of socialism. I say this not as an outside observer, but from a lifetime of experience. So that you do not feel that the perspective I relate is skewed, here is my work resume. Beginning in gradeschool, I delivered newspapers, sold ice cream (where a lesson was learned about eating profits), mowed lawns, and sold little hot pads (my siblings and I made) door-to-door. In my teen years I moved on to farm work, construction labor, retail clerking, union factory production line assembly, chemical process operation, and laboratory work. As an adult I have experienced every aspect of small business operations, inventing, teaching, building, medicine and surgery, and, obviously, writing.

From this vantage point, and looking at work as if thinking matters, it seems clear to me that the primary danger to society is the something-for-nothing attitude that is swelling in the ranks, the sentiment that business is the enemy, and work is what we can get away with. Certainly there can be irresponsibility by business owners. But businesses cannot survive long in this fashion since they have no benefits and entitlements. There is no business unemployment, no paid vacation, and no retirement. A business cannot quit today and find another job tomorrow. Business must face the reality of producing something real and of value day in and day out, and do so with the resources available, or they die. Business must face the cold, hard, economic reality that something does not come from nothing.

Many politicians attempt to convince the public that they can give them something for nothing. To buy votes, they promise worker's rights, guarantees, and entitlements. Unions do similarly. Both effectively deny that employees are in fact businesses selling their product, labor. As such, workers should have to face the same hard economic realities as any business—either produce a worthy product, or risk survival. When work is seen in the hard light of this reality, we become more productive, creative, and take responsibility. That attitude, in turn, can result in not only security, but a sense of worth that can only come from seeing work as a friend.

Standing in the way of the friendship between work and worker, and a sustainable economy, are artificial structures that create an attitude of entitlement. Consider, for example, the false logic of unions. What if all grocery stores got together and decided how to price our food? How about if they decided to only be open from 9:00 until noon, or shorten their open days to only three a week? What if all automobile manufacturers, gasoline stations, clothing stores, utilities, and restaurants did the same? Why, that would be an outrage. There are monopoly and fair trade laws that expressly forbid such rigging. By colluding, they remove competition and free enterprise—and with that our opportunity to make choices.

Are not unions de facto monopolies? When employees get together and fix a wage, benefits, hours and forbid firings under threat of strike, they remove the employer from a freely competitive manpower marketplace.

An employee's services are no different than a product. Workers should be able to market services to the highest bidder (called a job search) just like a company should be able to sell its product for the highest price it can, and buy its supplies (including human services) at the lowest cost. Just as a consumer has the right to not buy a product if they feel it is priced too high, a company (consumer of human services) should not have to purchase an employee's time if they feel the price is too high or the employee's work product is not satisfactory.

An employee—or union, or government—does not have a right to force an employer to pay certain wages or benefits any more than an employer can force customers to purchase products they don't want at a price they don't want. By interfering with the free enterprise labor process, unions can force employers out of competition. When that happens, employees kick the legs out from under their own chairs.

Legal Meeting of Union Officials

"Let's all agree to charge our customer, the company, the same."

Illegal Meeting of Company Officials

"Let's all agree to charge the customer the same."

Some may argue that if unions weren't around, there would be worker abuse. That fear is a carryover from the early days of the Industrial Revolution when there were few industrial jobs compared to the spate of immigrants. Companies cannot now underpay or abuse workers, not only because there are laws preventing such, but also because that is not how companies can keep good employees. Employees are also free to leave and go to another employer if they are unhappy or feel their services are worth more. If an employer is foolish enough to abuse good employees and under-reward them, they will be spelling their own demise.

The effect of unions (or socialistic government) on personal initiative can also be counterproductive. If a person feels that once they are a part of a union that they can then thumb their nose at the company and work at a mediocre pace, a basic human need is unfulfilled. I once worked in a unionized factory on my way through school. If I worked hard or fast I was firmly pressured by my comrades not to "kill the job." Tokenism was the modus operandi. The unwritten rule was to stretch things out and maintain a lower performance standard so there wasn't increased pressure on fellow workers. On the other hand, those who could find a place to hide and take a nap were considered clever, cute, sort of heroes for sticking it to the 'evil' company.

MINIMUM WAGE LOGIC
1. Force all companies to pay a minimum wage.
2. All companies must raise the revenue to pay the higher wage by increasing the price of products by at least a proportional amount.
3. Employees with the new minimum wage pay for products at a higher price at least proportional to the wage increase.
4. Net effect: no gain.

Not one of my clever coworkers would ever tolerate such behavior when their money was at stake. Not one would go to a hair solon, sit in the chair, be draped, and then pay a stylist who clipped a section of hair, then went into a back room and read a magazine until closing time. Yet workers who do essentially the same thing at their jobs fully expect to be paid.

No economy can survive if ambition, creativity, initiative, drive, and competition are suppressed. Guaranteed rewards for mediocre work deny a basic human need for creativity, ambition, and pride. Although an employee may be temporarily financially advantaged and secured by guarantees, it is counterproductive. The thing sought in order to have a happy and full life—a guarantee—is the very thing that will eventually deny a happy and full life.

Socialism and unions create a lot of fuss, great anticipation of benefit, but net a zero—if not negative—balance. For example, if all companies across the country were forced to increase pay, there would be no net gain to employees. Companies must create the additional revenue for the higher wages by increasing the price of products the employees and their families must in turn buy. In effect, this then offsets the buying power of the increased wage. Net result? No gain for employees.

This is the same ultimate result from government interceding like a union and increasing minimum wage. Companies do not create wage money out of thin air or have a bottomless vault they can just dip into whenever needed. Raising the minimum wage sounds good on a political platform, but when companies proportionately increase the cost of their goods or services to pay the increased wages, the buying power of employees is reduced by the same amount their wages were increased. The net effect is votes for socialist demagogues, and that's about it.

The socialistic attempt to level the playing field denies the hills and valleys in the field. There will always be inequities. That's okay as long as there remains opportunity. Life is not about guarantees; it's about challenges. If a person is not making enough money, enough stuff is not filling their garage, or they don't have enough days off, then

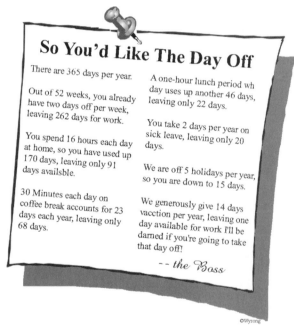

So You'd Like The Day Off

There are 365 days per year.

Out of 52 weeks, you already have two days off per week, leaving 262 days for work.

You spend 16 hours each day at home, so you have used up 170 days, leaving only 91 days availsble.

30 Minutes each day on coffee break accounts for 23 days each year, leaving only 68 days.

A one-hour lunch period wh day uses up another 46 days, leaving only 22 days.

You take 2 days per year on sick leave, leaving only 20 days.

We are off 5 holidays per year, so you are down to 15 days.

We generously give 14 days vacction per year, leaving one day available for work I'll be darned if you're going to take that day off!

-- *the Boss*

©Wysong

they have the freedom to change that. Employers are not the problem. In a free society, individuals are their own problem. For greater rewards, all that is necessary is harder and smarter work. If that does not do it, then find a job where it does. Another option is to start a business, hire employees, and prove they can be treated, benefited, and rewarded better.

We are entering a world economy where there will be many job casualties. Being out of work can be a disastrous life experience and can take a toll on physical and mental well-being. It will be an increasing challenge to keep a job as companies are pressured to justify every pay-check in order to stay competitive in a world market. To remain valuable, workers will need to shift their attitude from one of entitlement broker, to that of vendor. Workers must understand that they are in the business of selling their services. Like any business, they must make their service valuable, important, and in a constant state of improvement. Otherwise, who will want to buy them?

If out of work, make finding a job the job. Don't study about how to create an inflated resume or deceive in an interview. Be honest, be yourself, and give a clear picture of your ambition, abilities, and short-comings. Employment is like marriage. Unless a real ugly relationship and a divorce are desired, be straight up front.

Develop a skill. If you don't have one, make ambition, honesty, and energy your skill. If that doesn't work, try this: Tell a prospective em-ployer you are willing to work for free for a time to prove yourself. Why not? What's the difference between that and going to school? School is work without pay; in fact it's work that the employee (student) must pay for. Any new job is like school for a time anyway. So why should an employer, someone who can create income for you (a school doesn't), pay employees to learn if a school doesn't? We should be thankful if a new employer does not charge for the training.

If such an offer is made to a new employer, you will certainly have their attention and a good shot at an opportunity. If that doesn't work, pester them. Pestering tells them you are not or-dinary and are determined. That's what employers need and can't find.

When you land the job, give it your all; don't stop looking for work just because you found a job. Don't settle in or ponder workers' rights. Politics may be waxing socialistic, unions may preach rights, but there are no such things as guarantees in the business world. Work hard, don't measure work or hold back. Think about what can be done to help the company compete and survive, not about how little can be done for the most wages and benefits.

Above all, be sincere... even if you don't mean it.

As I write this and observe two of my children laboring over college coursework as they live at home, I am reminded of the remarkable paradox between school and work. Students diligently go to class during the day and then come home and continue to work evenings and weekends. They work with urgency, meet deadlines, and stay up into the night. To do all this work *they* pay thousands of dollars for tuition and books. All they receive in return is a report card. In contrast, many graduates will land a job and expect that job to pay for their entire life and yet would never think of doing homework, sacrificing a break, exceeding deadlines, not having to be reminded, or going above and beyond the minimums of a job description. School is seen as a rite of passage, a ticket to high wages and benefits. In fact, it is only the beginning, just a key to open the door to where real work begins. Considering that only 40 out of the 168 hours in a week are spent on the job, and that 40 hours must support the whole 168, with the prevailing attitude of entitlement it's a wonder how any employer survives.

The key to job success is to think supererogation—give more than expected. Ask for increased responsibilities. Bring jobs to completion quickly even if unpaid time is necessary. If there is free time on the job, clean, organize, repair, help others, and learn skills that will increase your usefulness to the employer. Do these things because of pride, to be a shining star in the workplace, a great model for others to follow, and to be indispensable. Take pride in the workday by doing the best that can be done even if *you think* it may be of more value than what the wage might be.

If you deserve a raise, don't read a book on how to ask for one, make it crystal clear by performance that it is deserved. Time does not create a reason for a raise; increased performance that brings increased value to the company does. Make yourself invaluable by creating more than you earn and most employers will reward accordingly if they are capable.

Keeping a job is about respect. Respect for self and for the employer. The way to show that respect is to be diligent, honest, work hard, and make supererogation a word taken to heart and applied every day. Such qualities are so rare that those who possess them have the best job security there can be.

Why? Because these qualities are almost impossible to find. Instead, employers have to struggle to keep workers on task and prevent the ruination of their businesses. As an employer in a small business I have experienced many fine and good hearted fellow workers, but also things

I could have never imagined. In one case we had developed a device that would require assembly when the customer received it. So we decided to make an instruction video. The person put to this task decided to do it after hours and add a little flair to the film. So he set the camera up to film himself as he threw in a bunch of crazy antics including shedding all his clothes. He then sent the video to a female customer. Another employee was tasked to take a load of recycling to the recycling center and instead took it home, burned it in his yard, and used the time to plow his driveway with the company truck. A salesman who assured us of his good Christian character developed his own brand of a competing product, copying verbatim our literature and labels, while still on our payroll. A trusted employee was allowed to use a company residence with his father. They then proceeded to get into a bloody drunken brawl and trash the home. A burly large male employee tried for a legal heyday by claiming that horseplay among the guys was sexual harassment because one of them touched him. Two employees had a regular affair in the bathroom. Several have spent time on the Internet with dating services, their own Internet businesses, and on porno sites. Occasionally there are those who, once hired, feel they have a right to all company property. They simply help themselves to money, products, tools and equipment. Most of these folks have moved on, but how they will ever make a living is a mystery.

In this age of downsizing, outsourcing, and bankruptcy, guaranteed job security has become a thing of the past. It is a difficult and tragic circumstance to be looking for work in our middle or later years. On the other hand, we must empathize as well with owners and managers who must contend with the things they do from unscrupulous workers, as well as make hard, life-altering decisions by releasing employees in order to keep a business viable.

On the bright side, there is no lack of jobs. But there is a lack of people who dig in with all they have once they find a job. Not just for a 30-day spurt during a probationary period, but for the duration. The problem for many is that hard work builds a future; laziness pays off now.

Work is one of life's best friends. Treat it well and it will return the favor. But the usual thinking is that work is just a necessary burden. Let's rethink that a bit. Isn't it through work that money is created that permits all the comforts, security, and many of the circumstances for joy and leisure in life? Why think negatively of something that brings so much, even survival itself?

The reason in large part lies in the fact that we're independent creatures. Work can obligate us and give the feeling that we are not in control and that we are victims of the selfish interests of others. Whether real or imagined, that view of work can make life very unpleasant and even take a toll on mental and physical well-being.

If the money reward is the only objective at work, that creates a duty-bound misery. This brings to mind a personal experience. While going through school, I worked in a large industry that paid and benefited generously. But the prevailing attitude was that the company owes everyone, never does enough, is unfair, and on and on. People weren't quitting, though. They knew they could never get similar compensation elsewhere, so they would stay and then moan and plod through the motions of work. They were prisoners bound by golden handcuffs.

There was also an 'us versus them' tension that cast a negative gloom over the entire workplace. This was, in part, fed by the socialism imposed upon the employer through unions and government regulations that created a sense of entitlement in workers. Socialistic politicians and media are also always on the ready to feed the ever present desire of workers to think of themselves as victims. Since business was supposedly only about money, the 'company,' and those in management who made the most money were looked upon with envy and viewed as the enemy. Once such propaganda sets in, it swells like yeast to infest and overcome workers so that they think in terms of what they should get and demand, not what they should be giving.

But giving is better than receiving. This is a life rule that does not switch off when a person punches in at work. To go to work with a 'what's in it for me' attitude turns a person into a ghost looking for a body to inhabit. Any job can be like licking stamps all day long or flunking high school over and over. It's up to us.

Work occupies a majority of the active life of everyone. It would be a shame to waste so much of life in an activity that brings dread rather than hope, optimism, fulfillment, and fun. When you love what you do, you're alive. (Jobs.com) Work should be more like a hobby than a sentence. It should be a cycle of perpetual challenge and fulfillment, like being on a treadmill where as soon as you get to the end of it you begin again. Ambition at work should be like love, intolerant of delays, distractions, and rivals.

The solution to work doldrums primarily lies with the employee. The enjoyment we derive from an activity has everything to do with our attitude toward the activity, not the activity itself. Work must be approached as if we mean it, as a challenge to do our very best so that we can walk away feeling a sense of pride. Challenge and accomplishment is never the path of least resistance. We should not work like a horse just when the boss is riding us. We can't hold back and be like the person who, upon hearing that work never killed anyone, said he was not going to take the risk.

We are creative beings and if we do not exercise that creativity we are miserable regardless of the wages and benefits we may receive. Work is the perfect place for creative release. One should never go to work without an objective for the day. There is always opportunity to improve, increase efficiency, save costs, and enhance quality. The self-respect that comes from achieving a goal is the best pay of all. Anyone can be a millionaire at that.

Working hard and doing well at something is the only way to make good things happen in life. A good result at work brings a feeling of honesty and worth. These are essential psychological nutrients we all need every day. If a person permits time to pass without them, he will suffer a malnourishment that turns life itself rancid. Nobody can feel good about himself or herself knowing that they are, in effect, stealing wages.

If fulfillment and happiness are not part of work life, things won't change for the better upon retirement. Health fails and life is shortened in a retirement where nothing productive lies ahead for each day.

People, money, and dreams will fail us in life. Work, on the other hand, can be a lifelong companion, one that will never let us down if we put ourselves in control by working hard and like we mean it. It can, for as long as we permit, bring a sense of worth, purpose, and meaning if we treat it like the good and loyal friend it can be.

LIFE WISDOM FROM BILL GATES*

Rule 1: Life is not fair - get used to it!

Rule 2: The world won't care about your self-esteem. The world will expect you to accomplish something BEFORE you feel good about yourself.

Rule 3: You will NOT make $60,000 a year right out of high school. You won't be a vice-president with a car phone until you earn both.

Rule 4: If you think your teacher is tough, wait till you get a boss.

Rule 5: Flipping burgers is not beneath your dignity. Your Grandparents had a different word for burger flipping: they called any chance to work an opportunity.

Rule 6: If you mess up, it's not your parents' fault, so don't whine about your mistakes, learn from them.

Rule 7: Before you were born, your parents weren't as boring as they are now. They got that way from paying your bills, cleaning your clothes and listening to you talk about how cool you thought you were. So before you save the rain forest from the parasites of your parents' generation, try delousing the closet in your own room.

Rule 8: Your school may have done away with winners and losers, but life HAS NOT. In some schools, they have abolished failing grades and they'll give you as MANY TIMES as you want to get the right answer. This doesn't bear the slightest resemblance to ANYTHING in real life.

Rule 9: Life is not divided into semesters. You don't get summers off and very few employers are interested in helping you FIND YOURSELF. Do that on your own time.

Rule 10: Television is NOT real life. In real life people actually have to leave the coffee shop and go to jobs.

Rule 11: Be nice to nerds. Chances are you'll end up working for one.

*(Although I have not been able to verify that this Internet circulated quote is actually from him, it is unlikely that he would disagree with its wisdom.)

SECTION I

Thinking about. . .

SOCIETY

IN THIS SECTION: *Although freedom is everyone's desire, once we left the woods and decided to pack together into society, imposed order became necessary. Order requires rules, and rules infringe on freedoms. The only way to strike the fine balance between freedom and the necessary limitations upon it is to apply thinking and the long view. If we do that, the world can come to unity, there will be no unfair discrimination, no despotic governmental oppression, decency, safety, and justice will prevail, and all people will be free to achieve their potential.*

53

GOVERNMENT

BEFORE PEOPLE GATHERED into complex societies, government was very simple. The might of the patriarch, matriarch, or the strongest member of the group maintained order. Those who disagreed were clubbed into submission or could move on into the vast untamed wilderness. As agriculture developed and food could be stored, people transitioned from hunter-gatherers to farm-based communities. Numbers swelled and leisure permitted more time for amour. Thus was born civilization.

Rubbing shoulders with increasing numbers of neighbors brings problems that need an arbiter, a central authority. Unfortunately, rather than people getting together and rationally devising a social order, rule by bully continued. Aristocracies were formed and obedience to their edicts was assured through brute force and fear. A few public beheadings, burnings at the stake, a disemboweling in the central square, and corpses skewered on stakes around the city went a long way in making citizens compliant no matter how malign the dictatorship.

With time, the desire for freedom among the masses grew. Great minds began to reflect on the proper form of government. The ancient Greek philosophers are generally credited with introducing the concept of democracy. Later, the English limited the power of kings with the Magna Carta and the House of Commons. Having lived for millennia under despotic rulers, freedom, and a voice in the shape of society must have been an exhilarating prospect for the ordinary citizen. [1]

Society has been toying with the balance between freedom and the rule of law for thousands of years now. Each of us would like total and absolute freedom, but would really rather that our neighbors have some constraints. We know our own hearts and minds, but do not know and are usually suspicious of the motives of others.

This brings us to the central issue at the core of government: is man basically good or is he bad? By 'good' and 'bad' I mean, can humans be trusted to look after the interests of their neighbors and society as a whole, are they always selfless and honest? After thousands of years of evidence, the answer is pretty clear. We are not altogether a very trustworthy lot. The longer our leash, the more nasty many of us are and the more trouble we get into.

So constraint (government) is clearly a necessary evil. It is also necessary because there is evil. In an ideal world, people would self-govern. Kindness, selflessness, generosity, and ethics would obviate the need for laws and punishment. But such is not the world of our reality. Humans cannot be trusted and must be controlled in order for everyone to at least have the opportunity for some measure of freedom, peace, and security. Government fills that role, but must be carefully and thoughtfully designed and monitored.

I would like to venture into this topic from the perspective of what the best form of government could be, its responsibilities and limits, and how people who would destroy peace and security should be dealt with. I do this not just because it is interesting, or that I want to add yet another opinion, but because the subject again demonstrates so vividly how misled the majority can become and how clear and open thinking is the solution.

It would seem that the ideal government would be the least government so that people could have maximum freedom. This would mean that people would need to be trusted. Most certainly they should be—we just better not trust the devil in them. So governmental rule is the price to keep the devilish nature of humans in check.

As we grow into adulthood, it is natural for the tensions of roiling youth to manifest in an uncertainty and suspicion about authority. We come to just plain object to others telling us what to do. When we are young we never cease to be amazed at the stupidity of our elders; as we add years to life we come to be amazed at how much those elders learned in the intervening years.

Some stay in this cynical and rebellious mode for life. Universities are particularly suited for propagating this idea because abstract theories about freedoms and equality can be advocated without experiencing the consequences of their real world applications. For those who leave the university and the protest marches, life out in the real world begins a new stage of intellectual awakening—or should.

The strong libertine and socialistic current today is a manifestation of this university-type thinking. It attempts to deny the necessity of rules and embrace the naiveté of youth. When we are twenty we feel we have no heart if we do not extend blanket understanding and compassion to rule breakers; when we are forty we have no brain if we do not see that rules, laws, and limits are essential.

A social and moral decision based only on compassion that makes us feel good about ourselves is irrational. Taken to its logical end: Rape could be justified because 'nobody is really harmed' and rapists have sexual needs; murder could be excused because people have a right to be upset and anyone can lose their head when really angry; theft and arson forgiven because kleptomania and pyromania are 'diseases.'

The enthusiasm and impatience in youth to right wrongs is both commendable and excusable. A child does not have the knowledge or experience to measure social, health, environmental, political and economic ramifications. But in the adult world things should be different. Attempting to fix the symptoms of hunger, poverty, economic inequality, and other social problems using shortsighted, libertine, and socialistic principles may seem compassionate and understanding, but such fixes do not address the underlying causes and real solutions.

LEFT TO OUR OWN CHILD-LIKE DEVICES of shortsighted compassion and freedoms, the very fabric of society would eventually unravel. There must be rules and limits. The ideal government to effect that would be an all knowing, all wise, benevolent dictator; a kind and selfless person who governs with pure reason, wise foresight, flawlessly determines guilt, and punishes and deters the bad guys with perfect justice.

The best benevolent dictator to yet come along filling that bill is a paper one, a constitution. What a clever idea. Great minds can sit down soberly and confer on defining a perfect governmental dictator. It's like creating the ideal person on paper, a ruler who governs with perfect justice, protects freedom, allows some flexibility and adaptation, does not grow old, become inept, and does not have an ego that might take over and change things for nefarious or selfish reasons. A constitution is a contract, too, because it assures all citizens that government will behave in a certain way into perpetuity. We don't have to worry about its mood, health, hormone surges, insecurities, megalomania, favoritisms, biases, or ambition.

How Communism/Socialism Works

At Work   At Home

In contrast, some would argue that communism/socialism—from each according to ability, to each according to need—is a better idea. What could be more fair than everyone working as hard as they can and everyone having all their needs taken care of? But the necessary subtext for this idea is that it presupposes that people are inherently selfless—that they will indeed work as hard as they can and willingly donate the fruits of their labors to be redistributed. They aren't. So communism (used interchangeably with socialism here) theorizes the way society ought to be (one gigantic, selfless commune), not the way it is (self-serving and dangerous). Treating the world as we would like it to be is to live a fantasy. That's not what grown up thinking adults should be doing.

Communism naively assumes that everyone will delight in being a team player and forget about individual desires. But the majority is not going to muster their full measure of ambition and creativity if they are not proportionately rewarded. Why break out a sweat at work if the rewards are spread to those who do no sweating? Why work hard if needs are taken care of no matter how hard you work?

America's early history taught a lesson that needs to be remembered. It seems that the colonists decided that everyone should put the fruits of their labors into a common stock, and withdraw only what was needed—communism. The problem was those capable of work resented their results going to women, children, and others not pulling their load, so they stopped working. Only about one fifth of the men worked and the others just freeloaded. The result was a famine in 1609 that dropped the population in Jamestown from 500 to 60. To solve this, leaders in Plymouth and Jamestown gave everyone a piece of land and permitted them to keep what they produced—capitalism. The result was bounty so great they even began to export.[2]

Since work is the thing that drives an economy and provides the money to distribute to all "according to need," if incentive is killed and people refuse to work, they must be forced to. Thus communism has never been able to function without the heavy hand of government. Some of the world's most oppressive and despotic regimes have emerged in attempts to implement this political ideology.

In fact, communism takes root because of oppression, such as in the autocratic czarist state. An economic blight swept across Russia in large part due to a selfish aristocracy. Their circumstances were quite different from a free society wherein people can earn their way to whatever station they desire and are capable of. A free society presents no cause for a communistic revolution. Economic differences are a symptom of freedom, not oppression. They are the sprouts from the seeds of liberty, not weeds to be scorned, trod upon, and used to incite riots.[3]

Nevertheless, there is always pressure to implement communistic ideas because they *sound* so fair and compassionate. Marxists tend to even adopt a presumptuous sense of moral superiority. Redistributing wages through an income tax, social 'safety nets,' welfare, and minimum wage laws are examples of beneficent communism in action. Such policies may seem fair and compassionate on their surface, but they can spell the beginning of the end for a free society. (These arguments are not to suggest that society does not have the moral duty to extend a helping hand to the truly helpless and needy.)

Socialistic actions spread over the masses siphon off individual initiative, the very stopper that allows the economic sink in a society to fill. Pull it and eventually there will be nothing left for government to dip into to redistribute. Politicians who try to impose communistic/socialistic principles to cure economic imbalance are trying to cure dandruff with a guillotine. They are often an especially slippery group of do-gooder self-promoters, who, under the pretense of intellect disassemble the very fabric of self-responsibility that holds a free society together. At best they are blind fools, at worst moral frauds. For citizens who wish to rise up out of their station, the solution is not a gift from government, it is freedom and opportunity.[4]

If communism seems fair on its face, so, too, does democracy. What could be more fair than majority rule? No dictators, no tyrants, no kings or queens, just 'we the people' ruling ourselves. Simple enough—or so it would seem.

Plebiscite (majority rule) is neither fair nor rational because 51 percent of the people could vote to do away with the other 49 percent. Also, there is the tacit assumption that voters are informed. But such people are a rarity. Uninformed voters create government by ignorance, leaving the informed minority at the mercy of the uninformed majority. Rule only by consent of the governed gives no assurance of a rational or sustainable government.

Another fallacy of democracy is that voting is said to be a patriotic duty. The duty is to become informed enough to vote intelligently. If a voter is not informed, they should not vote. In fact, why should it not be illegal to do so? A nation that expects to be ignorant and free is expecting something that cannot be.[5]

In a democratic republic such as America, is it not obvious that no voter should be allowed to cast a vote unless they can pass a test demonstrating their knowledge of the Constitution? They should also be able to pass a test proving that they understand the issues and the positions of each candidate. A monitored voter literacy test should be given to every eligible citizen who desires to vote. Why not? We do it for driver's licenses. Maintaining freedoms and integrity to the Constitution are at least as important as driving a car. Steering a nation is no less important.

People elected should have ethical character, high intelligence, a clear vision of the Constitutional principles of individual responsibility, and be one of the people, not an imperious career politician type. Unfortunately, political races in America increasingly look more like popularity contests of debutants where paper mache figures move across a sound stage saying whatever will gather votes. For some politicians, the most important qualifications are some degree of cultivated English and the ability to discern and pander to hot button issues. Politics has become the second oldest profession by copying the first as closely as possible.

Selfish uninformed voters in a democracy make the important unimportant and vice versa. For example, how many politicians would ever get voted into office if they ran on a platform of: Making everyone pay an equal share of taxes; putting a limit on the weight of a vehicle being used for personal transport; prohibiting voting without a passing score on a voter's literacy test; limiting the size of homes; penalizing people for families beyond a certain size; installing a luxury tax on all non-essential goods; placing a moratorium on all urban sprawl; requiring that all criminals pay restitution to victims and earn room and board while incarcerated (see below); fining all land owners who do not properly maintain their property; requiring that all people who are able bodied earn their own sustenance and support their offspring; charging people per pound of garbage and requiring everyone to recycle and compost; prohibiting the manufacture of any commodity that cannot be reused or recycled.

Each of these policies may be rational and serve the long-term interests of society, but the majority wants no part of it. They insist on their freedom and right to not have their lifestyle disturbed no matter whether it destroys society or not, and that is what they will vote for.

Because of the general ignorance and shortsighted view of most of the public, democracy can become nothing more than a gangplank to eventual totalitarianism and economic blight. American voters endorsing socialism and increased taxation present such a clear and present danger.

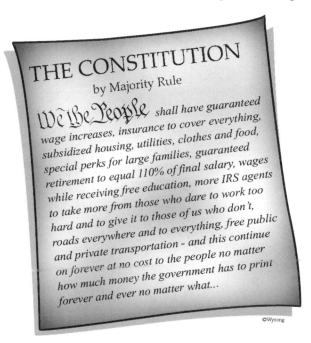

Cries of injustice often arise because of the economic disparity that exists. On its face it hardly seems just that the wealthiest five hundred people in the world have a net worth that exceeds that of the poorest three billion.[6] At the same time, everyone feels that people should be able to exploit their talents, work to their hearts' content, and enjoy the spoils thereof—the Constitutional guarantee of "the pursuit of happiness." But the latter is not possible without the former. If economic unevenness exists in a free society (all other things being fair and equal), it must be seen for what it is: a manifestation of the inherent inequality among people. People should not get to 'have' things; they should get to earn them. People are not doomed to 'have not;' they make the choice to not earn. The most important freedom is the ability of people to move up and down the economic scale, not the guarantee of economic equality. This is not to deny that help should be extended to people who find themselves in an impossible and hopeless situation over which they have no control. In fact, if there is to be economic intercession, it should be helping the bottom pull themselves up, not dragging the achieving top down.

Those who have earned Constitutional "happiness" (economic security) also usually attain the time and resources to think about the greater good and a higher purpose. A free enterprise system makes it possible for the common person to rise up out of a mundane hand-to-mouth existence and have the power of a king to do good. Earning "happiness," not having it guaranteed, also teaches valuable lessons about cause-effect relationships that are essential tools in personal success and in valuing the world. So, the existence of success honestly earned in a free society is not a problem needing a solution; it's reason for celebration. It means that freedom for the common person to earn Constitutional "happiness," and to reach out to make a better world is alive and well.

Regardless of the form of government, money is needed to run it. When we enjoy benefits such as roads, military protection, and social order, there are bills to pay. Public schools have a price, policemen need wages, sidewalks need to be constructed, roads graded, and a border defense maintained. Paying those bills with tax revenues is both necessary and fair. Taxes also help keep government in check. A government that has to ask its citizens for taxes is a government that will be held accountable. Without motivation by rulers to win the favor of the public, the needs of the people are too easily dismissed or ignored. Some of the world's most oppressive regimes have emerged in nations where rulers are awash in wealth from natural resources.

Since everyone in society should have to pay for the benefits and services they receive, the question of how to tax is quite simple. There should be a use (toll) tax where it can effectively be applied. For the remaining costs, government should tally its bills, divide the total by the number of citizens, and come up with a per capita fee, a citizen tax. Send the bill to every adult monthly or yearly. What could be more straightforward or just? What other club or organization that brings benefits—not even approaching those in the American citizen club—does not charge dues?

POLITICS AND COWS

Liberal - You have two cows. Your neighbor has none. You feel guilty for being successful. Instead of giving your neighbor one of your cows, you cry and then write to your congressman, demanding that he pass legislation for government programs to help your neighbor get a cow. You convince a pop-star to put on a concert to raise awareness for the cow-less, who couldn't attend because ticket prices are so expensive that only people with 3 or 4 cows come. You wear a pin that signifies that you care about cow-less people and condemn those who have more than one cow—but you are careful to keep your cows.

Conservative - You have two cows. Your neighbor has none. So?

Religious Right - You have two cows. Your pastor finds a Bible verse that proves you have a right to them. Your pastor has an affair with the milkmaid who has no cows. You send a donation.

Socialist - You have two cows. The government takes one and gives it to your neighbor. You form a cooperative to tell him how to manage his cow.

Communist - You have two cows. The government seizes both. You wait in line for hours to get your cow's milk. It is expensive and sour.

Capitalism - You have two cows. You sell one, buy a bull, and build a herd.

Democracy (*American Style*) - You have two cows. You vote for politicians who promise to give cows to everyone. Government taxes you to the point you have to sell both to pay for all the cows being given away and to support a man in a foreign country who has only one cow, which was a gift from your government.

Bureaucracy (*American Style*) - You have two cows. The government takes them both, shoots one to prevent overpopulation and grazing on wetlands, milks the other, pays you for the milk, and then pours the milk down the drain.

American Corporation - You have two cows. You sell one, lease it back to yourself and do an IPO on the 2nd one. You force the two cows to produce the milk of four cows. You are surprised when one cow drops dead. You spin an announcement to the analysts stating you have down sized and are reducing expenses. Your stock goes up.

American Non-profit Corporation - You have two cows but don't admit it. You run television ads and send mailings pleading for people to send more cows to you. You raise your salary so all the donated cows do not create a profit and you retain your non-profit status.

American Unionized Corporation - You have two cows. The union has a meeting and demands one employee per teat plus longer breaks and more vacation. One of the cows doesn't get fully milked and its udder explodes because all the milkers were having a grievance committee meeting. OSHA fines you for unsafe working conditions and the union goes on strike because you sent your other cow overseas to get milked at a fraction of the cost. You're picketed with "Milk American" signs and demands that you retrieve the exported cow and divide it and the exploded-udder cow among the workforce to cover pensions. You go bankrupt, the workers are out of work, and there are no more cows.

Politically Correct Corporation - You have two bulls. You must rename them bovine Americans and treat them equally with the female. Employees are regularly maimed and killed attempting to milk them.

French Corporation - You have two cows. You go on strike because you want three cows. You go to lunch and drink wine. Life is good.

Japanese Corporation - You have two cows. You redesign them so they are one-tenth the size of an ordinary cow and produce twenty times the milk. They learn to travel on unbelievably crowded trains. Most are at the top of their class at cow school.

German Corporation - You have two cows. You engineer them so they are all blond, drink lots of beer, give excellent quality milk, and run a hundred miles an hour on paths with no speed limits. Unfortunately they also demand 13 weeks of vacation per year.

Russian Corporation - You have two cows. You have some vodka. You count them and learn you have four cows. You have some more vodka. You count them again and learn you have eight cows. The Mafia shows up and takes over however many cows you really have.

Taliban Corporation - You have all the cows left in Afghanistan, which is two. You don't milk them because you cannot touch any creature's private parts. Then you kill them and claim a US bomb blew them up while they were in the hospital. You send radio tapes of their mooing.

Californian - You have a cow and a bull. The bull is depressed. It has spent its life living a lie. It goes away for two weeks. It comes back after a taxpayer-paid sex-change operation. You now have two cows. Only one makes milk. You try to sell the trans gender cow. Its lawyer sues you for discrimination. You lose in court. You sell the milk-generating cow to pay the damages. You now have one rich, transgender, non-milk-producing cow. You change your business to beef. PETA pickets your farm. The Rainbow Coalition makes a speech in your driveway. Socialists call for higher farm taxes to help "working cows." An aspiring presidential candidate calls for the nationalization of 1/7 of your farm "for the children." Illegal immigrants demand a law giving your farm to Mexico. The L.A. Times quotes five anonymous cows claiming you groped their teats. You declare bankruptcy and shut down all operations. The cow starves to death. The L.A. Times' analysis shows your business failure is a Republican president's fault.

(Adapted from Internet circulated e-mail.)

But no, rather than do something rational and consistent with Constitutional principles (such as the right to the "pursuit of happiness"), politicians have done a very slippery thing: tax citizens based upon income. It is no fairer to base tax on income than it is for a gas station or grocery store to charge based upon the size of your last pay stub. If there are those who work especially hard and do well, why on earth should they be forced to pay a larger share of the common costs of running a government? The focus of government should be to protect the freedom to pursue the American dream and achieve success, not punish it. But that's exactly what the scaled income tax does.

U.S. TAXES

Accounts Receivable Tax	Real Estate Tax
Building Permit Tax	Recreational Vehicle Tax
CDL License Tax	Road Usage Tax (Truckers)
Cigarette Tax	Service Charge Taxes
Corporate Income Tax	Social Security Tax
Dog License Tax	Sales Taxes
Federal Income Tax	School Tax
Federal Unemployment Tax (FUTA)	State Income Tax
Fishing License Tax	State Unemployment Tax (SUTA)
Food License Tax	Telephone Federal Excise Tax
Fuel Permit Tax	Telephone Federal Universal Service Fee Tax
Gasoline Tax	Telephone Federal State and Local Surcharge Tax
Hunting License Tax	Telephone Minimum Usage Surcharge Tax
Inheritance Tax	Telephone Recurring & Non-recurring Charges Tax
Inventory Tax	Telephone State and Local Tax
IRS Interest Charges (tax on top of tax)	Telephone Usage Charge Tax
IRS Penalties (tax on top of tax)	Utility Tax
Liquor Tax	Vehicle License Registration Tax
Luxury Tax	Vehicle Sales Tax
Marriage License Tax	Watercraft Registration Tax
Medicare Tax	Well Permit Tax
Property Tax	Workers Compensation Tax

Taxes – For those who think the abolishment of the income tax would leave government without resources, consider the above. Not one of these taxes existed 100 years ago. Then, the United States was the most prosperous country in the world, had no national debt, the largest middle class, and only one parent had to work to support the family. Socialism has a price tag.

Once we've settled what government should be like and how it should be paid for, we must turn our attention beyond our borders. No matter how well we govern affairs in America, an unsettled world always looms ready to spoil things. If we set aside fears about loss of 'sovereignty' and conspiratorial notions about a 'new world order,' one must wonder why the world is divided up as it is in the first place. Why is it not one universal organization? The Earth is just one round globe. It is circular and by nature continuous. We all breathe the same air, drink the same water, and walk on the same ground. It seems silly to treat a circle as if it had beginnings and ends. Each of us individually needs some private space, but rights of territory beyond that do not serve the world's common welfare. Obviously, one benevolent world government with absolute authority, one set of rules, and an international court is the only way the world can ever have a shot at being at true peace.

The Logic of Income Tax

Such a world order of things will not come so much by design, but because information is flowing more and more freely around the world. As people learn that people everywhere are just like them, borders will increasingly become irrelevant. Commerce will also do much to effect this change. World summits, trade treaties, and accords all increasingly bring pressure against borders. A free world market sends workers to where the money is, and business moves to where labor is cheapest. With time, this will result in a leveling of the world's standard of living. We see this happening at present as third world countries industrialize, win markets, and increase their standard of living, while developed countries lose markets and wages plummet. Over time, as this unfolds, the desperate migration of people will abate, and at least some of the causes for war will disappear.

Human Evolution

One world where fairness rules, resources are properly managed, the environment is protected, and everyone has freedom and a fair chance in the pursuit of happiness is utopian. Particularly does it seem a distant dream when in a free society, such as America, government panders to ideas of multiculturalism—a hodgepodge of hyphenated Americans with no unified language.

But why not a one-world ideal? Can our conscience ever be at peace while there are those in the world who have no chance of a decent life just because they were born behind the wrong border or under the thumb of a tyrant?

Which brings us to the question of what free nations should do about despotic and oppressive regimes? Being a pacifist is the easiest thing in the world to be. But reason and ethics dictate that our hearts must be tempered with reality. We can't turn a blind eye toward, sidestep, or accommodate torture, murder, and other unspeakable crime while we sit comfortably in our homes excusing our inaction with responses born of moral smugness like, "we can't police the world," or "killing is a sin." That amounts to taking a leave of absence from ethics, not taking charge of it. Permitting suffering we could prevent in this life, in order to secure our place of bliss in the next life, is cause for shame, not moral pride. Until we have a new world where all nations, leaders, and peoples lead moral and just lives, those who are moved by conscience have no choice but to intercede to save those who are oppressed. However, if battles are fought, it is morally obscene to send primarily young innocent people who have no mature understandings, or played any part in politics, to be killed and maimed.

If Neighborhoods Were Like Nation-States

Not only must nations be held accountable, but so, too, must individuals. Rules and laws mean nothing if they cannot be adjudicated and enforced. Justice within society should not depend upon expensive lawyering, and the innocent should not be behind bars due to overly aggressive prosecutors trying to make a name for themselves. The legal and criminal system as it stands generates huge economic incentives, and, as we have seen repeatedly in this book, all it takes is money to nail bad ideas in place.

Let's consider the dilemma of what society is to do with criminals. Since prison populations are growing at three times the rate of the general population, this is no small problem. Certainly dangerous criminals must be secured safely away until such time as there is reason to believe they are no longer a threat. That, of course, is the theory behind the present penal system. But how does it make sense to lock people away in expensive facilities providing for their every physical need by sending the bill to society? Meanwhile, the victims of the criminals are left with their injuries and abandoned. Why does the criminal not have to repair the damage to victims or those left behind bereaved?

A secured restitution work farm would be a rational alternative. Criminals would be employed producing useful labor or goods in order to pay for the victim's medical bills, lost work, and incapacities. Moreover, the criminal must pay all the costs to society for investigations, trials, and room and board while incarcerated (a great motivation for those guilty to admit it and reduce the legal costs).

This is not to suggest a chain gang, but rather passable work and living conditions with the product of labor going where it should, to the victims and society. U.S. companies are always looking for a labor force. Well, here it is, right on our own shores, and numbering over two million.

The time it takes for economic restitution would by and large dictate the length of the term, unless the person is a clear threat to society. For example, if you attack another, incapacitating them, then you have to spend whatever time is necessary earning the money to take care of them. Those who take another's life must substitute their own life with a lifetime of productive work to repay society and the victim's family.

How can discipline be maintained on the restitution farm? Well, a hard day's work will leave little energy for much more than rest. As it is now, prisoners lollygagging in cells all day have nothing to do with their energy other than scheme more wrongdoing. Discipline could be maintained with the threat of an extension of stay and longer work shifts. As it stands, life in prison is cozy enough that many criminals prefer life there.

Such a system based upon restitution would both deter crime and offset the damage created by it. Unlike the death penalty, the restitution farm would not have the potential of unjustly taking the life of another since time would be provided for proof of innocence.

How Prison Works   **How It Should Work**

There is nothing better to sober someone up and drain them of the energy to think up evil deeds than a hard day's work. Even dog trainers and behaviorists know enough to exercise and tire an aggressive and fractious animal to make it more compliant. For minor offenders who have a stint in these restitution farms and are then released, they will come to know what work is. Experience they gain could actually improve their resume for work when released. Also, the word would be spread on the street that crime means hard work, not just prison condo living. If they repeat offend, then society will not be the one to suffer. Criminals should be self-maintaining, even a profit source, rather than an economic sinkhole.

SOCIAL AND GOVERNMENTAL PROBLEMS are not so complex and insurmountable as they may seem. Like all other problems, they only arise, remain, fester, and grow if we let emotion, money, selfishness, and short-term interests, rather than thinking, matter.

54

THE END OF CIVILIZATION

CIVILIZATIONS COME AND GO. As things are going, ours is probably no exception and will go as others before it did. But it does not have to be that way. Barring a natural cataclysm that could send us the way of the dinosaurs, there is no reason our society could not continue on indefinitely. Even improve.

That would, however, mean applying the SOLVER principles with a particular emphasis on the long-view. All actions and policies now must be measured in terms of their effects into perpetuity. Our problem, and that of every civilization that has preceded us, is that humans tend to behave as all other animals do: We want all we can get right now, with little regard for what we leave for our children and theirs.

The Constitution with its idealistic principles tied to practical rules, demonstrates that we have the capacity to formulate a civilization with staying power. That's because every aspect of it was crafted to protect the future. However, once the document was framed and nailed on the wall to display how smart we could be, we turned our backs and once again set about unleashing our shortsighted selfishness, under the guise of progress, compassion, fairness, and rights to every licit pleasure. The progressive view today does not defend and embrace standards and rules, it dissolves them. It is now considered enlightened in some circles to grant every person practically total freedom and unaccountability.

This track denies nature. All of nature has rules. Although unwritten and unspoken, in a primitive and savage way, right and wrong still exist there. The alpha wolf decides what is right in the pack because it possesses the physical and psychological power to exert its will. A tree may dictate what is right by exuding allelopathic chemicals into the soil out to its root perimeter in order to extinguish competing plants. A lion takes prey from a hyena and a hyena takes it from a leopard because that is the order of things and therefore the right thing. Instinct and physical attributes decree this form of morality in nature.

Society, the in-your-face conglomeration of masses of people possessing tools and weapons that can inflict damage far beyond that of mere fang and claw, requires lots of rules and lots of alpha enforcement. Otherwise, the population would regress to a might-makes-right brutal anarchy.

Today, even obvious crimes like murder, theft, rape, and business graft are being excused with clever manipulation of the legal system, 'understanding,' and 'compassion.' In large part, such accommodation of sociopathic behavior derives from a belief that we do not really control our destiny but are victims of our circumstances: genetics, upbringing, race, and socioeconomic class. This belief, in turn, springs from an even more fundamental belief that we are mere matter and as such do not have control. In other words, a decision to murder someone is really not our decision, but could be the consequence of chemical reactions and electrical discharges in our brains that in turn obey laws of physics and chemistry. This materialistic mind set could lead us to think that every movement, every act, should make us want to exclaim, "Well I'll be darned, look what I just did. I just don't know what came over me!" In other words, we have no free will because we are victims of neurological biochemistry. If we have no free will there is no point in punishing anyone for any act they may perform.

This belief in materialism, and the question of whether we have free will, are discussed at length in the companion book. So I will not explore it at this point beyond identifying these issues as underlying causes of much of the emerging attitudes toward rules and accountability. For present purposes, it is clear that we at least seem to make choices and have free will, and that some of those choices could clearly result in the demise of civilization.

It is evident to most people that crimes against others should be policed and punished. We want to be safe when we walk down the streets and sleep in our homes. But our efforts to get at the causes of crime are almost totally misdirected. Rather than encourage true intellectual and skill development, society attempts to lower standards, accommodate, and excuse. Typical examples are the public school system shifting downward the requirements for high school graduation, and colleges being forced to admit students with lower test scores than others. Rather than tighten controls on the media and entertainment so that standards of decency and morality are protected, there is a race to remove virtually all limits. The same people who would argue that we are victims of our circumstances seem to overlook that what people see and hear influences what they come to believe. What they believe is what they do.

But never mind all that. Ratings have become king. People respond more enthusiastically to horror, shock, fear, and celebrities than they do to good news and beneficial instruction. News casts will spend weeks on the death of Princess Diana, but ignore educating the world on the steps necessary to change the circumstances of hundreds of thousands dying of disease and starvation. The benefits to Iraqi citizens and the world from the overthrow of Saddam Hussein is virtually never heard while the media pummels the world audience with only the costs of effecting that change. The good news of people lifting themselves and their fellow man up to make a better world are ignored, while the worst of news is dredged from the depths of human depravity and featured over and over. The U.S. casts the recent Russian pressure on media to feature at least fifty percent good news as draconian, but it is at least a sane step in the right direction. Those permitted access to the public airways must lift society up, not just drag it down for the sake of dollars.

The end of civilization will not likely come because society degrades to the point that overt crime against fellow citizens is openly permitted. It will more likely result from ignoring the causes that erode the rule of law, such as short-sighted socialism discussed in the previous chapter, and the 'renorming' of social mores with entertainment that celebrates such things as vulgarity, violence, lewdness, indiscretion, disrespect, and open sex.

Aren't there lines we all sense that should not be erased? A proof that these lines do in fact exist is the emotional release from swearing and the humor of a dirty joke. People everywhere use these psychological tools that depend upon forbidden zones. Somehow we intuitively know what is off-color and profane. We sense what lends itself to a higher human standard and what degrades and threatens society.

When rock-n-roll began, Elvis's gyrating hips drove traditionalists and parents crazy. Sodom and Gomorrah had returned. Kids scoffed. The old fogies just didn't get it. For the young, rock-n-roll was way too cool and certainly no more than innocent fun. But today there is filthy language in rap and hip-hop, and sexually explicit entertainment even our young children can easily access. Try as I may not to be a mossback, there seems a clear a difference by way of degree between Elvis and music today that celebrates demeaning sex, murder, civil disobedience, and every manner of vulgar language.

At the present pace, where will it end? There are now films and video games of rape, murder, and torture. They are justified by some as 'artful free expression.' Really. Aside from not being able to discern any conceivable value in such entertainment, might it not be numbing and create insensitivity, particularly in our impressionable children?

Since children know that adults—moms and dads—create such entertainment, might they not feel that such behavior is validated?

We keep edging ever closer to the Roman Coliseum. In the special front row seats there, a person could enjoy hearing bones break, getting sprayed with some real blood, or having a lopped-off appendage land in the lap as a souvenir. The Romans worked hard to prevent boredom among the citizens. For over 400 years the cruelty and gore for man and beast in the arena took on every imaginable grotesque creative form in order to maintain the interest of audiences. The Roman Empire is no more. The moral degradation of its society and its failure to think long-range is in large part the cause of its demise.[1]

285

Clear standards seem to be vanishing fast in our entertainment 'coliseums.' There is now practically bare-fisted, few-holds-barred bloody competitive fighting on television. There is full-contact teen dancing that looks exactly like the sexual act. Gay and straight TV shows where free for all sex is the theme glut programming. Erection commercials are interspersed in family television programming. We're also treated to bare breast exposure, bumping and grinding, ignited horse flatulence, and bestiality jokes during the family formatted Super Bowl. The new wave of reality shows seems to have no limit in their reach for stupidity, shock, and horror. Now the average American TV-drunk home has more television sets than people so that none of this quality programming will be missed.

In the mayhem of shock and titillation, it is hard to get the needle on our moral compasses to point in any clear direction. Violence is now even applauded with a perverted, bloodthirsty fiendishness. If in doubt, pan the audiences at professional boxing, ultimate fighting, wrestling, and when fighting mayhem breaks out during the more tame sporting events. Consider even the packaging of war as "shock and awe" by government and media.

Sex, an act meant for committed adults capable of shouldering the responsibilities of family, is presented as a mere recreational thrill-ride for people of all ages. Even the President is excused on television when he gets caught on company time, on company property, swinging from the Oval Office chandeliers with an intern. Children get to hear about thongs, cigars, and sex act details that make parents blush, while the President is given a pass by large segments of the population because "sex is a personal matter."

The media, pandering to the cheap-thrill seeking masses, engage in a never-ending cycle (more like a downward spiral) of profiteering one-upmanship. Each new provocative display raises the ante and challenges the competition to push the envelope even further. The goal is to shut down the thinking forebrain of the audience and enliven the base instinct hindbrain.

It might not be quite so alarming if a large and profitable part of the audience were not children. They need education, rules, and time to develop conscience, not alluring entertainment. They are the society of the future and should be protected and nurtured accordingly. Instead they are being brainwashed with confusing smut, vulgarity, and every form of base biological, violent, and criminal urge. Without sufficient life context they are easily led to believe that that is what life is about, how it is celebrated, and what they should aspire to.*

Schools are tightly controlled because they shape the emerging buds of future society. In the larger classroom of the world, the media is emerging as the school. As leisure time increases, people feed more and more on entertainment. What a wonderful opportunity through the impact of story to raise the public's sense of right, dignity, conscience, reasons and ethics.

The old time, so-called corny movies were clear attempts to do just that. The good guys always won and everyone was decent except the bad guys. How far (down) we have come. Entertainers should see their unique powers of influence as something other than a profit opportunity to promote depravity and to pander to those who evidently love to be dumbed-down. But for too many, as George Bernard Shaw observed, "Virtue is insufficient temptation."

How do we judge what is or is not socially redeemable and will serve the long-term stability of society? Use the SOLVER extrapolation principle. Ask whether we will advance or degrade if the action being promoted were universally practiced. Will open and free sex without regard for age, gender, or responsibility and commitment create a better society? Will the celebration of crime, filthy language, fighting, disrespect for parents and authority, sexism, racism, ageism, and the like create a better and lasting society?

The answer is not difficult.

VULGARITY, VIOLENCE, CRUDENESS, disrespect, and easy sex are marketed like candy. Will this moral slippage lead to the end of civilization? All we can say is that it does not seem to be improving it. However, there has also been some trade-off between virtues lost and those gained. Perhaps the disassembling of arbitrary puritanical standards is necessary for society to find their moral footing and build something more solid and meaningful. So long as we do not get mired in this moral floundering, end up concluding that there is no right course, and that nothing really matters, we may escape our doom. Maybe the b-movies where the good guys wear white and the bad guys always lose is a fantasy. But it is a good one; an ideal that we should set before society to reach toward.

*I recently watched a movie called Idiocracy. It is available on DVD and I would encourage you to watch this humorous look at the dumbing down of society and where we are headed.

55

FREEDOM IS NOT EQUALITY

FREEDOM IS A GREAT IDEA and most societies have come a long way in advancing it. Unfortunately, it seems that all good ideas with a good start in principle and intention veer off once people lock on to them and they pick up steam. Once any idea is applied apart from reason, all bets are off.

For example, there are movements afoot to make schools multicultural in the name of freedom and equality. It's difficult enough to accommodate just Spanish, Chinese, Vietnamese, and Ebonics. What happens when the Bantus immigrate here with their 500 languages? No society can hold together if its population balkanizes into factions that cannot communicate with one another. At an airport a 90-year old white female American citizen in a walker is practically strip searched to prevent a terrorist attack, while a young Arab man carrying a Koran is allowed to pass so as not to profile. The media will occupy the airways night after night in discussions about somebody of note saying the "n" word. Pressure is on the military to give slight female soldiers the same front line hand-to-hand combat positions as muscled up men. In an attempt to not be discriminatory toward pets, they are now called companion animals (why not feline and canine Americans while we're at it), and their owners, *guardians* and *caretakers* rather than pet owners.

In the zeal to root out bias and insure freedom, we have confused freedom with equality. In attempting to make everything politically correct by being equal, we have lost our grip on reason. Changing terminology, proscribing words, making a law, or creating a social program will never achieve the objective of making people equal. But all is most certainly not lost since freedom is not the same thing as equality anyway.

ALTHOUGH RACE HAS BEEN WORKED and reworked to the point of creating racial fatigue, the issue that matters seems to have been lost. For example, slavery denied blacks their freedom. To right this wrong, both blacks and whites went through the throes of the Civil Rights era. Freedom means the ability to explore and pursue one's talents and to enjoy the rewards. Equality means two people are the same in all respects, sort of in a mathematical sense. Freedom is possible, equality is not. Since no two people are the same, no two people will have the same result from their go at life and thus cannot be equal in their relative stations. They can, however, be equally free. This simple truth is ignored in the racism debate.

The only thing about racism that can be solved is freedom, not results. Everyone should have the right to open a business, but everyone should not be guaranteed success. Everyone should be able to try out for a football team, but not everyone should be guaranteed to make the cut. So, quotas for each race in each sport, in each business, and in each school make no logical sense. People should be what they have earned.

Let's also face a reality nobody likes to talk about by considering the obvious answers to these questions: Do some Caucasians not prefer the company of African Americans? Do some African Americans not prefer to be with Asians? Would some Hispanic business people rather hire Hispanics than Russians? The answer is yes in each case, and no governmental policy is going to change these innate comforts, likes, or dislikes.

The American business community thrives in spite of racial preferences. There are all-Chinese, all-Vietnamese, all-Spanish, all-Greek, all-Jewish, all-Italian, all-male, all-white, all-gay, all-black, all-young, all-old, and all-female businesses. This practice not only does not impede success, it can help create it. It is de facto discrimination, but it does not really encroach on freedom. It's just an expression of the reality of inequality and preferences that exists between all people.

When someone hires another, picks a mate or friend, votes for a candidate, moves into a neighborhood, or chooses a school, the spectrum of variables are assessed with prejudice. This cannot be stopped, not does it need to be for people to have freedom.

By attempting to force racial melding, we deny the reality that birds of a feather flock together. That is not an anomaly; it is virtually a scientific law. There is a natural tendency for creatures to prefer to associate with those most like them. Build a big saltwater fish tank. Put in couples of a hundred different species of fish. Give them a few days. They are all fish, but they will all pair up with their own kind. Even within a given race, people will preferentially gather in their families and give preferences accordingly. It's just the way things are.

Notice that since the Civil Rights era, with full freedom guaranteed, races have reinitiated segregation. There are Hispanic, black, and Chinese clubs and causes. There is Black Pride Day, the United Negro College Fund, Black History month, black-only colleges, Martin Luther King Day, the NAACP, BET, Cesar Chavez Day, and so on. There are even reversions to native cultures and school curricula supporting such. The largest voting blocks for candidates come from voters of their own race. (Ironically, the most enthusiastic are those who clamor for "racial equality.") This tendency toward preferences and segregation does not mean different races cannot come together in peace and harmony; it just means that in the main they prefer their own kind. That does not need to matter.

What about the argument that some races have at one time been abused by another race as a justification for special treatment centuries later? The problem is that all people can claim historical subjugation. Japanese and German U.S. citizens can point to World War II imprisonment in America; the Chinese can bemoan railroad labor oppression; Native Americans can complain about loss of land, genocide, and forced internment on reservations; African Americans can point to slavery; immigrants can recall an existence that included child labor and wages less than would permit survival. Anyone can dig into their history and find abuse of their ancestors. Does that give anyone the right to special treatment by the descendents of the subjugators? If I am Jewish and my neighbor a German, should he now be mowing my lawn for free?

The racial issue has become the perfect excuse for government to further entrench socialistic practices. By the socialist's logic, no one should be better off than anyone else. The socialist is particularly guilty of confusing equality with freedom. The assumption that all people can be equal denies individuality and even biology. It is heterogeneity and variation in nature that create the potential for biological and social improvement, and in some instances survival itself.

In the clamor for political correctness, even the obvious difference among the races is denied. If there were no differences we would not be able to delineate race to argue about it in the first place. Differences are not only skin-deep. Races differ in many anatomical and physiological ways. These differences can be linked to environmental factors that helped shape their genomes. Eskimos are rounder, shorter, and fatter (170 lb. average) and have higher (warmer) metabolic rates than taller and skinnier Algerian Berbers (125 lb. average) living in the desert. This doesn't make one 'better' than the other, just better suited to different climates. The rounder Eskimo has less body surface exposed to the cold, and their higher body fat creates insulation and increased (warm) blood volume. The Berber needs no insulation and the greater body surface area helps cooling.

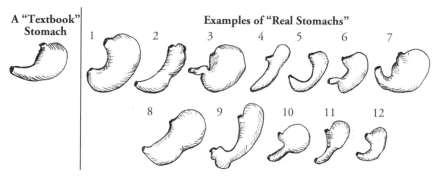

Human Stomach Variety – Everything inside a human varies from one person to another. Obvious differences among people are more than skin deep. (Williams, R. J. (1987). *The Wonderful World Within You: Your Inner Nutritional Environment.* Wichita: Bio-Communications Press.)

Races differ in body shape, eyes, noses, blood type, body hair (Caucasoids have the most, Eskimos the least, with many having no pubic hair whatsoever), hair texture, skin color, ear wax (98% of Northern Chinese have dry-type ear wax, 7% of American Blacks do), finger and hair whorls, brain size, shape of teeth, scent, birth defects, configuration of calf muscles, and disease susceptibility. Africans are vulnerable to sickle-cell anemia, the Pima Indians to diabetes, Asians are more likely to be lactose intolerant, and Caucasians are dropping like flies from atherosclerosis.

All dark skinned people (the melanin skin pigment shields against sunlight) who move to live above about 30 degrees latitude (top half of U.S.) are virtually assured of serious vitamin D deficiency (normally produced when the sun strikes the skin). With that arise myriad degenerative diseases and a greater risk of earlier death than for those who stay in southern latitudes.[1] This, not economics, access to medical care, or social circumstances is the reason black life expectancy in America is less than for whites. Denying racial differences is both wrong and deadly.

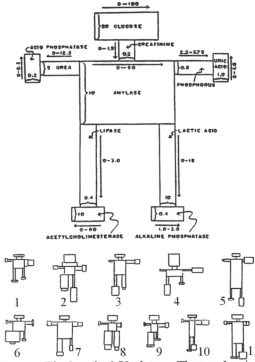

Human Biochemical Variety – The top drawing represents a human as if all biochemicals were average. The bottom drawings represent biochemicals as they really are from one person to the next. Obviously, differences among people are more than skin deep. (Williams, R. J. (1987). *The Wonderful World Within You: Your Inner Nutritional Environment*. Wichita: Bio-Communications Press.)

It is not by accident that certain sports have predominant races. Each sport requires certain physical skills. Since each race has different physical attributes (generally speaking), we would expect different races to predominate in different sports (generally speaking). Professional sport is about winning and it doesn't serve the bottom line to make those less capable first string for the sake of political correctness.

Similarly, some industries that require special skills might recruit those groups with those skills. Some may be better at heavy manual labor, others at speed, dexterity, repetitive work, mechanical problems, or math. There may be special social circumstances other than race here and there that account for the domination of one race in certain fields, but over time, particularly in a market economy where there is freedom, who is best and what is real statistically rises to the top. Differences are real. Whether they are innate or induced by culture is as hard to determine as answering the old conundrum, which came first, the chicken or the egg? Culture (through epigenetics) and environment can create mental and physical racial differences; racial differences in turn create physical aptitudes for different skill sets.

Why Racism Is Here To Stay
Birds of a feather will always prefer to flock together.

If we can delineate physical differences between the races, is there any reason not to believe that there might be some differences in mental skills? It is not as though the genetics governing the brain got locked away in a vault over thousands of generations while the genetics for every other physical attribute varied and sorted with the races. Variation among races does not end at the blood-brain barrier.

(Note: For those of you with racial sensitivities filed to razor edge, I said *different*, perhaps better suited for certain environments or tasks, not generally *inferior* or *superior*.)

Actually, it is not racist to argue that there are differences among races; it is racist to argue that there are none. Here's why. It is popularly argued that the predominance of a race in a particular field is due to such things as effort, commitment, sacrifice, diligence, and circumstances. That would mean, for example, that the predominance of blacks in certain sports is due to nothing more than determination. But then that would mean blacks could predominate over every other race in every other field using their 'determination.' That would make them a super-race. Any group claiming they are superior to all others in all categories is truly racist.

293

Thus, those who try to discount the innate differences in race to account for the way particular races tend to (generally speaking) rise to the top in certain areas of skill, and instead make an attribution to effort alone, box themselves into a racist argument of superiority. In effect they say: "Our race is the best at such and such because we work so hard at it, not because of any special physical feature." They don't continue with the logical consequence of this, namely: "Therefore, our race could be the best at all other endeavors if we just applied ourselves, so, our race is 'better' than yours."

About the only way an immaculately raceless and homogenous society could ever actually be achieved would be for intermarriage to be mandated. With enough time everyone would become 'gray' skinned, 'gray' gutted, and 'gray' brained. But even 'grayness' will not erase differences. In any given group, some will succeed more than others. Do we dare not succeed for fear of being 'succeedist?' Moreover, since virtually every person on Earth is as unique as their fingerprint, and therefore their own separate 'race,' we are all guilty of racism because each of us prefers ourselves to anyone else.

To make society perfectly equal, all traits for which people are discriminated against must be leveled, not just race. We would need laws that eliminate prejudice about weight, sex, comeliness, coordination, language, regularity of the teeth, intellect, height, neighborhood, occupation, amount of make-up, shape of the nose, color of the eyes, hairdos, dress, religion, ability to carry a tune, sense of humor, personality, shape of the feet, size of breasts or biceps, and running speed. Why does skin color get to enjoy such preeminent 'ism' status in public debate and policy when there is discrimination everywhere for just about everything?

Affirmative action would have to be applied to NBA basketball. The vast majority of first stringers on all NBA teams are African American. There is not a whisper of protest. Why isn't there a government program that forces all NBA teams to put a proportionate number of Caucasians and short people on the first string, reflecting actual population percentages? In this case there would be about nine Caucasians and short people for every tall African American.

If we're going to be fair in the affirmative action sense, English-speaking restaurants must hire Spanish-speaking waitresses, homely people must be able to win beauty pageants, a proportion of NFL linebackers would be required to be 90-year-old women, those with lowest IQs should be evenly distributed in highest corporate positions, and quadriplegics should be on our Olympic 100 meter dash team (and rig it so they win a certain percentage of time in order to be 'fair'); we must give mechanic jobs to some who test low in mechanical aptitude, make sure some who cannot carry a tune cut albums the rest of us are forced to buy, let those who have no technical or mathematical skills have an equal say in the space shuttle control room, and give the blind equal opportunity as air traffic controllers. If skin color is the only real difference between humans, why not? Obviously trying to be politically correct and denying the obvious leads to absurdity. But where does one draw the line once the Pandora's box of declaring everyone equal is opened? Facing reality, not bending to absurdity, is what advances the human condition.

The point is that although there are intractable differences between people, sexes, ages and races, that should have nothing to do with freedom. And, by and large, it no longer does. Although America lost its naiveté in the 1960's as it went through an age of enlightenment with regard to racism, Vietnam, women's rights, and environmentalism, what is done is done and should be put to rest. But social movements, like a train, are slow to get started—but once they pick up steam they continue way beyond their useful destination. By making equality the same thing as freedom, society assures itself that a sense of injustice will never go away no matter what is ever done.

Shelby Steele, a black research fellow at Stanford University, points out in *White Guilt,* that white society has made its residual shame for slavery and racism so controlling that it has lost any identity as a race other than: "I defer to other races."[2] (Notice that a White Pride Day or White History Month would be outrageously racist.) Steele goes on to argue that when, as a society, whites became more introspective in the 60s they came to define their morality in terms of race, gender, diversity, excesses of empire, big business, wealth, poverty, tolerance, the environment, and the like. Virtue on these 'big' issues became so popularized, so necessary and valid that it served like an indulgence granting a morality pass on all the small things—like sex, ethics, decency, work ethic, and personal responsibility. For example, notice that just about any sexual or ethical indiscretion of a politician tends to be given a pass if they are correct on the 'big issues' of race, affirmative action, militarism, and the environment.

Steele explains that after the overt garden-variety racism was put aside in America, black society floundered in its newfound freedom. The sense of community from having a common enemy was lost. Simply melting into white society did not do, since they clearly felt themselves different from white. Out of this black disorientation and a carryover sense of futility and pathos from slavery and pre-60s overt racism, was born the idea of global racism. This was a supposed universal and endemic racism that was so malignant and ubiquitous that nobody could escape it, and no solution could ever resolve it no matter how much whites put their shoulder into it or flogged themselves in contrite lamentations. The enemy was resurrected, victim status revived, an unearned sense of superiority emerged, and group black identity returned. This new, post–Martin Luther King version of racism has held public attention for the past forty years. It manifests as a hodgepodge of jerry-rigged, puritanically correct reactions such as quotas, affirmative action, entitlements, reparations, busing, inclusion, and multiculturalism.

With real racism essentially gone by the wayside (for society as a whole), global racism took up the flag. It became defined as an unavoidable burden all blacks faced. Any occasional overt racist act or word, any perceived inequality, or if matters related to race are not handled with utmost decorum and tippy toes, these events are taken as proof of this deterministic global racist force hamstringing blacks. But by and large, this was a rage in search of any true victims. Although blacks and other races may no longer be excluded from restaurants, pushed to the back of the bus, and hunted by white-robed bigots, they are being convinced by post-King black leaders that any inequality with whites was not of their doing, but rather was because they were pawns moved by forces much bigger than them. The power that could then be exerted on whites was derived not from being better, but from not being better.

Steele goes on to explain that races who define themselves by imagery of past evils and interminable preoccupation with race achieve nothing but a feeling of being aggrieved, entitled, and relieved from responsibility. He recounts from his experiences that the black pride mask is worn only for whites, and the heralded new global racist agenda had no real purpose other than reinforcing white guilt. In fact, the race card has become of such high value that it has become the black community's single greatest opportunity. Being non-white equals privilege and opportunism, as well as an excuse to escape common decency, decorum, and moral duty (in some inner cities, blacks have a 90 percent rate of illegitimate births), flout law (prisons hold them in vastly disproportionate numbers), avoid enculturation (English skills have decreased since affirmative action), and pass off personal responsibility (resulting in black cultural decline).

The more that whites can show themselves genuflecting to demands for race entitlement (particularly when the public relations cameras are rolling), the more the woundedness of race is affirmed in the public's mind and the more strident and militant the accusations. Even large corporations such as Toyota, Coca Cola, and Texaco are bullied into hundreds of millions of dollars in 'damages' if there is even a hint at breaching racial puritanical propriety. Moral relativism has come of age, but is certainly not applied to race. Everything is picayune relative to America's past moral infidelities.

The new hyped racism and "militancy of inferiority" (Steele) has only one purpose: white obligation. Simply being other than white is reason for rage regardless of the freedom and opportunity that exist. But the end result of promoting one's victimization is slavery because it means dependence (again) on the good offices of the white man and his magnanimity. On the other hand, there is also value in this for whites since they get no moral credit if the races lift themselves without white intervention. So it serves white moral justification to keep the race issue alive by throwing bones of atonement like affirmative action and quotas. This puts blacks in the position of "shuffling and bowing for a tossed coin" (Steele) and should be humiliating for the stigma of incapability it implies, not celebrated as victory.

People need respect for their talents and accomplishments, not tolerance because of color. Race, rather than excellence, should never be the criterion for achievement. To claim that there can be no equality without white intervention is to focus on whites as the only agents of change and to cast other races as intractably inferior, incapable, and perpetually weak.

Once a black militant himself, Steele writes:

> "Since the sixties, black educational weakness has been treated primarily as a problem of racial injustice rather than as a problem of blacks rejecting or avoiding *full* responsibility for raising their performance levels. Thus we get remedies pitched at injustices rather than at black academic excellence—school

bussing, black role models as teachers, black history courses, 'diverse' reading lists, 'Ebonics'… jerry- built African names… gimcrack educational ideas… multiculturalism, culturally inclusive classes, standardized tests corrected for racial bias, and so on. All this and no demand for parental responsibility, for harder work on reading, writing, and arithmetic."

In society's haste to achieve racial moral virtue, we have become alienated from the principles that address causes and create solutions. The race issue has become a currency to escape individual responsibility. Freedom has become redefined as equality in a sort of paradise where individuals have no responsibility. In that paradise where all human woes would dissolve in the holy water of tolerance, every hint or vestige of discrimination would be purged.

The disjunction between the race card and reason has become so outrageous that morality is twisted to mean dissociation with any part of society attached to the roots of racism. Even personal responsibility, which lies at the core of the Constitution and accounts for American success, is considered a white notion and therefore racist and rejected. The ongoing denial that freedom exists is necessary for both whites and other races in order to sustain racism as a valuable issue. That's because if there is freedom, everyone would be responsible for their own inferiority and for lifting themselves up from it.

So the race issue continues with claims of victimization by abstract systemic forces and by denial that freedom exists. Whites accommodate this charade, either out of ignorance or in order to sustain a false sense of morality. Races that shift responsibility to others only breed their own weakness. Those who help those who can help themselves only fool themselves about their virtue in doing so. In the end, everyone is deceived and distracted from the primary issue—individual responsibility.

It was good that America awakened to injustices for which it was responsible. They have been by and large corrected and are now being overcorrected. There is thus no utility in wallowing in the matter by either claiming victimization or beating breasts in contrition. We are back to what freedom means for each of us: reaching inside to find out who we are and what our best talents are. Nobody can be a better person without taking full responsibility for doing so.

It is also necessary to understand that we do not get to be equal to every other person on the planet. If someone is better than us at something, that's life. We can be better than them at something else. Differences do not make one person innately better than another. Differences are to be respected and put in perspective, not used as a cause for prejudice or an inferiority complex. Differences are what make us as a society more healthy, resilient, adaptable, and survivable. We should enjoy people differences. They make life more fun and interesting. As long as rights of opportunity are not being infringed upon, then racial difference is no issue at all other than something to celebrate.

> **Old Husband Tales***
>
> Supposedly, in the 1400's a law was set forth in England that a man was allowed to beat his wife with a stick no thicker than his thumb. Hence, "the rule of thumb."
>
> Supposedly, when the game of golf was invented in Scotland many years ago, it was ruled that it be "Gentlemen Only–Ladies Forbidden." Hence the acronym GOLF entered the English language.
>
> *Both of these interesting tales are untrue. We cannot simply accept what we hear.

MOST EVERYTHING SAID above applies as well to sexism. It, too, has ridden the wave of post-socially enlightened American contrition too far by confusing freedom with equality.

Men and women are different in so many ways. That does not make one an innately superior creature to the other, just superior in certain ways. Women can bear children and nurse them and men can't. That's one biggy. Men are usually stronger than women. Such biological attributes do make each of the sexes more suited to different tasks. If that is discriminatory, complain to politically incorrect *Mother* Nature.

Here are more differences (and don't get picky, these are generalizations and there are always exceptions):

1. Men average 5' 9" in height. Women average 5' 4".

2. Men carry 1-1/2 times as much muscle and bone and 1/2 the fat of women.

3. If asked, men add an inch to their true height while women subtract more than two pounds from their true weight.

4. Women live an average of 2,665 more days than men.

5. More than 8% of men are alcoholics compared to 3.5% of women.

299

6. Women remember details more effectively than men.

7. Men have a weaker sense of smell than women but are more sensitive to light and sound.

You can lift my weights if I can deliver your baby.

8. Men as bosses are more prone to use criticism and ulti-matums. Women more likely use a counseling approach.

9. Women develop cel-lulite; men are more inclined to big bellies.

10. 85% of women want to lose weight, 45% of men want to gain weight.

11. Most men put their pants on left leg first. Most women start with the right leg.

12. Men have double the risk of heart disease.

13. 71% of women spank children, 30% of men do.

14. The heaviest weight lifted overhead by a man is 560 lbs., compared to 286 lbs. for a woman.

15. The fastest mile run by a man is 3:46.32, for a woman it is 4:15.61.

16. Men commit 62% of violent crimes, compared to 38% by women.

17. There are 2,211 men and only 33 women on death row.

18. The chance that a man talks to himself is 1:12, compared to 1:7 for women.

19. 68% of men like the way they look in the nude, only 22% of women like the way they look nude.

20. 53% of men snore, 23% of women do.

21. The chance that a man is color-blind is 1:25, for women it is 1:50,000.

22. The chance that a man's best friend fantasizes about his wife is 1:2.5, compared to a chance of 1:6.6 for a man's best friend's wife fantasizing about him.

23. 37% of men have had an extramarital affair, compared to 29% of women.

24. The likelihood for a woman to go to a mall for entertainment is 10 times greater than for a man.

25. The likelihood for a man to spend a weekend afternoon watching a sports event on television is 10 times greater than for a woman.

26. The largest voting block for women candidates are women who think sex discrimination is unfair; the largest voting block for men are men who think sex discrimination is fair.

27. The success rate for men who use the pickup line "Hi" in a bar is 7%, whereas the same pickup line for a woman nears 100%.

The uniqueness of men and women is sure and obvious. Each sex should nurture and celebrate who they are, not pretend they are one another. Women who understand this can own themselves and exude security and intelligence. They need not feel they must play superman in a bra or waste time attempting to erase indelible differences so as not to be viewed as a pawn of patriarchy.

Out of innate differences between the sexes spring children. How could anything be more correct or fundamental? Mom and dad differences make a wonderful complement, changing the 1 + 1 man-woman bond equal to more than 2. To competently face the Herculean task of rearing a family, that kind of math is needed and is certainly not by accident.

THE LAST -ISM I WOULD like to address has not yet become popularized, fashionable, and beaten to death. Ageism is perhaps cruelest because of its subtlety and the way it creeps up on all of us. It's like being born one race and totally assimilated into that culture, only to gradually turn into another race and be shunned by your original race. When we age we keep moving from one age group to another—accepted into a new one, ostracized from the previous one.

Anatomy of An Older Person's Brain

Reflect for a moment. Regardless of your age, think back to the you that was on the grade school playground. Notice that the you that was inside the child playing on the swings has not changed, just the shell has. This should help us empathize and understand that age does not really turn people into different creatures at all. That elderly person bent and shuffling along, inside, in their own mind, is still the same person they were when they were riding a tricycle.

Old people are just children trapped in failing body machines. If they seem removed and distant, it's because they are physically handicapped, bored with the folly of many of life's activities, or have acquiesced to being excluded. Age makes one wiser, not different inside, or insensitive to how others treat us. The tragedy for the elderly is that they not only endure a failing body, its limitations, and pain, but younger society ignores and discards them.

To our own detriment we carry this bias against the aged with us when we ourselves get older. If a person figures that by age 40 they should not be trying to beat their record in the 100-yard dash, that it is futile to try to create a better physique by age 50, by age 55 they should be retiring, or that by age 70 sex life should be over, then so it will likely be. This is not to say that we should not accommodate the limitations of age, just that we should not be old folks in our dotage before it is forced upon us.

On the other hand, there is little that can't be done at any age. We can always begin a new career, gain new knowledge, become a community leader, make a better world, and find new friends. Even as our body does inevitably decline, we can stave off or minimize that decline as much as possible and even achieve new physical, mental, and social feats. It simply requires not ever giving up, and certainly not surrendering to popular biases about age.

THIS SECTION SHOULD AT LEAST RAISE the suspicion that society is moved by preconceived ideas that have not been examined carefully. We too easily attach to sound bites and movements that simply make us feel good for the moment and justify how we wish to behave. Consequently we are mired in a social froth of government, taxes, criminal justice, entertainment, and isms that have little to do with the real world and lasting solutions. Solutions require that we pay particular attention to the fact that in the end we are responsible for what we make of life. Freedom to be the best we can be—which does not mean being 'equal' to everyone else—is the greatest gift we will ever receive. But it is merely the starting point. Squandering it by claiming victimization and not taking responsibility for ourselves is not enlightened or politically correct, it is a life wasted.

SECTION J

Thinking about. . .

FAMILY

IN THIS SECTION: *Each of us comes from a family, we are part of a family, and we can create a family. It is the foundation of life and the cornerstone of society. Marriage, sex, and children are not rights to do with as we please, mere entertainment, or things to serve only selfish purposes. A more sober and rational view grounds us in realistic expectations, reveals the ethical responsibilities family implies, and brings us the sense of belonging, security, love, and happiness we all yearn for.*

56

SEX

SEX IS A MANY-FACETED THING. It has its utilitarian aspect—procreation—but it is also enjoyable and important for ego, bonding, social interaction, and health.

From a biological perspective, we can be thought of as little more than disposable packages of immortal genes: we carry the genes of our parents, we die, and our genes continue on through our children. We are in the grip of powers serving ends beyond our own.

In the beginning, prior to civilization, a few people in the wild with the urge in their loins to go forth and fill the Earth could have at it with little consequence. Life could be a concupiscent breeding frenzy. But with billions of people on one finite planet, thinking must now intercede. Although popular culture would have everyone believe they should have at it with gusto, sex has serious ramifications.

Most importantly, since sex can create a helpless child, there is implicit responsibility. Those partaking should be fully prepared for the potential consequences linked to this very adult act. Teens and young adults unprepared for marriage, commitment, and financial responsibility are not ready for children and therefore, by inference, not ready for sex. This is in spite of the devil-may-care attitude evident in teen magazines, movies, and television. Child pregnancies, ruined lives, disease, abortions, and unwanted and abandoned children now plague our world because sex is promoted as innocent recreation. The ability to do something and the fun of doing so does not make the right. Survival of our species depends on reining in impetuous biological desires and acting with conscience and a sense of responsibility to the rest of society.

In our ancient past, procreating at a young age was vital since people were not expected to live long. Children needed to be weaned and reared before the parents died. Modern society and long life make no such early procreation demands, but sexual capability at a young age remains and the fervor to 'do it' is the most intense during youth. The sexual constraints necessary in modern society must overcome our hormone-driven biology better fitted for the 'club-em–and-drag-em-by-the-hair' days.

The problem is that sex is too much fun. That's not by accident. If it were a chore, the species would have died out long ago. On the other hand, if sexual fun becomes a preoccupation, the rest of life suffers. Society's constant titillations and abundant leisure creating time and energy for more focus on sex makes it challenging to keep things in perspective.

This modern circumstance is in sharp contrast to life in primitive societies where day-to-day survival, not sex, was the number one priority. In a PBS documentary that examined a hunter-gatherer society, I was struck by the premarital instructions to the new wife by the new husband and relatives: "Feed the pigs regularly and be happy about it; pull the weeds in the garden; carry the water; don't try to find another husband; share your food and don't hide it; gather the tubers from the garden and cook them well; don't complain; weave and repair the nets and baskets; feed the baby when it cries." Not a word about sex.

WOMEN

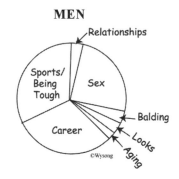

MEN

Pie Charts of Thoughts

306

The emotional and psychological entanglement created by a sexual relationship is complex. It's not just an orgasm thing. People who attempt to treat sex as casual miss an important point—sex is the ultimate intimacy. To treat it otherwise makes it no more fulfilling than a cough, sneeze, or bathroom visit. Sex is a means to connect to another person, and connection is critical to a happy and fulfilling life.

Security, self-worth, and esteem are also intimately linked to sex. A fulfilling sex life creates socio-psycho-ego equilibrium. An unhappy one can cause frustration, depression, and a loss of a sense of worth. When libido ebbs or sexual dysfunction occurs in later years, many people feel that life has pretty much ended. This is the primary reason Viagra is the most successful pharmacological agent ever invented and why advertising it and its brand name offspring flood the media.

The sexual act is a reflection, a metaphor of what a long-standing relationship can mean—each partner fulfilling the needs of the other to bring pleasure to both. Sexual intimacy for a few moments can relieve the fundamental loneliness of being human and bring an altered state of consciousness, transcendence, and unity.

The psychological and social complexity related to sex is yet another reason it is inappropriate for children. Regardless of age, sex bonds and creates feelings of obligation and rights. In a child's world where independence has not been achieved, rights and obligations with regard to those outside the family don't fit. Similarly, kids may be able to have and enjoy money, but they are hardly capable of earning it, investing, handling an IRS audit or the potential consequences of a fiscal disaster they could create. At a time in life when learning and exploration should be preparing a young mind to meet the challenges of adulthood, the interjection of sex is like a detour and dead end that offers no upside. Instead it preoccupies young minds and emotions with obligations, jealousies, and bodies. Sex is serious business and kids are not ready for serious business.

One last point: Sex is healthy. Studies show that disease resistance is increased and longevity extended in a fulfilling adult sexual relationship. This is likely due to two reasons. One is that feeling loved brings a sense of well being that actually boosts the immune system. The second, getting back to the biological aspect, is that the body senses an end to

307

one of its important purposes for existence if reproductive acts do not take place. That sends the message to the body that life is no longer important, so it slips into a weakened and vulnerable state.

So there you have my birds and bees talk. The long and short is that we should not partake if we are not fully capable of shouldering the potential responsibilities. When we are ready, we should have fun but not get too preoccupied with it. Shared with someone with whom

> *"I always look for a woman who has a tattoo. I see a woman with a tattoo, and I'm thinking, okay, here's a gal who's capable of making a decision she'll regret in the future."* -Richard Jeni

there is mutual commitment, sex is healthy, life extending, psychologically fulfilling, gives us a sense of connection, and permits us to experience an important aspect of love, life's ultimate high.

57

BEING IN LOVE

AS CHILDREN WE ARE WEANED on Cinderella and acculturated by an endless parade of romantic fantasies in novels, television and movies. It would be easy to assume that if we are not madly in love there is something wrong with us.

The euphoria of being in love is like an hourglass, with the heart filling up as the brain empties. The object of our affection is perfect; any problems we see in them will disappear because of love; we feel more alive than ever; our sense of self worth is at its peak; we don't get sick (immunity is actually strengthened during the phase); and we even look better. It is indeed one of life's pure joys.

But the dizziness ends—for everyone. That's why the stories about the spoony prince and princess never go on to talk about what happens next. The altered state of consciousness resulting from the shower of love chemicals that bathe the brain can only last for about two years. From a biological point of view, this is long enough to conceive a child and for the man to be held in the relationship while the mother and child are most vulnerable.

Since sex is primarily for the purpose of procreation, men are inclined to bond to women for short periods of in-love engagement, and then move to the next opportunity for being in love and disseminating genetics. There are longer-term considerations for a woman. She may end up with a child that will be her responsibility to suckle and nurture. Being at such risk, she is inclined to be more deliberate in her selection of a mate since long-term security and stability are of utmost importance for her and the child she will bear.

Men are the initiators of relationships and women more choosy and careful. This is not because of tradition, but because of these innate differences. Women flaunt their looks and sexuality; men flaunt their money (security) and strength (protection). Note how our hunter-gatherer origins are manifest in the way men are inclined toward sport and career (hunting, protecting, and providing), while women are inclined toward shopping, housekeeping, nurturing (gathering, sheltering, child rearing). It's all a human version of a mating dance.

Even the male and female sexual responses mirror these fundamental differences. The man is quickly aroused and more easily fulfilled, whereas the woman is slower to arousal, giving her more time to opt out if she determines the guy is a real loser. None of us have to think through these things. It is just who we are at our core; behaviors emanate from there.

In a pre-civilized world in which survival and perpetuation of the species was the imperative, moving to the inner urge of spreading seed far and wide was fine and dandy. But today's world is one in which stable, peaceful relationships and families, as well as intelligent population control are necessary for the very survival of the species. New rules are in order, the first being that mind, not gonad reflexes, must take priority.

310

Without realizing that the in-love altered state of consciousness will inevitably pass, and acknowledging the fundamental innate differences between the sexes, people are doomed to frustration when the intense feelings masking differences and excusing foibles abate. Then couples sense that they may have made a mistake and are missing out on the one true love that lasts forever. But the search for the perfect sustained love relationship is quixotic and doomed, like trying to nail Jell-o to the wall. If people understood that the euphoria of being in love is only sustained for a short period of time, they could then approach relationships with, so-to-speak, full disclosure so that relationships could be rationally built with realistic expectations.

A long-standing, intimate, and exciting relationship requires creative adaptation and needs to be continually nurtured as it evolves. It is a work in progress, never truly finalized. Instead, people feel betrayed when in love feelings ebb and tend to blame their partners for failing. If resentment builds, thinking about one another in a sexual way can fade like a memory. Studies have shown that if couples stop thinking erotically about one another for about five years, the ability to do so cannot be recaptured no matter how hard they may try.

The solution is not more closeness. The exact opposite is usually what is needed. Once a compatible mate is found and each has agreed to be locked to the marital ball and chain, mates need to be given slack. Two is not really one. Wedlock should not be more lock than wed. A woman's family orientation (nurturing), although different, complements a man's occupational (hunting) endeavors. A division of duties and interests and separation to accomplish these is normal and harmonious in the context of a stable family.

A warm and amiable relationship with unanimity of purpose is a realistic hope. However, we-ness, if taken to extreme, can hasten the demise of erotic zest and intimacy. By attempting to negate differences, neglecting independent friends and interests, and always attempting to think and feel as a unit, couples lose sight of the individuality that sparked the original interest in one another. Mary Sarton wrote: "Clutching is the surest way to murder love, as if it were a kitten not to be squeezed so hard, or a flower to fade in a tight hand."

311

The fundamental human problem of being a distinct individual who is ultimately alone can uniquely find a solution in a long-standing intimate relationship between two individuals who maintain their identity. However, the constant effort by couples to shape and mold one another into a cookie cutter version of one another is a tyranny that will demolish intimacy and fulfillment. Bonding and intimacy must not be taken to mean limitation of freedom or abandoning privacy. Everyone needs his or her own non-relational sphere of existence that should not be questioned or challenged. The knowledge that a free and independent person voluntarily chooses us also brings a sense of pride, affirmation, validation, and self-esteem. Such cannot come from feeling obligated and forced to conform to we-ness.

Curiously, therefore, the desire to be in love is at odds with itself. Falling in love and courting is like a wrestling match, the goal is to get as close as possible and win. But winning is at odds with the goal. After all, what is passion but a desire seeking fulfillment? But fulfillment satisfies desire. Unless the relationship is understood to be cyclical, with an endless series of desires and fulfillments that must be nurtured to be sustained, passion will end.

It is a paradox in life that satisfaction of any kind sows the seeds of discontent: we lust until we conquer and obtain, treat that which we have conquered with casualness, disrespect, or even contempt, and then set our sites on new horizons. But if relationships are understood to be a natural series of arousal, passion, fulfillment, satisfaction, and then a degree of disinterest, unrealistic expectations need not burden nor doom the relationship.

A sustained intimate relationship requires an act of will to maintain the attraction. In this regard, once one imagines that another person is no more than an extension of themselves, they let their guard down and can lose the dignity that privacy affords. For example, a mate may complain about their personal faults to a partner. The partner may not see them, but most certainly will if they are continually highlighted. It's like commenting to a friend on the tipped ear of another person. Your friend may have never noticed it, but now that is all they can see when they look at the person. People must permit their mates some fantasy even if they do not see themselves in such a favorable light. We can pretend we are perfect without saying it or acting like we think it. In this regard, Alfred Hitchcock's remark applies to either sex: "A woman, I always say, should be like a good suspense movie: the more left to the imagination, the more excitement there is."

It is also the duty of any person who expects another to remain faithful to them for a lifetime to be the best they can be. Letting oneself go because there are supposedly no obligations once locked into marriage, or because a mate tells us they "love us just as we are," is a crime against self and a betrayal and injustice to the partner.

Time itself can also wear thin the desire for intimacy unless a conscious effort is made to not let it happen. Simply remembering the physical and mental features in a mate that originally elicited the attraction can prove to be a powerful stimulus. A man in his 70s may see a certain look in the eyes of his elderly wife that reminds him of the special attraction that originally brought him to her. She, when seeing his glances, may recall her fondness for his strong assertive and confident personality. This, in turn, causes her to look at him in that special way again which in turn stimulates his pride and confidence. And on the cycle goes. Such seeking out of comely characteristics in the other (not succumbing to the ever-present human tendency to be critical) can be an ongoing strong aphrodisiac that nurtures and sustains intimacy.

When people come together voluntarily to embark on a life-long relationship, they must accommodate rhythms. These include desire, euphoria, fulfillment, frustration, boredom, self-doubt, and disappointment. Accommodating this reality and not the fantasy of a continual in-love experience is an achievable objective that can bring inner peace, happiness, and the answer to a lonely existence.

58

MARRIAGE—THE UNION OF OPPOSITES

BEFORE A MAN AND WOMAN decide on the commitment of marriage, they must face certain facts. Topping the list is differences. Not just between two people, but between the sexes themselves. In the early going of a relationship when romantic love and sexual desire are blinding, contrasts seem unimportant. But after the euphoria ebbs, unless the couple have common interests on which to focus, such as children, differences can drive wedges into a relationship—and they do. Three-fourths of all divorces occur after the first three years of marriage.

It seems obvious that we should choose a mate like we choose a good friend. Since you like yourself and get along with yourself more than anyone in the world, finding a companion that is most like you in as many respects as possible will create the best prospect for long-term compatibility. Internet dating services have built multi-million dollar businesses by employing this principle.

On the other hand, a mate that is your opposite may be fun, interesting, and challenging in the beginning when hormones obscure vision and forgive just about everything. Down the road in a relationship, after the brain returns from vacation in the gonads, those cute little quirks noticed early on become glaring and annoying problems. Tolerating them is not as easy as once imagined, and changing another person is next to impossible.

Married couples commonly move from their romantic love bond to the busyness of family life. These new activities can draw the couple close since the family is an important and shared goal. But when the children leave and retirement approaches, the things that distracted each from the other's differences must then be faced squarely. The golden years that could be peaceful and contented can turn into a bitter entanglement with each partner barely tolerating the other. Many remain in the relationship only because they see no other option.

Choose wisely going in. You get along with you best, so find another close facsimile of you.

With that said, likeness between the sexes can only go so far. The differences are immutable and go deep into the bones of DNA sequences. Culture does not create these differences by imposing pinks and blues on infants or giving them boy or

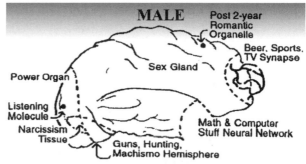

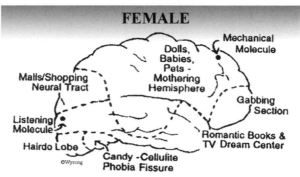

girl names. Given two stacks of toys, girls will usually show a preference for the dolls and will play house, the typical mothering instinct. Trucks, dinosaurs, and sports symbolic of the typical hunting and protecting instincts, intrigue boys. Without any nudging whatsoever, given equal access to various toys, I have watched with amazement as each of my children made these choices clearly and irrevocably. The movement afoot to discount such man-woman differences, as if we now know better than the countless billions of people who have preceded us through eons of time, and in silly repudiation of differences that are innate and obvious, only creates doomed expectations.

Many primitive societies recognize the basic gender differences and are structured accordingly. For example, the South American Yanomama keep men together in separate housing where they discuss their hunting forays and other manly stuff. Women house together and discuss family matters. The sexes come together as necessary to procreate.[1]

The differences between men and women deepen as each plays the role in a relationship they naturally must. First, man and woman meet and fall in love. They fulfill each other's needs for affection, security, and worth. In the beginning the only role to play is to swoon over one another. They marry. The husband becomes absorbed in his work (hunting/protecting). The wife

feels neglected and unfulfilled (or vice versa, if you must). She has a child (no vice versa here please) and becomes absorbed in its care (mothering/nurturing). The child diverts some of the mother's love and affection, so now the husband feels neglected and unfulfilled. Paul Valery wrote about this last circumstance: "God created man and, finding him not sufficiently alone, gave him a companion to make him feel his solitude more keenly."

If the two don't understand this evolution in the relationship, if they fail to continually work to satisfy one another's needs, resentment, bitterness, animosity, and even hostility and separation can result. The dream of a lifelong, loving, and close family can become the nightmare of divorce courts, child custody battles, dating turmoil, emotional trauma to the children, support payments, and destroyed assets—not to mention the toll on health.

> "My wife and I took out life insurance policies on each other -- so now it's just a waiting game." -Bill Dwyer

As discussed in the previous chapter—and worth repeating—making a man-woman relationship work requires the understanding that the super-charged infatuation and euphoria of romantic love will pass.

If it didn't, society would crumble as couples spent days dreaming of one another and nights breeding the planet into oblivion. This is not to say that sexual fulfillment does not remain important and that love cannot continue, just that the in-love fervor will not continue to excuse or solve all problems.

Not recognizing innate man-woman differences, and not allowing and accommodating them, can create tensions and stress that make life miserable and negatively impact health. Harmony may simply be a matter of sitting down and rationally discussing needs, expectations, differences, space needed, and areas where adjustment is possible. As basic as this sounds, such pow-wows are a rare occurrence. Rather, innuendo, smirks, jabs, insults, outbursts, sarcasm, nagging, and silence prevail in many troubled marriages. Mates too easily resent their partners not living up to their expectations but may never tell their partner what those expectations are.

So where lies hope for this unlikely union called marriage? It begins with thinking, not fantasies. Understanding and tolerance of innate differences between the sexes is essential. At the same time, each will also need to compromise biological imperatives to a degree to fulfill the needs of the other. Rather than assert differences, couples need to find areas of common-ality and agreement to build on and enjoy with one another.

Why Female Polygamy Doesn't Work

Finally, don't take advantage of familiarity or a marriage contract in order to nullify common decency. Mates deserve to be treated with at least the respect afforded a stranger—or the cat or dog. We would not berate, criticize, ignore, and constantly disagree with a stranger we meet, so why do it to someone who has given us their life commit-ment? Additionally, to the degree it is possible, without totally giving up our own identity, we should look for and welcome those hints that suggest how to satisfy the desires of a mate.

Many a marriage could be saved if couples would keep in mind that no woman was ever bludgeoned for listening empathetically to a husband's frustrating day at the office, remarking about his 'studliness,' or being astonished at his wisdom; no man was ever shot while doing the dishes, complimenting a hairdo, or marveling at the daily grind his wife accomplishes at work or at home. Neither is ever hated for loving touch.

Ultimately we tend to want to be with people who make us feel good about ourselves. Partners who accommodate differences and make a concerted effort to bolster the self-esteem of one another are forging a long and fulfilling union.

FOR SOME FINAL WISDOM on man-woman relations and marriage, here's what some kids have to say about it.

KIDS INTERVIEWED ON MARRIAGE

How Do You Decide Who To Marry?
"You got to find somebody who likes the same stuff. Like, if you like sports, she should like it that you like sports, and she should keep the chips and dip you like coming."
–Alan, age 10   "No person really decides before they grow up who they're going to marry. God decides it all way before, and you get to find out later who you're stuck with."
–Kirsten, age 10

What Is The Right Age To Get Married?
"Twenty-three is the best age because you know the person FOREVER by then."
–Camille, age, 10   "No age is good to get married at. You got to be a fool to get married."
–Freddie, age 6

What Do You Think Your Mom And Dad Have In Common?
"Both don't want any more kids." –Lori, age 8

What Do Most People Do On A Date?
"Dates are to use to get to know each other. Even boys have something to say if you listen long enough." -Lynnette, age 8   "On the first date, they just tell each other lies and that usually gets them interested enough to go for a second date." Martin, age 10

What Would You Do On A First Date That Was Turning Sour?
"I'd run home and play dead. The next day I would call all the newspapers and make sure they wrote about me in all the dead columns." –Craig, age 9

When Is It Okay To Kiss Someone?
"When they're rich." –Pam, age 7   "The rule goes like this: If you kiss someone, then you should marry them and have kids with them. It's the right thing to do."
–Howard, age 8   "The law says you have to be eighteen, so I wouldn't want to mess with that." –Curt, age 7

Is It Better To Be Single Or Married?
"I don't know which is better, but I'll tell you one thing. I'm never going to have sex with my wife. I don't want to be all grossed out." –Theodore, age 8   "It's better for girls to be single but not for boys. Boys need someone to clean up after them." –Anita, age 9

How Can A Stranger Tell If Two People Are Married?
"You might have to guess, based on whether they seem to be yelling at the same kids."
–Derrick, age 8

How Do Married People Make Kids?
"The dad gives the mom an egg to swallow." –Matt, age 5   "I don't know cause my mom told me something and it must be a lie." –Tina, age 6

How Would You Make A Marriage Work?
"Tell your wife that she looks pretty, even when she first gets up and looks like a truck."
–Ricky, age 10

(Modified from an Internet circulated e-mail.)

59

DIVORCE

WHEN TWO LIVES INTIMATELY INTERTWINE in marriage and invest so much emotionally, separation is traumatic at best. If children are involved it is often a disaster. What follows is not so much a how to, or how not to, but a heads up about the realities of divorce.

The mate with whom the past is shared is a connection to personal history, giving a sense of grounding, belonging, and purpose. When there is a separation, connections are severed not only to the mate but also to the shared history. It is like tearing off one's skin. Since marriage is in large part an effort to not be lonely, divorce represents a failed attempt that then amplifies the sense of loneliness.

In an ideal world divorce would never happen. In an ideal world the choice of a mate would be perfect and people would never change in their likes, dislikes, and desires. However, this is not an ideal world and people are not perfect. In a free society children may choose life partners at an age when they have no real idea what life is even about. Lack of life experience causes them to see others through hope and illusion, whereas if they could only open their eyes, the end is there in the beginning. Also, with age, experience, and education people may grow apart in life goals. There could be any number of reasons why people feel the need to separate, including just the inability to remain happy within the marriage when there is really no significant problem and no fault with either party.

Often, however, sufficient reason to separate from the security and history of an existing marriage does not occur until a person is attracted to a new person who seems to be an answer to discontent. Although no new mate ever solves one's personal problems, life is what we imagine it to be. The prospect of a new life, like a horse breaking from the gate, is almost impossible to contain. Once a person projects a new life through another person, the acute pain of divorce is usually chosen over the perceived chronic pain of not being able to have the new life. Whether it is true or not, emotion chokes out reason and divorce is seen as creating the least pain.

"I'm leaving you.
If you were watching Oprah, you'd know why."

People who are happy and content in a relationship may believe things will never change for them, or for anyone else for that matter. But life is change, so no one should get too smug or judgmental towards those who do change and then divorce. Also consider that everyone 'divorces' others throughout life. We leave our parents, move away from communities, change friends, switch girlfriends or boyfriends, leave fellow workers for another job, or fire an employee. These acts all sever relationships to one degree or another. So no one can be self-righteous and 'without sin' with regard to separating from other people in life.

The difference between divorce and other interpersonal breakups is not so much a clear matter of morality. It's just that marriage is far more entangled emotionally, biologically, historically, economically, and legally than, say, a friendship. It's better to think, "There but for the grace of God go I," than to self-righteously condemn divorcees.

People going through divorce need understanding, empathy, and compassion every bit as much as those who have lost someone to death. The pain they feel is real and awful enough without other people's sanctimonious condemnation. Nobody has the ability or right to peer into the hearts and minds of others and cast stones at them for choosing friends and mates, or for moving on from them.

That being said, divorce is a decision that haunts people in one way or another for the rest of their lives. A divorce is never really final. Remnants of it will remain forever, particularly if the parties do not make a special effort for civility, and when children are involved.

Unfortunately a legal fight—fueled by an adversarial legal system—is too often used to vent emotions when trust and communication end. Money and property are thrown into the mix reducing what beauty there was in the relationship to the ugliness of a closeout sale with the parties scrambling for all they can get without regard for the feelings or rights of the other. Love, trust, and friendship are reduced to an ugly legal battle over marital assets. In some cases, the bitterness and hate created in this battle are more tolerable than the guilt or pain of the separation itself, so the parties drag it out. The legal battle may also be stoked if one of the parties finds it to be the only remaining means of access to a lost mate. In any event, surviving a contentious divorce is a feat of no small magnitude.

One thing is certain: divorce grows people up quickly. It forces a person to come face to face with some hard realities regarding relationships, economics, expectations, ethics, and the legal system. But they are hard lessons to learn by this means. Soldiers in the line of battle grow up, too, but there are better, kinder, and gentler ways.

Next to the death of a loved one, there is nothing quite so emotionally devastating as divorce. For some, the living reminder of a mate doing fine without them is worse than if the mate had died. Regardless of the circumstances, both sides hurt and it will take at least two years to recover. In the meantime, being decent, respect-ful, and humane to someone we have been so close to should be the utmost priority. More is at stake than just hurt feelings.

For divorced individuals, the death rate from cancer equals that of those married who smoke a pack or more of cigarettes a day. Cardio-vascular disease and strokes double, premature death is up to ten times more likely, death from pneumonia is more than seven times greater, susceptibility to acute conditions (immune suppression) such as infec-tious disease, parasites, digestive problems and trauma is increased, and rheumatoid arthritis and osteoarthritis are increased. Psychiatric visita-tions are up to nine times more frequent; hospitalization is as much as 21 times greater. The risk of suicide is four times greater (divorce being the number one risk factor), and automobile fatalities triple.

Children can suffer for a lifetime if parents don't handle divorce well. Fighting and attempts by parents to poison a child against the other are disastrous. Children need assurance that they are not at fault and will be cared for unconditionally. They need love and a sense of stability during this time of crisis. If the rocks in their lives—the parents—start hammering at one another, the child's world crumbles.

Additionally, children can be their own cause of problems in later life. Many use a divorce as a selfish opportunity to manipulate parents, gather sympathy, or as a cross and excuse for not living life well. For children who see a divorce as about them, or who use it as an excuse for not getting about their own lives, life span may be shortened by as much as 10 years, alcohol and drug abuse are increased, and girls are 60% more likely to divorce, and boys 32% more likely.[1]

Although divorce may give a new lease on life for some, it can also be one of the worst experiences life has to offer. Its commonness does not diminish this fact. People must be wise and do their due diligence before going into marriage and then expend considerable effort to make it work. Although emotions tend to rule relationships, thinking is what matters in choosing a mate, staying in a relationship, and getting out if necessary.

60

THE FAMILY NEST

THE BREAKDOWN OF THE TRADITIONAL family structure is one of the most difficult and important problems society faces. If families do not take responsibility for themselves, society must step in. Although that may sound okay in theory—and is in fact what socialism/communism is ostensibly about—it does not work in practice. Society is nothing more than a gigantic family and if people cannot shoulder the responsibility for smaller families in specific, they certainly won't be able to take care of the bigger society family in general. Trying to make a healthy society family while ignoring the responsibilities of individual family units is like trying to eat soup with a fork.

Way back when humans were few and far between on this planet, family was about the only society there was. Family created a labor pool that helped with hunting, gathering, defense, and shelter. The utility of the family continued with the advent of the agricultural age. Farming was just not very workable as a solo enterprise. Retirement was a figment of the imagination without kids to take over. The more progeny, the more productive the farm was and the easier life became. The family farm and the family trade (later in the pre-industrial era) were often the default occupations for children. Social roles were neat and defined. People knew what they had to do to survive and they knew what the future held. The family gave life continuity.

Not today. A brave new landscape of options and freedoms split families apart. Schooling for myriad occupations, easy travel, instant communication with the world, the prospect of limitless success, the advance of socialism, and the popularity of 'me' pop psychology seems to make the family increasingly obsolete. But our basic biological and psychological design is still matched to our genetic roots in a prehistory in which family was necessary for survival.

Children are the most tragic victims of the modern flip attitude toward the family. There is just no substitute for loving, caring parents. The damage to abandoned children is enormous. The brain will not even develop normally if the child does not experience touch and love. The 'blood is thicker than water' bond within families creates a 'cushions on a couch' feeling of security, and a sense of belonging, love, comfort, and hope. People are healthier physically and psychologically in the secure family nest. If this is not provided, then that is a hole the person spends life trying to fill—manifesting in all sorts of aberrant insecurities and endless chats with therapists.

The extended family of the past may end up being the most workable model for the future. In the extended family all generations are either in the same home or nearby. The sense of belonging in that arrangement must be wonderful. Think of the support, the shared responsibilities, and the potential

Skipping The Family Part

leisure. There would be ready-made babysitting. Varied talents would be right there to take care of most eventualities. Parents and grandparents would provide a pool of wisdom to draw from. The strength and energy of the young could help the elderly; the experience of the elderly could help the young. When someone became ill there would be a fleet of caregivers. When dying, one would have loved ones alongside. When birthing, all would experience the joy. Shared use of materials would decrease the tax on resources—fewer garages to fill with stuff. Everyone would not need to go cut down more woods to have their own home. Young children would have older ones to play with. Practical education from the family community would be of immense value. Shared children would decrease the urge to have one's own, or at least so many of them.

There would be problems, of course, since no two people can ever agree on everything. But the blood/love bond would help soften the differences and be a motivator for peaceful resolution. Even conflict within the group that is resolved with justice and love would become an invaluable learning experience for all and deepen the sense of family community.

As the world continues to fill and crowd, extended families may become a necessity. Our family, the whole thing, might become our family's responsibility rather than society's. Why not? Family is the reason we exist and is an inherent responsibility. As world resources dwindle and governments learn that social programs must be funded by something other than political idealism, what is the other viable alternative to people taking care of themselves and their own? As people are crammed into tighter and tighter spaces, would we rather be pooled with those we do not know, or with our family?

Discounting the value of family and its inherent responsibility to itself as resulted in society being overrun with tens of thousands of abandoned children. Failed family structures require replacement with loving surrogates such as properly monitored adoption programs, mentoring, and foster care. For the very young, at least through early grade school, a parent or loving surrogate at home should be a mandatory thing, not an option. Young children require love and security to help them develop into loving, well adjusted, and secure adults. Children are the foundation of the future. Like the foundation to any significant structure, they must be constructed and tended with the utmost intelligence and care.

Unfortunately, people insist on freedom to have children, rear them as they choose, couple, disconnect, and behave as if consequences from their actions belong to somebody else. Freedom can only exist in tandem with responsibility. Spewing out children who are not properly cared for and who then become burdens or menaces is the blowback from thinking of freedom only, not responsibility and consequences. Disassembling the family creates a yawning vacuum of authority not adequately replaced by society. Like modern medicine that does nothing to prevent disease or build health, but rather attempts to just pick up the pieces, the new socialistic landscape does little to cultivate good people; it just punishes them when they go bad.

Sooner or later government will have to take the bold move of enforcing the ethical obligation parents have to their children. The only other option is to regulate copulation (a virtual impossibility) or shift responsibility to the rest of society (the present solution that does not work). Once people have children, they lose certain freedoms. Parents can never walk away from the responsibility of the proper rearing of their children. If they do, then they must foot the bill for others to do the parenting for them. A thinking society should not shift the burden to others as if 'others' were some bottomless vat of resources to repair all the damage people create from exerting their freedoms.

THE WORLD OF TODAY'S COLLEGE-BOUND KIDS

- They were prepubescent when the Persian Gulf War was waged.
- They were 10 when the Soviet Union collapsed and have no memory of the Cold War.
- Are too young to remember the space shuttle exploding.
- Tiananmen Square is meaningless.
- Bottle caps have always been plastic screw off.
- Atari and vinyl albums are before their time.
- Record players, 8-tracks, BETA, Pac Man, and Pong predate them.
- Most have never seen a 13-channel TV set in black and white.
- They don't know about cloth baby diapers.
- They have never heard the "Help me, I've fallen and I can't get up" commercial.
- Michael Jackson was never black.
- Jay Leno has always been the Tonight Show host.
- Popcorn comes from a microwave.
- They have never seen Larry Bird play basketball.
- They never thought about Jaws when swimming.
- The Vietnam War is ancient history.
- They don't know who Mork is.
- They never heard: "Where's the beef?", or "I'd walk a mile for a Camel."
- They don't know who J.R. is or who shot him.
- MTV has always been there.
- They have never used a typewriter or lift-off tape.

Today's Generation - Young people are particularly vulnerable to artificiality. It is easy for them to not recognize their true origins. Their environmental and social origins deeply root them in nature and family. Although technology may fill many needs in our modern world, it proceeds without conscience and without consideration for the physical and mental health of those who create it.

327

61

HAVING BABIES

WHEN FIRST OUT OF COLLEGE I interned in Boulder, Colorado during the height of the hippie era. The establishment was increasingly being viewed with cynicism and the back-to-nature theme was coming of age. While there, friends of mine wanted to have their second baby at home because of a bad experience in the hospital with their first child. They were worried about the dangers and asked if I would help. I agreed.

It turned out to be an uneventful and beautiful experience for them and a remarkable and moving one for me as well. I was hesitant at first, nervous about all of the possible things that could go wrong, and aware of my potential liability. But after everything worked out, and considering the sheer wonder and beauty of the event, it seemed like the right thing to have done.

Word got out and within a couple of years I delivered two more babies for friends who wanted to birth at home. Later, I delivered two of my girls as well. All of these experiences were without problems. Yes, they could have been disasters, but the odds were way on my side.

I'm not sure I would volunteer to do this again other than in an emergency. Although the risks of home delivery may be statistically small, the legal threat to an attendant is enormous.[1]

Nevertheless, over 80% of all the babies in the world are delivered either by women alone, a family member, or midwives. World population obviously does not suffer. Our high-tech obstetrical suites, fetal monitors screwed into scalps, drugs, and cesarean sections only seem necessary to us now because we are used to medical intrusion. As for whether that intrusion is necessary, or even very smart other than in high-risk situations, consider that the United States ranks between 16th and 22nd in the world in terms of newborn deaths.[2]

We've been brain-washed to believe that giving birth is a disease to be treated, rather than a natural process to be watched. Although Cae-sarean sections account for about 40% of all births in the U.S., researchers argue that most of these are un-

Okay, we're ready, you can push now.

necessary and that fewer than 6% of births need be Caesarean sections.

You may wish to consider having a baby at home with an experienced midwife or at a birthing center. Now I know I have no uterus and arguably no valid opinion on this matter, but consider that there are 30% fewer deaths and 31% fewer low birth weight babies with midwife assisted births.[3-7] Being as close to all aspects of the birth as possible is an experience that is one of life's most remarkable treasures. Husbands, and even children, should be a part.

Two more baby pearls. First, give your baby the food it was meant to have, breast milk, from a mom who is eating right. (See previous section.) The evidence now in hand demonstrating that feeding processed formula (arguably junk food) to newborns is inferior to breast milk is significant enough that formula feeding should be banned unless there is simply no other option.[8] Breast feeding is one of the few opportunities in our modern world that a person gets to have the true, raw, natural food that he or she is genetically designed to have. The rewards are increased intelligence, decreased likelihood of degenerative diseases in later life, proper body development, enhanced immunity, and decreased likelihood of allergies and autoimmune diseases.

Secondly, sleep with your baby. That is what it wants and what will make it happiest, most secure, and healthiest. This is the way families have always slept until the new modern ways.[9] A baby will even synchronize its heart to the mom's when cuddled at night.[10] It also makes breastfeeding through the night convenient for both mom and child. Keep them in the family bed until they decide to leave.[11] You will never regret it—and no, the parent's sex life does not have to end. Where there is a will, a way can be found. As you will learn from the experience of sleeping with your children, it is the way things were meant to be.

Having a child is a rare life and love experience not duplicated by any other. The experience is healthiest and safest for all involved if intelligence is interjected. That means trusting and respecting nature.

Meet Your New Boss

62

CHILDREN

IN THE BEGINNING, having children was just a byproduct of sexual instinct. Later it was a means to increase manpower for survival (hunting the mastodon, tilling the fields). Having children was an important part of life, even what one aspired to. Children were potential workers. A strapping daughter was great, a strong son perhaps even better.

Having children is also an expression of love between mates. How more intimate can two people be than to literally mix their biological (genetic) essence into a tangible package that both can love with equal enthusiasm? Children also help cement the marital bond through the shared common interest in their rearing.

Bearing children in today's world is serious business. It's not just a diversion from boredom or a means to satisfy our insecurities and ego fantasies. In modern civilization things are different than in the bush or on the farm. The world already has more than enough people for its resources. Also, usually in modern societies children do not help parents with their burdens, they add to them.

Nevertheless, having children is such a joy that some parents keep repeating it without a full understanding of the long-term responsibilities and consequences. New parents fall in love with their babies and toddlers and the experience gives unequaled meaning and purpose to life. So, it is reasoned, if a little is fun, a whole lot more will be even more fun.

Some keep the production line running until they realize their biological machinery is nearing exhaustion. By that time they will have a household of teenagers and young adults not quite so cute, dutiful, malleable, and compliant. Parents can become overwhelmed by what they have created: Well I'll be darned, the cute little dolls that were so obedient and fun to play with grow up to be independent and self-willed adults.

Procreation is not recreation. The cord between child and parent is never really broken. Playing goo-goo with babies is short-lived; responsibility (at least the feeling of it) is forever. The worry for children never ends regardless of their age.

"But, I don't know how to act my age. I've never been this age before."

Having and rearing children is a place for thinking and conscience. Michail Levine wrote, "Having children makes you no more a parent than having a piano makes you a pianist. Certainly, would-be parents should be educated on child rearing as well as on the impact population pressure has on the world. In fact, nobody should be allowed to have children without such training. It's pretty crazy that such an important responsibility requires nothing more than capable (and always willing) genitals.

Modern sex education classes take a stab at this but are focused more on coitus and condoms than conscience, social responsibility, the psychological impact of sexual intimacy, and the long-term duty and meaning of bearing children.

Here's a sex education addendum. Before becoming Mr. or Mrs. Fecund, consider the following realities:

1. Babies grow up to be adults. They do not remain cuddly, cute, and compliant. Yes, you will be god to them for about 12 wondrous years, but that's it. Then you will face the rest of their lives with responsibility without authority—they want you there to provide for them and pick up the pieces, but don't want to follow your advice.

2. You will not make your children what you want them to be. They are not your toys, something to solve some ego or insecurity problem you have, or a glob of clay waiting for you to shape into your perfect view of a child (modeled after you, of course). They will not change from the first time you can discern their personality in the crib until they die of old age. Don't try to spank them into submission or conformity to your dream of what they should be. It will not change them, but it will leave you with memories to regret. All you can do is provide a healthy and loving environment for them to be what they will be. The rest is up to them.

3. You will never stop feeling a sense of responsibility toward them regardless of their age. You will never stop feeling guilt that you should have done more when they were young, even if you did all that was humanly possible at the time.

4. Children are a dramatic departure from a single's life and take a huge amount of energy and effort. With children in hand, it is no longer all about you. They require total devotion. If you have children when you are biologically ready in your teens there will be plenty of energy to raise them, just not a whole lot of savvy to go along with that. Young parents are still kids

"Have any self-validating and agrandizing anecdotes about when you were a kid this morning?"

themselves and have not yet even figured out that the world does not rotate around them. Having children when young means they will be raised and gone while you are in your thirties. On the other hand, if you have children in your thirties you will have plenty of energy to begin but will be running out of steam in your forties and fifties. But age brings much more life wisdom to help in their rearing. Having children when you are quite young is therefore not a good idea; having them when you are quite old isn't either. My vote, however, is to have them when you are older (not too), smarter, less egocentric, more mellow, are not thinking bar-scene, and can really appreciate and savor the things around you more. A child is something to savor.

5. You will never stop feeling as though they should listen to you (rightly so), but they will pretty much stop when they are about 12.

6. The more you do for your children when they are older, the more you impede their own independent development. Love is turning them loose, not providing for their every need. Life is a series of lessons that come from experiencing failures and successes. Parents who insist on providing for every need thwart the development of their children and rob them of life itself. Failure, pain, and mistakes are successes—if we let children experience and learn from them.

Now

Later

7. Children grow faster than we can keep up with. About the time we come to understand and adjust to a particular stage in their lives, they have moved on. We will always be behind, thinking of them in terms of a previous molt. If we do not adjust and respect their new mature stage, but keep them in our mind where they no longer are, they will move on to friends who see them for who they really are.

8. Each child brought into this already overpopulated world places an enormous burden on the carrying capacity of the Earth.

9. Worrying about teenage hormone-driven kids—who might do what you did when you were that age—is hell.

We can have no good understanding of what we're getting into with parenting until we live the experience of having and raising children. We may think we do since we were once children ourselves, but being a child and raising one are two entirely different matters. This is particularly true when children become young adults, insisting on adult freedoms but being still incapable of shouldering any of the responsibilities. It is also a mistake to think you know what parenting is when you just have infants, toddlers, or youngsters. It should be a requirement that before anyone has children they must have raised children through and into the adult years. An impossibility, of course, but nonetheless a good idea to give would-be parents true insight.

With all that said and the caveats highlighted, there will never be another time in life when you feel so important and are so needed as when raising your family. There is also no affinity you can have for another to equal that for your child. Watching the development of children, when for them all things in the world are fresh and new, is like reliving these discoveries and joys.

Several children later, these are some of the lessons I have learned. Would I like to experience rearing all my children again? Yes, in a heartbeat. Did I do everything as well or as intelligently as I now perhaps could and am telling you to? No.

Such is life.

63

THE EMPTY NEST

HERE'S THE PROBLEM. You have a baby. It's cute and cuddly beyond your wildest dreams. It's the apple of your eye and you're completely sure there has never been another quite like it. You feel protective to the degree that you'd give your life for this little creature you've created.

At the same time, this genetic miracle you've created adores you. It's a real love-fest. As your little miracle grows you get to relive childhood and innocence through its experiences. Watching it learn and develop makes you bubble with pride. Its first smile, steps, words (or facsimile thereof), and first potty alone are marvels. Each advance further convinces you that what you've created is one-of-a-kind. You see the opportunity to shape and mold a being into perfection, just like you, or how you wish you could be.

The sensory delight can be overwhelming. Moms who nurse never have an equal experience of intimacy. Bathing an infant, holding them, sleeping with them, and listening to and smelling their pristine breath, feeling their soft succulent skin, and kissing their drooling sweet lips (if you were to open a baby's head and peer inside—now I'm not recommending you do this—you would find one giant drool gland) are not equaled by any other life experience.

The work and attention required by infants is all consuming. It's a tiring job. So you long for them to grow out of diapers and feed themselves. But once that happens, you miss what has passed. It's one of those 'can't live with it and can't live without it' deals. Time does not stand still so they continue to grow and you lose the infant. They still have the same you, but you don't have the infant anymore. How is that fair?

Now your infant is a toddler, presenting a whole new series of developmental adventures. Their thrill with new toys, watching them play with others, their endless cute antics, and their amazement of discovery is constant entertainment. You are even more convinced that what you have created is destined for something really great. Their absolute devotion to you and dependence has the effect of catalyzing the love bug infection. They are still a lot of work at this young age, even a pain in the butt at times, but you dread them getting older. Can't live with it, can't live without it. But regardless of what we want,

they continue to grow and become a young child. Your infant is gone, now your toddler is gone too. How is that fair?

Now you have a school-aged child, precocious to be sure and certainly smarter and cuter than all the rest. You beam with pride at school conferences. They become a little more independent, but you are still the center of their lives. All is well and the love affair continues. But you miss the infant and toddler and they do not come back. No problem. You've got lots of pictures and videos to capture all the magic moments.

Now

Then your totally dependent child passes into puberty and develops an independent spirit. They likely won't even want to be seen with you in public. Not that they don't love you, it's just not cool. You can't pick them up anymore (no more "uppy me"), and hugging and kissing might become uncomfortable for them. They spend more time with friends than with you and seem to use you more just for food, clothing, shelter, and play money than as the central being in their lives. You realize they must become independent, grow, and mature to face the world, but why now?

Years Later

Why so soon? It was only yesterday they were spitting up on you or peeing in your eye when you changed their diaper. It was just a few moments ago they were underfoot constantly and you were their omnipotent, omniscient god.

But that's gone. That infant, toddler, and youngster are gone forever. Your pubescent teenager doesn't even remember the thousands of hours you've invested in them and the love you've shared. It's embedded within them, but not an active memory like it is with you. They're different now, but you're the same—complete with all the vivid memories and the same feelings. Their feelings have changed, however. They are preparing to leave the nest.

You long for the infant.

No problem. You've got the pictures and tapes and recordings. So you dig them out to re-experience what you have lost. But the vivid recollection does not help. It doesn't make you content or sate your longing. It doesn't bring them back. It only amplifies the pain by making the loss so real. Back the memorabilia goes. It hurts too much.

It's tough to see your children grow up and go away. It's like having to live through a series of deaths. Each stage, each incarnation of your child 'dies'—to be replaced by another and another until they are all gone and fully apart from you. They are now creating their own nest; you have an empty one.

I know (intellectually) that this is what life is all about. But I still have a lot of trouble with the loss of my babies. At times it's just too hard a dose of life's reality.

All I can say is enjoy your children to the full. It passes so very quickly. There is no solution other than to continue to shuck out a never-ending stream of progeny—which is certainly not wise. Anyway, you can't do it forever and you would be not only just forestalling the inevitable, but multiplying it as well.

For self preservation, it's best to resist looking back too much and mourning. But for me, right now is a tough time since my youngest are now leaving home—a home filled with reminders of them— and off to college. I love these new semi-adult creatures too and would not trade them for anything, but I also love the ones who have gone, the toddlers and infants, who will never return.

I also know that this is just life moving forward, a series of passages with endings and beginnings. I know that happiness requires that we always keep a sense of future, and challenge ourselves with new goals. But moving on, living the moment, and looking forward can be tough when you have loved so much those who are leaving you behind.

I know this may sound like a lamentation, and it is to a large extent. But it is also a forewarning to those who have not had children and to those who have only young ones. The bottom line is to be smart, not naïve, about having children. It is a lifelong adventure. Love them as much as you can. Their time with you will pass soon and you will only be left with the doubt that you ever loved enough no matter how much you poured into it.

(To my children: Consider this a love letter from Dad to you and all your past molts and incarnations.)

SECTION K

Thinking about. . .

LIFE LESSONS

IN THIS SECTION: *Life presents many surprises. Some are pleasant, even wonderful. Some are painful and tragic. We can learn from these events, even learn from the experiences of others to try to carve out a better life and avoid the bad parts. As we look back we will often think, "If I only knew then what I know now." This Section gives a heads up on what life brings. You can learn from this or repeat it all for yourself and then say one day, "If I had only listened to what I read in that (this) book!"*

64

EXPERIENCE

No matter how reasonable the counsel or compelling the argument, we too often must live the experience and feel the pain before we really apply wisdom in our lives. For example, there is nothing like saying the wrong thing at the wrong time and feeling the embarrassment, or the empathy for the pain we have caused another, to teach the wisdom of zipping it or putting things another way the next time.

The value of experience was brought so vividly to mind for me when I experienced a car accident. A lady ran a red light and I broadsided her in the middle of the intersection. Decades later I can still see her car rolling up on its side exposing the undercarriage. I remember how fast it happened and how helpless I was at that moment. I was only going about 40 mph but the sick crushing pain from the impact of my body on the dashboard and windshield stays with me to this day. Hobbling around on crutches for weeks nursing a knee injury is not something I wish to repeat, either.

I gained a lot of respect for tons of moving vehicle and the cold and unyielding reality of momentum and inertia. Up until then, the danger of automobiles was an abstraction. I heard about it, studied it in driver's education classes, saw the statistics, passed terrible accidents on the road, and even lost relatives and friends to car accidents. It was still all theory; it wouldn't happen to me. Well, yes, I realized it could, but it was a long shot because I thought I was a good driver and in control of things.

Experience indelibly taught me that it *can* happen to me and that I better drive and live defensively. I knew before the accident that I should pay attention to cross traffic even if I had the green light, but after I *really* knew! That experience I was fortunate enough to survive created a sense of caution and wisdom that may have more than once helped me avoid even greater disasters. That is the useful takeaway, not that life was unfair ("poor me") or that God shouldn't have let me experience the pain.

It is not by reading books or listening to lectures that the old become wise (which has caused me pause more than once as I have worked through this book of words and counsel). It is in the school of hard knocks that people grow, mature, and become sage. The more dramatic the life experiences, the more profoundly we are shaped.

How We Insist On Living

We could read every book in the world and speak to every person. But we will never know the true meaning of the death of a parent, spouse, or child, getting divorced, having children, being imprisoned, abject poverty, marriage, sex, being robbed, having a fortune, being lost in the wilderness, life-threatening or debilitating illness, growing a successful business beginning with nothing, being down-sized, or losing or gaining freedoms until we live through such events.

I'm not suggesting we must experience all things. That's where intelligence comes in. Hopefully we can be smart enough to learn some things from afar. But in most instances we can't seem to really know until we live the experience. Experience gives an edge not obtainable by any other means.

As a young person I hated to hear, "You don't have enough experience," or "When you get older you'll understand." It was frustrating because it was a defeat I could not overcome other than by the addition of years. Yes, it is an advantage to the older generation. But life is not even. (It is, however, fair.)

This explains why age and experience should be respected more than any other credential. The passage of years brings an accumulation of experience that always brings a measure of wisdom proportional to the amount of experience. If someone 'has been there and done that,' we should pay heed far more than if someone is just giving advice because they heard or read such and such somewhere.

The trick to defeating the inexperience disadvantage is to experience as much as possible as quickly as possible until we have come to realize that experience is the best teacher. Then we can reach out for the wisdom of others and learn from their experience. That's where intelligence comes in: not always having to put our hands on the hot burners or feel the pain for every choice in life. At the very least, if we will not learn from others, we should learn from our painful experiences and change behavior.

Those who do not learn from others or from their own experiences miss the fullness of life and invite so much unnecessary misery. Even the lowliest of animals learn from stimuli. Nevertheless, our prisons are full of those who refuse to learn regardless of the stimulus. Political systems continue to repeat the same oppressive and dehumanizing control over populations. Environmental ruination marches on in spite of the lessons of history and the obvious fact that we should not foul our own nest. The stupidity of insisting upon our right to repeat mistakes is everywhere.

Being a thinking person means paying attention to our own and others' experiences and then changing. The difficulties in life are often painful, but look at such experiences as gifts—the best way of all to learn life's lessons and become a better person.

65

EDUCATION

EDUCATION IS A LIFELONG DUTY and adventure. It means learning, growing, and applying knowledge. Certain fundamentals must be gained, but education is not about settling in on a list of beliefs, closing the book, taking a test, and getting a degree. An open mind is forever essential or we make ourselves vulnerable to errors that could jeopardize the planet and ourselves.

Mental growth is an ongoing endeavor and a basic human requirement for happiness. Continuous intellectual development is necessary to be interesting to others, properly function in society, and to contribute to improving the world.

Although school should teach us how to think in this way and train us in practical skills and critical thinking, it does not. Instead it occupies students with endless irrelevancies, minutia, and the politically correct agendas of educators and text writers.

As such, modern education stands in the way of enlightenment. So the sooner a student can get out of school and set about educating themselves (assuming they do) and gaining experience in the real world, the better. As it is, the more important lessons gained in school have little to do with books and lectures. Things such as genuine concern from a loving teacher, fear of a bully, and infatuation for a classmate all create indelible lessons we remember for a lifetime. On the other hand, the only lesson most kids take away after learning the Pythagorean theorem and the date of the battle of Gettysburg is that learning is boring and seems to be a waste of time.

Personal initiative, individual study, successes, mistakes, fear, challenge, and pride of accomplishment out in the real world are the best teachers. This and its companion book encapsulate the important issues we face in real life and have taken over 100 chapters and almost a thousand pages to cover in abbreviated form. The fact that essentially none of this material is covered in formal schooling is a testament to the failure of modern education.

Without sufficient life experience (which creates little hooks in the mind to which details can attach), or a specific need to apply information, learning by rote goes into short-term memory long enough to pass a test and is then lost. As mental calisthenics, coursework is fine. As training for life it is woefully inadequate. Children are taught how to read (barely) but they are left unable to distinguish what is worth reading. School teaches about things, not reasons.

If in doubt about the utility of modern education, ask employers whether new graduates (other than from trade schools) bring to the workplace anything other than tools they don't know how to use. Bosses joke about how they can expect to see whiteout on computer monitors and have to put stamps under lock and key so they are not used up on faxes when new grads come on board. About the most an employer can hope for is to find an employee who is motivated, eager to learn, and a self-starter (all rarities). From there the employer is faced with all the costs of training—something school should have already done.

In the meantime, the educational system takes a big chunk out of tax dollars and teachers get relatively good salaries and great benefits. (Overcompensation for the poor teachers; undercompensation for the good ones.) Although graduates are not ready to hit the ground running, educators—who use the absurd lecture, note-take, regurgitate pedantry—mislead students into believing that they are receiving real training that can immediately command high wages and benefits. This not only does a disservice to the student but forces employers to repair the damage and bring new graduates back down to earth. Mark Twain had it right when he said, as I recall, "Education is not as sudden as a massacre, but it's more deadly in the long run."

Understandably, students spending years burdened by mountains of memorization are exhausted by academic demands and feel entitled to a reward, even though they intuitively know that the majority of what they have memorized is worthless. Most graduates see education as a price paid, a certificate for entitlement, and a burdensome part of their personal history, not an active and engaging part of their future. The result is a population that associates education only with school—a necessary but distasteful right of passage. People are left unmotivated to learn and grow, and workplaces fill with overpaid, under-skilled employees.

Schools should effectively teach the academic basics. Very general courses in all the disciplines can give students a broad overview of what knowledge holds. But what is the point of years of study in algebra and geometry, in a foreign language, or in scientific detail when 99.999% of those learning it will never use it after graduation? In the meantime, schools dump people into society who don't know how to balance a checkbook, avoid credit card debt, spell, write a clear letter, prepare meals, fix a plugged sink, sew a button on, check the car oil and tire pressure, or change the furnace filter.

Such a practical education could be accomplished easily within 6-8 years of school, but beginning at an older age. Too much education is wasted on the young. School days should be shortened and not begin in the early morning when growing bodies and minds should be sleeping. By compressing school time, teachers would be forced to hit the high points that students need and are more likely to retain.

Specific training for specific careers should follow these 6-8 years with lots of hands-on practical experience and emphasis on problem solving. Before a student is released into the workforce they should be able to accomplish a job with competence. As things presently are, most degrees do not signify useful skills other than book reading and test taking.

WHY COLLEGES DON'T WORK

Multiple choice history test question:
Colonization encouraged trade, industry, and the manufacturing of items such as:
    a. weapons, pottery, silks, and leather products
    b. pottery, silks, weapons, and fine artistic metalwork
    c. fine artistic metalwork, tools, pottery, and silks
    d. tools, weapons, pottery, and fine artistic metalwork

Preparing my daughter for the world - This is a sample question from a test she was given by a history professor. The course is required for her degree in a business related field. History is an immensely interesting and important subject, but a student would be lucky to discover that under such tutelage. To obtain this kind of 'education,' students incur tens of thousands of dollars in costs and then expect to receive high salaries. What possible value could such trivial information bring either the student or their prospective employer?

©Wysong

Also, coursework in intellectually challenging topics should be interspersed in the school curriculum. Topics such as philosophy, science, religion, marriage, family, metaphysics, politics, sociology, ethics, and logic should be subjects everyone at least touches upon. Such coursework would make it clear that education is not something achieved, it is a process. The most important takeaway should be the

SOLVER principles: Self-responsibility, Open thinking, Long view, Virtue, Evidence, and Reason. These principles encourage synthesis, original thinking, and hands-on learning, not dull memorization of ideas or facts to be nailed into the brain.

Teachers should be accomplished in the real-world field they are teaching and be accountable at all times. If there is any occupation that should be under pressure to achieve performance standards at all times, it is teaching. Instead, unlike any other career, mere time (tenure) can lock in a bad teacher for a lifetime. The best formula for souring young minds on education is to force incompetent and unlikable teachers on them. Education is not about teachers and their security—it's about properly training young minds and motivating the intellect of the next generation.

These are all nice ideas, but education is too institutionalized, governmentized, unionized and tenurized to change any time soon. It likes itself the way it is: very comfortable and secure for all who feed from it. Never mind whether students, the workplace, and society are benefiting as they should from it.

TEACHING MATH THROUGH THE YEARS

Teaching Math in 1860: A logger sells a wagonload of lumber for $100. His cost of production is 4/5 of the price. Write an essay about what his profit is.

Teaching Math in 1960: A logger sells a truckload of lumber for $100. His cost of production is 4/5 of the price, or $80. What is his profit?

Teaching Math in 1980: A logger sells a truckload of lumber for $100. His cost of production is $80 and his profit is $20. Your assignment: Underline the number 20.

Teaching Math in 1990: By cutting down beautiful forest trees, the logger makes $20 but is now out of work. What do you think of this way of making a living? There are no wrong answers.

Teaching Math in 2000: A logger sells a truckload of lumber for $100. His cost of production is $120. Find an accounting firm that will determine that his profit margin is $60.

Teaching Math in 2010: A greedy logger sells a truckload of lumber for $100. Here is contact information for lawyers who will sue loggers for discriminating against conifer and deciduous Americans. Your question: Do you e-mail an attorney or use your cell phone?

(Adapted from an Internet circulated e-mail.)

There is no grand conspiracy to keep education boring, irrelevant, and expensive. It's just that those who write curricula and who teach know no better and find it easiest to stay in the same groove in which they were taught. Charles Chesnut observed, "...popular education is merely a means of forcing the stupid and repressing the bright, so that all the youth of the rising generation might conform to the same dull, dead level of democratic mediocrity."

Love of children and wanting to teach are certainly important, but not enough. Students who go through high school, then college, then graduate school to become teachers are still students of the school kind. School students teach others how to be school students, not what life is really about or how to succeed in it.

A teacher entrusted with the future of the world (children), must have lived out in the work world and proven their ability to be successful at it. Particularly should this be so at the high school and college levels. Instead, too often those who were incapable or nonproductive in the workplace find a home in a teaching position. We must change the aphorism: Those who can, do; those who cannot, teach. It should be: Those who can, teach; those who cannot should go do something else. One on-line university has the right idea. Their advertising for professors says, "If you haven't done it during the daytime, you can't teach it at night!"

Speaking of the Internet, that may be the catalyst for a solution to education's problems. It creates a realistic alternative to the traditional classroom format. Education will not change from within because it is too comfortable with itself like all embedded institutions. The free market of Internet choices may create the pressure all institutions pay most attention to—economics. That will force the system to either become relevant and efficient or die a quiet death as their tuition and tax resources dry up.

Parents are not above blame or absolved from educational responsibilities just because kids can be pushed off to school. Educators cannot be trusted and school is not just a convenient baby sitter. Education, like goodness, begins at home. Home schooling or 'un-schooling' (an actual movement you can search out on the Internet) are options every parent should explore. At the least, parents should engage with children when they get home from school. Children learn best by experience and example, and parents are in the best position to put what is being taught in school into practical context. Meaningful learning in youth is like engraving on stone, and competent parents who follow the SOLVER principles are the best sculptors.

THE TRUTH ABOUT COLLEGE

College is rooms you rush to and fro from for four years to memorize things. The rest of the time you party and drink. Less than one-tenth of one percent of what you memorize is of any value. Professors don't know how to tell you which is the stuff of value. So they test you on it all. If you fail to forget all the stuff that is not important you get to be a professor and stay in college forever.

To make your stay easier, it's best not to major in the sciences where you will be held responsible for knowing actual facts. If, for example, you major in mathematics, you're going to wander into class one day and the professor will say: "Define the cosine integer of the quadrant of a rhomboid binary axis, and extrapolate your result to five significant vertices." Since this sort of information will prove essential to you in adult life, if you don't come up with the exact answer, you fail. The same is true of chemistry. If you write in your exam book that water is comprised of wet atoms, you will be flunked. You must come up with the same answer all the chemistry scientists have agreed to. Professors are extremely snotty about this.

So you should major in subjects like English, philosophy, psychology, and sociology—subjects in which nobody really understands what anybody else is talking about, and which involve virtually no actual facts you have to be sure about. For example:

ENGLISH: This involves writing papers about long books you have read little snippets of just before class. Here is a tip on how to get good grades on your English papers. Never say anything about a book that anybody with any common sense would say. For example, suppose you are studying Moby Dick. Anybody with any common sense would say that Moby Dick is a big white whale. So in your paper you say Moby Dick actually represents the competing interests of Russia and America in Antarctica—which is big and white. Your professor will think you are wonderfully insightful and creative. If you can regularly come up with lunatic interpretations of simple stories, you should major in English.

PHILOSOPHY: Basically, this involves reading a lot of big books by guys in robes who lived thousands of years ago. When you can decide that you do not exist, or that if you do it does not matter, you go get some lunch. Major in philosophy if you plan to take a lot of drugs.

PSYCHOLOGY: This involves studying mice in mazes and talking about dreams. Psychologists are obsessed with mice and dreams. You may be required to do an experiment to test how fast mice can learn to push buttons for food compared to your roommate. If the mice beat the roommate, that is highly predictive of your roommate becoming a psychology professor. If you like mice and dreams, and above all if you dream about mice, psychology should be your major.

SOCIOLOGY: Sociology professors want to be considered scientists, so they spend most of their time translating simple, obvious observations into scientific-sounding code. If you plan to major in sociology, you'll have to learn to do the same thing. For example, suppose you have observed that children cry when they fall down. You should write: "Methodological observation of the sociometrical behavior tendencies of prematurated isolates indicates that a causal relationship exists between groundward tropism and lacrimatory behavior forms." If you can keep this up for fifty or sixty pages, you will get a large government grant.

(Modified from an Internet circulated e-mail.)

66

LIFE IS UNCERTAIN

Expectations in our early years go a long way in determining our happiness. Certainly setting lofty goals and working hard to achieve them is important. But that is not the ethic promoted in the modern world. We are led to believe that things come easily, we can avoid unpleasantness, we are entitled, immediate gratification is only a few dollars away and—perhaps most delightful of all—we are the focus of other peoples' attention and interest. Moreover, when young, we assume that if we jump through the hoops of going to school, landing a job, getting married, having children, and making big bucks we will live happily ever after. Life can seem so certain when we are young and look forward.

Entertainment presents a Pollyanna ideal in which people are physically perfect, apparently don't worry, are certain of their life's course, always have fulfilling love and companionship, are secure in themselves, and seem to have abolished all negative aspects of life. Commerce exploits these fantasies by attempting to convince us that their products and services are the means to a perfect life. Surgeons reshape bodies, closets bulge with every new fashion, impoverished ghetto children wear $150 sneakers, zillionaires glut themselves with the best that money can buy, and therapists are used as a substitute for personal reflection, learning, healthy life choices, exercise of conscience, and self-responsibility.

But as time marches on, an idealistic life is not our life. We make mistakes, we hate to take risks, we are uncertain, financial security seems elusive, there isn't time to interact properly with those we love, our face has a new wrinkle, our hairline is receding, problems continue to mount, and we do not feel as though we are gaining more control, but rather losing it. When we contrast real life against the ideal marketed to society, we can feel failure, inadequacy, bitterness, social alienation, and hopelessness. All because we are chasing a fantasy, an unreal mythology about how life should be, rather than how it is.

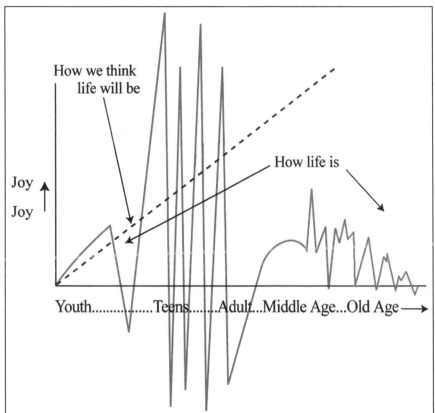

The Ups And Downs Of Life - We think, starting out, that life will be peaches and cream. Then the wild ups and downs of the tumultuous teenage years hit. As life moves on through the adult years there are fewer highs and more lows as the impact of the baggage we accumulate disappoints us. In old age there arc few surprises any longer in life and thus the wild swings level out and we see the world more clearly for what it is. Understanding this natural progression helps us put things in perspective and focus on things that will bring true meaning to life.

This is the reality:

• Pain, difficulty, and failure are part and parcel of being alive. (Notice even movie stars, sports heroes, moguls, and presidents face crises and tragedy.)

• The future cannot be programmed, it is uncertain.

• Any accomplishment requires hard work and dedication, both to achieve and maintain.

• Everyone is not looking at us, we are not the center of other peoples' universe, and it's not 'all about me.'

• No matter what you do, you cannot avoid the above.

• None of this will ever change.

We can't perfect life and then get it to stand still. Of course we would like to grip some experiences forever, such as our children's early years of innocence, winning at sports, the love and adoration of parents, receiving an honor, being in love, and good friendships. While we're saving and savoring all these things, at the same time we would like to be able to remove the pain from the loss of a loved one, the incapacity of illness, the loss of a critical sale or game, or rejection by a friend. Confusion and uncertainty are season ticket holders on the roller coaster of life. Life is a flow of events, a never-ending succession of peaks and valleys. Although we may attempt to deny this and work against it, we will not succeed. But that is okay.

How We Think Life Is...

How It <u>Really</u> Is...

It is best to be aware of and accept life's uncertainty. If we know we will be faced with the unexpected then we will not be unduly surprised and can set about making the necessary adjustments rather than whining and beating our chests in despair. Much better to label events as failure, tragedy, success, or happiness, and see them for what they are: momentary happenings that will be replaced with yet others. By not embracing too tenaciously that which will not remain (everything), we open ourselves to new adventures, challenges, and joys, and avoid the trap of always looking backward with regret or longing.

We get a grip on reality when we see life as a process, a dynamic with unpredictable curves, stops, reverses, and new paths over which we may not have control, and some choices over which we do. Part of that reality is that life's uncertainty and challenges are what we need to become better people. Without forks in the road we cannot exercise choice and conscience. Without trying times we do not reflect on who we really are—people who are here for the purpose of becoming, becoming better people.

67

THINGS MOUND UP

PEOPLE SPEND MUCH OF LIFE busily moving toward goals of less work, less burden, fewer problems, and more peace, happiness, and freedom. We assume that school, raising a family, and succeeding in a career will bring the reward of leisure, fun, and a more carefree life.

What we do not take into account in this appraisal is that nothing goes away completely. Everything we do in life, every contact we make, every choice, mounds up. The junk in the garage and closets starts to take on a life of its own like some alien creature pupating and swelling uncontrollably. These bulging incubators in our homes are a metaphor for what is happening on a grander scale in the rest of our lives.

The more life activity, the more the mound grows. Social contact creates personal responsibilities and history to consider. If there are children, they are a concern for life. Children compound into grandchildren to worry about. At work there is the burden of fellow workers or employees. Money in excess of that necessary for day to day needs, and the goodies purchased with it, become a chore to manage. Worse yet is consumer debt because, of course, we had to have all the trinkets pronto.

All life choices queue up behind us like railroad cars as the years march on. They aren't easily disengaged or disposed of. Almost everything is retained—at least in the mind and conscience. Over time the length of the train becomes an enormous burden to pull. The dreamed of devil-may-care golden years can turn into worrisome and obligating toil as steam is lost chugging along life's track. Or we may find ourselves accelerating toward some as yet unknown calamity. The momentum and mass of all the railcars we've stacked behind push us down a hill no matter how hard we pull on the brakes.

This realization leads some to decide to drop out entirely, move into the woods, build a hut, and live off the land. Most of us have envied Thoreau's life at one time or another.[1] But if we were to move to Walden Pond we would replace modern living problems with others—like what to eat today, to name just one not-too-little problem. No matter where we are, life is about challenge and that cannot be avoided.

If we understand that every life choice comes back to give pleasure, regret, or responsibility, we can make life choices more wisely. That will mean not permitting ourselves to be swept along in the commercial stream and always putting conscience first. By so doing we can have the smallest mound possible to manage, fewer regrets, and time to work on being the better people we are meant to become.

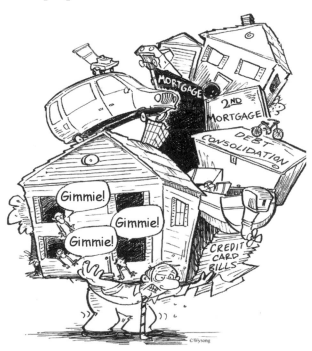

The Golden Years

68

MURPHY'S LAW

MURPHY'S LAW IS: If anything can go wrong, it will. Then there is Otoole's Commentary on Murphy's Law: Murphy was an optimist. A related law is the Law of Selective Gravity: An object will fall so as to do the most damage. Corollaries to these laws are:

• The chance of the bread falling with the jammed side down is directly proportional to the cost of the carpet.

• If there are only two programs worth watching, they will both be on at the same time.

• If you don't need it and don't want it, you can have tons of it.

• A monetary windfall is always accompanied by a new expense of the same or greater amount.

• If it's good, they discontinue it.

• If everything is coming your way, you're in the wrong lane.

• When the plane you are on is late, the one you are connecting to is always on time.

• No matter which side of the fire you move to, the smoke will come your way.

- The easiest way to find something lost is to buy a replacement.
- To find the difference between a weed and a valuable plant, pull on it. If it is a valuable plant it will come out easily.
- There is no limit to how bad things can get.

That's meant to be funny. And it is, but only because we all suffer under the burden of Murphy's Law and its corollaries. Just when we have arrived at a winning life formula, one of life's spoilers always seems to come along. That fact is so dependable that we really have no other choice but to laugh at it and roll with the punches.

Good advice. I wish I could always follow it. But sometimes it seems the world is just conniving against me. The latest devil's play I notice is how everyone times their driving to interfere with mine. This morning I drove to the end of the driveway hoping to be able to pull right out onto the road. But no. Mrs. Smarty Pants down the road has evidently been watching me and waiting to drive down the road so that I have to stop for her before I can pull out. There's not another car in sight, and not another one will pass on our remote road for another ten minutes. When I patiently wait the

ten seconds for her to pass (it feels like ten years), I drive on to the office. But before I get there I come to an intersection with a stop sign. No cars anywhere in sight, except Mr. Smarty Pants who evidently has been timing his morning in order to make me wait another ten seconds for him to go by. Such events are far too typical to be just chance.

And you thought you were having a bad day.

So, if you are feeling that the world is stacked against you at times, you aren't alone. You aren't the only one who goes to the store and gets the only cart with a wobbly wheel out of the 75 that are there. Me too. You aren't the only one to try to dig a hole in the ground and hit a gigantic root dead on center. Me too. You aren't the only one who tries to do a home repair project and never has the right tool with you, is always missing one screw, and always has one nut that will not come off. Me too.

By definition life does not course in a straight line. Even if it did it would intersect other people's lives that are not accommodating or conveniently avoiding ours. Such collisions and the setbacks they cause are unavoidable because our agenda is never perfectly in accord with others.

You aren't the only one who makes mistakes.

But rarely does a bad circumstance befall us for which we are not in some way responsible. So, difficulties and failures are not a reason for despair. Murphy is often just a reminder for some honest self-evaluation and adjustment that could save us from an even bigger catastrophe later.

Life intelligently lived is a continuing educational process meant to refine us. Without things going wrong we do not learn. Without making mistakes we can't profit from them. All sun makes a desert. Adversity and setbacks teach us humility, that we are not invincible, that it is not all about us, that we are not perfect, above the law, or superior to others. Those are lessons we must learn to fare well.

So don't let life's problems get you down or put you in a helpless mode as if you are being singled out or are a victim without control. No one, no matter how seemingly perfect their life, does not have ups and downs. We must see the valleys in life for what they are, a better vantage point from which to plan scaling the mountain.

That may seem a bit glib, as if not being defeated by life's difficulties is really that easy. After all, we all learn early on that life is not easy, that there are highs and lows and that everyone has problems. But when life does not go as we wish or plan, it is easy to react emotionally. We can feel out of control, victimized, and as if our problems are unique in human experience.

But our problems are never unique. Others have endured more and overcome. Besides, we all have the best tools to minimize Murphy in our lives. They are the SOLVER principles: Self responsibility, Open mindedness, Long view thinking, Virtuous intent, Evidence first, and Reasoning.

69

LIFE'S PREDICTABILITY

IT IS A WELL-KNOWN FACT that young children go through predictable stages. The times at which they potty train, walk, cut teeth, speak words, smile, read, write and then get pubescently cocky are all pretty precisely worked out. Parents need only pick up a book and all this development is laid right out in chart form.

But it is not generally understood that such predictability continues through adulthood. It's easy to assume that once we're in control as adults we can bend life in any direction and stop or start any stage we like. Not so. How we think and behave as adults and seniors, and the challenges we face, are predictable. It is the reason age groups throughout adulthood tend to focus on similar activities and have similar sentiments and problems.[1-3] Here are examples of some adult stages as we proceed through life:

• The desire for and pursuit of a career

• The urge to blaze new trails 'obviously' better than your parents'

• The desire to have children and mold them into perfect creatures just like you

• The shock that your children, who think you are the center of the universe, turn into teens who think they are

• The disorientation of an empty nest when there are no longer little munchkins running around adoring you

• Mid-life crisis when we realize our mortality

- Health and body failures regardless of the best efforts
- The realization that we are ultimately alone
- Concern about future security for retirement
- Desire for legacy
- The nagging of conscience for all the foolish things done in the past
- Difficulty in managing all the things accumulated in life
- Expecting respect from the young whippersnappers
- Desire for simplicity and freedom from so much responsibility
- Cynicism toward those with less life experience
- Difficulty finding things in life that are fantastic and exciting
- The realization that we are not as special as we once thought
- The desire to be close to family, home, and community
- The discovery that all of our big plans in life were really quite silly and only love and goodness are important

When we get really old we joke with friends about how the medical insurance is finally paying off, that we sing along to elevator music, got cable for the weather channel, enjoy the tales of friends' surgeries, have a party and the neighbors won't know it, and take satisfaction in the fact that the things we buy won't wear out. Then, in the final stages we can have even more fun, like the three retirees who were playing a round of golf. One said to the other, "Windy, isn't it?" The second man replied, "No, it's Thursday." The third man chimed in, "So am I, let's go have a beer."

Don't be surprised by the turns life takes and the discovery that the new trails you think you are blazing have already been well trodden. Also, don't be shocked when what you thought was forever suddenly ends or what you never imagined would happen, does. We will be chagrined more than once in life finding ourselves doing things, behaving, and thinking just like the older folk we said we would never be like (or like the younger folk we should no longer be). This is good reason to observe and listen to the older generation to see what lies in store.

Welcome life's new doors and determine to make each entrance, sojourn, and exit the best it can be. It is the twists, turns, peaks, and valleys that create the opportunity for us to grow and show our mettle.

When all is said and done, the sense of goodness we knew was important in our earliest childhood memory ends up being the only thing worth pursuing throughout all of life. Everything else is a diversion, temporary, and superfluous.

70

FINDING HOME

IT IS COMMON FOR YOUNG ADULTS to look for greener pastures. They think that surely they can do better than their parents. I was no exception. After graduating from college, I gathered my little family and went west. Colorado seemed like a beautiful place to live. There were mountains, milder winters, wilderness, and lots of perfect skiing. It would be all I imagined and more.

But it was not long after I arrived that the giddiness subsided as I became swallowed up in the day-to-day activities of work and life. There was not much room to enjoy the romantic reasons for the move. To find a job in Colorado, I found myself in Denver, a city about fifty times bigger than my hometown. In three years in Colorado, I skied twice.

One weekend I decided to take a backpacking trip with the family up the mountains into the 'wilderness.' After driving for four hours, we found ourselves trekking up a mountain on a two-lane footpath of backpackers. I could have found more private natural areas ten minutes from my home back in Michigan.

The Rocky Mountains are an incredibly beautiful place and I'm sure there are remote areas. I just didn't have the time to find them. Everyone, it seemed, was moving to Colorado for the same reasons I did and it was becoming more like a park than wilderness. This is not really to criticize Colorado, just to point out that problems—like the big city population one I tired of in Michigan—can follow you.

Many people move because of social problems created by their own personality, or because of pickles they create by not thinking through life choices. Problems we create follow us. They don't shred and break off along the road to a new destination.

Additionally, living away from where one has grown up is difficult for many people. It can be tough to develop a sense of belonging. The little things from home such as family, friends, history, and familiar geography create a sense of belonging and security hard to duplicate elsewhere. Some scientists even argue that the unique magnetic, solar, and lunar circumstances peculiar to the place of birth are implanted in us, creating a sense of uneasiness only resolved by migrating back home. These are also the factors possibly underlying the homing mechanism in migrating animals.

When I finally did move back to Michigan the sense of home was quite overwhelming. There is not much color in the semi-arid desert on the eastern plains abutting the Rockies where all the big cities are. So as I drove into Michigan in the early summer, the green was overwhelming, like a verdant fluorescence bathing my eyes with soothing familiarity.

My new job was back in the college town from which I had fled. But that didn't last long either. It was but a few years before I moved back to the small city I was raised in. None of these moves were consciously a decision to come home. Nevertheless, it was a little humbling, even embarrassing, to find myself back at the starting line of the greener pasture quest I set out on several years earlier.

There was an unmistakable comfort in being back in the place of my childhood where all was familiar. By then I had also come to realize that happiness is something we make for ourselves within our little private sphere. Changing geography does not create it and may even stand in the way.

I still fantasize that there must be, somewhere, that perfect place to live that I'm missing out on. But I have come to respect the inherent draw of my place of birth and know that I cannot disengage from it with impunity. Traditional Navajo felt similarly. They would bury the umbilical cord of their children in the floor of the hogan so the child would always be drawn to home. Pauline Whitesinger, a Navajo Big Mountain Elder, wrote: "In our traditional tongue, there is no word for relocation. To relocate is to move away and disappear."

On the other hand, we should not be afraid to explore and find circumstances more suited to our liking. For example, some people struggle with heat or cold and need to be where climate is more suited to them. For some, the only way to pursue a career they love is to move. So it is a matter of motive. If there are objective reasons that another place will help our happiness that is one thing. If we believe location in and of itself creates success or solves personality problems, we will find ourselves as disappointed as standing in line trying to get tickets at a sold out Super Bowl game.

Life is something we create for ourselves, and as such it has a way of following us around. The greenest grass is not likely in the distance. It is under our own feet if we nurture it properly.

71

LEARN FROM HISTORY

HISTORY TELLS US THE RESULTS of putting theory into practice. It cuts to the chase. Looking back on our own individual history—called experience—gives us better savvy to face what lies ahead. Experience helps us to know in a very personal and definitive way what works and what does not. No one would say that if they could take their history with them and live life over that they would not be able to do a better job of it.

We can't do that, but we could listen to those who have lived more life than us and then use their life wisdom to guide our own. But no, we think we know better so we don't listen. We insist on making our own mistakes, suffering our own bruises, and then complain that life is not fair.

Society as a whole does the same thing. The history of the world is experience in grand storybook form. Society can read it for entertainment, or learn from it and save repeating the same mistakes over and over.

One of the reasons we do not pay attention to history as we should is because we think we are different from people of the past. Our heady time of technological pyrotechnics creates a smugness that leads us to presume that pre-modern era humans were unsophisticated stone-age brutes. But a closer look tells us that is not so.

As far back as written records go, clear back to the Phaistos disk printed by a printing press using a syllabary of 45 signs (one sign for each syllable) 3,700 years ago, there is clear evidence that humans were as innately intelligent, or more so, than we are today.[1] The ideas underlying our Constitution were in large part borrowed from the Romans who borrowed from the Greeks before them. Much of today's engineering can be traced back to the Minoans who predated the Greeks. Romanesque and neoclassical Greek architecture can be seen everywhere in our present culture, and particularly in Washington D. C. If we removed all words derived from Latin, we would lose half of our dictionary. As archeologists dig deeper and deeper into the strata of our history there is every reason to be humbled.

About the time that humans abandoned hunter-gatherer nomadic life and developed iron-based statehood, extraordinary intellectual progress blossomed. Look at the great structures of incredible size, engineering, and intricate detail that were created without one power tool or machine. The Taj Mahal, the Greek Parthenon, ancient Rome, and the Pyramids are examples of such marvelous tectonics. Around the world there are also unbelievably immense megaliths. Some stones comprising these structures are so gigantic that it would have taken 30,000 men to move one a single inch. Yet they were moved hundreds of miles over land and then elevated dozens of feet in the air. Structures in Europe, Mesoamerica, and the South Pacific are made of thousands of stones weighing tons each, and were somehow hewn to fit so tightly that a playing card cannot even be inserted anywhere in the joints. We, with all of our smarts and technology, cannot replicate these feats yet to this day.

People in the past were intelligent with respect to their technology, but they were not so clever that they could not destroy themselves through environmental devastation, or by senseless warring. It is a mistake to assume that their demise was due to a lack of sophistication. We do well to respect their intelligence and learn from reflecting on their mistakes. Otherwise, their history will be a prologue for our future. Just as our own experience shapes who we are, the present circumstances of society are the legacy of the past. If we want to know the future we must therefore look to the past. There is nowhere else to look; that is our crystal ball.

Here's an interesting piece of history demonstrating how closely we are tied with the past.

Notice that the space shuttle has two solid fuel booster rockets on the sides of the gigantic main fuel tank. Why are these the size they are? Surely this was determined by sophisticated science... or was it?

As it turns out, Thiokol, a company in Utah that must ship them to the launch pads, makes the tanks. The mode of shipment is by rail. The tunnels the trains must pass through and the width of the rail cars dictate the thickness of the tanks.

How We Learn From History

What determines the width of the rail cars? It's based on the track. The track is exactly a standard gauge of 4 feet, 8 inches.

What a weird dimension. Why is this the distance between rails? Because the first American and Canadian rails were built by expatriated Englishmen and that's how they did it in England. But why did they do that in England? Because the first railroads were built by those who built tramways and that's how they did it.

So why did the tramway builders do it that way? Because they had the jigs, templates, and tools used to build wagons and that was the wheel spacing for the wagons. Why this wheel spacing for wagons? Because the wheels needed to fit into the ruts on roads so they wouldn't break.

So where did the ruts come from? Imperial Rome etched those ruts with their war chariots, the wheels of which carved roads all over Europe, including England.

Why 4 feet, 8 inches? Because that's the width of the rear-ends of two Roman war horses.

So, the dimensions of the space shuttle, a crowning achievement of human technological advance, are based on a horse's ass.

History indeed casts long shadows and our link to it is inextricable. But that does not mean we are doomed to repeat it. We can break our obstinate habits and pay special attention to the experience of our own lives and that of others. That will give us wisdom beyond our years. We can also pay attention to the bigger picture of society's experience and create a new history for our children, one of reason, fiduciary responsibility, compassion, and hope. Nothing is stopping us from changing the course of our lives and the downward spiral of civilization other than doing what is right, doing it now, and going about it as if thinking matters.

72

SHAPING THE FUTURE

THE FUTURE IS UNKNOWN but is shaped by the actions of humans each day. However, the complexity of our modern world makes it seem as though our individual concerns and voices are too puny to make a difference. So we tend to live for the moment *carpe diem*, dream about what might be, and assume somebody else, somewhere else, pulls all the strings.

Yes there are movers and shakers but they are flesh and blood like everyone else. All they did was decide to make a difference and then act.

Each of us can, too.

Technology and machines have brought us so much comfort and security that it is easy to believe that is where our hope for a better world lies. But technology has no conscience and is not deserving of our faith. If anything, technology devoid of conscience has become the number one threat to our very survival.

The degree to which development of technology has been given precedence over development of character is exemplified by the hopes tied to the space program. As I write this, the famous astrophysicist, Stephen Hawking, received headline news because of his warning that the only way we may survive as a species is to colonize space. After we turn the Earth into a gigantic paved landfill, or just before the Earth is vaporized by modern weaponry, we would just hop on spaceships bound for a new planet to plunder. It's like hoping to move to a new house when the grass gets too long and the stinky dishes pile up too high at the kitchen sink.

There is no sci-fi paradise in our solar system. The nearest hope, the star Alpha Centauri, is over 25 trillion miles away. If we tried to make that daunting trip at anything much less than the speed of light we'd die of old age long before we got there. Even then we might be foiled since that star may not have any planets that are just right. Not just any rock orbiting a star will do. We are finely tuned biological machines designed for this specific Earth habitat. The size of the planet relative to the size of the star, and the distance from it all combine to make the right conditions. The air, water, food, solar and lunar cycles, magnetic forces, and climate of Earth determine our health. Vary them and disease and death result. Protracted time in space, or on a planet not exactly like this one, would either be lethal or a miserable, disease-ridden sojourn.

It's fun to dream about greener pastures somewhere 'out there,' or visitations from superior aliens who will coach us to a better world. But a better life is not about quick fixes, salvation by aliens, or by 'experts.' A better world and a better us is an internal—not external—thing. Our best space program is one directed at making spaceship Earth the paradise it could become. It's about us picking ourselves up by our own bootstraps, reaching inside to listen to the inner voice, and doing things right. It's work and it takes thinking, but that is what all good things require and is our only true hope for the future.

73

THE OTHER LINE ALWAYS MOVES FASTER

OUR FAST-PACED WORLD can give us the feeling that everything is a race and that winning and losing defines every moment of the day. In the important matters of life, winning is a proper goal. The key word there is *important*. The problem is that most things in life, particularly the ones we stress about day-to-day, are not really important in the larger scheme of things.

We tend to take meaningless events as personally as if our value is diminished if others get ahead of us once in a while. For example, being in the slow line is frustrating. But that is the way things are; some must always be last. Who says we get to always be ahead? If we always get to be the first, then others always have to be last. Where is that written?

Have you noticed that the guy weaving in and out of traffic, tailgating, speeding, honking, and flipping everyone off ends up beside you at the red light? Even if he were to get ahead, how much time would be shaved off? One minute, five at most? The same could be said for grocery lines where you desperately search for the shortest one, but then, to your horror, discover that the 'idiot' in front of you needs three price checks, has 56 coupons to redeem, and is paying with change that has to be counted out.

In the greater scheme of things will the few moments of time we are stressing about really mean anything? Are our days so packed with meaningful activity that a few minutes' delay will make a difference? Think about how many one minutes and five minutes we have during the course of a day that are a waste, when we are basically doing nothing. Is creating more of this time by being obnoxious in traffic or rude in lines worth the stress and the knowledge that we have been a jerk?

Arrives home

Why We Must Hurry

Chill. Relax a little. Make it a daily challenge to let others win and be first where it does not matter. Yield in traffic, open the door to let others pass first, be content with the longer line, wait your turn, and let others go ahead of you. Rush only to do a good deed or an act that will brighten another person's day. Do not let the frenetic pace of modern life sweep you along. Get your bearings on what matters, see things in perspective, and let others beat you in meaningless races. Be patient and feel (and be) like a winner compared to all the other foolish people hurrying to wait, or rushing home to do nothing.

74

LITTLE THINGS ADD UP

GREAT WONDERS OF THE WORLD—such as the pyramids, the space shuttle, utility grids, dams, waterways, skyscrapers, and computers—come to be one little bit at a time. Moreover, flesh and blood people just like you and me created such apparent impossibilities. They were just patient and persistent enough to make them piece-by-piece.

Look at the great castles, cathedrals, and other monuments of days gone by that were built before there were even light bulbs, electricity, bulldozers, cranes, power drills, or jackhammers. The intricate detail of these structures is astonishing and their scale overwhelming. Yet they were apparently done with little more than primitive hammers and chisels, one chip at a time. All it takes for great feats is being content with one chip at a time and an eye to an end result that can bring pride.

Great knowledge, wisdom, and physical ability come incrementally as well. If one were to examine each of the increments in the lives of notable people, no one big deal would be discovered. We gain knowledge by listening, reading, and observing one day at a time. Wisdom comes from reflecting on experience and knowledge gained one day at a time. Athletic skill comes from practice one day at a time. Those who then become accomplished are not something other than normal humans. If anything deserves honor and respect, it is the work and persistence, not the person.

Any of us can accomplish great feats and be of great skill. All it takes is a goal and a willingness to work on it in doable increments and not get too anxious about the end result. Life itself can be a great accomplishment, or something that just takes up time and space. Each step, each day is a choice each of us makes. We can look back and say we should have, or we can begin, stick with it, work on it one day at a time and say, I did.

Life's magic is desire, persistence, and patience. It is not genetics, genius, or luck. It's about sweat, sacrifice, and small victories.

So, do you want to be a doctor, lawyer, pilot, engineer, musician, author, craftsman, parent, leader, or just accomplish something that really seems worthwhile? Start today, begin one step at a time, and take delight in the accomplishment of each of those steps. Does it seem like you could walk around the world? No. Can you take one step at a time and walk around the world (with a few boat assists)? Yes.

Bit by doable bit, all seemingly impossible feats result from the accumulation of one stone, brick, or bolt at a time.

Great feats are really not that at all. They are just the accumulation of small easy steps. The fantastic accomplishments of man are nothing more than small parts all added up. Great people are those who understand this.

75

GROWING UP

WHEN WE ARE YOUNG CHILDREN our parents fulfill every need and define our world in what seems to us as absolutes. We never again have it so simple, easy, or well packaged. Growing up and away from that secure nest is no small task. Some fight it to their dying breath.

As a child we feel we are the center of other people's universes. Parents, relatives, teachers, and other adults create that self-centeredmess (spelled correctly) with their love and nurturing. Although that is important to our early development, we can't let it go to our heads. Unfortunately, it's easy to get comfortable with the notion that everything is about us. Growing up means coming to understand that it is not.

As our bodies and brains mature, our horizons should stretch. Questions we once did not have will come to haunt us with uncertainty. If we ignore these new and indefinite horizons and questions, we remain intellectually a child. It is no better to accede to society's accepted answers and subjugate ourselves to 'experts.' We remain children when we pirouette around our responsibility to seek truth by looking for a sufficient payload of unjustified beliefs to keep everything well defined and sure. Substituting experts and the consensus view for our parents is just like moving back home. We leave our genetic mommies and daddies and move in with the mommies and daddies society puts in their place.

Growing up for real means to use our own mind and heart to search for as many answers as we can, always remaining open to truth, and conceding that there are some things we may never fully understand.

On any clear night look into the sky. It should be a humbling experience and give perspective. The Earth is just a small planet in just one galaxy among millions. Our planet receives only 2 billionths of the light energy from our average star/sun and there are trillions of suns in the universe. We are infinitesimally puny in the greater scheme of things. No matter how much we would like to think so, it is ridiculous on its face to assume we are the focus of the universe.

Adulthood means humility and admitting human ignorance. There are no omniscient moms, dads, experts, or other authority figures we can rely upon for all the answers. When humans proceed as if they know everything, as if their brain speck defines the universe, harm results. War, disease, oppression, poverty, and environmental degradation can all be linked back to those who position themselves as having authority and truth, and to millions of complicit human lemmings who let others be their surrogate mommies and daddies.

Growing Up Is Not About
Finding New Mommies And Daddies

WYSONG

Adulthood is a continuing process requiring search, openness, change, and self-reliance. It means malleability and a willingness to put the SOLVER principles first in life. It will never be as easy as just taking another's word for it, regardless of their credentials. Since belief is the seed from which all human activity, good or bad, arises, each of us must take responsibility for developing our own humble and reasoned philosophy of life. We must be especially wary of any unexamined belief that owes its existence to the mere words of another frail and faulty human. We are really not free to embrace any belief we fancy any more than we are free to believe two plus two equals seven. (This timely and interesting idea that—we are really not free to believe as we choose—is developed fully in the companion book.)

If we let our conscience and our desire for truth guide us, and we recognize that the search for truth is a continuing endeavor, we have the best hope for a better world, and a grown up and better us.

76

ALONE

Perhaps the most difficult of all life lessons is to come to the realization that each of us is ultimately alone. To ever truly grow up, every person must face this reality.

But it's hard, having been reared as we were. We start as the apple of our parents' eyes, have doting relatives and teachers who make us feel special, and are taught that God is personally watching over us. A secure job, social aid programs, and a mate and children of our own continue the feeling of being cared for and important.

But along the way we are slapped with reality—if we choose to be awake. We leave the nest and must fend for ourselves; our parents divorce or die; family members strike out on their own or die; we leave the embrace of school; organized religion turns out to be a faulty human institution; we get sued for no just cause; friends abandon us; salespeople defraud us; government does not come to our rescue and may even treat us unjustly; our mate fails us or dies; we lose our job; our children leave the nest with barely an acknowledgement of the pain, sacrifice and hero-ism we went through in their rearing. What are you left with? You.

That litany may seem like a real downer. It need not be. It is reality, and reality is what we all must come to grips with if we are to succeed in life. Success is the upper. Understanding that we are ultimately alone does not mean we cannot have pleasant, even wonderful relationships. It just means that we are ultimately responsible for ourselves and our own fulfillment. You are the CEO of your own life and the buck stops with you.

With that understanding comes reflection about who we are and why we are here. Looking inward instead of outward to rely on others allows us to become what we can become: the best we can be. That is our real destiny, and we can only discover it when we understand that we are ultimately alone.

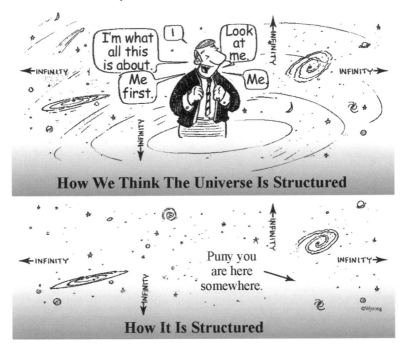

How We Think The Universe Is Structured

How It Is Structured

Although we are alone in terms of responsibility for ourselves, we are joined at a fundamental level with everyone and everything. (The scientific basis for this will be discussed in the companion book.) That holistic sense, however, is only realized through grown-up, adult outreach and love, as opposed to self-centered and dependent expectations as if the world circles us.

It is strange but true that only when we learn that we are alone and that others do not owe us, can we express selfless love. That love, in turn, is the only way that our desire to be loved and not feel alone is fulfilled.

77

HOPE

ENVIRONMENTAL DESTRUCTION, billions of people starving or living hand-to-mouth, natural disasters, insane dictators, terrorism, corporate greed, urban violence, unprincipled politicians, and unreasoned governmental policies can make the world seem hopeless. But there are lilies among the debris and pond scum. You and I are those beautiful flowers waiting to blossom.

We can go about our business keeping our nose out of trouble only to have catastrophe befall us because the big players—business, institutions, and government—are not playing fair. The world at large is now the stage upon which we all are players. Like it or not we must think of the world-scale big picture. We are not independent islands. We must be interested and engaged. But how can one puny person be anything other than a pawn or victim of such large forces?

We are all empowered because we are made of the same organic stuff those who cause the problems are made of. If one person can mess things up on a world-scale (consider the impact of Attila, Napoleon, Hitler, Ossama), one person can make things better (consider Gandhi and Mother Theresa). Feeling hopeless and victimized can be self-fulfilling. Not only does pessimism and shrinking from difficulty cause torpor and permit evil to spread like a cancer, it also robs life of joy, fulfillment, and even health. Difficulty creates challenge, and challenge is the opportunity for us to be truly alive.

Hope resides in action, in feeling like we can make a difference, and that our deeds and words do matter. And they do. Our actions and thoughts can have impact worldwide. This can happen from direct contact networking—since everyone in the world is only about 5 or so networked people removed from everyone else—and from more ethereal mechanisms we are only beginning to understand such as holography, morphic resonance, and quantum reality. We are, in fact, part of one interconnected living whole. Losing hope based on just the events we personally see and hear is not justified. That's because we cannot know the truth of the reporting (bad news is a profit center for the media), but also because the reality we can know is only a tiny speck of the total reality.

Never Give Up

Consider this as well. Have you ever met anyone you would consider fundamentally evil, bad, or ill intentioned? Yes, there are jerks, but once you get to know them they seem to be the decent sort as well. (Even mass murderers on death row get marriage proposals.) Have you not found that once you get to know almost anyone, no matter where they are or what they have done, that they seem to have the same basic goodness as you? That is the thread that holds the world together, the underlying and too often inchoate urge within us all to be good people and do what is right—something never heard on the evening news. It is that thread of goodness that is our hope and which should be nurtured.

Our best hope is to choose to live life as if we have brains—as if thinking matters. We should not fear departing from the unthinking masses and doing the acts and spreading the message of goodness. It is something every single one of us can do. It may, in fact, be the real reason we are here in the first place. The worst-case scenario is that we try to make a better world and the world does not get better or even explodes one day from a meteor or nuclear fusillade. So we tried. We did the best we could. We attempted to act intelligently, selflessly, lovingly, and responsibly. Are we not better for it? By living a life of such meaning have we not been alive, healthy, and purposed? Might it not accrue to our betterment if this is not all there is?

As bleak as things may seem at times, there is always hope. It resides in each of us reaching out with love, searching for truth, and trying to improve the world. We don't need hope; we are the hope.

SECTION L

Thinking about. . .

SELF IMPROVEMENT

IN THIS SECTION: *To not explore the fullness of the gift of life by improving oneself is a waste and a tragedy. Here are ideas and motivation to become the best you can be.*

78

PAYING THE SUCCESS PRICE

THOMAS EDISON performed thousands of experiments to get to a desired end point. He would say, "I have not failed. I've just found 10,000 ways that won't work." He also said, "The reason a lot of people do not recognize opportunity is because it usually goes around wearing overalls and looking like hard work." * One artist credited his success with his determination to do 10 more drawings each time his art instructor would assign the class a certain number of sketches. One football great came 15 minutes early to practice and stayed 15 minutes late. The result? Thirty minutes a day made the difference between ho-hum and greatness.

It's easy to assume that the success of those who rise to the top is due to some kind of special gift, or that they were just lucky. But in most cases that is not true. The real talent is the will to pay a higher price in personal effort than the competition. The winners in life may make everything look easy but behind that look of grace and ease are thousands of hours of fumbling, blundering, losing, awkwardness, toil, error, and sweat. Hard work is the alchemy for success.

*Go to Thomasedison.org for an astonishing account of the amount of effort put forth by America's most prolific inventor.

A probe into the history of any successful person will reveal these common themes:

• Make a plan to achieve a goal, and then do it with urgency, enthusiasm, and persistence.

• There must be the will to *prepare* to win.

• Success is never final and failure never fatal; you must simply move on with the commitment to succeed. There are no short cuts, just long work.

• Adapt and change as necessary to achieve the goal.

• Don't fear competition or losing; use them as opportunities to learn and become better.

• Every day improve.

• There are no secrets, there is only work.

• If you want to win, you've got to leave everything on the playing floor.

• Desire and intention are the most dynamic of our faculties; they do work.

• Be willing to make the effort, pay the price, and get at it—now.

Here are some aphorisms that repeat these lessons in clever ways:

• You're never a loser until you quit trying.

• Triumph is the result of a little "umph" added to "try."

• The only time you can't afford to fail is the last time you try.

• The doors of opportunity are marked "PUSH."

• The smallest action is greater than the greatest intention.

• Ideas bring in nothing unless carried out.

• The only way to coast is by going downhill.

Larry Bird, who eventually turned out to be one of the greatest NBA basketball players of all time, admitted to very little natural talent. But did he work! One time, when playing an NBA all-star game, he had to step to the line for free throws. At this point in his career he was shooting over 92% in free-throws and leading the entire league. He missed both shots. Reporters following him to the locker room afterward noted Larry's sullen attitude in spite of the fact that his team had won the game. They assumed it was the missed free throws and asked him why he thought he missed them, Larry responded, "It's my fault. I didn't take my 100 free-throw practice shots today."

Preparation, practice, determination, effort, belief in oneself, willingness to adapt, changing, and always learning and improving are the keys to success. Ernest Hemingway reportedly went back through his manuscript of *The Old Man and the Sea* eighty times, grooming and editing it. Virgil spent twelve years working on the *Aeneid* and was perfecting it up until he died. Leonardo da Vinci spent twelve years on *The Last Supper* and often would be so absorbed in the work he would forget to eat. Michelangelo's *The Last Judgment* was preceded by more than two thousand preliminary sketches.

We can make a difference, we can become better people, we can improve the world, we can be the healthiest our genetic potential permits, we can achieve and succeed. It all directly depends upon how much fuel we are willing to put in the engine.

Life is about challenge, not just to survive, but to survive well. Mediocrity can become greatness if we are simply willing to pay the price of hard work.

79

CHANGE—
A WONDERFUL THING

WE CAN SAFELY WAGER that just about everything we hold to be true at this point in time is wrong or incomplete. That is what history teaches. Since we are likely wrong on most things, why would we not be open to change, even seeking it? A sixth century Chinese proverb says, "We will end up where we are going if we don't change direction." Why not be willing to give up at any moment who we are in order to become all that we can be?

By tenaciously holding to present beliefs, progress weeps. Society owes its advance to those who have dared to differ, not to conformists. But "psychosclerosis" (hardening of the intellect) and "neophobia" (fear of new ideas) are at epidemic levels and always have been. Nobody is immune regardless of their station or credentials. In fact, the more expert, pompous, and sure someone is, the more likely they are infected with these intellectual diseases. Will Rogers said (roughly), "It's not what they all know for sure, but what they know for sure that just ain't so that's bothersome."

Belief is difficult enough to overturn when it is just treasured ideology. But today, belief is almost always coupled with an economics that has grown out of it. Effecting change under these circumstances becomes almost impossible since people will not give up the flow of fortune or livelihood easily. For money's sake, people will keep a death grip on the status quo long after the quo has lost its status. Why else does Earth polluting industry remain in place, socially ruinous politics endure, oil-dependent transportation continue, and a life-robbing health care system flourish?

Even science (which is supposed to mean open discovery) does not welcome change that challenges conventional thinking. Proving and supporting existing theory and the consensus view keeps scientists plenty busy and with abundant grant money. Scientists believe their

work is a search when in fact it is more like institutional rubber stamping. If there is out-of-the-box discovery that does not conform to accepted dogma, and if it is important enough to threaten funding or profits, it is cast aside as an anomaly and not pursued with open-minded vigor.

Scientific progress proceeds as follows: new ideas are first ignored; then if they persist they are ridiculed; then the proponents are persecuted; and finally, when public outcry and the market make it wise to convert, science takes credit for the discovery and claims it as their own.

The chronicle of intolerance is endless. Hundreds of years ago a Renaissance scientist, Galileo, was put under house arrest for life for publishing the heretical idea that the Earth moved. Semmelweiss, the 19th century Hungarian obstetrician, was thought insane for arguing that doctors delivering babies should first wash their hands when coming from the autopsy room where they were carving up cadavers with bare hands. Physicians used to denounce midwives as witches and many continue to spurn them today in spite of their proven advantages. Albert Einstein complained about attitudes toward his new ideas: "Fashion abides over every age without people realizing tyrants rule over them."

Although the card-carrying intelligentsia would have us believe that conformity to accepted dogma is progressive and informed, consistency is the refuge of the unimaginative. In fact it's hardly worth an intelligent person's time to be part of the majority. By definition, there are plenty of people to do that. In fact, if you find yourself on the side of the majority (even within a little group that has broken from another majority), you can almost count on being incorrect. The majority are usually not right, so, we must be wrong (in the majority view) in order to be right.

Change can be messy since institutions must be torn down to build new ones in their place. It is always easier and tidier to leave things as they are. But change is exciting and fun because once the mind is expanded to the dimensions of a new idea, it never returns to its original size. So be an iconoclast and shake the foundations of ideas that "just ain't so." Followers are never remembered; truth-seeking rebels are.

80

BEING THE BEST YOU CAN BE

MOST PEOPLE DO NOT GROW in the mental department much beyond the 13-year-old stage. What they learn by this age is sufficient to get them by, so that's where they remain. Also, in our modern age, people have changed from *being* something, to *having* things. Instead of inventing, they buy inventions. Instead of playing the sport, they watch pay-per-view. Instead of being healthy, they get a pill. The result is a neutral gear where a person becomes a mere repository of goods and services. But life is funny that way. There is no such thing as status quo or neutral. Either we advance or we fall behind. This applies to business, relationships, society, employment, and physical and mental health. Use it (and grow it), or lose it. It's not the easy road, but what worthwhile in life is?

The body and mind are designed for growth. We can always learn a new physical skill. Strength, coordination, and speed can all be increased. It takes work, but it can be done. The body thrives on signals telling it that it is alive, needed, and must improve because of the demands placed upon it. Challenging the body (within reason) is a key to keeping youth and health.

Even with our most concerted efforts we use only a small fraction of a brain designed with incredible capacity. But if we don't use it, it gets all stupid, mushy and bigoted ("I know this or that is so because that's what my parents told me when I was 13").

Here is some brain weightlifting to start growing impressive brain muscles:

• Learn a new word every day. Words are the framework from which thought can be expressed. Keep to the tiny vocabulary erector set you had at 13 and that will be the level of your intellect and your ability to make something of life.

• With age, life experience permits us to learn much more efficiently than when in school as a child. So get high school chemistry, English, biology, government, history, or algebra books and study them. The ability to understand the material will have greatly improved and you'll be surprised at the fun of really mastering a subject and seeing how it all makes sense and fits together.

• Read lots of non-fiction. Listen to educational tapes. Watch educational television. Join organizations that are doing something worthwhile. Associate with smart people and let it rub off.

• Self-teach something like building a home, fixing the plumbing, preparing your own taxes, learning a sport, cooking nutritionally, sewing, and painting. Be slow to hire someone to do something you could learn to do. To learn something new and accomplish a thing you have not done before is one of life's great treasures. Why pay someone to take it from you? Look at it this way, as the comedian Jim Carrey quipped, "They are a carbon-based life form just like you." If they can do it, so can you.

• Find sites on the Internet to engage others in intelligent discussion on topics that interest you. But don't assume that just because you can talk uninterrupted in a chat room that you should be saying anything. Put something intelligent, informed, and rational under your cap first. Until then, make ears and eyes the primary organ of communication.

• Express your view in writing to politicians or anyone else who is rubbing your smarts the wrong way. Win others with the force of your knowledge and reason. Above all, be ready to admit error. The only real mistake is the one from which we learn nothing. Welcome and embrace the discovery of your error. No one is perfect and it is only by discovering imperfections that we can improve.

• Don't overlook the *physical* needs of the brain. It is an oxygen and good nutrition glutton. So get plenty of fresh air as well as exercise to help expand the vessels that deliver this essential brain fuel. Sleep and nap for rejuvenation. Eat plenty of high quality protein and use supplements such as essential fatty acids which can significantly enhance cognitive and motor subscales of mental development. (See Health and Food Sections, as well as my book, *Lipid Nutrition*.)

Begin today to grow a better you and never stop. Don't let age, lack of education or any other excuse stand in the way. Be the best you can be, starting now.

81

DO SOMETHING, SOMETHING HAPPENS

THE LAWS OF MOTION in physics dictate that all things in the universe move toward a state of rest. Once at rest they stay there unless acted upon. A ball rolls along the ground and finally stops. It stays there unless some force again acts upon it. Creatures are alive and dynamic but inevitably move toward a state of rest (death). All molecular motion in the universe is inexorably moving toward the same state of stillness.

This principle of motion also applies to living. If we want something to happen in our lives—have more friends, excel in a sport, make more money, be healthier—we must take the bull by the horns. Good things do not spontaneously generate; they happen because we take action.

Look about you. Everything that you have can be traced back to a decision to do something. I marvel at the tall trees now gracing my yard that began as seedlings. I can remember thinking that I would never really get to enjoy anything from the puny six inch starts and questioning whether to even plant them. But I resisted the strong urge to do nothing, and instead did something. Amazingly, wonderful big trees that I now can enjoy happened. Relationships blossom, houses get built, products get invented, financial security grows, and books get written (I have had to keep reminding myself) because people do something. Do more, and more will happen. That's how to fill life with wondrous things.

A corollary of "do something and something will happen" is: "do nothing and nothing will happen." Whose fault will that be?

We can sit back and make wishes and bemoan our lot in life, or we can make things happen. The choice is ours. But it takes energy, will, persistence, action, and alacrity. Pushing the gigantic

Bob laments why nothing good ever seems to happen in his life.

boulder of life along is not an easy task. But the reward is something accomplished. Isn't that what life is about? The grave affords plenty of time for rest. Now is the time for action.

Think about what you would like in life. Now start to make it happen. Not tomorrow, today. Not later in the day, now. Start typing, pick up the phone, get off your duff, and do something. Begin and stick with it. Even a poor plan violently executed is worth a thousand plans put off until next week. The most important cause of success is doing the thing you should do, right now, whether you want to or not.

On the other hand if you argue for your limitations, that is the best way to make them yours. Even if you do not succeed at something, or make an error, the experience is enriching and will sharpen your tools to make your next go at it more likely to succeed. None of this is to even mention the enormous physical and psychological benefits of taking control of life.

How simple, wise, and true: If you are not happy with your life, if you want something you have never had, then do what you have never done. Do something, and something happens.

> *"Twenty years from now you will be more disappointed by the things you didn't do than by the ones you did. So throw off the bow lines, sail away from the safe harbor. Catch the trade winds in your sails. Explore, Dream, Discover."* -Mark Twain

82

CHANGE THE WORLD

THE WORLD CAN CHANGE because single individuals like you and me decide to do it. It doesn't have to mean running for office or organizing protests. Just doing whatever small thing you can in your own life can make a difference. If it is a good idea, it may catch on without even telling a soul.

In biology there is a recently discovered phenomenon called morphic resonance. It is the instantaneous transmission of ideas, beliefs, skills, and even physical characteristics to others far distant and not connected in any material way.[1] For example, after monkeys on one island decided to wash their food, monkeys on other distant islands began doing the same. In controlled studies people and animals that learned how to solve puzzles somehow transmitted the skill to new test groups who were able to arrive at solutions more rapidly.

Inventors run into this phenomenon all the time. No matter how novel an invention may be, it is usually under development by someone else at the same time. Examples include the atomic bomb, printing press, rockets, the first airplane, electricity, and countless others. Businesses experience it in naming new products. Lo and behold, when a trademark search is done another company has come up with the same name. Morphic resonance helps explain cycles of fashion, product trends, new ideas, and argot. There is more at work here than advertising.

An example I have recently noted is children saying "I love you" to parents. It is done in the hearing of friends without the slightest embarrassment. If I had done that as a child, my buddies would have ridiculed me into nerd oblivion. With our youngest children, frequent "I love you" expressions seemed special and unique to our family. Neither my wife nor I had heard it being done in other families. Then, as the kids got older and we started mixing with their friends and their parents, to our astonishment they were all doing it. We didn't learn it from them, nor did they learn it from us—directly.

Much of the change we see in the world may be the result of the 'contagion' of morphic resonance. The zeitgeist of a society originates with one and can spread like wildfire, unseen, unspoken, unheard, unprinted, and without electronic transmission into the consciousness of the whole.

Pay attention and notice how trends spread beyond the means of any physical mechanism. It's as though thought itself instantly transmits throughout society. No, this is not hocus-pocus. Modern quantum physics argues this to be a scientifically plausible idea. (More on this fascinating topic in the companion book.)

So do not underestimate the power of your thoughts and actions beyond the immediate circumstance. As Gandhi exhorted, "Be the change you wish to see in the world." Do what is right in your own little domain regardless of how insignificant it may seem. You will most certainly impact those around you and may even instantly transmit to the whole of humanity creating the seed for a better world.

You are only one, but still you are one. You cannot do everything, but you can do something. Because you cannot do everything you should not shrink from doing that which you *can* do.[2]

83

GROWING GOOD PEOPLE

IF SOCIETY IS EVER TO ADVANCE, people must be nurtured properly, taught correctly, and then stand on their own two feet to take responsibility for their own actions. What can be done to grow such people?

Let's start at the beginning. At age seven months in the womb, humans begin language coordination in response to what they hear through the mother's belly wall. Some 52 muscles learn to respond to the various phonemes (a phoneme is a basic language sound like 'b' in boy and 'm' in man) of the language surrounding the mother. The emotional state of the parent imprints itself on the baby growing in the womb, as do things like music and other environmental conditions. Poor nutrition, drugs, and even topical lotions and pollution spill right through directly to the fetus via the placenta. Parenting and nurturing better people obviously begins way before the bassinet.

At eighteen months the child has a brain one-third the size of an adult but with the same number of synapses (neural connections). Neurons have fingerlike tendrils that relay information—outgoing from the nerve cell through axons, ingoing by way of dendrites. It is the number of synapses that appears to determine intelligence, not the number of neurons.

Astonishingly, a six year old has about five times more synapses than adults. These trillions upon trillions of connections in youngsters are waiting to be imprinted by the environment, parents, and society.

This is probably the reason that beginning in the first millennium the Roman Catholic Church initiated children into the sacraments at age six or seven. (It is remarkable how so many 'new' scientific discoveries were anticipated by the intuitive traditions of the past.)[1]

Beginning at about age twelve, the fatty myelin sheath covering the unused neural tendrils are literally dissolved, absorbed into the cerebrospinal fluid rendering the neurons functionless. Some 80% of the functional neural brain mass present at age 6 is gone by age 14 as a result of disuse. To make matters even worse, consider the fact that of the remaining 20% of the brain, we only use 5%. That means we are running on only about 1% of the full potential we began with.

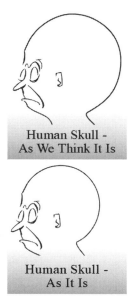

Human Skull – As We Think It Is

Human Skull – As It Is

This retrogression (devolution) of the brain applies only to the neocortex, that big part of the brain with all the folds and grooves that humans are so proud of. The more 'primitive' parts of the brain, the 'reptilian' brainstem and limbic system responsible for stimulus-response and emotion-cognition, remain intact and do not experience this loss. In other words, our ability for fight-flight (running from predators), self-awareness (look at me), sex (fun stuff and children-hatching), eating (wouldn't want to miss that), and road rage (essential in modern

Human Skull – What We Use

living) are never at risk. Our ability to be intelligent about all that base reptilian stuff, however, is in decline throughout our adult lives.[2]

Is it not clear which parts of the human brain are in full function today? Just watch a little television, listen to 'with it' music, go to movies, and pick up some of the tabloids at the grocery counter and you'll see that the primitive human brain *stem* has suffered no melt-down. But that three-pound blob on top of it, the so-called seat of intelligence, is evidently just filling up space.

The ability to make and hold neural connections in the smart part of the brain is not due to what can be beaten into our kids with rules, instructions, and performance pressures. Those connections grow from what they experience around them without even realizing it. Neither the child nor the parents are aware of at least 95% of the imprinting a child receives. Who we are as parents emotionally, ethically, and intellectually in our day-to-day routines—not what we pretend or preach—is picked up by our children as their most important lessons and is then neurally connected. So telling a child to be something we are not doesn't do. If we want better children we must be better people.[3]

This idea also speaks to the importance of a loving and nurturing family nest. We learn love, in large part, by experiencing it. The erosion of the family in our libertine society thrusts the child into a peer group for imprinting. This surrogate family begins with technological births in hospital wards, and then continues with isolating infants in their own bedrooms, pseudofood in bottles with plastic nipples, television, day-care, broken homes, and on to public school. The raising of children by society rather than families results in a premature unfolding of development accelerated through exposure to adult themes pressing in from everywhere. Menstruation is beginning in eight-year-old girls (partly the result of hormone-type pollutants in food), there is an outbreak of pregnancies in nine-year olds, and violent sex crimes among children under the age of 10 are becoming too common.

Children are being thrust into full operational adult thinking way before they are capable of handling it properly. That is, in large part, why some 70% of teenagers are functionally illiterate: They may be able to learn, but cannot interpret meaning. They have not been properly imprinted (and have also experienced the diminution in neural connections mentioned above) and they don't have sufficient life experience or proper social context for intelligent decision-making.

So yes, home, family, and parents contribute to the development of children. On the other hand, nature plays a big part, too. Any parent raising a child into adulthood will see that the personality of a person at 40 is pretty much identical to their earliest infancy. So parents should not be too quick to take the blame for a child gone bad. Grown ups should also not spend a fortune in therapy whining about how their parents didn't love them enough. We may lose important neural connections in childhood, but once we realize who we are—very early in childhood—the ball is in our court.

There are people with essentially no brain in their skull (compressed to a thin membrane from hydrocephalus) who excel intellectually and ethically. So, as an adult, buck up, take responsibility for yourself, and make good use of the neural connections remaining. We are not victims. Even though we are left with only 1% of our mental potential we can make a lot of good use of that. It means reaching inside for the goodness that is there and extending that to our fellow humans. It means not following the conscience of others but learning what is already within and being true to that.

Our children don't need money, videos, signature shoes, and pressure for grades and sports performance. The inner needs of children are met if they are raised in a pigpen, as long as there is love. If that critical emotional relationship is not there, children will seek it in peers, including some of the perverted media models. Then we have the ethically blind (other children, idols, and profiteering media) leading our blind children. This is not the proper incubator for the adults of the future, it is the formula for the collapse of society.

What, then, is the best stimulant for growing good people, particularly with the popular indoctrination they get elsewhere that everyone is a victim, and any failure in life is the fault of somebody else? It is that greatest of all intelligences, love. That is not a platitude. Love requires an expansive and wise mind. Even with the puny 1% of our brain that we use, the capacity for love is infinite. Love means growing to be the best we can be, extending ourselves to others selflessly, and taking responsibility for ourselves. When that is done, the perfect model is created to grow good children as well.

84

WORDS

IF THE ONLY TOOL POSSESSED is a hammer, there is only so much one can do. Add a saw and the possibilities dramatically increase. Add some nails, screws, screwdriver, wrenches, crowbar, level, router, jigsaw, and drill with bits, and now we're talking serious possibilities.

Words are the tools of thinking. The more we have, the more things we can do with our mind. Why do large vocabularies characterize outstanding men and women? The best answer seems to be that words are the instruments by which people grasp the thoughts of others and with which they do their own communication.[1] Small vocabulary means small mental input and output; large vocabulary means large input and output.

To add more to your cerebral tool chest costs nothing but a little effort, but effort is a price few people wish to make. For most, the vocabulary they possess at the age of 13 is essentially the same at 80. There are more than 800,000 words in the Oxford English Dictionary, but the average American uses no more than 12,000. Even a reasonably well-educated college graduate will seldom have command of more than 20,000.

The words used reflect the depth of the mind. A healthy vocabulary makes a person interesting and challenging to partners and it sends the message in the workplace that you are not ordinary and should be respected. There is no downside to growing vocabulary, but there is unlimited upside. Those are the rare odds to always look for in life.

Here are ways to start adding word tools to your repertoire. First, do a lot of reading. Reading teaches new words and how to use them well. Keep a notebook, enter the pronunciation and definition of new words, and copy the sentence in which the word was found. Periodically go back and review. Make it a point to use these newly found tools in speech and writing. That will help embed them into memory and make them a part of your working vocabulary.

Buy books and audio programs that teach new words. If you subscribe to Reader's Digest, be sure to pay attention to that little section on building vocabulary. Check the inside back page of The Atlantic, where new words are listed each month. Go to dictionary websites and subscribe to their free on-line word of the day e-mail lists. Pay attention to the speech of others and note new words. If you don't know the meaning, go home, look the words up, and enter them in your little book. When reading, mark the words you want to learn and look them up later. Don't read without a pen in hand.

Watch intelligent television such as the book reviews on C-span, and commentator and editorial programs. Listen for new words and observe how smart folks use them. Don't watch TV without a notepad nearby. Before long, errors will stand out (they said "nucular," not "nuclear," or "vetnarian," not "veterinarian"). Even those who are intellectually superior make mistakes you may catch and that will in turn give you confidence that you need not be in awe of anyone.

Finally, although it may seem daunting, study a dictionary. Really. Begin with the "A's." A thesaurus and a dictionary of etymology would be good, too. Just do a little at a time. Many of the words will already be familiar so it will go fast. Little things, as noted in a previous chapter, can add up to really big things that can make a huge difference in your life. So just begin. Mark the words you do not know and want to add to your tool chest. Go back and keep reviewing them.

Use memory aids like finding something in the word that reminds you of something. The mind is like a gigantic framework to which new things must hook in order to be retained. It's easier to hook something new to an existing crossbeam than to hope it will remain by setting it off all by itself in the thin air of your brain.

For example, *armamentarium* means a gathering of drugs, tools, or other things to be used for a task. It sounds like, and is derived from, arms. Arms, you know, are all the weapons an army has at their disposal. To be armed is to have all the things needed to go to war. So the "arm" part of *armamentarium* is the memory trigger for the

The Evolution Of Vocabulary

meaning of the word. It doesn't have to make sense. It can be nonsense as long as it hooks to your existing mental lattice and triggers memory. *Immigrant* has the "in" sound, so remember that an *immigrant* is coming "in" to the country. An *emigrant* goes away from, "e"-xits the country.

When thinking about a new word, think of what general category it falls under. For example, *frugal* and *impecunious* both fit under money. *Metaphysics* and *deductive* both fit under *philosophy*. When trying to recollect the words, these are the headings to look under to find them. Arrange new words in your notebook under these headings. File cards may work better because they can be deleted, added, and rearranged easily. By being your own lexicographer the information becomes tailor-made to you and is much more likely to be retained.

Just as the body needs exercise to keep its strength and flexibility, so does the mind. Growing vocabulary is like doing reps and sets for neurons. It is a lifelong adventure that will open up never ending intellectual doors.

Begin today. One word at a time, one dictionary page a week, one book a month, whatever you are comfortable with—just don't get too comfortable. Nothing good comes easily and "no pain, no gain" applies to growing mind muscles just as it does to body muscle.

Words can be fun, too. My favorite big word is "sesquipedalian." It means, of all things, tending to use big words. Or, if you go to medical school you can learn about a surgery connecting the gall bladder, hepatic duct, and intestine called, hepaticocholecystostcholecystenterostomy, and a respiratory disease caused by the inhalation of silicate or quartz dust called, pneumonoultramicroscopicsilicovolcanoconiosis.

85

GENIUS

MOST OF US THINK GENIUS is unachievable. We perceive it as a gift we are either born with or not. If not, then we are supposed to be content to look with awe upon those who have the gift, as if they were from some other planet.

Most certainly there are those who are born with special talents. Some, from infancy, have remarkable skills in language, math, music, and memory. The source of these precocious skills is a mystery. It is difficult to believe that it is the result of some random mutation, recombination of genetic material, or atavistic quirk. Evidence shows that it is something else entirely, but I will leave that to discuss in *Solving The Big Questions*.

Be that as it may, these odd forms of genius are not what seem to drive the world forward. Few leaders, entrepreneurs, and movers and shakers now considered to be geniuses were child prodigies. In fact, many were considered slow, distracted, average, misbehaving, and possessing poor attention skills in school.

What makes these slow-comers geniuses? Work. Lots of it laced with persistence, a thirst for knowledge, desire, belief in self, and a sense of mission. Since these are traits anyone can achieve, we are all candidates for genius status. Genius in the making is all around; we just don't recognize it because it's all dirty and sweaty.

IQ tests used to determine genius rely on questions that can be answered correctly with sufficient study. Merely improving one's vocabulary can move the score into the genius range. In other words, even IQ genius can be learned.

Real world genius is about doing something, not waiting for something to happen. What we do to separate ourselves from the pack is to do it quickly. So a sense of urgency is critical to genius. Anyone can do almost anything given enough time. It is those who get there first who become the geniuses. Genius is creativity,

What Genius Really Looks Like

a lot of reliance on the knowledge and skills of others, tens of thousands of man-hours, and a tenacious will to get it done, and get it done now. Look into the history of any successful person and note that these are the common, banal, unremarkable, sweaty causes for their genius.

Given that truth, most geniuses, if they are honest with themselves, are embarrassed by the title. There is even reason to be resentful because the moniker diminishes the hard work by presuming the accomplishment was unearned, a gift of genius. The term also sends the wrong message, namely that if you are not a genius by birth, you can never do genius things.

The term genius should therefore be restricted to children with talents unearned. All the other geniuses (the vast majority) should be called hard workers instead.

You can be a hard worker (genius) too.

86

LISTEN AND LEARN

No matter where we go, there are too many wide-open spaces...surrounded by teeth.

Listening, not thinking about what we will say, is a lost art. Talking, on the other hand, too commonly reveals a mind that has not had sufficient input. Abraham Lincoln once remarked, "He can compress the most words into the smallest ideas of any man I ever met." Socrates, wise to the waste of time the mouth causes in the learning process, would make students wait three years before they could even ask a question.

There is no learning when the mouth is engaged. "Listen, or your tongue will make you deaf." (Cherokee proverb) Learning by listening provides the necessary fuel for good colloquy. Unfortunately, people are like barrels in that the less they have in them the more noise they make. A mind enriched with experience, listening, and learning has some hope of creating words of interest to others. Even then we must be ever mindful of how dangerous a little bit of knowledge is—and what we have is always a little bit compared to what there is. Otherwise we risk being as edifying to our listener as a leaky faucet dripping into a tin dishpan at the head of the bed when they want to go to sleep.

Talking strokes ego and satisfies insecurities. We come back to that basic human problem of thinking the universe circles around us. We may think the world is our vast lecture platform to affirm our importance, but we are usually the only audience that is impressed.

It takes most of us a few times of putting our foot in our mouth and suffering embarrassment to realize that silence is often the wiser course. A closed mouth gathers no feet. The wrong thing said at the wrong time can produce a scar that never heals and can destroy relationships. Hurtful things said by another are embedded in memory forever. So why risk wounding others with thoughtless words (a risk that increases in direct proportion to the amount we speak) unless you enjoy being a lifelong enemy and always being held in the mind of another with resentment? Better to be like a new bottle of ketchup and wait awhile before anything comes out. Or, perhaps

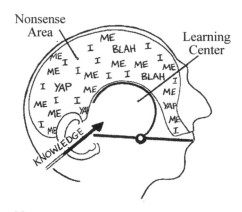

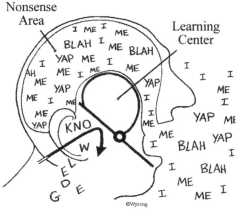

even better, when in question as to whether to speak we should give ourselves the benefit of the doubt and keep silent.

Talking is a fine art. It requires empathy, sensitivity, and informed intelligence. If in doubt, don't. Just be silent unless what you say builds up the listener. If what you are about to say will embarrass, belittle, or otherwise demean it's better to stay quiet. The consequences of bad word choices last a lifetime. Remember what mom said, "If you can't say anything nice…"[1]

The exception is when important issues are at stake. Then the truth must be told. But if the goal is to win a mind and not create an enemy, careful calculation, sensitivity, empathy, and kindness are required. Easier said than done when emotions run high, but it is wise counsel nonetheless.

When sufficient information, experience, and useful ideas are gathered you can write letters, articles, a book (whether or not it ever gets published) or memorialize your life and thoughts in a private diary. Writing permits conversation in a more calculated and thoughtful way with fewer chances for gaffes. It can also expose errors and weaknesses in your thinking. This is particularly so if you put the masterpiece down for a few days or longer and read it later

"I am listening... A person has to listen very carefully to hear only what he wants to hear."

with a fresh eye. When I do that I never cease to be amazed at the stupidity of the writer. This exercise will make it painfully clear why we should always be reluctant to speak with authority off-the-cuff.

You may be thinking that I've been doing a whole lot of talking about not talking. True, but the difference here is that you don't have to listen. When you get tired of me you can just slam the cover without hurting my feelings. On the other hand, I get to live the fantasy that you are savoring every word. How wonderful it is.

87

MIND OVER MATTER

NEGATIVE EXPECTATIONS YIELD negative results. Positive expectations yield positive results. This is most remarkably evident in sports. If you throw an object, shoot a basketball, or hit a tennis ball it will go where you want if you are absolutely focused and sure of the outcome. You, in effect, can will the object to its destination. This can be tested just around the home by throwing things in the basket. If you miss, note that you were unsure before and while you were throwing. If you score, you were sure, focused, and confident before and during the toss. Visualizing the outcome makes it happen ("Be the ball").

The power of the mind is the reason some athletes excel while others do not. Once the basic skills are in place and the neuromuscular coordination embedded into memory as a result of determined practice, the only thing remaining is will and focus.

It has been proven that some people are able to tap into powers intrinsic to the mind that result in superhuman feats (a mother lifting a car off a child), movement of objects using only thought (psychokinesis), seeing the future (clairvoyance), and distant healing. If these things are true, little wonder the mind can enable great athletic skill or force an outcome in our lives.

Power of mind applies far beyond motor skills. It can make the difference between success and failure in almost everything we do. But it is essential that the attention be unconflicted with no fear, uncertainty, or holding back. Some believe the power of the mind with such focused attention is unlimited. If that is true and we can tap into it, humankind will experience a revolution that will make all former technology seem like child's play.

So don't think that hitting life's targets is a matter of chance or luck. Success is always within our hands. It is no more than a matter of gaining the skills, making a commitment, and then exerting focused confident attention to the goal with the sure expectation of the result.

88

LOOKING GOOD

ACCORDING TO TELEVISION commercials, a man is supposed to have a wooly pate, six-pack abdomen, and Adonis features. A woman should be buxom, svelte, made-up, in the latest fashion, and puffy-lipped.

Let's put looks in perspective. Do people really care that much about how we look? Are other people thinking about us, or really only thinking about how they compare to us? Does our appearance preoccupy the minds of others? Do we spend time thinking about how others look? If not, why should they be spending time thinking about how we look?

This is not to say some care and grooming are not in order. We have a responsibility to present our possessions to the world in a neat and clean condition. Our yard should be cared for (there are even ordinances to that effect), the home should be in order, and our person should be presentable. The personal care I'm talking about is the basic care that makes a person look 99% as good as they can look. Unfortunately our narcissistic culture spends billions of dollars and countless hours in anguish fussing and primping to achieve that other 1%.

The majority of our beauty is inherent. It has to do with bone structure, proportions, how we carry ourselves, our demeanor, intelligence, and personality. It is who we are, not the façade we create. Ovid said: "When the disposition charms, the features are pleasing." Athenaeus concluded: "Beauty when unadorned is adorned the most."

Think about it. Have you come to know and love anyone because of the amount of his or her hair, bicep size, eyeliner, or silicone? Window dressing may turn a few more heads but will never be the cause of an important or lasting relationship. Superficial and fake window dressing is not why we are attracted to others, so why would we think it would be the reason they are attracted to us?

Take the before and after commercials of men with and without hair. Of course all the gals just can't keep their eyes and hands off the guy with the gorgeous mop. The balding guy is presented as pathetic, doomed to a lonely life without hope of any possible relationship. Really? Why then are just as many guys without hair in contented relationships as those with hair? As opposed to the commercials, in real

life do we see the mate to the hairy guy adoringly running her hands through his hair and just unable to keep her eyes off his curly locks? Notice how before and after photos of men with and without hair look like the same person. One does not look younger than the other and one is not more handsome. Women swoon over Sean Connery with or without his toupees.

"After implants, a personal trainer, Viagra, Rogaine, liposuction and Botox, she left me for an older guy."

Before getting too excited about remodeling yourself to perfection, keep in mind that facelifts, implants, liposuction, and drugs are not without medical risks. A little cosmetic 'tune-up' could result in a lifetime of misery and disfigurement.

Creative hair parting and obvious plugs, make-up that could paint a barn, plastic surgery scars like tree-rings, and facelifts that look like they could shatter with a sneeze, run the risk of drawing attention to the very thing one is trying to conceal, insecurity. This is not to say that things that bother us should not be fixed or improved. Why let a two-inch cyst rest on the end of the nose that obscures vision and distracts everyone around you? But everything in moderation. Plastic surgery can give peace of mind if expectations are realistic. But some get addicted and take it to its extremes. The results can end up gaining attention for the wrong reasons—people look at us not because we look so good, but because we look plastic and shallow.

Real beauty and attractiveness is without device and has to do with who we really are inside and what we make of ourselves. Being the

> *"I was so ugly when I was born, the doctor slapped my mother."* -Henny Youngman

best person we can be is cheap, safe, lasting, and honest. The most beauty we can ever achieve comes from staying in shape, being healthy, grooming in moderation, growing the mind, and reaching out with love and compassion to others. Make the most of time in this way, and time will return the compliment.

89

PROTECTING YOURSELF

THERE ARE TENS OF THOUSANDS of murders each year in America, about one every twenty-one minutes. Homicide is the second leading cause of death in the general population aged fifteen to twenty-four years, and the first cause of death for black males between the ages of fifteen and twenty-four. More teenagers and young adults die from gunshots than from all natural causes combined.

It is reported that five percent or more of all high school students carry guns to classes. One million semi-automatic guns are made in the U.S. each year and are replacing the handgun as the preferred weapon. Millions of AK-47 rifles are imported from China… and they don't go to the military.

If the social fabric unravels, we're pretty much on our own. Government protection, if widespread breakdown occurs, is extremely limited. In the 1992 Los Angeles riots, police were quickly overwhelmed. In some areas they simply withdrew, leaving the citizens at the mercy of crazed mobs. The 2005 New Orleans anarchy following hurricane Katrina is another reminder. So don't plan on help from 911 or the troops. You must prepare to be able to defend yourself.

Here are some specific things to do for protection. These may be unnecessary if nothing ever happens, but if something does happen you will forever thank yourself for taking measures now while there is opportunity:

1. Secure your neighborhood—talk with neighbors about the possibility of violence coming to the neighborhood and what to do. Begin neighborhood watch programs and get a list of neighbors and telephone numbers so that you can readily communicate. During widespread rioting, gangs in Los Angeles left all areas where there was determined resistance and instead went in search of places that offered easier pickings. Residents rolling dumpsters into the road, illuminating the intersection in front of the barricades, and standing armed behind them kept one neighborhood intact. Hour after hour vehicles filled with predatory gangs approached the barricades but moved on once they determined the area was not going to be an easy target. The threat of "frontier justice" left the neighborhood unscathed.

2. Secure your home—security includes fences, floodlights, alarms, good locks, deadbolts, unbreakable windows, and metal doors.

3. Be prepared to be self-reliant; store a supply of canned goods, dried foods, the new MRE military rations, and other non-perishables. Dried fruits, dried meats, and whole grains have good shelf lives. Purchase a water filter that can be used to purify drinking water. Also, consider a first-aid kit, home generator, cellular phone, battery operated radio, and an assemblage of camping equipment including stove, lanterns, coolers, sleeping bags, tent, and other basic survival gear.

4. Prepare an escape route. Know where you can go and how you can get there under your own power if violence threatens the neighborhood. Predetermine a rendezvous point with your loved ones.

5. Have portable money. Maintain a supply of cash. Have traveler's checks and currency on hand. Even some bullion gold and silver coins are a good idea in the event the banking system fails or currency becomes worthless.

Relocate to safer areas. Even the Marines know when to retreat. If in a high crime area consider moving to a more remote city or rural area. Also consider a climate that would not threaten you if you were forced to live outside for a period of time.

Get tough. Be prepared to defend yourself against an attacker. This is something that could happen at any moment walking down any American street. Eat healthy and exercise. By so doing you will likely be more fit than your attacker. By engaging in a regular aerobic and weight training fitness program (as discussed in a previous chapter) you can be a force to reckon with. Being able to run away is a great skill, and even hand-to-hand defense measures such as employed by the elite military can be learned. Talk to local martial arts teachers about quick-study personal defense classes.

Every time we hear of a shooting our thoughts go to gun control. That's because emotion always precedes rational thought. Yes, if all guns could be outlawed—and everyone followed the law—our problems would be solved. Unfortunately, only the good citizens would follow such a law, the criminals wouldn't. So under such a law the bad guys would have guns, the good guys wouldn't. People who have self-defense sprays, stun guns, real guns, or other weapons at least have a fighting chance.

Be politically astute. Support law, order, and policies that encourage education and self-reliance. Socialism and libertine pressures will always exist in society. It is up to citizens to recognize the naiveté of these ideas and their danger to the ultimate safety and fabric of society.

If you let yourself be vulnerable you will likely be victimized. Ignoring danger does not make it go away. Don't assume that just because you have never been attacked it will never occur, or because your community has always seemed a place of stability, security, and justice that it will remain that way.

90

SELF-SUFFICIENCY

AS OUR WORLD BECOMES MORE COMPLEX and we are distanced from nature and the sources of life, we become more vulnerable. Reflect for a moment on how dependent we are on electricity, heat, gasoline, water faucets, and stores stocked with food. If any of these things were interrupted, our very survival would be at risk.

In the not-too-distant past, just 50 years ago or so, a large percentage of the population occupied family farms. Some of my fondest childhood memories are of spending time at my grandparents' farm where cows were milked, eggs gathered, a garden tended, and wood cooked food and heated the home. Garbage was thrown to the pigs and chickens, water was hand-pumped, and an outhouse with catalog pages for toilet paper was quite an adventure. Just a few decades prior to that there was no electricity, and horsepower came only from horses. People took care of themselves with the resources available outside their back doors.

Today we have traded self-sufficiency for convenience, comfort, ease…and dependency. As population grows, our vulnerability can only increase as we are caught up in the complex commercial web we create for ourselves. I shudder when I visit a big city and think about how precarious life is there. If all of a sudden the power is gone, or gasoline is not available, or food is not delivered to the grocery store, there would be desperation, pandemonium, and terror. This unintended consequence of industrialization and commercialization is good business—making people dependent on goods and services—but really bad for us customers if supply is interrupted.

It is only prudent to have a plan and think about things that can be done to be self-sufficient, at least in terms of basic needs to stay alive. Not only might you survive and be able to help others if infrastructure crumbles, but there are important psychological benefits right now from not feeling helpless.

How can we gain control when we are in fact so dependent? First, do the obvious. Reconsider living on or below a flood plain, on an active earthquake fault line, near a volcano, below sea level next to the ocean, underneath an avalanche zone, and anyplace from which there is no exit. Stay fit enough to run, jump, lift, swim, crawl, and walk.

We can also become less dependent by learning how to do things usually hired out to others. Such capabilities include gardening, mechanics, carpentry, plumbing, sewing, and meal preparation. Learn what foods are edible in your back yard or nearby forest. As mentioned in the previous chapter, put together a survival kit. You can learn survival skills even while living in a high-rise apartment in the middle of Chicago or New York.

Alarmist? Extremist? Is this silly to do when you've lived your whole life without such a need? Perhaps. Perhaps not. Who knows what circumstance could interrupt our comfortable and secure lives? Good thinking demands that we use foresight and take preventive actions, not assume disasters only affect others.

SECTION M

Thinking about. . .

BEING GOOD

In This Section: *Before one can begin the journey to a successful life, a road map and ground rules are necessary. Most fundamentally, human life and health must take priority. If we begin with that premise, ethics can make sense and not be subject to the vicissitudes of libertine relativism. Commonly recognized, but rarely admitted, the universe not only has inherent laws that define and govern the physical world, but the world of choice as well. The ethical/moral laws embedded in the universe cannot be altered, and consequences from violating them are certain. To understand what these ethical standards are does not require consulting with others. They are indelibly written within each of us like involuntary heart rhythm and respiration. Unlike those physiological processes, however, the laws of ethics are there for us to either heed or ignore. Life is about choices, and they are all ultimately ethical and moral choices. Nothing is truly neutral since all things are interconnected, if even by a very thin and long thread. How we spend our time and energy either contributes to the improvement of the human condition, or subtracts from it. There are always good things that can be done and if we are not doing them, that is also a choice. Listening to the voice within, being true to it, facing reality, and keeping long-term consequences always in mind provides the best direction for a life well lived.*

91

LIFE IS MATH

2+2=4. THE PURITY OF THIS SIMPLE EQUATION reflects the order, rationality, and beauty inherent in nature. The formula never changes, is absolutely reliable, and crosses all language, age, gender, political, and historical boundaries. Unlike our endlessly conflicting ideological ideas, it is something all people can agree on. Wars are not fought over whether 2+2=4. That's because the equation is clear, unequivocal, and backed by evidence, not an abstract idea backed by belief and faith. Math is a model for addressing life as if thinking matters.

Math allows us to do the seemingly impossible like invent computers and put men on the moon. It is the language of the universe, even permitting us to 'see' things in deep space far beyond our vision and to peer into the tiny quantum world where matter disappears and waves, subatomic particles, and probabilities reign. There is no uncertainty or ambiguity if the math is solved correctly. The answer will always be the same.

2+2=4 is a metaphor for all of reality. The equation is a reflection of what fundamental reality is and is not. It is order and predictable truth; it is not random and irrational. Truth does not depend upon the opinions of a legislature, courts, police, parents, teachers, or ministers. Mathematical purity is just there whether or not we obey it.

Discovering the certainty in nature is what science is all about. The more we learn, the more it becomes clear that law governs everything in reality.

Moreover, all of out technological progress rides on the shoulders of the laws of motion, electricity, gravity, nuclear physics, chemistry, and the correct answer to 2 + 2. The more we know about these laws and obey them, the more we can create and the better we can keep our machines working.

This presents an interesting and logical conclusion. Let me express it with the formality of a syllogism so its simplicity can be clearly seen:

1. All activities in reality are governed by laws.

2. Humans perform activities.

3. Therefore, all human activities are governed by laws.

Now I know this seems absurd since any one of us can do almost anything we choose at any given time. We can stop whatever we're doing right now and go give money to a poor family or slip in their back door and steal whatever they have. Free will seems—at first glance—to negate our neat little syllogism. I will spend this and the next chapters trying to convince you it does not.

We may treat life as if we can make five, six, or even more out of 2 + 2. That's what lying, cheating, stealing, defrauding, and faking it are. We think we can add together zeros and get something for nothing, or put in just a little and get a lot out, or not do the work but get the reward. If that kind of math were used to put a man on the moon, he might end up on Pluto or in the ocean—dead by either route. Faulty ethical equations don't usually get people to a good destination in life either.

As for what the laws of ethics are, they are not in a book or reducible to a universal equations. They are by and large within and situational. It may seem like a contradiction to say that a law is situational, but all laws are that way. A leaf is heavier than air and should fall straight to the ground. But that is not always the case. They can go diagonally, horizontally, and even vertically. It all depends on the situation, including the shape of the leaf, its weight, whether it is wet or not, the wind, altitude, temperature, and humidity. Ultimately though, the leaf must fall. Similarly, the correct ethical choice in a given situation can depend on many variables and long-term effects. But ultimately there is only one correct choice.

Our innate sense of the math of ethics makes Hollywood billions of dollars. That industry has thrived by entertaining us with stories condensing the math of life into a brief movie. The good guys eventually prevail and the bad guys get their due. That's the ending we applaud because it adds up.

It is a correct 2+2=4 solution that makes us feel good because we have an internal ethical calculator that goes haywire if things don't compute.

True, it may seem at times that we can cheat the math of ethics. We think we can get something for nothing, or do wrong and suffer no penalty. We might rob a bank and escape the pursuers. We could think we got away with it if nobody saw us. But that would be just a temporary perturbation in the equation, a little glitch in the calculation on the way to the final result. The final result will always be, 2+2=4. Any undue temporary gain will always be eventually offset by loss or penalty that will negate the benefit so that the right result, 4, will always emerge. Life cannot be cheated. What we put in, we get out. It adds up unerringly and perfectly. How could it be otherwise? The universe is perfect and unerring.

Since we are an integral part of the unerring universe, we are ultimately held to that same standard. Every blood corpuscle, bone cell, muscle fiber, and neuron in our bodies is made of molecules and subatomic particles that must obey the laws of the universe. The thing that we identify as self does not transcend these components and set apart from the rest of the universe that must obey law. Free will may permit choice, but it cannot deny the consequences for wrong choices.

Those of us who have lived enough years see this truth because we have experienced in real time the equation balancing out. Those in their youth, on the other hand, are easily deceived because they are in the early part of the equation and think they can cheat the math. They naively think that cleverness will conceal wrongdoing and that time will erase memories and any pangs of conscience. But time is merely the opportunity for the scales to be balanced, for the surety of the equation to work out, and a subtraction in the form of a penalty to be levied. Unjust gain is always just a temporary minuend from which paybacks will be exacted.

Remember those dreaded red marks the teacher would make on our math papers in school? The same corrections happen in life if we try to cheat the ethical math. In some cases the penalty is obvious by way of physical injury, monetary loss, ostracism, or even death. These can be meted out by society, or they may occur independently. Something we think we got away with as a child may not revisit us with a price until later in life when we reach a better state of understanding. Regret, guilt, and remorse for something we cannot correct because of the distance in time, or the irreparable damage done, may be the most awful of all penalties to pay. This understanding helps us see that we are our own best policemen, that we should correct our own papers, or better yet, listen to our inner ethical voice and get it right the first time.

Unfortunately society as a whole seems increasingly bent on denying ethical math and bringing us all along in a fraud. We see huge movements afoot to challenge and deny standards. All mores are seen as disposable and open to debate. To see what I mean, just watch TV, surf the web, and open your junk mail and Internet spam.

This morning I opened yet another letter from a dignitary in Nigeria. It seems that my name has been discussed with great regard in the highest circles in that country. I learn that the Royal Princess Abdulla Takyumony Grace III, the Royal Highness of Mt. Royale Timbuktu, (or whatever) needs my help. She has been separated from her vast treasures by a coup. Her emissary needs me to sign some papers as an "esteemed" person to help this poor damsel in distress recoup her millions. If I do, they will give me 20%. If I participate, all the transactions will give me perfect security since the prestigious law firm, Dewey, Cheatum, and Moore will handle them. Fair enough. I agree with everything, especially the part about me being esteemed and getting all that free money. If I do a little digging though, I find that this is a fraud bulk-mailed to tens of thousands. If I were to follow through I would need to deposit some money that is "guaranteed secure" (just as a formality) to get my share of the Princess's millions. Hey, what's a few thousand when the return is millions? I could even end up in Nigeria penniless (as some have) when it is all over.

I just e-mail these generous folks back, "Shame on you for trying to defraud me. Find something honorable and decent to do with your life." (Unfortunately this tact did not work. Instead it put me on a mail list and I now receive emails from damsels in distress all over the world wanting to give me money.)

In my daily load of junk mail is a big red envelope with a large officious notice: "MONITORED SPECIAL DELIVERY." It looks like it is from the IRS, CIA, or the like. It says, "Monitored identification code on enclosed documents." How could a person not open that? Inside is a questionnaire. It seems they want my answers to questions about an air filter. Me buying their filter is not important, just my answers to the "monitored" questions. More lies, more fraud.

The trick seems to be tricks and how many of them people can get away with. This mentality of defrauding as many people as possible pervades the media, marketing, politics, commerce, and even the professions. Many instances of this have been detailed in previous chapters. Modern medicine, nutrition, pet feeding, government, and environmental and social issues are viewed merely as profit centers or opportunities for short term benefits, not as responsibilities to bring the world to a better state that only truth can deliver. It's like everyone wants to pretend that there is really no right or wrong, that standards are purely arbitrary. As long as a deal is greased with money, we supposedly can thumb our nose at the whole idea of ethical absolutes.

Nonetheless, the underlying laws in the universe (including the ethical ones) remain and they exact their price regardless of our agendas. Modern ethically challenged society is like a car dealer who tries to close a sale by saying how much money can be saved by not changing the oil and ignoring the low oil light indicator. A person might save a few dollars, the inconvenience of oil changes, and prove for the moment that car maintenance 'ethics' is just so much nonsense. The price paid later when the pistons seize up and the engine has to be replaced is the inevitable balancing of the ethical ledger. Such is life if we allow ourselves to be fooled by society's Hansel and Gretel witches who would lure us with cookies of instant gratification and quell our fears with promises that there is no downside.

As math is true, so must we be true. We are anchored to an exacting ethical existence that demands goodness in every respect. Doing what is right in our lives has no downside. It will always ultimately get us to the correct answer to the equation, the peace and fulfillment of a life well lived.

92

ETHICS

LAWS AND ENFORCEMENT exist in every culture. However, such culturally relative artifacts are not what holds societies together. Without the inner sense of right and wrong (ethics) and the personal suffering people experience from not obeying it, all would be lost. If everyone thought might makes right and the trick in life was getting away with whatever we could, a brutal pandemonium would reign. The British philosopher, Clifford, concluded: "What hurts society is not that it should lose its property, but that it should become a den of thieves."[1]

We normally look to books, institutions, prominent luminaries, and tradition for moral rules. But when the huff and puff is sifted away, all such rules turn out to be the creations of humans. The natural question should then be: Who are other people to tell us what to do? There is no law written across the sky demanding that some people be rule makers and everyone else rule followers. Yes, rules laid down in society in order to maintain order are necessary. But those rules may or may not be ethical.

Let's not get the reality of ethics confused with failed attempts at it. For example, when religions ruled the world, right and wrong were clearly defined. Was that ethics? Not really. It was just a system of rules imposed by people who figured they had a hot line to God. Through history, hundreds of thousands of religious leaders have dialed the same number but have all gotten a different message.

All the contradictory views about right and wrong do not prove that there are no ethical absolutes any more than getting lost in the middle of a city proves the destination desired is not there. Nor do the ghastly things done by arbiters of morality void ethics—like burning people at the stake for heresy, removing tongues for blasphemy, and disemboweling inquisitive seekers who gaze into the sky and speculate about planetary movements.

Clerics pronounced the Earth to be flat, motionless, and destined for an apocalyptic end. They have attributed disease to devils, and taught that boring holes in the skull to let evil spirits out was the cure for mental illness. The failures of people and institutions that have traveled the deeply worn path of conviction and piety establish only that people are fallible.

Science makes errors too, but we don't discard it. We continue to explore nature to find its laws and get nearer to its absolutes. People changing their minds, as well as ignorance, are to be expected in the march toward scientific—and ethical—truth.

Even animals display forms of ethic. Bands of carnivores don't normally eat their young or turn on one another when they get hungry. They could, they are free to do so, but they don't. Pets and farm animals also don't normally harm one another or turn on their caretakers. They are not taught such rules and they do not reason on what to do; it is innate. Ethics (dos and don'ts) in one form or another evidently extends throughout nature.

Although history may suggest that there are no carte blanche ethical absolutes that can be applied to all people regardless of circumstances, that conclusion does not preclude that there may be ethical absolutes for us individually given the particular circumstances of our situation. Just because we are confused and do not see at a particular moment a clear course of action, does not mean we are justified in any choice. Moral uncertainty is simply a holding pattern waiting for more data.

I would like to propose that, in spite of all the failed attempts at ethics, there must be such a thing as ethical absolutes. I say that because we are a part of the universe, and absolutes are what our universe is made of. We can end a dispute about the length of a fish by measuring it. There are tried and tested mathematics, and laws of chemistry and physics upon which everyone agrees. The rules governing inertia, magnetism, gravity, chemical interactions, and geometry have universal consensus. There are no Jewish or Muslim laws of algebra or gravity.

Banks in all 192 countries exchange currencies and agree on the numbers. If there is a dispute, there is a rational mathematical basis for coming to agreement. Similar agreement occurs in the sciences of engineering, automobile manufacturing, and computer electronics. People everywhere exchange parts, technology, and know-how. Scientific laws we discover are always testable and repeatable. That's why we can build dams that hold and motors that run, again and again with certainty. On the other hand, people bitterly disagree on what is ethically right or wrong and are willing to kill one another over beliefs for which there is no evidence whatsoever, other than, "somebody told me."

If we dig deep enough in the treasure chest from which we find true scientific laws, why would we not also find sure and true laws governing human behavior? I am not talking here of a law like stopping at a red light, but a law of process within each of us that lays out right and wrong choices based upon the circumstances. There is no reason to believe that a universe that reveals predictable law in every place we can check, has a void that permits arbitrariness and excuses any sort of activity just because we have free will. Arbitrariness, uncertainty, and dispute in science are only signals that we have not yet uncovered the real fundamental truth. That should drive further investigation. It is not justification for people to believe whatever they like. We press onward because we intuitively know, and experience has taught us, that there is truth to be found.

Ethical truth should be every bit as real and inescapable as rules governing the beating of a heart, the program in a computer, and the orbit of the moon. The rules science discovers are used to build bridges, put men on the moon, and do brain surgery. To the degree we discover and obey such laws, technological advance can occur and bring us the wondrous benefits of the modern world. Why can't we use the same process of discovery to bring us closer to the even more wondrous benefits of a world in which everyone is in tune with ethical law?

One way to know if you happen upon a law is to violate it and see if there are consequences. If there is ethical truth, it must exact penalty for disobedience just as there are consequences for not operating or maintaining the lawnmower properly. Although it is typical for us to think that the world 'out there' is different from our will, and that we can set our own rules, such is not the case. Law, whether ethical or physical, must extend to all activity, from the chemistry of liver metabolism and the forces in our ball and socket hip joints, to our decisions about how to behave at work today. This is not to suggest that ethical law would negate free will. We can decide to ignore the law of truth and jump off a cliff; we can decide to ignore the law of truth and rob a bank, then get shot trying to escape or suffer the pangs of guilt for life.

What about the argument by materialists that ethics is mere artifice, an invention of the material human brain and its invented culture? They say that ethics is subjective and in the eye of the beholder. By this reasoning there is no *right* ethical choice just like there is no *right* painting, color, or sound. But  things only seem subjective because we try to apply blanket laws to situational matters. There is a right painting, color, and sound for a *particular* situation. A fire engine red car is the correct car for a particular person, given the premise that preference can take precedence. Similarly there is always a right ethical choice given a particular situation, and assuming our starting premise that long term human welfare must always take precedence.

Belief in an anything-goes relativism is also self-contradictory. A belief in relativism is a belief. A belief is a sure thing, it is not relative. Saying that one believes in relativism is as self-contradictory as believing that one can prove there is no such thing as proof.

Moreover, for the materialist, the argument of arbitrariness fails because a mind that is solely brain matter would be governed by fixed physical laws: If the mind is mere chemistry, it should behave like every other test tube and create predictable results. But it doesn't.

If the brain is matter, but does not behave in predictable ways like all other matter, what is going on? The answer lies in the underlying nature of physical reality itself. Evidence from quantum physics shows that matter (including brains) is not really substance all the way down. Neither are the laws that govern matter made of matter. The laws of motion, for example, cannot be put in a box, weighed, or viewed under a microscope. Atoms—with their textbook billiard ball electrons and nuclei—are not fundamental material units. They are infinitely reducible to pieces so small they cease to be pieces and resemble something nonmaterial—like a thought. Thought cannot be reduced to matter or its laws, but matter and its laws can be reduced to thought. Thus the thoughts that create ethics are not confined to the sort of precision of mathematics, but that does not mean they are not subject to law.

Understandably these are difficult concepts. I will explore them with more detail and proofs in *Solving The Big Questions*. But for now, understand that just because something like ethics cannot be put on a scale and weighed is no reason to dispute its reality. If matter and the laws governing it are actually non-material and yet we can come to agreement on truths about the physical world, then there is no reason why the non-material sphere of ethics cannot be reduced to certainty as well.

The parallel between scientific and ethical truth is also manifest by results. Think of Truth (big T) as the all-embracing underpinnings of reality, not in the way opinionated people toss truth (small t) around unattached to any evidence other than their desires, faith, and beliefs. Mere claims about truth get us nowhere because that which is asserted with no supporting evidence, can also be dismissed without evidence. Big T Truth, on the other hand, applies to every spin of an electron, every apple that falls from a branch, and to every thought, word, and deed. Physical truth and ethical truth aren't two different things. There is just one Truth with different manifestations. If we ignore any aspect of Truth, consequences are sure. Don't duck under a low hanging limb, get a knock on the noggin; don't duck under a wrong ethical choice, get a knock as well.

If we apply bad science that does not reflect underlying physical truths—we scientifically lie—disharmony and discord result. Engines quit, floors collapse, bridges buckle, and planes will fall out of the sky. Why? Because what is mechanically incorrect—inconsistent with scientific truth—doesn't work. If we apply improper math to our budget, too much month remains after the money runs out. Don't keep gas in the car and end up stranded along the road. We have to get things right. No fudging, no sloppiness, no arbitrariness. Nothing that is wrong, no matter how small, ends up being right or okay.

Whenever ethics is violated, there is also a penalty, in some form or another, at one time or another. The penalty may range from a death sentence, to just the private pangs of guilt. The danger with ethics violations is that consequences are usually delayed, but gratification can be immediate. For the ethical cheater, this creates a trap because the bog entered just gets swampier the further in one goes. Delayed consequences do not deny the existence of ethics any more than a car that is running perfectly fine with dirty oil proves that what the owner's manual says about oil changes can be ignored.

Cheating at ethics is like cheating at science. As discussed in earlier chapters, eating the wrong foods may make our taste buds do somersaults, but the long term degenerative disease consequences from violating physical, environmental, and genetic laws will eventually come. Drugs can create euphoria, not changing the filter in the furnace saves money, and sitting on a couch and not exercising is easiest. Pleasure for the moment, without consideration of the scientific laws being broken, does not mean disaster will not come later nor does it deny the existence of the laws. Similarly, when we deny ethics, and the SOLVER principles that should be employed to properly exercise ethics, we may not experience any immediate harm. That does not mean a price will not be exacted later.

Now then, it is one thing to argue that there must be fundamental ethical standards, it is quite another to lay out what specifically is right or wrong. Although we would like a precise formula laid out for us, like dos and don'ts for children, such is not possible. That's because trenchant divisions between right and wrong, honest and dishonest, proper and improper, leave little room for the unforeseen. Fixed rules cannot always be made to conform to the complex dynamics, and infinite possibilities and circumstances of life.

For example, is it wrong to lie if the Gestapo knocks on the door and asks if the innocent person hiding in your back closet is there? Is it wrong for a bus driver with a full load of children to veer from hitting a semi if it means running over a child playing on the shoulder of the road? Is torture wrong if it means getting the location of a bomb that could kill a thousand people? Is killing in a war to stop a brutal dictator from torturing and murdering citizens justified? Is lying about being disloyal to a friend or loved one okay if you know the person might commit suicide if they found out? Is it okay to steal if it is the only way to keep your family alive?

But such quandaries and the fact that the right course of action cannot always be laid out like the assembly instructions for a piece of furniture we purchase in a box, still do not make ethics arbitrary. In this regard, ethical law is not unlike scientific law. The laws of hydrology may demand that water run downhill. But there are circumstances that seem to deny those laws, such as when momentum and pressure force water uphill. Hydrology and gravity are not denied when a city's eight story high water tower fills, an artesian well flows out of the ground, or water in a siphon hose flows uphill. One just has to take into account all the surrounding factors that interplay before drawing conclusions. Similarly, ethical laws are never really denied. One just has to understand all the variables that influence a given situation before drawing conclusions.

In order to reason toward truth on any matter we must begin with reasonable premises. Scientists must begin with the assumption that they can believe what they see and that logic can be trusted. Only when these assumptions were given priority over religious proclamations and ethereal philosophy did science advance. Likewise, if we are to attach reason to ethics, it must begin somewhere other than from mere proclamations. Beginning nowhere reasonable gets us to no reasonable place. Only by anchoring ethics to the reasonable premise that healthy human life over the long term should be given priority can we gain any bearings. This is the premise that has been used throughout this book and permits us to achieve the potential of thinking. Otherwise we are mired in opinionated froth, exactly the thing the world seems to insist upon.

If we again look to the real world model that science explores, we can see what means should be used to reveal ethical truth. Scientists use intuition, reason, and experience. On the road to discovery, they may begin by intuiting that a certain mathematical formula will work, or that two chemical compounds may interact in a certain way. Then they reason on their idea to see if it accords with other evidence they know. Finally, they perform experiments and observe the results (gain experience) to see if they are right.

Intuition, reason, and experience also tell us what is ethically right and wrong. Take rights of property for example. People everywhere intuit rights of property. If I am eating an apple, you don't get to jerk it out of my hand and finish it off. Such does not need to be learned from a book or outside authority any more than we need a book or teacher to understand 2+2=4, or that a ball will roll downhill, not uphill. We can then reason that without rights of property society would disassemble into battles over apples. We also evaluate ethics in terms of our experience (previous experiments) in which apples were unfairly taken from us or we took them from others. So how we arrive at ethical truth is just like how we arrive at scientific truth.

Consider how the consequences of violated ethics can disrupt the world. The home is like a microcosm of society. If a child is honest and does not steal there is homeostasis and peace in the home and the world is at rest. On the other hand, if he breaks ethical law and steals from dad's wallet left out on the dresser, the home would be disturbed with mom and dad now having to ferret out the thief. Immorality in a home is like having a worm in an apple. If the child admits to the crime, there is a chance for return to near normalcy. But things will never be quite the same. The parents' trust, which depends upon confidence in truth, is now off center. By lying, the problem is further compounded and discord in the home will continue to fester like an open wound. A violation of ethics may enter like a pinprick only to spread like a weedy vine.

If riveters cheat on a bridge and skip some holes, one day the bridge may collapse. Workers who get lazy or sloppy on an assembly line turn out products that anger customers and could end the business upon which their wages depend. CEOs who violate good accounting practices and fiduciary responsibility to stockholders, in pursuit of a selfish lavish lifestyle, can end up behind bars nursing guilt. Politicians who lie and demagogue only ruin the very country from which they derive their power. Social decline, economic instability, war, deaths, torture, and starvation all usually start with unethical actions. It is estimated that every day about 75,000 people die of starvation. Yet at the same time there is enough food in the world to feed everyone. This atrocity occurs because people along the line of supply and demand believe that ethics can be ignored.

There is often even a confluence between consequences from disobeying scientific laws and disobeying ethics. That's because there is only one bank of truth, and ethical and scientific truth come from the same vault. For example, the bridge riveters not only cheated by not doing what they had agreed to, but cheated as well on the physical laws that needed to be obeyed for the bridge to stand. The bridge falling is the physical consequence; the lives lost and the jailing of the riveters is the ethical one.

Truth is ubiquitous and must be obeyed for consequences to be avoided. Perhaps that's why the same basic rights and wrongs eventually emerge from every society. Truth ultimately rises to the top ethically, just as it does mathematically and scientifically. There is no latitude for cheating it. If physical or ethical laws are broken, no matter how small the infraction or how cleverly concealed, there will eventually be negative repercussions. From the perspective of ethics, all violations are as wrong as stealing from the poor box. Right and wrong are forever.

Think about ethics when politicians say what they know full well to be untrue. It applies when children do not fess up to the truth because they do not want to disappoint or because they fear penalty. It is there when salespeople try to scam, or when companies create false and misleading advertising just to turn dollars. Ethics even applies to inactivity, for it is the law at work that causes the unsettling guilt when reflecting on the day and realizing that we could have done something more or better.

Setting aside reason, ethics also reaches deep within to the essence of our character. Life turns out not to just be about the choices we make and the consequences that result, but rather whether we make decisions on the wrong grounds. Saving a pedestrian's life by pushing him out of the way of a speeding automobile has no merit for us individually if it were done so that we could pick his pocket during the mayhem. Ethical truth is not just about obeying the law that says we should not steal, or not doing it for fear of being jailed; it's also about not doing it because we sense the wrongness of the act. It just doesn't feel good. Ethics turns out to be about choice, not obedience to a command.

We can never close the book on ethical obligations. That is the way of Truth and the laws of reality. Escape from them is never possible. That's why a sharply honed sense of ethics creates a sense of culpability that extends to all suffering and death we did nothing to prevent today. We come to realize that any time or money spent on anything other than the necessities for our survival has, so to speak, the blood of an innocent child on it. We can no more take a vacation from ethics than we can from the laws of inertia or gravity.

We are all in an ethical race. Our incomplete understanding of ethical truth or our inability to comply with it does not deny its existence. Getting near ethical truth is just like getting near scientific truth. It is a process whereby as knowledge and experience grow, so does certainty. Life is clearly not about how much money we make, how many pleasure highs we can have, or whether we can gain power over others. It is about those quiet and private battles that go on within and combine to create the moral wealth of a society. It is the caring, concern, and love we feel and the degree to which we can let it dominate life.

Not everyone is equally endowed with moral wisdom and ethical intelligence. Some pass ethics off to others and their institutions to solve. Some have convinced themselves that staying within the law—or however the law can be finagled—fulfills their ethical duty. For example, a defense attorney can feel elated if he gets a serial murderer off using a technicality within the law. Others go about life as Groucho Marx quipped, "Those are my principles. If you don't like them I have others." But how we behave toward truth, or our denial of it, does not affect its reality.

In science there are only two assumptions required. One is that the universe is governed by predictable laws. The other is that we can trust reason. Those two assumptions are required in ethics as well, but there is an important guiding corollary: All decisions must be made giving priority to long-term human life and well being. The constant struggle, dialectic, and dilemma as to how to live bigger than self and make decisions that embrace the welfare of all humankind is in large part what makes us human and sets us apart from mere matter obeying mechanical laws.

Where there seems to be no clear course of action, we are left with conscience, the topic of the next chapter. Although it is underused and often ignored, it is an effective personalized filter for life choices telling us how to be in accord with truth, become the best we can, and answer the question of whether humans can be a worthwhile addition to the universe.

93

CONSCIENCE

WHEN WE WERE CHILDREN our parents told us what was right and wrong, school had its rules, and church had its sins. To be good, all we needed to do was obey all the dos and don'ts. If we did this, we were led to believe we were following conscience.

This view of conscience can carry into and through adult life so that one's perception of right and wrong is shaped primarily by the dictates of others. Is conscience just a product of nurture? Are we mere blank moral slates at birth to be written on by others, or do we have an inherent sense of ethics from the get-go?

Take a moment and think back to the time of earliest self-awareness. See if you do not agree that ethics has always been present within you. Have you not always made choices influenced by it? Conscience is like a homing instinct within a migrating bird breaking from the shell. Conscience is like an innate ethical compass and explains why society throughout time has had the same basic ethical grounding. Conscience and ethics are inescapable parts of being human.

We spend a lifetime tinkering with our conscience, testing its limits, compromising, suppressing, denying, ignoring, and passing it off to outside moral purveyors. We do this out of sheer laziness or in attempts to cheat life and gain unfair advantage. I am reminded of the storekeeper who kept the change the customer forgot to pick up, and then, out of good conscience, divided it with his business partner.

Perhaps we take the materialistic view that conscience is a mere epiphenomenon of brain atoms. This line of thought permits scientists to perform virtually any macabre experiment. Animals by the millions are cruelly tortured in laboratories around the world because cries of pain are considered to be nothing more than spark discharges across neurons. To materialistic scientists and laymen alike, conscience can be just troublesome and inconsequential baggage that makes us feel bad when all our other parts can feel so good.

As argued in the previous chapter, ethics cannot be reduced to amoral, deterministic atoms. Yet conscience is at our core and always ready to be consulted. In fact, as a Dutch proverb says, "In the courtroom of the conscience, a case is always in progress." Trying to ignore it is like reading a book on a sinking ship. We are painfully reminded of its presence when we flout it. Pangs of guilt from a violated conscience remain with us for a lifetime, teaching us to listen up when it speaks. Conscience is like a shadow that in midday, at the moment of infraction, scarcely is noticed underfoot. But in the evening of our lives how monstrous and terrible is the long shadow troubling our memory. Indeed, everything changes in the world except our good deeds and bad deeds. The bad ones are the only memories not forgotten. Unlike any other wound, time never erases nor heals them; it just makes them more painful. They are like a rough tooth to the tongue and stick in our memory like chewing gum to the sole of a shoe.

Discovering our true conscience requires reaching within to decide what is *our* conscience, as opposed to something seeded there by another person. Somebody else's rule sheet is not *our* conscience. Some societies practice cannibalism, infanticide, suicide bombing, or convoluted rituals because someone at some time decided such acts are of good conscience. The further the guru is in the past, and the less his words are tied to evidence, the more sure people are about the authority. But real conscience is not contingent upon where or how we are raised, and it most certainly can never contradict the facts. Although conscience should be tuned to the truth, we too often tune to somebody else's station, or just turn off our ethical receiver altogether. Nevertheless, truth and ethic are always there transmitting to us, always available for us to listen in.

Conscience is commonly marginalized into ethical meaninglessness by assuming it is dependent upon the whims and seasons of human desires and hopes. For example, military leaders instill patriotic 'conscience' into soldiers. Each side in a conflict sees it as moral and in good conscience to kill the enemy. Attorneys will defend the guilty and prosecute the innocent and do so in line with their trained legal 'conscience.' Physicians prescribe drugs and practice surgery and other therapies that may do more harm than good. But they do so in good 'conscience' because this is what medical school taught and it is in line with conventional standard of care. If a patient dies as a result of therapy, the doctor can take comfort in thinking he has done all that can be done as defined by accepted medical standards. If a food manufacturer makes food composed of a variety of synthetics and food fractions, and tortures it into nutritional oblivion to give it shelf-life and consumer appeal, that's considered fine as long as it meets certain regulatory requirements and the label is designed properly. The company will suffer no problems with 'conscience' regardless of the health consequences so long as their product is legal to sell.

On the other hand, consumers feel they only need to follow all the societal norms to be of good 'conscience.' Let doctors take care of health, the government take care of the economy, the military take care of security, the attorney take care of disputes, the accountant take care of finances, the church take care of ethics, and the food industry take care of food choices. Sit back, watch TV, overeat, pay the bills, and follow the rules. All is well and 'conscience' is served because the rules are being followed.

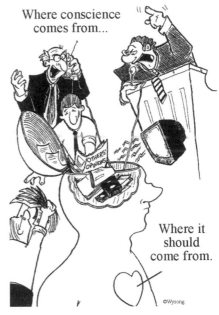

Where conscience comes from...

Where it should come from.

©Wysong

If we were to deny outside moral authority from society, school, religion, government, or parents, and be left alone with only our own conscience, would we become thieves and murderers? Rather than indulging amoral freedom, we would find the inner voice of conscience far more demanding than even the most strict outside ethical code.

Besides, if one is looking for virtue, it is found in choice, not obedience. Plato so wisely said, "Good people do not need laws to tell them to act responsibly, while bad people will find a way around the laws."

Sometimes a clear path to right is not always evident no matter how much we soul search. The infinite circumstances and nuances of life can create constant dilemmas. But it is that very element of uncertainty that helps us in our training to be better people standing on our own feet. If morality were reducible to a precise formula there would be only two choices in life: know the formula; follow the formula. Although that is what much of religion has tried to do, this approach can reduce people to followers, not free moral agents. We are not here to be robots, but rather thinking people, ever searching our inner sense of ethics and meeting all challenges.

Perhaps our most difficult task in life is to be sure we are not just moo-ing along back to the barn to be milked by the conscience merchants. Surrendering to others makes us vulnerable to their self-interests. The end result all too often is that we become pawns, victims, experimental subjects, tools, resources, and profit centers of others. Rather, our objective should be to become full human beings and help to bring the world to a better place by listening to our own cultivated inner voice.

Conscience is well defined as being innate; it is an instinct that serves as an ethical guide. Abraham Lincoln said, "When I do good I feel good, when I do bad I feel bad." We will never come to know our conscience, however, until we free ourselves from the imposed consciences of others. This is not to say the views of others should not be considered, just that all of us are at least as justified in deciding what is right and wrong for ourselves, as someone else is in deciding it for us. This does not mean just dropping out and being self-willed. To the contrary, it means taking on the heavy lifting of being informed and exercising judgment. A conscience nurtured by search, openness, self responsibility, and a commitment to reason, evidence, and truth (the SOLVER principles) is a heavy burden, but one each of us must shoulder.

Exercising conscience is not an easy task because it means looking within to a most fearsome and demanding place. There is nothing quite so humbling and terrifying as coming to know the good that lies within and how much we are capable of doing or becoming.

94

THE LONG VIEW

THE ABILITY TO SEE LONG-TERM consequences and then act with wisdom early is in short supply. We are just not very good at doing the difficult and painful things that make sense for the long haul. We would rather have our rewards now and hope there is no price later.

People eat every manner of processed synthetic junk because it's easy, quick, and gives the taste buds a thrill. We live sedentary lives that are comfortable, easy, and bring the most immediate pleasure. Riches are feverishly pursued without regard for what gets in the way. The feelings and lives of others are callously used as stepping-stones for personal gain and ego satisfaction. A 2-trillion dollar medical system focuses on health crises and symptom relief without addressing fundamental causes. Industry disregards resource depletion and pollution for short-term bottom line. The halls of justice are perverted by legal tricks and manipulated for treasure. Government moves in whatever direction will gain the most votes without regard for reason.

Hindsight will be a cruel master.

Our mindless pursuit of instant gratification is a struggle between the beast in us and our better senses. Animals and children think only in terms of their immediate needs. Adult humans must think further ahead than that if we are to survive as a species. But that requires intelligent reflection, knowledge, and the ability to extrapolate to future consequences. It's harder than just fulfilling whatever urge we may feel at the moment.

Extrapolation is an intellectual tool that can yield profound wisdom. It's a matter of making judgments based upon, but beyond the facts now known to be true. Using the long view can serve to assess politics, religion, scientific theory, philosophy, health, and social issues. It is a key SOLVER principle we have used again and again throughout this book. It is the opposite of the failed philosophy of deontology, whereby morality is measured by simply following rules regardless of their consequences.

Here's how extrapolation can work. If I find that pollution from my factory destroys oxygen-producing plankton, I might think that is no big deal since the ocean is so huge and my pipes are so small. But if I extrapolate to the potential devastating effects if all factories did what I was doing, the conscionable thing to do would be to stop my pollution and support regulation that stops others as well. Long view extrapolation helps us nip potential disasters in the bud.

Here are more examples:

• Short view: People should be able to have as many children as they wish. Having children is a right.

• Long view: Unbridled reproduction would mean that eventually population would outstrip resources, resulting in massive starvation, disease, and death.

• Short view: Immigrants should be encouraged to speak their own language and their children should be taught to do so with public dollars.

• Long view: Since there are hundreds of languages and dialects, eventually schools would collapse under the burden of attempting to teach them all. Also, society would not be able to converse with itself and would fall like a modern Babel.

• Short view: It makes me feel good when I make life easy for my children by taking care of their every need.

• Long view: True love is to help children prepare for independent living in the difficult adult world, not pamper them into a uselessness that will make them vulnerable to great calamity as they grow older.

• Short view: I can do so little, therefore I will do nothing.

• Long view: If everyone throughout history took that position, no human progress would have ever been made. Even the space shuttle and the great pyramids were developed little by little.

• Short view: Everyone should have free healthcare and a guaranteed minimum standard of living.

• Long view: The dollars to fund such social programs must come from the productive sector. But if the fruits of their labor are stolen from them, incentives will disappear, productivity decline, and all will suffer.

By carefully reasoning an assertion or action out to its nth degree to see what the result will be, the correct present course of action becomes clear. We achieve lasting happiness, health, and peace by being smart enough to see beyond our noses to the eventual outcome of actions.

Some instant thrills may have to be forgone. But the lifelong dividends from an intelligent life are worth the little sacrifices along the way. For example, eating right and pursuing a healthy lifestyle now can keep us out of the hospital and nursing home in our later years and help prevent painful, incapacitating, and debilitating diseases. As I watch people I knew in their youth who are now in their middle or later years, crippled and living on drugs, surgeries, and doctoring, I reflect on their earlier attitudes. You've heard it: "What the hell, if smoking doesn't get you, something else will." "Exercise isn't any fun." "If something goes wrong, doctors can fix it." "If I'm out of shape a little nip, tuck, and silicone will fix it." Their life philosophy was nothing more than a justification for a continued course of momentary pleasure.

People don't want to be inconvenienced or expend effort for something that lies in the abstract future. We hate to wait. We can learn too late that inconvenience is not as painful and limiting as is disease, war, economic collapse, or environment ruination.

Unlike the rest of the physical and biological world, which moves primarily to the rhythms of natural law and instinct, humans have a unique fiduciary responsibility. As individuals and as a society, we can face virtually every decision in either of two ways. One is that we myopically do what the crowd does, is expedient, what gets rid of the problem for the moment, or gives the most pleasure the quickest. That is the way to a wrecked life and wrecked world. The other option is to live a contemplative life, to intelligently and dispassionately reflect on long-term benefits and consequences and not fear departing from what the masses are doing. In other words, exercise our conscience to effect solutions without being driven to them. That is what is called living life as if thinking matters.

How We Look Ahead

95

BEING REAL

ALL EVIL—THAT WHICH WORKS against a good world and good us—can be thought of as nothing but a kind of lie. Falsehood is discord with the underlying truth of the universe.

Reflect back through the many topics in this book. We find again and again in our society that the most popular views are usually wrong. Trying not to get faked out is like a full time job.

Genuine people, valuable products, and good ideas are scarce because being real, taking an ethical stand, and creating genuine value is hard work. We are always looking for the easy way, the short cut, and the reward without the work. Feigning knowledge is easier than doing the homework. Pretending to be busy at work is easier than putting a shoulder into it. Faking virtue is easier than living an ethical life. Practicing political demagoguery gets more votes than telling voters what they need to hear. Life experiences teach us, as Andrew Carnegie reflected in his later years, "to pay little attention to what men say and just watch what they do."

We want the look, the goods, the persona, and the adulation right now, minus the necessary sweat. Modern instant gratification culture fosters this something-for-nothing mentality. Tenured jobs, fat corporate salaries, union guarantees, entitlement programs, the stock market and lottery, plastic surgery, inheritance, and anabolic steroids can bring easy and instant success.

In the business world, faking it has become the standard Groucho Marx spoke of: "The secret of life is honesty and fair dealing. If you can fake that, you've got it made." All of the superficial, air-brushed, blow-dried charm being marketed to us from every direction is only a fool's gold. If we fall in line the commercial world gets our dollars and in return we get hokum and a degraded world for our children.

Not only does commerce pretend to be what it is not, so do people everywhere. Hypocrisy is cheaper, quicker, and easier than being the real thing. It is a funny thing how we clamor for freedom, but then when we can do as we please, we imitate one another. People run away from themselves into the shells of other people. But the cloak of an artificial persona is a fabricated thing that covers a soulless being. Such a person is like a tree without leaves or a home with no pictures on the walls.

Borrowed character only serves to show the poverty of the borrower.

The fake smiles that turn on and off like a neon sign, the glad-handing, the brags, and the empty promises fool nobody. As Dr. Seuss so wisely counsels, be who you are because "those who matter don't mind and those who mind don't matter."

Lying, faking it, and hypocrisy never work because truth always prevails in the end. The prizefighter with all the tassels, fancy footwork, and big mouth, but no real skills, gets decked. The basketball player with the garb and clever dribbling gets cut if he hasn't the competitive heart. The gussied-up aspiring socialite attempting to convince others she is beautiful, rich, famous, and of station deceives only herself.

"I want our first date to be special... let's not spoil it by being ourselves."

Cinderella's wicked stepmother and awful sisters are hated, not because they were homely, but because they were hypocrites. Cinderella did not pretend to be more than she was; she was self-effacing, if anything. We love her not because of her beauty but because she was humble, genuine and even willing to be thought of as less than she was.

447

Being honest to ourselves and others is difficult in a world that is working hard night and day to make us everybody else. So it is a courageous venture to grow up and actually turn out to be who we really are. Being oneself is like a protest. On the other hand, if we fake it often enough we get to believing the lie. Hypocrisy is not so much a danger in its visibility to others, but in its invisibility to self.

An interesting way to look at our responsibility to be who we are is to loosely apply the philosophical concept of negation developed by the 19th century German philosopher, Hegel. In his study of being (ontology) he argued that we are in large part defined by what we are not, not what we are.[1] In other words, if you defined all things in existence other than you, what is left over is who you are. So if we try to be those things other than what we are—to be who we are not—we in effect zero ourselves out.

DESIDERATA

Go placidly amid the noise and haste,and remember what peace there may be in silence. As far as possible without surrender be on good terms with all persons. Speak your truth quietly and clearly; and listen to others, even the dull and the ignorant; they too have their story.

Avoid loud and aggressive persons, they are vexations to the spirit. If you compare yourself with others, you may become vain and bitter; for always there will be greater and lesser persons than yourself. Enjoy your achievements as well as your plans.

Keep interested in your own career, however humble; it is a real possession in the changing fortunes of time. Exercise caution in your business affairs; for the world is full of trickery. But let this not blind you to what virtue there is; many persons strive for high ideals; and everywhere life is full of heroism.

Be yourself. Especially, do not feign affection. Neither be cynical about love; for in the face of all aridity and disenchantment it is as perennial as the grass.

Take kindly the counsel of the years, gracefully surrendering the things of youth. Nurture strength of spirit to shield you in sudden misfortune. But do not distress yourself with dark imaginings. Many fears are born of fatigue and loneliness. Beyond a wholesome discipline, be gentle with yourself.

You are a child of the universe, no less than the trees and the stars; you have a right to be here. And whether or not it is clear to you, no doubt the universe is unfolding as it should.

Therefore be at peace with God, whatever you conceive Him to be, and whatever your labors and aspirations, in the noisy confusion of life keep peace with your soul. With all its sham, drudgery, and broken dreams, it is still a beautiful world. Be cheerful. Strive to be happy.

(Max Ehrmann, Desiderata, Copyright 1952)

We are all born originals, but try our best to die copies. How silly it all is because if we are ourselves we have no competition. By pretending to be someone else we lose ourselves. By pretending to be more than we are, we become less. It is far better to be who we are to ourselves, and less than we are to others. If we are unhappy with ourselves—and we all are to one degree or another—then we must do the work, make the mistakes, learn, and grow to be what we aspire to. That makes for a beautiful and true person, one forged with honesty and hard work.

> *"Sincerity is everything. If you can fake that, you've got it made."* -George Burns

If our world is to ever advance, it must edge toward the honesty that is reality. Unfortunately our institutions and popularized beliefs follow selfish agendas that bring superficial and short-term benefits. Only pretenses are made about truth. Gaining the discernment to cut through to the truth (which usually means being wrong in the eyes of the masses) and become part of the solution is no little task. But it begins at home, with honesty in our own lives and in our own person—being true to ourselves.

SECTION N

FINIS

IN THIS SECTION: *To become better people and to make a better world requires setting aside cherished beliefs, facing reality, and, a most difficult task, change. By using the SOLVER principles, not only do our underlying problems become manifest, but truth has a chance of being brought into focus, and with that, hope for a better and brighter future.*

96

CHANGE

ONE OF THE MOST FRUSTRATING THINGS we can experience as we open our minds and grow is the world's resistance to change. Democrats, Republicans, atheists, Catholics, Baptists, humanists, polygamists, sloppy people, lazy people, capitalists, socialists, racists, overeaters, undereaters, junk food eaters, video addicts, sugar and starch addicts, rude people... and on we could go, just want to stay where they are. They are addicted to their mindsets. If you speak to anyone and ask why they think and behave as they do, they will give various justifications, including dogmatic assertions about how they believe they are right. If you try to suggest that they may be wrong and should change, they will bristle, like any addict who has their supply threatened.

Everyone seems to be stuck in ruts. We all see this failing in others, but tend to be blind when looking in the mirror. We want to continue on our merry way, expect others to change, and demand that 'somebody' needs to fix problems that occur in the world that interfere with our comfort zones.

But all of us can't be as right as we think we are. The thousands of beliefs people hold contradict one another. Since there is only one truth, we are probably all wrong. Well, that is to say, all except one. Maybe. It is highly unlikely that there is even one of us absolutely right. But that doesn't matter. The point is, since we refuse to change, and owning the one absolute truth of the universe is the only reason not to change, we all, in practice, behave as if we think we own the truth. The absurdity of this is self evident.

It's easy to see the problems in the world and how things could be improved. In large part, that is what motivated me to write these 97 chapters. But it is maddening to see that it does not happen. That's because people don't seem to care about real solutions. What's important is whatever beliefs they hold, no matter how insane they are. It's enough to make you want to grab the whole world and slap it up side the head.

It was not until I got to this point in the book, the end, that I got the feeling that all might be for naught. Even if I could lead all the horses in the world to water, that does not mean they would drink. If what I said did not accord with what people already believed, what I said would simply pass most people by. This sobering thought just kind of snuck up on me.

So, in winding up the book's effort to 'save the world,' I will try to address this last, daunting, and most important task: explaining why people don't want to change and what can be done about it. (By doing so, I am not suggesting that I have 'the truth,' and that I am not inclined to resist change as well. It is a universal problem.)

My first tactic will be to make us feel ashamed. Think of it this way. The only thing that sets us apart from instinct-driven animals is our intelligence and conscience. When we don't use those faculties to take actions for the betterment of our individual lives and the world at large, but rather just fall into a pattern we don't veer from—like an instinct— we are little more than slugs. If we will be human, and not be slugs, we have the capacity to transform the world to a peaceful paradise. All that is necessary is to seek truth honestly and openly, and then change. But we don't. That's as crazy as an instinct-driven rat eating poisoned food out of a box that is clearly marked "Poison." So, unless we wish to be nothing more than an animal, we should seek and welcome change.

If shame does not move us, perhaps belittling will. When we refuse to change, but rather just believe and do what we have been told, we are a child, we haven't grown up. In infancy we are trained to think and behave in certain pat ways. As children we are forced into obedient behavior by parents, teachers, religion, and society. We try to avoid mistakes, behave and get answers right, score well, and make brownie points. We learn the rules and follow them closely to solve problems quickly. We become response-able (not a typo). There are no rewards for challenging rules, initiative, creativity, and long-view thinking. The pats on the back are for conformity and doing it NOW. Ours is not to question, look to the long view, nor to change things.

As we continue in schooling we become narrowed and specialized, boxing our minds in even further. We are rewarded with degrees if we parrot the professors' mindsets. When we join the work force we are given a job description and again are rewarded for obedience and routine. Our livelihood and success come to depend upon working well within the status quo and keeping business as usual. This, then again, reinforces conformity and a crowd pleaser mentality. We try not to make waves in order to keep the support and respect of our friends and superiors, and not be viewed as weird and maverick.

The obedient, repetitive, day-to-day living from infancy up to and through adulthood helps keep us as children. Just because we add years, have bigger toys, and can push our weight around, doesn't mean we are truly adult.

Wanting *immediate* results and pleasures is also a child mentality. Children learn early on to look at their immediate situation and react to it as they have been taught. If they do as they are told, and do it immediately, they get milk and cookies. If they don't, they get punished. In adults, this short-view, pleasure seeking mentality precludes reflection, contemplation, and critical thinking, the prerequisites to change.

Our refusal to change makes us mere epigones, inferior imitators of full humans. In contrast, a true adult human is moved by intelligence and conscience, reflects on history, weighs all the facts, and projects out into the future. An adult makes decisions and forms mindsets without regard to what they may have been taught, or the milk and cookie rewards. It should be a matter of self respect. Why on earth would we not want to be adults and be fully human?

Now, to further shock us into our senses, I will bash religion. Not religion in the sense you are thinking, but rather the idolatry that we all engage in. It's called materialism. We are so surrounded by, dependent upon, and rewarded by material Newtonian machines that we tend to ignore things that are conceptual, philosophic, and ethical. We devote ourselves to that which responds quickly to a plug, button, switch, or cursor. Our impatience is being filed to a razor's edge as we expect faster and more of everything. We just don't have time to change our Pavlovian behavior, think beyond immediate rewards and punishments, and do anything that might yield a payback years into the future. Worshipping at the shrine of matter reduces us to dutiful, nonthinking lemmings.

453

To pile insult on injury, consider how cowardly we are when we are unwilling to change. Fear of the unknown is in large part to blame. We like to stay in the middle of the herd. We are leery of the new and don't want to depart from our routines, security, and comforts. We like the security of the 'known,' even if the 'known' has nothing to do with truth and reality. This behavior links back to when we were in the bush. We stayed on the beaten path, not wandering off into the hinterlands where dangerous creatures (new ideas) may lurk. Abraham Maslow wrote, "You either step forward into growth, or you will step backward into safety."

Finally, to cap off this litany of insults, we are a lazy lot. It's always easiest to leave things as they are, not clean up messes, and not do work before its time—work that may never bring a reward, or if so, only in the distant future.

It's difficult to activate all those neurons in the big front part of the brain and make them interlink with conscience and heart. Better to be fainéant and just let the autopilot pain and pleasure reflexes in the hindbrain and spinal cord do all the work of living for us.

So there are powerful forces at play keeping us at home in our comfortable mindsets. Yes, we can take initiative, be creative, and rearrange things, but only within the bounds of accepted patterns. The resistance of the world to breaking its oil glut addiction is a perfect example. Oil is a finite resource (it will run out), is damaging to the environment, and causes international instability. Rather than change the mindset and aggressively create better and independent energy technologies, we just try to make more fuel efficient cars and more clever oil drilling techniques. Only if the price of gasoline becomes ridiculous, or we begin choking on our own fumes, do we demand change.

Changes that would mean shifting our behavior are resisted even if those changes can obviously benefit us or the rest of the world. No matter the merit of a change, about 10% of the population will vehemently resist it, 80% will change only if forced or it is economically advantageous, and only 10% will embrace it and implement it regardless of how it might disrupt their lives.

Yes, by leaving things as they are we can earn a living, even rise to positions of prestige in our community or nation. But that does not mean we are truly being human. To be human means to disengage the autopilot and think openly, listen to and follow conscience, and make changes that serve the long-term interests of ourselves and the rest of humanity.

How can we shift our minds and behaviors away from the fearful, crowd pleasing, lazy, materialistic, animal instinct, child-like, hindbrain, automaton mode that refuses to change? We need to shift our behavior toward the list on the right:

NONCHANGERS	CHANGERS
Having/Possessing/Materialistic	Reflective/Internally driven
Faster/Bigger/More	Open minded/Moved by logic and fact
Greed/Profit/Market share	Seek to be in touch with reality
Credit/Debt	Self reliant/Creative/Take responsibility
Consumerism/Convenience	Critical/Discerning
Me centered/Selfish	Long view perspective
Short term view	Altruistic/Humane/Sensitive
Resistant to reason/Oblivious to reality	Seek meaning and purpose
Symptomatic relief/Bandaids	Discern distant consequences
Feel entitled/Blame/Justify/Socialistic	Sense a duty to the future
Status/Success/Appearances	Use talents
Superficial/Entertainment oriented	Philosophic/Deep/Spiritual

Most of us start with the characteristics reflected on the list to the left. To own the characteristics on the list to the right, characteristics that offer the most promise for bettering each of us individually and the whole world, requires us to be changers.

To see the need for change requires us to first of all open our minds to the real world, all of it. However, most of us don't do this because we have created our own little realities by opening our eyes only to that which fits our preconceived beliefs. We should be moved to have an open mind because that is the only honest mind there is. Honesty in turn requires that we reach forward into the front part of the brain and down into the heart to activate the goodness that is there.

Also, our intuitive sense, our conscience, tells us there is more to life than its mechanics and that we have a responsibility to serve more than our immediate selfish needs. Listening to that voice, believing it, understanding that we can only muffle it so long without suffering consequences and terrible pangs of guilt, is a reality it is wise to face as early in life as possible. That voice also tells us we have duty. Surely the sad state of world affairs and our experiences with others individually tell us that change is needed and things could be better. The world is headed for disaster and all about us we can see people in self-destructive modes of living—drugs, laziness, obesity, debt, violence, needless disease, compulsive consumerism, inactivity, narcissism, and so on. History proves that our voice, our actions, no matter how seemingly small, can make a difference. All change begins with one.

Since the mindset we have is riveted in place by repetitious thematic messages from family, friends we choose, the media, our religious group, and work environment, and those rivets are in turn welded by our experiences and rewards, the pattern must be changed. Breaking our mindset addictions requires a conscious effort to recognize the patterns that are threatening us and their belief etiologies.

For example, people everywhere are under the belief (mindset addiction) that more access to modern medical care will mean more health. If all we do is listen to our doctor, watch medical hype on television, remain ignorant of our body's natural mechanisms, read drug advertisements, and marvel at the short term effectiveness of medical intervention, we will continue in that belief, even if our health is failing. The reality that must be faced is the fact that our health is failing. That should lead to a conscious effort to find out why by letting in all the facts and information—as I did in the previous section on modern medicine. Reading more widely, exploring, learning, and experimenting will reveal that the prior belief in medicine and the patterns it produced in our lives were wrong. From there we should discard the old belief and institute a new, more holistic view of health that respects natural balances and puts responsibility where it belongs, on us, not doctors and government programs. Then new patterns in lifestyle, eating, and treatment approaches can not only reverse disease safely, but expand health itself. We create a solution for ourselves, rather than just continue to wallow in a belief addiction that ruins health.

Because beliefs are so potentially deleterious, even deadly, we need to make a conscious effort to scrutinize every one of them. We should go through the same mental process we did with medical beliefs, and examine political, environmental, religious, industrial, social, economic…all beliefs. Then, in the light of full disclosure, let them fall, change our mindsets and institute new living patterns.

Change—betterment—will not come if we don't make a conscious effort to get off our high horses of assumed truths. Otherwise we will fail to notice what we fail to notice. Ambition (it is not "too hard"), fearlessness of truth, sensitivity to conscience, facing reality, activation of intelligence and all the SOLVER principles (Self responsibility, Open mindedness, Long view thinking, Virtuous intent, Evidence first, and Reasoning) can serve us so well.

Personally, I have always found it most helpful to understand that the sources of the beliefs that drive our behavior are other fallible people with their own belief baggage and personal agendas. That should embolden us—if for no other reason than pride—to freely shed them. We can then strike out for better ideas (that remain malleable) earned on our own and paid for with the currency of facts and reason.

Change is our only hope and should be welcomed with enthusiasm, not avoided and dreaded. Truly, the only sustainable consciousness is a learning and growing consciousness. Our crises, the individual ones and those facing the planet, can be but passing storms. But they can only be prevented from organizing into a horrific cataclysm if we have the insight, courage, and ambition to change. Although crises in themselves stir an awakening (disease, smog, war, escalating fuel prices, rampant teen pregnancies, starvation, etc.), the scale of the importunate problems now facing the planet is such that we cannot afford to wait until we are threatened or uncomfortable. If we do not act on the wisdom of foresight, some of our problems will be irreversible.

The incredible world-wide communication now possible, particularly by means of the Internet, lays bare bad ideas and unites those of a higher consciousness. Increasingly there is no excuse for ignorance. It is no longer possible for wrong political, health, religious, economic or other ideas to linger under the assumption that the masses will remain shielded from the truth. All beliefs that trap the minds of humans are being exposed to the scrutiny of reality. Hopefully this exposure will eventually burst all the false belief bubbles permitting individuals to improve their lives, and humanity to unite and create real planetary solutions.

There is a light at the end of the tunnel. Our willingness to change is the only thing that will make sure it is not the beam of an oncoming freight train, but rather the dawn of a wonderful new era.

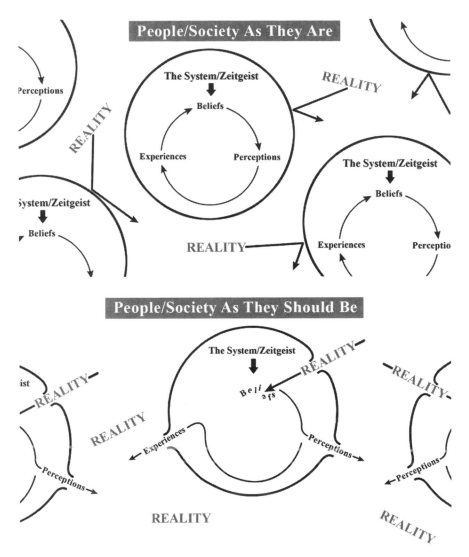

People/Society As They Are

People/Society As They Should Be

Mindset Bubbles - Belief systems (zeitgeists) embed beliefs which in turn create perceptions that lead to experiences that reinforce the beginning beliefs. These systems perpetuate themselves only because they remain insulated from reality. Around the world and within each society a variety of mindset bubbles exist that are insulated from reality. They clash with one another in war, they waste the lives of those devoted to them, and bring immense harm to the planet, societies, and individuals. If a false belief is exposed to the facts and evidence of reality, the belief dismantles. Once exposed to the light of reality, our perceptions and experiences no longer reinforce the wrong belief. A new, truer, zeitgeist can result that is more in tune with reality.

97

END AND BEGINNING

Imagine driving on a mountain road, cruising right along enjoying the scenery. As you break over the crest of a hill the road takes a hairpin turn. Unable to react in time, you go tumbling down the mountainside. When you awaken, you find yourself in a hospital at the foot of the mountain. You're in the intensive care unit plugged into IV bags and monitors alongside other wreck victims. How relieved you are that medical technology is there to put you back together.

When your wits return you look out the window and see heavy equipment shoring up the hillside that you and others have excavated rolling down the slope. Looking down the street you can see numerous wrecked vehicles behind tow trucks all lined up waiting for repair. It's amazing what mechanics are capable of these days.

You will have a long expensive recovery and your new car was nearly totaled. But you have insurance and there are special government programs to cover the rest. If that fails, there are fleets of attorneys who will sue the hospitals and garages. Sure, taxes are high, but social programs are the only right thing to do for all the victims who keep cascading over the cliff.

Nobody is redesigning the road at the top of the hill, changing the speed limit, placing warning signs, or erecting crash barriers on the hairpin turn. All the money and resources are being consumed down at the bottom repairing the damage. Besides, if no more cars came crashing down the cliff, the garages and hospitals would go belly-up, people would lose jobs, and politicians would not have causes they needed more taxes for. Why, my goodness, a whole way of life would be changed. Can't have that.

Such a scenario may seem ridiculous. Surely, people couldn't be that shortsighted. But they are, only on a grander scale. The whole world is beset with problems that aren't getting fixed. The lion roaring at the door catches our attention but the termites gnawing in the walls are ignored. We just keep attempting repair after the fact.

Health, peace, the environment, economics, society, and politics are all cars tumbling off cliffs. At the bottom of the hill are political demagoguery, symptom-based medicine, environmental disregard, socialism, scientific and religious close-mindedness, capitalism without conscience, functional illiteracy (people can read and write but either don't do it or do it only for fun), dependency, and bigotry. We exert our best technology and drain resources to apply Band-Aids. Status quo is protected, short term gain prioritized, desire rules as king over reality, and real solutions go by the wayside.

This sad state of affairs creates enough bad news to gladden the heart of any prophet of doom. As much as it may fill us with despair, it is nothing new. Notice how well Gandhi's seven deadly sins sum it up:

Politics without principle

Wealth without work

Commerce without morality

Education without character

Pleasure without conscience

Science without humanity

Worship without sacrifice

As bad as things may seem, there are glimmers of hope here and there. Love, compassion, heroism, and intelligence can be found. Unfortunately rationality is too often suffocated by the ever-present drone of the closed-minded masses, the enticing rattle of modern-age trinkets, the grip of deep-seated unexamined beliefs, and a greedy and selfish few who always seem to have far too much influence.

Although we may sense that there must be solutions, we may feel too insignificant to make a difference and then allow ourselves to be swept along in the system. If we have permitted that system to influence us to any extent we will also have adopted at least some elements of the materialistic philosophy. Determinism, relativism, and fatalism are the most insidious of its irrational creeds and foster pessimistic, cynical, and hopeless people who have become like lands with no harbors.

The companion volume on the "Big Questions" will root out and expose the nefarious materialistic philosophy as the pretender of truth it is. There it will be proven quite conclusively that we are not mere matter and that the choices we make and the efforts we put forth to be better people are important, even central to our life experience. But that is a long story and you need to learn about it from the beginning by reading that book. For now, at least leave room for suspicion that you are more than a machine and are not confined or doomed to its hapless machinations.

As bleak as things may seem at times, we must realize that most of the woes that threaten or befall us are of our doing. We are our own worst enemies. But when we come to understand that every single bad idea that visits misery on the world begins with a single person, we should also realize that good ideas can begin the same way. No beneficial change has ever occurred that did not begin with an idea, from one person, who was willing to insist that it happen. Any one of us can be such a person. We can follow or we can lead. Following will only get us to where we are going.

Humankind has the power to *safely* prevent and reverse most disease (but chooses not to), eliminate hunger (though we haven't), harness all the clean and renewable power we need from sun, wind, waves, chemistry, and geothermal (yet we don't), achieve peace (we fail to), and destroy all life (well on our way). A world of beauty, bounty, health, compassion, love, and peace is mere decisions away.

Such a paradise may seem fitting only for hope or prayer, but the dream is entirely within the realm of possibility. All that is necessary is to come to the understanding that such a new world is not something we purchase or that can be given to us. Its potential is not out there somewhere; it is within. We find it by committing to truth, daring to be 'wrong' by departing from the crowd, and pursuing truth using the

SOLVER principles: Self-responsibility, Open thinking, Long view, Virtue, Evidence, and Reason. When this is done—when we live life as if thinking matters—the wonderful possibilities are without limit.

By way of reminder, a special website is in place for you to ask questions, make comments, and view any updates on the topics in these books. Go to: www.asifthinkingmatters.com

CREDITS AND RESOURCES
FOR FURTHER THINKING

HEALTH

5. We Live In A Unique Time

1. Wilson, E. *The Diversity of Life.* Cambridge: Belknap Press of Harvard University Press, 1992.

2. Hambrech, R., et al. Essay: Hunter-gatherer to sedentary lifestyle. *The Lancet,* 366 (2005), 560-561.

3. Cordain, L. Origins and evolution of the western diet: Health implications for the 21st century. *American Journal of Clinical Nutrition,* 81 (2005), 341-354.

6. Being Health Smart

1. Milton, K. Diet and primate evolution. *Scientific American,* 263 (1993), 86-93.

2. Tooby, J., et al. The past explains the present: Emotional adaptations and the structure of ancestral environments. *Ethnology and Sociobiology,* 11 (1990), 375-424.

3. Wysong R. L. *The Synorgon Diet – How to Achieve Healthy Weight in a World of Excess.* Midland: Inquiry Press, 1993.

4. Schroeder, H. A. Losses of vitamins and trace minerals resulting from processing and preservation of foods. *The American Journal of Clinical Nutrition,* 24 (1971), 562-573.

5. Eaton, S. B., et al. Paleolithic nutrition revisited: A twelve-year retrospective on its nature and implications. *European Journal of Clinical Nutrition,* 51 (1997), 207–216.

7. The Illusion Of Youth Health

1. Cordain, L., et al. Origins and evolution of the western diet: Health implications for the 21st century. *American Journal of Clinical Nutrition*, 81 (2005), 341-54.

2. Pathobiological Determinants of Atherosclerosis in Youth (PDAY) Research Group. Natural history of aortic and coronary atherosclerotic lesions in youth. Findings from the PDAY Study.

3. Strong, J. P., et al. Prevalence and extent of atherosclerosis in adolescents and young adults. *The Journal of the American Medical Association*, 281 (1999), 727-735.

4. Wysong, R. L. *Lipid nutrition: Understanding fats and oils in health and disease.* Midland: Inquiry Press, 1990.

8. The Good Old Days

1. Eaton, S. B. M.D., et al. Special Article – Paleolithic nutrition: A consideration of its nature and current implications. *The New England Journal of Medicine*, 312 (1985), 283-289.

2. Bryson, B. *A Walk in the Woods.* New York: Broadway Books, 1998.

12. The Female Hormone Problem

1. Berger, E. Cancer: Looking beyond mutations. *Houston Chronicle,* 27 Jun 2005, 1.

2. *Healthy and Natural Product News.* Feb 1999, 20.

15. Healthy Dos And Don'ts

1. Sebastian, A., et al. Estimation of the net acid load of the diet of ancestral preagricultural *Homo sapiens* and their hominid ancestors. *The American Journal of Clinical Nutrition*, 76 (2001), 1308-1316.

2. Benson, C. J., et al. Acid-evoked currents in cardiac sensory neurons: A possible mediator of myocardial ischemic sensation. *Circulation Research*, 84 (1999), 921-928.

3. Simonsen, L., et al. Impact of influenza vaccination on seasonal mortality in the U.S. elderly population. *Archives of Internal Medicine*, 165 (2005), 265-272.

4. Hatchett, R.J. Public health interventions and epidemic intensity during the 1918 influenza pandemic. *Proceedings of the National Academy of Sciences,* 2007. Retrieved from the World Wide Web www.pnas.org/cgi/doi/10.1073/pnas.0610941104.

5. Raju, T., et al. Protective effects of quercetin during influenza virus-induced oxidative stress. *Asia Pacific Journal of Clinical Nutrition,* 9 (2005), 314-317.

6. Kiremidjian, R. M., et al. Supplementation with selenium and human immune cell functions. Effect on lymphocyte proliferation and interleukin 2 receptor expression. *Biological Trace Element Research*, 41 (1994), 103-114.

7. Null, G. In pharmaceuticals we trust. *Townsend Letter*, Feb/Mar 2007, 128.

8. Weingart, S. N., et al. Looking for medical injuries where the light is bright. *The Journal of the American Medical Association*, 290 (2003), 1917-1919.

9. Eaton, S. B., et al. Paleolithic nutrition: A consideration of its nature and current implications. *New England Journal of Medicine*, 312 (1985), 283-289.

10. Hawkes, J. S., et al. The effect of breast-feeding on lymphocyte subpopulation in healthy term infants at 6 months of age. *Pediatric Resources*, 45 (1999), 648–651.

11. Wysong, R. L. *Directory of Alternative Resources*. Midland: Inquiry Press, 2008.

MODERN MEDICINE

16. The Medical Profession

1. Zuger, A. Are doctors happy? Reprinted from Christian Medical & Dental Associations (CMDA). Excerpted from Dissatisfaction with Medical Practice. *New England Journal of Medicine*, Jan 2004.

2. Null, G., et al. Death by medicine. *HealthE-Living News*, Jul 2004.

3. Hartman, C., et al. Efficacy of bilateral prophylactic mastectomy in women with a family history of breast cancer. *New England Journal of Medicine*, 340 (1999), 77-84.

4. Saul, A. W. Medline bias. *Journal of Orthomolecular Medicine*, 20 (2005), 10-16.

17. The Greatest Threat To Health

1. McKinlay, J. B., et al. Cities and sickness: Health care in urban America. *Urban Affairs Annual Reviews*, 25 (1983).

2. London School of Hygiene & Topical Medicine. US ranks last amoung other industrialized nations on preventable deaths. *ScienceDaily*, 8 Jan 2008.

3. Bates. Drugs and adverse drug reactions: How worried should we be? *Journal of the American Medical Association*, 279 (1998), 1216-1217.

4. Moore, T.J., et al. Serious adverse drug events reported to the Food and Drug Administration, 1998-2005. *Archives of Internal Medicine*, 167 (2007), 1752-1759.

5. Lazarou, J., et al. Incidence of adverse drug reactions in hospitalized patients. *Journal of the American Medical Association*, 279 (1998), 1200.

6. Center for Disease Control. Unintentional poisoning deaths – United States 1999-2004. *MMWR Weekly*, 56 (2007), 93-96.

7. Institute of Medicine. *To err is human: building a safer health system*. Washington, D.C.: National Academy Press, 2000.

8. Alberti, K.G.M.M. Medical errors: A common problem. *British Medical Journal*, 322 (2001), 501-502.

9. Vincent, C., et al. Adverse events in British hospitals: A preliminary retrospective record view. *British Medical Journal*, 322 (2001), 517-519.

10. The Joint Commission on Accreditation of Healthcare Organizations. A follow-up review of wrong site surgery. *Sentinel Event,* 24 (2001).

11. Associated Press. Botched surgeries lead to injury. *The New York Times,* 29 Nov 2007.

12. Zhan C., et al. Excess length of stay, charges, and mortality attributable to medical injuries during hospitalization. *The Journal of the American Medical Association,* 290 (2003), 1868-1874.

13. Groopman, J. *How Doctors Think.* Boston: Houghton Mifflin Company, 2007.

14. Hart, J.T. The inverse care law. *The Lancet,* 1 (1971), 405-412.

15. Starfield, B. Is U.S. health really the best in the world? *The Journal of the American Medical Association,* 26 (2000), 483-485.

16. Null, G., et al. Death by medicine. *HealthE-Living News,* Jul 2004.

17. Bates, D. *Los Angeles Times,* 8 Jan 2001.

18. Null, G. In pharmaceuticals we trust. *Townsend Letter,* Feb/Mar 2007, 128.

19. Bates, D. W., et al. Drugs and adverse drug reactions: How worried should we be? *The Journal of the American Medical Association,* 279 (1998), 1216-1217.

20. Willman, D. The new FDA: How a new policy led to seven deadly drugs. *Los Angeles Times.* 20 Dec 2000, 1.

18. Don't Surrender To Medical Care

1. Ritter, T. *Say No to Circumcision: 40 Compelling Reasons.* Aptos: Marketscope Books, 1996.

2. Nordenberg, T. Direct to you: TV drug ads that make sense. *FDA Consumer Magazine,* Jan/Feb 1998.

3. Vincent C., et al. Reasons for not reporting adverse incidents: An empirical study. *Journal of Evaluation in Clinical Practice,* 5 (1999), 13-21.

4. McKenzie, J. Conflict of interest? Medical journal changes policy of finding independent doctors. *ABC News,* 12 Jun 2002.

5. Wysong, R.L. The surgery placebo effect. *Wysong E-Health Letter,* December 1994.

6. Wysong, R.L. Placebo surgery. *Wysong E-Health Letter,* March 1999.

7. Wysong R. L. Cancer, the missing point. *Wysong E-Health Letter,* #956.

8. AMA criticized for letting drug firms pay for ethics campaign. *Washington Post,* 30 Aug 2001.

9. Elliot. Six Problems with pharma-funded bioethics. *Studies in History & Philosophy of Biological & Biomedical Sciences,* 35 (2004) 125-129.

10. Do free samples sway your doctor's prescribing for you? *Medical News Today,* 29 Jul 2005.

11. Dodd, M.L., et al. Pathological gambling caused by drugs used to treat Parkinson's disease. *Archives of Neurology,* 62 (2005), 1377-1381.

12. The medicalization of everyday life. *New York Times*, 2 Jan 2007.

13. Are you finally catching on to phony diseases? *Public Library of Science Medicine*, 11 Apr 2006.

14. How drug companies deceive you. *Washington Post*, 30 May 2006.

15. Heath, I., et al. Selling sickness: The pharmaceutical industry and disease mongering. *British Medical Journal*, 324 (2002), 886-891.

16. Berenson, A. Health news cholesterol drug not effective in study. *AOL News*, 15 Jan 2008.

17. Avoid the tonsillectomy! *British Medical Journal*, 329 (2004), 7466.

18. Boe, et al. Screening digital rectal examination and prostate cancer mortality: A case-controlled study. *Journal of Medical Screening*, 5 (1998), 99-103.

19. Yearly prostate cancer test unnecessary in men with low PSA. Annual Meeting of the American Society of Clinical Oncology, 20 May 2002.

20. Benefits of routine screening for prostate cancer are questionable. *Agency for Healthcare Research and Quality*, 2 Dec 2002.

21. Woolf, S. Screening for prostate cancer with prostrate-specific antigen – An examination of the evidence. *New England Journal Of Medicine*, 333 (1995), 1401-1405.

22. Broder et al. The appropriateness of recommendations for hysterectomy. *Obstetrics & Gynecology*, 95 (2000), 199-205.

23. Null et al. Death By Medicine. *HealthE-Living News*, Jul 2004.

24. Bollinger, R.R., et al. Biofilms in the large bowel suggest an apparent function of the human vermiform appendix. *Journal of Theoretical Biology*, 249 (2007), 826-831.

25. Hammaren-Malmi et al. Adenoidectomy does not significantly reduce the incidence of otitis media in conjunction with the insertion of tympanostomy tubes in children who are younger than 4 years: A randomized trial. *Pediatrics*, 116 (2005), 185-189.

26. Paradise et al. Efficacy of adenoidectomy in recurrent otitis media. *Annals of Otology, Rhinology & Laryngology* Supplement, 89 (1980), 319-321.

27. Hibbert et al. Critical evaluation of adenoidectomy. *The Lancet*, 1 (1978), 489-490.

28. Robb, P.J. Adenoidectomy: Does it work? *Journal of Laryngology and Otology*, 121 (2006), 209-214.

29. Williamson, I.G., et al. Antibiotics and topical nasal steroid for treatment of acute maxillary sinusitis. *Journal of the American Medical Association*, 298 (2007), 2487-2496.

30. Vohr, B.R., et al. Beneficial effects of breast milk in the neonatal intensive care unit on the developmental outcome of extremely low birth weight infants at 18 months of age. *Pediatrics*, 118 (2006), 115-123.

31. York et al. Arterial oxygen fluctuation and retinopathy of prematurity in very-low-birth-weight infants. *Journal of Perinatology*, 24 (2004), 82-87.

32. Singh et al. Humanized care of preterm babies. *Indian Pediatrics*, 40 (2003), 13-20.

33. Talmi et al. Relationships between preterm infants and their parents. *Zero to Three*. Nov 2003, 13-20.

34. Neonatal ICU's not better than mother and breast. *People's Doctor Newsletter*, 11 (7), 3.

35. Use of broad spectrum antibiotics in neonatals leads to infection. *The Lancet*, (1989), 509.

36. Jimenez-Perez et al. Has the use of pap smears reduced the risk of cervical cancer in Guadalajara, Mexico? *International Journal Of Cancer*, 82 (1999) ,804-809.

37. Shingleton et al. The current status of the papanicolaou smear. *CA Cancer Journal for Clinicians*. 45 (1995), 305-320.

38. McCormick, J.S. Cervical smears: A questionable practice? *The Lancet*, 2 (1989), 207-209.

39. Pisano, E. Diagnostic performance of digital versus film mammography for breast-cancer screening. *New England Journal of Medicine*, 353 (2005), 1773-1283.

40. Epstein et al. Danger and unreliability of mammography. *International Journal of Health Services*, 31(2001), 605-615.

41. Whitaker, J. Do mammograms save women's lives? *Health and Healing*, 1993.

42. Mammography dangers. *Health Alert Newsletter*. 1 Jun 1993, 4.

43. Mammary cancer, screening mammography increases mortality. *The Lancet*. 28 Aug 1993, 549.

44. Epstein, S. S. et al. Danger and unreliability of mammography. *International Journal of Health Services,* 31 (2001), 605-615.

45. Reidy, J., et al. Controversy over mammography screening. *British Medical Journal,* 297 (1988), 932-933.

46. Anderson, I., et al. Mammographic screening and mortality from breast cancer: The malmo mammographic screening trial. *British Medical Journal,* 297 (1988), 943-948.

47. Wysong, R.L. Breast cancer screening. *Wysong E-Health Letter,* January 2008.

48. Wysong, R.L. Think twice about mammography. *Wysong E-Health Letter,* July 1996.

49. Wysong, R.L. Breast screening by hand. *Wysong E-Health Letter,* February 1994

50. Office of Technology Assessment, 1995.

51. Inzitari, D. et al. The causes and risk of stroke in patients with asymptomatic internal-carotid-artery stenosis. *New England Journal of Medicine*, 342 (2000), 1693-1701,1743-1745.

52. Barnett et al. Carotid endarterectomy – An expression of concern. *Stroke*, 15 (1984), 941-943.

53. Winslow et al. The appropriateness of carotid endarterectomy. *The New England Journal of Medicine*, 318 (1988), 721-727.

54. Warlow, C. Carotid endarterectomy: Does it work? *Stroke*, 15 (1984), 1068-1076.

55. Operating to prevent stroke. *The Lancet*, 337 (1991), 1255-1256.

56. Rolak, L.A. Carotid endarterectomy has never been shown to be any value to the patient. *Journal of the American Medical Association*. 258 (1987), 3514.

57. Warlow, C. et al. The appropriateness of carotid endarterectomy. *New England Journal Of Medicine* 318 (1988), 722.

58. Carotid stenosis – Debate over treatment. *The Lancet*, (1991), 1600.

59. Rennie J. Will mountain trekkers have heart attacks? *Journal of American Medical Association*. Vol. 261, No. 7, 1045.

60. Eye pad for corneal damage no effect. *The Lancet*, (1991), 643.

61. Whynes et al. Colorectal cancer screening and quality of life. *Quality of Life Research*, 3 (1994), 191-198.

62. Ahlquist et al. Accuracy of fecal occult blood screening for colorectal neoplasia. A prospective study using hemoccult and hemoquant tests. *Journal of American Medical Association*, 269 (1993).

63. Black et al. All-cause mortality in randomized trials of cancer screening. *Journal of the National Cancer Institute*. 94 (2002), 167-173.

64. Neale et al. Physician accuracy in diagnosing colorectal polyps. *Diseases of the Colon & Rectum*, 4 (1987), 247-50.

65. Bensen et al. The colonoscopic miss rate and true one-year recurrence of colorectal neoplastic polyps. *American Journal of Gastroenterology*. 94 (1999), 194.

66. Leiberman et al. One-time screening for colorectal cancer with combined fecal occult-blood testing and examination of the distal colon. *New England Journal of Medicine*. 345 (2001), 555-560.

67. Yale University. Colon cancer screenings may not pay off and could pose harm to some. *ScienceDaily*, 22 Dec 2007.

68. Kristiansen et al. Effect of the remuneration system on the general practitioner's choice between surgery consultations and home visits. *Journal of Epidemiology and Community Health*. 47 (1993), 481-484.

69. Woodward et al. Considering the effects of financial incentives and professional ethics on "appropriate" medical care. *Journal of Health Economics*. 3 (1984), 223-37.

70. Gosden et al. How should we pay doctors? A systematic review of salary payments and their effect on doctor behaviour. *Quarterly Journal of Medicine*, 92 (1999), 47-55.

71. Leape, L.L. et al. Relation between surgeon's practice volumes and geographic variation in the rate of carotid endarterectomy. *New England Journal Of Medicine*, 321 (1989), 653.

72. Chow T. et al. Microvolt T-wave alternans identifies patients with ischemic cardiomyopathy who benefit from implantable cardioverter-defibrillator therapy. *Journal of the American College of Cardiology*, 49 (2007), 50-58.

73. Sakala. Medically unnecessary cesarean section births: Introduction to a symposium. *Social Science & Medicine*, 37 (1993), 1177-98.

74. Koroukian et al. Estimating the proportion of unnecessary cesarean sections in Ohio using birth certificate data. *Journal of Clinical Epidemiology*, 51 (1998), 1327-1334.

75. Daskalakis et al. Risk factors predisposing fetal loss following a second trimester amniocentesis. *International Journal of Obstetrics and Gynaecology*, 108 (2001), 1053.

76. Sangalli et al. Pregnancy loss rate following routine genetic amniocentesis at Wellington Hospital. *Journal of the New Zealand Medical Association*, 117 (2004).

77. Roper et al. Genetic amniocentesis: Gestation-specific pregnancy outcome and comparison of outcome following early and traditional amniocentesis. *Prenatal Diagnosis*. 19 (1999), 803-807.

78. 1:500 miscarriages from amniocentesis. *Dr. Prescription for Healthy Living*. Oct 1990, 3.

79. Banta et al. Historical controversy in health technology assessment: The case of electronic fetal monitoring. *Obstetrical & Gynecological Survey*, 56 (2001), 707-719.

80. Toubia, Nahid. Female circumcision as a public health issue. *New England Journal of Medicine*, 331 (1994), 712-16.

81. Hellsten, S.K. Rationalizing circumcision: From tradition to fashion, from public health to individual freedom—Critical notes on cultural persistence of the practice of genital mutilation. *Journal of Medical Ethics*, 30 (2004), 248 - 253.

82. Hinchley, J. Is infant male circumcision an abuse of the rights of the child? Yes. *British Medical Journal*, 335 (2007), 1180.

83. Malone, P., et al. Medical aspects of male circumcision. *British Medical Journal*, 335(2007), 1206-1290.

84. Wysong, R.L. Circumcision and sexual dysfunction. *Wysong E-Health Letter*, July 1996.

85. Wysong, R.L. Circumcision and pain response. *Wysong E-Health Letter*, August 1995.

86. Wysong, R.L. Uncircumcising. *Wysong E-Health Letter*, September 1993.

87. Wysong, R.L. Gastric rupture from circumcision. *Wysong E-Health Letter*, April 1994.

88. Wysong, R.L. Let the buyer beware. *Wysong E-Health Letter*, #883.

89. Wysong, R.L. Genital mutilation. *Wysong E-Health Letter*, March 1996.

90. Goldberg, B. *Alternative Medicine: The Definitive Guide*. Fife: Future Medicine Publishing, 1998.

91. Stanford, J.L. Who profits from coronary artery bypass surgery? *The American Journal of Nursing*, 82 (1982), 1060-72.

92. Legorreta, A.P. et al. Increased cholecystectomy rate after the introduction of laparoscoptic cholecystectomy. *Journal of the American Medical Association*, 270 (1993), 1429-1432.

93. Curfman, G.D. Shorter hospital stay for myocardial infarction. *New England Journal of Medicine*, 318 (1988).

94. Klotter, J. Infection Epidemic in Hospitals. *Townsend Letter*, 232 (2002), 33.

95. Harvey, E.B. et al. Prenatal x-ray exposure and childhood cancer in twins. *New England Journal of Medicine*, 312 (1985), 541-545.

96. Herzog, P. Risk of cancer from diagnostic x-rays. *The Lancet*, 363 (2004), 340.

97. Patja, A. et al. Serious adverse events after measles-mumps-rubella vaccination during a fourteen-year prospective follow-up. *Pediatric Infectious Disease Journal*, 19 (2000), 1127-1134.

98. Strickler, H. D. Contamination of poliovirus vaccines with simian virus and subsequent cancer rates. *Journal of the American Medical Association*, 279 (1998), 292-295. 40 (1955-1963)

99. Wysong, R.L. Vaccine safety. *Wysong E-Health Letter*, #926.

100. Wysong, R.L. Vaccines for everyone. *Wysong E-Health Letter*, September 1994.

101. Wysong, R.L. Autism may be linked to measles vaccine. *Wysong E-Health Letter*, #985.

102. Wysong, R.L. Dangers of measles vaccines. *Wysong E-Health Letter*, January 1994.

103. Wysong, R.L. Childhood vaccine dangers. *Wysong E-Health Letter*, April 1994.

104. Wysong, R.L. Polio – Risk from vaccination. *Wysong E-Health Letter*, July 1996.

105. Faguet, G. *The War on Cancer: An Anatomy of Failure, a Blueprint for the Future*. New York: Sprinter Publishing, 2005.

106. Wysong, R.L. Cancer. *Wysong E-Health Letter*, September 1987.

107. Wysong, R.L. A better approach to cancer. *Wysong E-Health Letter*, September 1990.

108. Wysong, R.L. Is common sense or research needed to cure cancer? *Wysong E-Health Letter*, #937.

109. Wysong, R.L. More cancer treatment failure. *Wysong E-Health Letter*, #978.

110. Hildreth, N.G. et al. The risk of breast cancer after irradiation of the thymus in infancy. *New England Journal of Medicine*, 321 (1989), 1281-1284.

111. ELF magnetic fields and breast cancer, immune function, Parkinson's disease and multiple sclerosis. *Nutrition Update*, (1993), 8.

112. EMFs (electromagnetic fields) increase breast cancer risk. *Science News,* 18 Jun 1994, 388.

113. Mills, J.L. et al. Risk of neural tube defects in relation to maternal fertility and fertility drug use. *The Lancet,* 33 (1991), 853.

114. Werler, M.M. et al. Ovulation induction and risk of neural tube defects. *The Lancet,* 344 (1994), 445-6.

115. Van Loon, K. et al. Neural tube defects after infertility treatment: A review. Fertility & Sterility, 58 (1992), 875-84.

116. Tests ordered by doctors often inappropriate - Support staff frequently changes orders - Support staff usually right. 37% physicians had not ordered right tests. *Science Impact,* 2, 2.

117. Physicians lack sufficient knowledge in treating chronic pain. *Townsend Letter,* 227 *(2002),* 2.

118. Ross, C.E. et al. The impact of the family on health: The decade in review. *Journal of Marriage and the Family,* 52 (1990), 1059-1078.

119. Siegel-Itzkovich, J. Doctors' strike in Israel may be good for health. *British Medical Journal,* 320 (2000), 1561.

120. Robert S. Mendelsohn, M.D. *Confessions of A Medical Heretic.* Chicago: Contemporary Books, 1979.

121. Vincent, C. A. The human element of adverse events. *Medical Journal of Australia,* 170 (1999), 404-405.

19. "But We Live Longer Today"

1. Flanders, J. *Inside the Victorian Home.* New York: W.W. Norton and Co, 2003.

2. Faguet, G. *The War on Cancer: An Anatomy of Failure, a Blueprint for the Future.* New York: Sprinter Publishing, 2005.

3. Mann, N. J. Paleolithic nutrition: What can we learn from the past? *Asia Pacific Journal of Clinical Nutrition,* 13 (2004), S17.

20. Dollars Don't Make Health

1. The Troubled Healthcare System in the U.S. The Society of Actuaries: Health Benefit Systems Practice Advancement Committee. 13 Sep 2003. Retrieved from the World Wide Web: http://www.soa.org/

2. Starfield, B. Doctors are the third leading cause of death. *Journal of the American Medical Association,* 284 (2000).

3. McKinlay, J. B., et al. The questionable contribution of medical measures to the decline of mortality in the United States in the twentieth century. *Milbank Mem. Fund Quarterly Society,* 55 (1977), 405-428.

4. McKenzie J. Conflict of interest? Medical journal changes policy of finding independent doctors. *ABC News.* 12 Jun 2002.

5. Doctor threatened for not telling patients to lose weight, *Washington Post*, 24 Aug

6. Groopman, J. *How doctors think.* Boston: Houghton Mifflin Company, 2007.

7. Null, G., et al. Death by Medicine. *HealthE-Living News,* Jul 2004.

22. Germs Don't Cause Disease, We Do

1. Ananthaswamy, A. Urinary tract infections 'protect' against stillbirth. *New Scientist*, 14 Nov 2002.

2. Wysong, R. L. Salmonella enteritidis infection from eggs. *Wysong e-Health Letter,* Sep 1999.

3. McKinlay, J. B., et al. The questionable contribution of medical measures to the decline of mortality in the United States in the twentieth century. *Milbank Memorial Fund Quarterly,* 55 (1977), 405-428.

23. From Where Does Healing Come?

1. Wysong, R. L. *Directory of alternative resources.* Midland: Inquiry Press, 2008.

2. *Los Angeles Times*, 8 Jan 2001. Based on a 1998 University of Toronto study.

3. Boschert, S. Episiotomies do more harm than good. *Family Practice News,* 35 (1995).

4. Argentine Episiotomy Trial Collaborative Group. Routine vs. selective episiotomy: A randomized controlled trial. *The Lancet,* 343 (1993), 1517-1518.

5. Shy, K. K., et al. Effects of electronic fetal-heart-rate monitoring, as compared with periodic auscultation, on the neurological development of premature infants. *New England Journal of Medicine*, 322 (1990), 588-593.

6. Intrapartum electronic fetal monitoring. *Guide to Clinical Preventive Services, Prenatal Disorders* (2nd ed.), 1996.

7. Chaparro, C. M., et al. Effect of timing of umbilical cord clamping on iron status in Mexican infants: A randomized controlled trial. *The Lancet,* 367 (2006), 1997-2004.

8. Lozoff, B., et al. Long-term developmental outcome of infants with iron deficiency. *New England Journal of Medicine,* 325 (1991), 687-694.

9. *Commonwealth Fund*, 20 Sep 2006.

10. McKinlay, J.B et al. The questionable contribution of medical measures to the decline of mortality in the United States in the twentieth century. *Milbank Memorial Fund Quarterly,* 55 (1977), 405-428.

FOOD

24. The Best Food

1. Berry, W. *What Are People For?* New York: North Point Press, 1990.

2. Mann, N. J. Paleolithic nutrition: What can we learn from the past? *Asia Pacific Journal of Clinical Nutrition,* 13 (2004), S17.

3.   Hildes, J. A. et al. The changing picture of neoplastic disease in the western and central Canadian Arctic. *Canadian Medical Association Journal,* 130 (1984), 25-32.

4.   Rowling, J. T. Pathological changes in mummies. *Proceedings of the Royal Society of Medicine,* 54 (1961), 409-515.

25. Food Ethics

1.   Ratsch, C. *The Encyclopedia of Psychoactive Plants: Ethnopharmacology and Its Applications.* Rochester: Park Street Press, 2005.

2.   Tompkins, P. *The Secret Life of Plants.* New York: Perennial, 1989.

3.   Harpignies, J. P., et al. *Visionary Plant Consciousness: The Shamanic Teachings of the Plant World.* Rochester: Park Street Press, 2007.

4.   Buhner, S. H. *The Secret Teachings of Plants: The Intelligence of the Heart in the Direct Perception of Nature.* Rochester: Bear & Company, 2004.

5.   Mann, N.J. Paleolithic nutrition: What can we learn from the past? *Asia Pacific Journal of Clinical Nutrition,* 13 (2004), S17.

6.   Cordain, I., et al. Origins and evolution of the Western diet: Health implications for the 21st century. *American Journal of Clinical Nutrition,* 81 (2005), 341-354.

7.   Associated Press. Vegans sentenced to life for starving. *AOL News,* 9 May 2007.

8.   Eaton, S. B., et al. Paleolithic nutrition: A consideration of its nature and current implications. *The New England Journal of Medicine,* 312 (1985), 283-289.

9.   Hambrech, R., et al. Essay: Hunter-gatherer to sedentary lifestyle. *The Lancet,* 366 (2005), 560-561.

26. Healthy Weight

1.   Mattson, M. P., et al. Intermittent fasting dissociates beneficial effects of dietary restriction on glucose metabolism and neuronal resistance to injury from calorie intake. *Proceedings of the National Academy of Sciences,* (2003), 6216-6220.

2.   Holloszy, J. O., et al. Long-term calorie restriction is highly effective in reducing the risk for atherosclerosis in humans. *Proceedings of the National Academy of Sciences,* 101 (2004), 6659-6663.

3.   Wysong R. L. *The Synorgon Diet – How to Achieve Healthy Weight in a World of Excess.* Midland: Inquiry Press, 1993.

27. Healthy Eating Ideas

1.   Carter, G. Endocardial damage induced by lactate, lowered pH and lactic acid in non-ischemic beating hearts. *Pathology,* 21 (1989), 125-130.

2.   Wysong, R. L. Optimal Health Program. Retrieved from the World Wide Web: http://www.wysong.net/PDFs/ohp.pdf

3.   Wolfe, D., et al. *Naked Chocolate.* San Diego: Maul Brothers Publishing, 2005.

MENTAL HEALTH

29. Hopelessness

1. Peterson, J. Farmer John Productions, 1990. Retrieved from the World Wide Web: http://www.angelicorganics.com/

30. Depression

1. Johnston-Wilson, N. L., et al. Emerging technologies for large-scale screening of human tissues and fluids in the study of severe psychiatric disease. *International Journal of Neuropsychopharmacol,* 4 (2001), 83-92.

2. Corruption in drug companies. *Wysong E-Health Letter,* #992.

3. Kondro, W., et al. Drug company experts advised staff to withhold data about SSRI use in children. *Canadian Medical Journal,* 170 (2004).

4. Hayes, C. E. The immunological functions of the vitamin D endocrine system. *Cellular and Molecular Biology,* 49 (2003), 277-300.

5. Wysong, R. L. How the sun is absolutely crucial to your health. *Wysong e-Health Letter,* #975.

6. Wysong, R. L. Light, the ultimate health food. *Wysong Health Letter,* 10 (8); Light, time and health. *Wysong Health Letter,* 4 (11).

7. Grant, C., et al. *Burton Goldberg's* Curing Depression, Anxiety and Panic Disorder. [CD-ROM]. Do No Harm Productions, 2006.

8. Wysong, R. L. Therapeutic benefits of pet ownership. *Wysong e-Health Letter,* #826.

35. Touch

1. Schwartz, S., et al. The realm of the will. *Explore,* 1 (2005), 199-207.

2. Swartz, S. A., et al. Infrared spectra alteration in water proximate to the palms of therapeutic practitioners, 15 Nov 2006. Retrieved from the World Wide Web: www.stephanaschwartz.com?PDF/Healing%20Final%20Report.pdf

36. Music As Healer

1. Hanser, S. *The New Music Therapist's Handbook.* Boston: Berklee Press, 1999

2. Music and performing arts professions. The Steinhardt School, New York University. Retrieved from the World Wide Web: http://education.nyu.edu/music/mtherapy.

3. Careers in Music Therapy. Berklee College of Music, 2007. Retrieved from the World Wide Web: http://www.berklee.edu/careers/therapy.html.

37. Humor

1. Labott, S. M., et al. The physiological and psychological effects of the expression and inhibition of emotion. *Journal of Behavioral Medicine,* 16 (1990),182-189.

2. Rider, M. S. et al. Effect of immune system imagery on secretory IgA. *Biofeedback Self Regulatory,* 15 (1990), 317-33.

3. Wysong, R. L. Humor heals. *Wysong e-Health Letter,* #902.

PETS

38. Pets As Life Savers

1. Pets: Good for what ails us. Retrieved from the World Wide Web: http://www.wysong.net/scientific74.shtml.

40. The Myth Of 100% Complete Pet Foods

1. Zaghini, G., et al. Nutritional peculiarities and diet palatability in the cat. *Veterinary Research Communications,* 29 (2005), 39.

2. Pion et al. Myocardial failure in cats associated with low plasma taurine: A reversible cardiomyopathy. *Science,* 237 (1987), 764-768.

3. Spitze, A. R., et al. Taurine concentrations in animal feed ingredients; Cooking influences taurine content. *Journal of Animal Physiology and Animal Nutrition,* 87 (2003), 251.

4. Childs-Sanford, S. E., et al. Taurine deficiency in named wolves (Chrysocyon brachyurus) maintained on two diets manufactured for prevention of cystine urolithiasis. *Zoo Biology,* 25 (2006), 87.

5. Pet Food Recall/Tainted Animal Feed. U.S. Food and Drug Administration, 16 May 2007. Retrieved from the World Wide Web: www.fda.gov/oc/opacom/hottopics/petfood.html.

41. Feeding Pets As Nature Intended

1. Zoran, D. L. The carnivore connection to nutrition in cats. *Journal of the American Veterinary Medical Association,* 221 (2002), 1559.

ENVIRONMENT

42. Industry Vs. Earth

1. Wilson, E. *The Diversity of Life.* Cambridge: Belknap Press of Harvard University Press, 1992.

43. Population

1. Population. U.S. Census Bureau, 11 Apr 2007. Retrieved from the World Wide Web: www.census.gov/prod/www/abs/popula.html.

2. Ehrlich, P. *The Population Bomb.* New York: Ballantine Books, Inc, 1968.

44. Modernity's Deception

1. Hambrech, R., et al. Essay: Hunter-gatherer to sedentary lifestyle. *The Lancet,* 366 (2005), 560-561.

45. Animal Rights

1. Relationship between Animal Abuse and Human Violence. Oxford Centre for Animal Ethics, 2007. Retrieved from the World Wide Web: www.oxfordanimalethics.com.

2. Gawrylewski, Andrea, 'The Trouble with Animal Models: Trials and Error', *The Scientist* 21-7 (2007), 45-51.

3. Qureshi, B. The reverse effect. *Journal of the Royal Society of Medicine*, 83 (1990), 131-132.

4. Rowland, D. *The Nutritional Bypass: Reverse Atherosclerosis Without Surgery*. Parry Sound: Rowland Publications, 1995.

47. Respect For All Life

1. Trewavas, A. Aspects of plant intelligence. *Annals of Botany*, 92 (2003), 1-20.

2. Tomkins, P. *The Secret Life of Plants*. New York: Perennial Library, 1989.

3. Harpignies, J., et al. *Visionary Plant Consciousness*. Rochester: Park Street Press, 2007.

ECONOMICS

48. Doing Good With Business

1. Komlos, J. *The Biological Standard of Living in Europe and America, 1700-1900: Studies in Anthropometric History*. Aldershot, England: Variorum Press, 1995.

2. Fishback, P. *Government and the American Economy: A New History*. Chicago: The University of Chicago Press, 2007.

49. The Global Economy

1. Agheuli, B., et al. *Role of National Saving in the World Economy: Recent Trends and Prospects*. Washington D.C.: International Monetary Fund, 1990.

2. Roberti, P. *Financial Markets and Capital Income Taxation in a Global Economy*. Netherlands: Elsevier Science B.V., 1998.

3. Murphy, C. *Global Institutions, Marginalization and Development*. New York: Routledge, 2005.

50. The Power Of Money

1. Nimmo, W., et al. *Clinical Measurement in Drug Evaluation*. New York: John Wiley & Sons, Inc, 1995.

SOCIETY

53. Government

1. Dunn, J. *Democracy: A History*. New York: Grove/Atlantic Inc, 2005.

2. Middleton, R. *Colonial America: A History, 1565-1776.* (3rd ed.). Malden: Blackwell Publishing, 2002.

3. Pipes, R. *Communism: A Brief History.* London: Weidenfeld & Nicolson, 2001.

4. Hout, M. *Inequality at the Margins: The Effect of Welfare, the Minimum Wage, and Tax Credits on Low-Wage Labor Markets.* Berkeley: Russell Sage Foundation, 1997.

5. Project Vote Smart. Retrieved from the World Wide Web: http://www.vote-smart.org/.

6. Adams, J. *Thinking Today As If Tomorrow Mattered.* San Francisco: Earthheart Enterprises, 2000.

54. The End Of Civilization

1. Terpstra, N. *The Politics of Ritual Kinship: Confraternities and Social Order in Early Modern Italy.* Cambridge: Cambridge University Press, 1999.

55. Political Correctness

1. Luca, L., et al. *The History and Geography of Human Genes.* Princeton: Princeton University Press, 1994.

2. Steele, S. *White Guilt: How Blacks and Whites Together Destroyed the Promise of the Civil Rights Era.* New York: HarperCollins Publishers, 2006.

FAMILY

58. Marriage - The Union Of Opposites

1. Chagnon, N. *Yanomamo - The Last Days of Eden.* Orlando: Harcourt Brace & Company, 1997.

59. Divorce

1. Dangers of divorce. *Physician,* Sep/Oct 1997, 15-17

61. Having Babies

1. Olsen, O. Meta-analysis of the safety of home birth. *Birth,* 24 (1997), 4-13.

2. Turnbull, D., et al. Randomized, controlled trial of efficacy of midwife-managed care. *The Lancet,* 34 (1996), 213-218.

3. Boschert, S. Episiotomies do more harm than good. *Family Practice News,* 35 (1995).

4. Argentine Episiotomy Trial Collaborative Group. Routine vs. selective episiotomy: A randomized controlled trial. *The Lancet,* 343 (1993), 1517-1518.

5. Shy, K., et al. Effects of electronic fetal-heart-rate monitoring, as compared with periodic auscultation, on the neurological development of premature infants. *New England Journal of Medicine,* 322 (1990), 588-593.

6. Intrapartum electronic fetal monitoring. *Guide to Clinical Preventive Services-Prenatal Disorders.* (2nd ed.), 1996.

7. Chaparro, C.M., et al. Effect of timing of umbilical cord clamping on iron status in Mexican infants: A randomized controlled trial. *The Lancet,* 367 (2006), 1997-2004.

8. Wagner, M. Technology in birth: First do no harm. *Midwifery Today*, 2000. Retrieved from the World Wide Web: http://www.midwiferytoday.com.

9. Arms, S. *Immaculate Deception: A New Look at Women and Childbirth.* Berkeley: Celestial Arts, 1985.

10. Russek, L., et al. Interpersonal heart-brain registration and the perception of parental love: A 42-year follow-up of the Harvard Mastery of Stress Study. *Subtle Energies,* 5 (1994), 195.

11. Thevenin, T. *The Family Bed.* New York: Perigee Books, 1987.

LIFE LESSONS

69. Life's Predictability

1. Levinson, D. *The Seasons of a Man's Life.* New York: Ballantine Books, 1978.

2. Sheehy, G. *The Silent Passage: Revised and Updated.* Riverside: Pocket Books, 1998.

3. Sheehy, G. *Passages: Predictable Crises of Adult Life.* New York: Bantam Books, 1984.

71. Learn From History

1. Bookalam, P. *The Phaistos Disk: Written Word of an Oral Culture.* Hicksville: Exposition Press, 1982.

SELF-IMPROVEMENT

82. Change The World

1. Sheldrake, R. *A New Science of Life: The Hypothesis of Morphic Resonance.* Rochester: Park Street Press, 1981.

2. Elliott, S. *The Grassfire Effect.* Nashville: Broadman & Holman Publishers,

83. Growing Good People

1. Norman, E. *The Roman Catholic Church: An Illustrated History.* Berkeley: University of California Press, 2007.

2. Pearce, J. *The Crack in the Cosmic Egg.* Rochester: Park Street Press, 2002.

3. Pearce, J. *The Biology of Transcendence: A Blueprint of the Human Spirit.* Rochester: Park Street Press, 2002.

84. Words

1. Labov, W., et al. *Atlas of North American English: Phonetics, Phonology and Sound Change.* Berlin: Walter de Gruyter GmbH & Co KG, 2006.

86. Listen And Learn

1. Pearce, J. *From Magical Child to Magical Teen.* Rochester: Inner Traditions, 2003.

BEING GOOD

92. Ethics

1. Clifford, William K. *The Ethics of Belief and Other Essays.* New York: Prometheus Books, 1999.

95. Being Real

1. Marcus, H. *Hegel's Ontology and the Theory of Historicity.* Cambridge: MIT Press, 1989.

INDEX

Einstein, Albert, 391
Elderly, 302
Elvis, 285
Employees, 240
Empty nest, 336
End of civilization, 282
Endorphins, 157
Entitlements, 296
    American, 240
Entrepreneurship, 241
Entropy, 56
Environmental, 368
    crises, 207
    devastation, 368
    ruination, 343
Environmentalism, 208
Enzymes, 61
EPA's superfund, 212
Epidemics, 106
Epidural blocks, 114
Episiotomies, 114
Erectile dysfunction (ED), 82
Eskimos, 291
Ethical, 137
    absolutes, 427
Ethics, 428
Etymology, 405
Evolution, 222
Exercise, 37, 157
Expectations, 317
Experience, 341, 367
Extrapolation, 287, 443
Eye pad, 84

F

Faith, 432
Family:
    extended, 325
    farm, 324, 420
    nest, 324
    structure, 324
Fast-paced world, 374
Fat, 66
Fatty acid supplements, 63
FDA, 78, 190
Fear, 454

Feces, 105
Fetal monitoring, 84
Fever, 67
Fibroblast, 57
Fiduciary, 225
    responsibility, 225, 444
Financial:
    affairs, 247
    responsibility, 250
Finding home, 364
Fish, 63
    out of water, 18
Fluoroscopy, 85
Food-borne, 106
Food:
    forage, 67
    living, 61
    local, 66
    manufacturer, 440
    pyramid, 118
    raw, 61
    variety of, 63
Formula, 64, 192, 329
Fortified, 191
Freedom, 265, 288, 298, 326, 327
Free:
    enterprise system, 273
    range, 62, 131
    will, 424, 425
    world market, 277
Fresh air, 67
Fulfillment, 312
Full spectrum light bulbs, 157
Future, 371

G

Galileo, 391
Gall bladder, 85
Gandhi, 399
    seven deadly sins, 460
Garbage, 67
    dehydrated, 189
Generators, Ion 67
Genetic life limit, 58
Genius, 407
German, 290

Immigrants, 255, 443
Imprinting, 402
Imprints, 400
Inactivity, 436
Inclusion, 296
Independent development, 334
India, 239
Industrial Revolution, 15, 207, 255
Industry vs Earth, 207
Infant, 89
    mortality, 74, 89, 114
Infanticide, 217
Inferiority, militancy of, 297
Influenza, 106
Information, 277
Inhumanity, 234
Injury, 61
In love experience, 313
Insecurities, 409
Instant gratification culture, 446
Intelligence, 220
Intermarriage, 294
International trade, 249
Internet, 349, 394, 457
Intuition, 434
Investing, 247
IQ tests, 408
Irradiation, scalp, 85
Irrelevant, 277

J

Jamestown, 269
Japan, 218
Japanese, 290
Jefferson, Thomas, 238
Job:
    casualties, 257
    security, 261
Joint, 138
Junk mail, 427
Jurassic Park, 25

K

Kind deed every day, 159
King, Martin Luther, Jr, 296
Knowledge, 376

L

Labels, 232
Labor force, 280
Lab tests, 62
Lactose intolerant, 292
Language coordination, 400
Laparoscopic cholecystectomy, 85
Las Vegas, 217
Latin, 368
Laughter, 174
Lawyering, 278
Leaf from tree, 58
Legal system, adversarial, 322
Lexicographer, 406
Levine, Michail, 332
Libertine, 267, 419
Libido, 307
Life:
    expectancy, 90
        after age 40, 74
        at one year of age, 74
    is joined, 126
    is math, 423
    is uncertain, 351
    maximum potential, 90
    predictability, 361
    span, 90
        average, 87
        of around 22 years, 32
        maximum, 57, 138
Light, 66
Lighting, 61
Lincoln, Abraham, 409, 441
Line always moves faster, 374
Listen and learn, 409
Little things add up, 376
Logging industry, 211
Loneliness, 320
Long-term benefits, 445
Long view, 442
Longevity, 89
Looking good, 414
Los Angeles riots, 417
Love, 382, 403
    euphoria of being in, 309
    us just as we are, 313
Loving touch, 318

M

N

BY THE SAME AUTHOR

Solving the Big Questions as if Thinking Matters

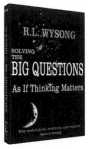

Nothing could be more fundamental than the questions of: Where did we come from? Why are we here? Where are we going? Nothing could be more true than the fact that virtually no one has answers they can rationally defend.

If we do not know our origin or destiny, then we cannot know how to properly live. The world's precariousness, and the prevailing sense of futility and meaninglessness are symptoms of either having no answers, or having the wrong ones.

Experts in religion, philosophy, and science have reached no consensus in spite of thousands of years of trying. So the average person either latches onto some convenient and attractive belief propped up with desire, hope, and faith, or gives up and ignores the topics altogether.

This book offers the promise of turning that all around. The key is to put honest thinking and evidence ahead of materialistic, religious, scientific, or philosophic ideologies. Pursuing truth in this way, and without fear of where it might lead, is arguably our highest responsibility.

When we approach the big questions as if thinking matters, we are led to exactly where the world needs to go, a place of honesty, truth, confidence, solutions, and love. Dr. Wysong masterfully teaches us how to reach within, use our own minds, consider honestly all the evidence, and remain open-minded. The result, although unpalatable to any who have the sureness of untested beliefs, is beautiful in its simplicity and wonderful in the hope, meaning, and purpose it brings.

The Thinking Person's Master Key to Health

This-one hour CD encapsulates over 30 years of Dr. Wysong's thought and research on health, medicine, and prevention.

Few people realize that the modern paradigm of health care is dangerously flawed. The solution is not cheaper drugs, lower medical insurance rates, or free universal health care. More of the same is not the solution.

As Dr. Wysong proves, using the medical profession's own scientific literature, modern health care is the number one killer in modern society. That's because doctors are not taught about what creates health, but are rather immersed in a technology that focuses on naming diseases and treating symptoms. Medical intervention flouts the body's own healing mechanisms and introduces disruptions in the form of surgery and allopathic drugs that usually do more harm than good.

Dr. Wysong explains that the key to health is to understand our genetic roots in prehistory and respect them. By (figuratively) returning to the wild we tune to our proper place in the natural order of things and permit our minds and bodies to reverse disease and achieve the true health we were designed for.

This is not yet another formula of dos, don'ts, and rigid arbitrary rules. Rather, Dr. Wysong employs the highest ideal of teaching: helping those who want to learn reach within to understand and obey what they already intuitively know.

In this thought provoking, information pregnant discourse, you will learn how to make day-to-day choices so you, your family, and pets can achieve optimal health.

Lipid Nutrition:
Understanding Fats and Oils in Health And Disease

Fats in foods and fat on the body have become national obsessions. With due cause. Research is showing the far-reaching deleterious effects of obesity as well as relationships between lipid (fat and oil) consumption and a wide range of health concerns.

In this book, Dr. Wysong brings a surprise and reveals that fats are not the nutritional demons popularly assumed. The key to health is not to avoid dietary fat and jump on the cholesterol-checking and drug band wagon. Lipids are a part of every cell and are essential components of hormones and body regulators. Even cholesterol (in its natural state) is critical to health. If it is not eaten, the body produces it. Dr. Wysong provides the understanding necessary to avoid such popular and professional myths.

Natural fats are not something to avoid, but rather to seek and cherish. The real villain is food processing. Heat, light, air, hydrogenation, and time are the enemies of healthful fats. Not only does processing destroy important fats and oils, but it can convert them to dangerous disease-producing toxins. Dr. Wysong explains how to choose foods that are protected from these dangers.

Read carefully, Lipid Nutrition can be one of those rare books which replaces the reading of dozens of others. Whether you are a person just concerned with better health and nutrition, or a professional seeking keys to prevention and treatment, Lipid Nutrition will prove to be a wonderful aid to understanding and a valuable resource for making healthy decisions.

The Synorgon Diet:
How to Achieve Healthy Weight in a World of Excess

Healthy weight is not just about calories, diet, eating too much, and exercising too little. Such things are symptoms of an underlying problem, not the true cause of the epidemic of obesity.

Dr. Wysong explains that humans and animals in the wild do not become obese, nor do they have to think about preventing it. Except when body fat is needed for insulation or hibernation, wild creatures remain trim and fit. Understanding how they achieve this is the key to understanding what we must do in modern society to maintain healthy weight.

494

In this book you'll learn:
- How to lose weight without dieting
- Prehistory essentials for healthy weight
- Why excess weight is not a lifestyle right or private matter
- The real dangers in modern processed foods which are being kept secret
- Fats and oils in the diet that are critical to diet success
- An essential kind of exercise
- A one-day diet plan that guarantees success
- Why an understanding of such things as pollution, recycling, and deforestation is required
- Natural foods that can raise your metabolic rate so you burn more calories while at rest
- How to turn off a powerful but little known physiological obesity switch
- Hundreds of foods you can eat all you want and not become obese

The Synorgon Diet is the long term solution to excess weight and provides the philosophic filter through which all other diet plans must be understood and judged.

Wysong Directory of Alternative Resources

This is where to turn to find alternative resources to achieve health and a better life. Although alternative ideas are usually sought only after conventional mainstream choices fail, they should be given equal billing. After all, every bad idea in history was at one time thought to be convention and mainstream. We will never advance if we do not probe the edges of what is believed to be certain.

This Directory provides information and choices for all who seek a better world and wish to prevent and reverse disease safely by being in tune with nature.

Assembled for over a decade, the Directory is the place to turn when you don't know where to turn, or just want to be a more enlightened and healthy citizen.

Subjects include:
- Health & Disease
- Alternative Medicine
- Food & Nutrition
- Environmental
- Consumer Help & Protection
- Family Help
- Survival & Self Defense
- Political Action
- Travel
- Index

The Truth About Pet Foods

For more than fifty years people have been filling their pets' bowls with processed foods. This is done with full confidence that manufacturers have things all figured out. After all, the label says, "100% complete and balanced."

It would seem that the case is closed on pet nutrition. But this exposé, by a veterinary surgeon, clinician, teacher, researcher, and food scientist, tells another story. Pets exclusively fed processed foods are in jeopardy. Untold thousands of animals have suffered disease and death at the hands of this modern feeding practice. Neither nutritionists tweaking percentages, so-called "natural" foods, or eliminating boogeyman ingredients have solved the disaster.

Such disease—cancer, arthritis, obesity, dental degeneration, and so on—is not always immediate, but rather insidious and progressive. So the cause—singularly fed processed food—is not identified as the culprit it is. The tragedy is that modern degenerative diseases are not only largely preventable, but in many cases reversible by simple dietary and life-style changes.

In an easily read format, Dr. Wysong explains what's wrong and what to do to take control of pet health. Along the way, readers will learn how to better care for their own and their family's health as well.

This is a provocative, no-holds-barred look at one of the world's largest food industries and its regulatory sanctions. But it is fair, documented, logical, thought provoking and definitely eye opening.

Dr. Wysong gives readers the knowledge necessary to prevent and reverse the epidemic of degenerative health problems ravaging pets and their caretakers.

Rationale For Animal Nutrition
An Interview With Dr. R. L. Wysong

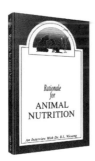

Rationale for Animal Nutrition is the seminal book that started the natural pet food movement.

Although nutrition is thought to be a completed science, it is not, neither in theory nor practice. Rationale for Animal Nutrition addresses the incorrect ideas and unsettled issues, and goes far beyond the standard, protein-builds-muscle and vitamin-A-is-good-for-the-eyes, nutritional pabulum.

Dr. Wysong's experience in veterinary surgery and medicine, nutritional and food science research, and building and running food manufacturing facilities gives him the 'in the trenches' insight to take issue with a wide variety of common nutritional givens. These are some of the myths he challenges:

- Processed packaged pet foods are "100% complete and balanced"
- Synthetic nutrients are the same as natural
- Better digestibility equals better food
- Supplementing commercial pet foods is dangerous

- NRC requirements are well founded in fact
- A food's merit can be determined by its list of ingredients or analyses
- Foods in paper bags can have a six month or greater shelf-life
- Modern nutrition is better than that of our ancestors
- More technology and more medicine will mean less disease
- Science knows what nutrients we require

Dr. Wysong gives readers fundamental, philosophic understandings of their place—and that of their companion animals—in the natural order of things. This empowers people with the insight needed to make independent, healthful decisions when confronting the confusing and dangerous commercial marketplace.

Wysong E-Health Letter

Short periodic e-mail postings containing provocative thoughts, new health research findings... and more. Just e-mail wysong@wysong.net and say "Subscribe." FREE

The Creation-Evolution Controversy

Who has not wondered about the origin of the universe and life? And, for certain, this is a question that should be taken with the utmost seriousness and sense of duty. After all, how can we know why we are here or what we should be doing if we do not know where we came from?

Although religions have their belief (creation), and materialists have their belief (evolution), beliefs are not what truth is about. This is a book of daring adventure between these two emotionally charged belief systems. Rather than advocate, Dr. Wysong pits one belief against the other using the only weapons that should be used if truth is the objective: reason and evidence.

Dr. Wysong's rational, philosophic, and scientific probings make this book a reservoir of thoughtful and factual information that will not draw dust on your bookshelf.

Now in its twelfth printing, this 1975 book has been read worldwide, is widely cited on the web, and continues to be used in schools. It has helped lay the groundwork for a rational dialogue between religion and science and remains current to this day because of its even handed treatment of the subject and because reason should never fall out of fashion.

All who profess a love of knowledge, thirst for answers about our origins, seek scientific and logical clarity, and can come to this subject with a truly open mind will find The Creation-Evolution Controversy refreshing, illuminating, and worthy of more than the usual attention.

ABOUT THE AUTHOR

DR. WYSONG is author of the companion book, Solving The Big Questions As If Thinking Matters, The Creation-Evolution Controversy, now in its twelfth printing, several books on nutrition, prevention, and health for people and animals, scientific articles on embryology, nutrition, health care, and surgical techniques, and monthly health newsletters since 1987. He has practiced veterinary surgery and medicine, taught college courses in human anatomy, physiology, and the origin of life, directed research for his health education and product development company, and guided the philanthropic non-profit Wysong Institute. Dr. Wysong may be contacted at wysong@asifthinkingmatters.com.